The Supreme Court, the Constitution, and William Rehnquist

The Supreme Court, the Constitution, and William Rehnquist

Steven T. Seitz

LEXINGTON BOOKS
Lanham • Boulder • New York • London

Published by Lexington Books
An imprint of The Rowman & Littlefield Publishing Group, Inc.
4501 Forbes Boulevard, Suite 200, Lanham, Maryland 20706
www.rowman.com

Unit A, Whitacre Mews, 26–34 Stannary Street, London SE11 4AB

British Library Cataloguing in Publication Information Available

Library of Congress Cataloging-in-Publication Data
Names: Seitz, Steven Thomas, 1947- author.
Title: The Supreme Court, the constitution, and William Rehnquist / Steven T. Seitz.
Description: Lanham : Lexington Books, [2018] | Includes bibliographical references and index.
Identifiers: LCCN 2018029974 (print) | LCCN 2018030670 (ebook) | ISBN 9781498568838 (electronic) | ISBN 9781498568821 (cloth : alk. paper)
Subjects: LCSH: United States. Supreme Court—Decision making—History. | Judicial process—United State—History. | Political questions and judicial power—United States. | Judges—United States—History. | United States. Supreme Court—Officials and employees—History. | Marshall, John, 1755-1835. | Rehnquist, William H., 1924-2005.
Classification: LCC KF8748 (ebook) | LCC KF8748 .S45 2018 (print) | DDC 347.73/26—dc23
LC record available at https://lccn.loc.gov/2018029974

The paper used in this publication meets the minimum requirements of American National Standard for Information Sciences—Permanence of Paper for Printed Library Materials, ANSI/NISO Z39.48-1992.

Printed in the United States of America

Contents

Preface

Long books should have short prefaces. I want to thank the Computational Modeling Laboratory, University of Illinois, where people ask questions seldom heard in traditional departments. In the instant case, the book began after a simple query: how could we computationally model Supreme Court decision makings, replicate them, anticipate them, have links to all the sources referenced in a case, while keeping appropriate sensitivity to subject matter, era, and composition of the Court? That is a tall order, but technological enthusiasts know it is only a short matter of time.

There are themes running through these decisions, but myopic focus on a case minimizes their cumulative importance. Misguided emphasis on the decision-making of individual judges along some faded line of liberalism-conservatism or other over-simplification move further from the intellectual foundations of American constitutional law. We need to understand how the Court developed various themes, such as interstate commerce, privileges and immunities, or how the Court unfolded the multiple prongs of justiciability. Charles Warren's great book *The Supreme Court in United States History* developed an historical picture by term, but the different cases each term made it impossible to trace how the Court treated similar problems over time. In his preface, Warren suggested he should have developed the book by themes, but development by terms was much more manageable when he started the book in the early 1920s. This book, and another to follow on clauses in the Bill of Rights, helps address this void. The task was much more difficult than it appears because it became necessary to review far more cases, concurrences, and dissents than ultimately referenced.

I need to offer special thanks to my family. They did not understand why daddy was at the computer all hours of the night. They eventually adjusted by crawling into the bed near the computer and waiting for the next break in work. I need to give special thanks to D. D., B. R. B., S. B., B. D., the rowdy boy, and Gretchen. Fortunately, their sleep schedule corresponded with my work schedule.

Chapter 1

State Sovereignty

This book is about core constitutional themes running through Supreme Court decision-making from the original Marshall Court through the Rehnquist Court. In his extraordinary work, *The Supreme Court in American History*, Charles Warren endeavors to picture the Supreme Court as the skin of living thought, using important cases before the Court from year to year. Warren argues that his development would have been more logical if it had traced developments of the doctrines formulated by serial decisions, but he chose to make the correlation between cases and yearly political events. With the Warren book still at our disposal nearly a century later, we turn back to the development of doctrines, tracing those logical thematic threads across the administrations now complete (John Marshall through William Rehnquist).

In *Democracy in America*, Alexis de Tocqueville juxtaposes the French legal system and its English counterpart. The French model is more rationalist; it takes the principles of a conceived future world and applies them to cases or issues before the court. A principle draws the present forward; the present speaks to the future. Barristers or French avocets make grandiloquent arguments applying eternal principles to today's problems.

The English model is theoretically the reverse. English law speaks to cases and controversies of the present from cases in the past. We call this *stare decisis*. This more utilitarian spirit possesses American law. SCOTUS (Supreme Court of the United States) says that it does not decide by abstract principle. It is a bad day, some say, when a decision becomes the subject of continued commentary. On a good day, SCOTUS drafts decisions narrowly so that only lawyers and jurists may perceive how they serve as precedent. The law unfolds slowly. It may show sensitivity to conditions in the world, or it may not. It is a living constitution expounded by Marshall and his heirs. It is also a Constitution where power not given is power not exercisable.

The truth falls somewhere between. Even originalists would accept certain fundamental rights not enumerated in the Constitution or Bill of Rights. We restrict the public taking of private property; thus, we assume the existence of property rights. The Fifth Amendment mentions private property once. That amendment restricts taking private property for public purposes without just compensation. Other rights inherited from common law and usually accepted by originalists include the right to marriage or the right of reproduction. These fundamental rights, not enumerated in the Constitution, are essential to ordered liberty and are historical components of Western civilization.

The development of American constitutional law is generally conservative. There are clearly eras where the development of law accelerates; other eras where the pace slows to a crawl. Focusing on individual court terms and the happenstance cases before the court each term can give a false impression of continuity and stability of constitutional law. Warren recognized the cadence issue but fell victim to the historicist view of the time; change in context or environment drives ideas and their application at successive moments of time. *Stare decisis* sinks to the level of another judicial rule rather than being the central rule of precedent-based legal systems. Following themes or constitutional clauses over time is a better tool to examine the continuity and stability of constitutional law; it helps us focus on where change does occur and why.

A popular conception of Court decisions elevates the importance of presidential appointments. If each Justice merely reflected the ideology, party, and policy preference of the appointing President, Court decisions should change as Court majorities change. In addition, the conception largely reduces the Chief Justice's importance to a vote. After Rehnquist joined the Court, for example, Republican Presidents made nine appointments (excluding Rehnquist's appointment to the Court and to the position of Chief Justice) versus four by Democratic Presidents. Under this scenario, Rehnquist has little causal effect on the direction of the Court beyond his conservative vote. The causal force would be presidential appointments. Reducing the Court to a shadow of the political process might be accurate, but it also makes the judicial portion of the separation powers relevant only in the sense that it is a legacy institution, that is, the accumulation and amalgamation of past generations of political decisions.

One clear exception to the popular scenario is *stare decisis*. The Supreme Court tries, as much as possible, to respect its prior decisions and use those as benchmarks for new cases. The use of precedents serves important functions in Court decision-making. The most obvious function is direction to lower court decision-making. If the direction of the Court changes nearly as fast as presidential turnover, lower courts could well make decisions using one set of rules while the Court is adopting another set. With this type of instability, more cases would move up the appeals chain as new rules demand overturning cases using older rules. The popular scenario, if that were the way the Court works, would politicize the Court and subsequently reduce its legitimacy as an independent branch of government.

Under *stare decisis*, judgments should show less variance than under the simpler political scenario. Stare decisis is not merely an internal constraint at a point in time, but a constraint re-exercised over time. It avoids chaos in the lower courts. It is a constraint that should guide future Courts, even as personnel and party change. A precedent, or which precedent to use, is still subject to the friends and neighbors effect among Court members. Precedents remain interred if four members do not bring a new instantiation before the Court. The Chief Justice may choose who writes a decision, but we seldom see an outlandishly grounded decision like Scalia's opinion in *Columbia v. Heller*, 554 U.S. 570 (2008).

Stare decisis surely involves interpretations, differentiations, and even what constitutional theme applies? What does a rightward swing mean in Supreme Court decision-making under these circumstances? What does a conservative swing mean? Labels presumably point to something. Arguing that they differ from former decisions sheds little light on the difference between those and these decisions. One of the oldest, most brittle forms of differentiation rests on the use of formalisms. We are familiar with many: local versus national, economic versus non-economic, traditional versus non-traditional, and so forth. This is the route often traveled during the Lochner Era (1887–1937). Three formalisms appeared often during this period: national sovereignty versus state sovereignty, individual versus state capitalism, choice versus determinism. These formalisms roughly correspond to states' rights, laissez-faire, and social Darwinism (Justice Holmes famous dictum in *Buck v. Bell*, 274 U.S. 200 (192) "three generations of imbeciles are enough").

Justice Rehnquist demonstrates an acute dedication to states' sovereignty. He favored injecting the Tenth Amendment whenever possible. He also tried to close use of the commerce clause as an unlimited grant of national authority: *NLRB v. Jones & Laughlin Steel Corp.*, 301 U.S. 1 (1937); *United States v. Darby*, 312 U.S. 100 (1941); then *United States v. Lopez*, 514 U.S. 549 (1995); *United States v. Morrison*, 529 U.S. 598 (2000). Rehnquist goes further. He elevates the Tenth Amendment and demotes the commerce clause by introducing more formalisms of his invention, some of which had remarkably short shelf-life, such as traditional versus non-traditional governmental functions. Rehnquist introduces the "traditional function" distinction in *National League of Cities v. Usery*, 426 U.S. 833 (1976). Nine years later, the Court majority not only abandons the "traditional functions" in *Garcia v. San Antonio Transit Auth.*, 469 U.S. 528 (1985), but the Court also overturns *Usery*. Rehnquist did not abandon *stare decisis* entirely, but his introduction of another layer of formalisms did not bode well.

Consider two variables that make possible modest change in the intellectual or ideological direction of the Court, under the assumption that stare decisis seriously limits intellectual or ideological change. First, what cases do at least four of the justices want to hear? This can enhance the important of certain types of cases while dampening the appearance of other types, often lest the result be an unfavorable decision. Second, new cases seldom present the same decisions as reached before; they contain some nuance or additional issue that requires a new application of an old principle. A deft selection of such cases may give a different majority the chance to slowly change or erode previous decisions. Both certainly happen, but the process of change is painfully slow and would only become apparent after long periods of incremental interventions. This is the hidden power of *stare decisis*. The search for and expectation of Court swings left or right might well be ignoring a big elephant in the room.

We have a glimpse of how it may happen that a new majority becomes more than the sum of its parts, but whither remains elusive. To observe a pattern or claim, a rightward swing requires some systematic direction discernible across incremental changes. Some eras stand out, such as the Lochner Era from 1887 to 1937, that imported an economic theory of laissez-faire, a doctrine of social Darwinism, and then kept the federal government at bay through the Tenth Amendment and the states at bay through the Contracts Clause. Although the Constitution has neither an economic nor social theory, both were apparent in Lochner Era decisions. Even so, the technologies of railroad and telegraph strained both theories, opening vast areas of decision-making not easily absorbed by laissez-faire.

Deep Congressional funding of the railroads, even though privately held, led to anomalies such as railroad throughways defined as "public highways." Soon the federal government required these public highways to host telegraph poles and lines. Long before the formal end of the Lochner Era in 1937, its logic had been imploding. A public interest could infect private property. The Interstate Commerce Commission of 1887, as strengthened by the Hepburn Act in 1906, formalized federal administrative regulation of interstate commerce. The Federal Employees Liability Act of 1908 permanently changed common law liability in the railroad industry. SCOTUS tried, and ultimately failed, to accommodate monopolies and trusts under a laissez-faire umbrella.

The administrative state occupied a permanent part of the legal landscape by 1972, when Justice Rehnquist entered the Court. Both federal and state governments increasingly relied on the administrative state, even though "bloated bureaucracies" became battle cries without a battle plan. Congress found itself in the awkward position that it rescued the remnants of laissez-faire competition from anti-competitive forces, within the economy, by using public policy. Adam Smith's hidden hand wore government-made gloves. Justice Rehnquist's judicial landscape was a world away from that of the supposed apostles of the self-made man.

Government intervention into the economic and social order had a century of practice and precedent before Justice Rehnquist took his seat on the Court. Arguing that Justice Rehnquist would tilt the windmills of Big Government in favor of capitalist competition would substitute fictional lines for the real lines of battle. Once government became the primary savior of capitalist competition, the myth of the hidden hand had been rudely exposed. A poorly developed public conception of the battle lines sought to explain a swing toward the right, but that conception was such a caricature of the real problem that it explained little. Justice Rehnquist could not bring capitalism back in a blaze of glory, no matter how slowly. Championing state sovereignty was never a path to capitalism. Big Government was already doing what it could to salvage competition from the destructive forces of competition. The interstate collusive power of corporations rendered the states relatively hapless.

If simplistic juxtapositions, individual versus state capitalism, state sovereignty versus federal sovereignty, do little to explain where Justice Rehnquist might have steered the Court, then what would? Labels like left or right, liberal or conservative, do more to obfuscate than illuminate. We develop below what may amount to a single-factor explanation of a complex history, namely, the shaping and sharing of sovereignty between the state and national governments. This, as we develop in the next section, is a debate that goes back to the early battles over the Constitution of 1787. There is a twist. There were three conceptual opponents on the constitutional stage: the central government, the state governments, and the individual. Hamilton and the Federalists wanted an energetic central government. The anti-Federalists wanted to preserve the sovereignty of the states. Proponents of individual rights wanted a large sphere around the individual that protected against the intrusions of government. Because the Founding Fathers were largely Federalists, the opposition anti-Federalists effectively absorbed both the states right proponents and the individual right proponents. Thomas Jefferson recognized this potential difficulty; he mustered the weak defense that a majority would never intrude on the rights of a minority because the majority recognized those rights as its own as well.

The simple question of state versus central governments becomes more complicated. Which of these two would better protect the rights of the individual? State rights proponents have long argued that they are the natural protectors of individual rights because they are closer to the people. The Civil War and the Civil War amendments made it clear that many no longer bought that argument. The national government would be the protector of individual rights. Virtually the same argument occurs in the 1960s, with the Civil Rights

Bills of 1964 and 1965, stewarded by the so-called liberal Court under Justice Warren. We argue below that it is this juxtaposition between central and state governments, coupled with which of these the individual rights proponents made coalition, that becomes the benchmark for what SCOTUS does when it changes direction.

THE RATIFICATION ERA

During the Virginia Ratification Convention (1788), the ardent anti-Federalist Patrick Henry rhetorically asked: "Have they said We, the states? . . . The question turns, sir, on that poor little thing—the expression, We, the *people*, instead of the *states*, of America." For Hamilton and the Federalists, "We the people" spoke to a grand economic empire on the world stage. The Federalists gave short shrift to the rights and liberties of ordinary people. On the other side, Jefferson's pastoral view precluded strong commercial ambitions. Jeffersonian democracy expected the recruitment of yeoman farmers into local political debate and leadership, because these were men of virtue and restrained ambition. Representatives had to be close to and trusted by ordinary people. The anti-federalists championed rights and liberty as they understood it, pastoral over commercial life, and representatives of limited ambition with ties to local communities. None of this would be possible under a federal constitution. State sovereignty became the core of the ratification debate.

The anti-Federalists clearly understood that the proposed Constitution would dramatically change the balance of power between the national and state governments. The Supremacy Clause suggests: "This Constitution, and the laws of the United States made in pursuance thereof, and all treaties made, or which shall be made, under the authority of the United States, shall be the supreme law of the land." Whether federalist or anti-federalist, both sides clearly understood that state sovereignty was at stake. As Madison (Madison, Letter from James Madison to George Washhington, April 16, 1787. 1920) wrote to Washington:

> Conceiving that an individual independence of the States is utterly irreconcilable with their aggregate sovereignty; and that a consolidation of the whole into one simple republic would be as inexpedient as it is unattainable, I have sought some middle ground, which may at once support a due supremacy of the national authority, and not exclude the local authorities wherever they can be subordinately useful.

Much of Madison's view would eventually prevail at the Constitutional Convention in summer 1787. Before the Continental Congress even considered the issue, Madison had convinced the 1786 Virginia legislature to invite all the states to join in Annapolis (September 1786) to discuss ways to reduce interstate conflict. Those attending the Annapolis Convention recommended holding a Grand Convention in Philadelphia in May 1787 to improve the Articles of Confederation. Madison then got the Virginia legislature to pursue the Annapolis recommendation and elect delegates to the Philadelphia Convention. Five states followed, but the remainder sought approval for a Philadelphia Convention through the existing Confederation Congress. It endorsed the Philadelphia Convention in February 1787. Altogether, twelve states (excluding Rhode Island) sent delegates to Philadelphia.

Madison reports the Confederation Congress instructions in Federalist 40 (Madison, Federalist # 40 1961). Those instructions have two parts: "Whereas" and "Resolved." These instructions would be vital to the charge that the Philadelphia Convention lacked the authority to propose a Federal Constitution.

> Whereas there is provision in the articles of Confederation and perpetual Union for making alterations therein, by the ascent of a Congress of the United States, and of the legislatures of the several States: and whereas experience has evinced that there are defects in the present Confederation, as a means to remedy which, several of the States, and *particularly the State of New York*, by express instructions to their delegates in Congress, have suggested a convention for the purposes expressed in the following resolution; and such Convention appearing to be the most probable mean of establishing in the States, a firm national government.
>
> Resolved, that in the opinion of Congress it is expedient that on the 2d Monday in May next, a Convention of delegates, who shall have been appointed by the several States, be held at Philadelphia for the sole and express purpose of revising the articles of Confederation and reporting to Congress and the several Legislatures, such alterations and provisions therein as shall, when agreed to in Congress and confirmed by the States, render the Federal Constitution *adequate to the exigencies of government and the preservation of the Union.*

The struggle over state sovereignty was far more than just theoretical. It was also more than a parade of ambitious men competing for national versus state power. The Articles of Confederation had a decade-long string of failures in its credits. First, the Articles required unanimous consent of the colonies before a bill would become law. This roadblock prevented effective interstate governance from the late 1770s into the early 1780s. The lengthy approval time highlighted serious border disputes among the various colonies.

The 1787 Constitution required only nine of thirteen state's approval before going into effect and in so doing dropped the unanimity rule. Second, the Articles did not transfer control over interstate commerce to the central government. The states battled one another with tariffs or other restrictions on the movement of goods and people across state lines. The commerce fights essentially closed markets among competing states, resulting in high prices for demand goods that were not reasonably procurable from neighboring states, and low prices for supply goods that now only marketed across seas. The 1787 Constitution transferred all control over interstate commerce, as well as any treaty-making authority, to the central government.

The third among many other failures was that of security. The insecurities arose in several circumstances. The Amerindian tribes, inside the states, beyond the state borders, or both were still a recurring threat to the colonists. As the colonists moved west, the Amerindians became increasingly recalcitrant of treaties and the struggles intensified. A second source of insecurity was the several Old World imperial powers keeping some form of military presence in the New World. The treaty (of Paris, 1783) ended the Revolutionary War but not all the battles between England and America. Confrontations between Spain and America continued in Southern regions of the New Nation. Anti-royal turmoil in France created tensions and new challenges between France and America. A third source of insecurity occurred within the several colonies, where poor farmers fought economic injustices and perceived threats to civil rights. Shay's Rebellion became more ominous when the Shayites stormed a national armory seeking guns stored there. The middle and upper classes, largely located in Eastern commercial ports, questioned whether the states could even maintain peace within their borders, let alone across state boundaries.

By 1787 a great part of the population and an even greater part of the elite recognized a need to change the Articles of Confederation. Even during its short life span, the Confederation had become a symbol of the trials and tribulations that followed the Declaration of Independence, even though the states did not ratify the Articles of Confederation until 1781. The government had not paid the Continental Army. Many state legislatures refused to pay, and the new Confederate Congress could do little about the problem. Other states, especially Massachusetts, put exorbitant taxes on land to raise the money needed to pay its veterans, but the tax drove many farms into foreclosure. When the state would not grant tax relief, the dispossessed farmers became Shay recruits. Other states, facing their own problems, would not assist Massachusetts' militia against the Shayites, and again the central government could do nothing. Massachusetts resolved its tax problem and defeated the Shayites, but the events sowed the seeds of discord and distress against state sovereignty. Many elites foresaw recurrent problems growing from state sovereignties. These elites saw a strong national government as the appropriate remedy. State sovereignty had failed its political exam.

Its post-Revolutionary War shortcomings aside, state sovereignty created greater disunity. A king's charter had set most of the colonial borders. After the Revolutionary war, state leaders were not eager to admit that the Crown had drawn their borders on a map in England for a king who claimed to own it all. Even if some colonial boundaries followed the natural terrain, other borders lacked any intrinsic coherency whatsoever. A foreign power had essentially made many of the colonies. State sovereignty rested on an artifice without its own raison d'etre. In any event, the Jeffersonians emphasized towns and townships as meaningful seats of self-rule.

The concept of democracy welcomes many interpretations. The early Puritans in Massachusetts often summoned the "sense of the community" in decision making, reinforcing the closed nature of these societies. Early home-rule, as practiced by the Puritans in Massachusetts, veiled intolerant religious sects, closed societies of people of like mind, working to build their own "city on the hill." Many such communities controlled who could enter the community and whom they would expel. It was also here, especially in Massachusetts, where the Salem Witch Hunts (1692) showed the heinous underbelly of closed societies (Popper, *The Open Society and its Enemies* 1945). The witch hunt epidemic that followed needed closed societies.

The anti-Federalists loosely linked people supporting home rule as well as people supporting state sovereignty. Deriving one's identity from what you oppose is easy enough. Most anti-Federalists came to use "democracy" as their mantra. A state government "becomes" more democratic because a national government allegedly cannot be. Through a sophistic use of Rousseau and Montesquieu, certain anti-Federalists heralded the states as being "close to the people." Thus, state sovereignty rests on democracy.

Home rule elite in the Massachusetts Bay Colony were mostly members of the clergy. Fleeing to the New World for religious freedom did not mean religious toleration. Various Protestant sects essentially closed their doors to those who did not agree with their interpretation of the Bible. The clergy had anticipated even greater control in the colony after the Glorious Revolution in England. The new king did indeed issue Massachusetts Bay Colony a new charter, but instead of greater local control, the charter put a substantially empowered English governor in place. It was the new governor who finally put an end to the "witch" arrests, imprisonments, and executions for alleged compacts with malevolent spectral spirits. The inquests into, and executions for witchcraft would thus come to an end, not by the conscience of the community, but by the secular powers of the king and his governor.[1]

The colonial experiment of local community control met an ignoble end. The anti-Federalists feared the states would meet a similar end if the country adopted the Constitution of 1787. They portrayed the plan for a combined union as undemocratic when compared with the thirteen postcolonial states. Still, the anti-federalists found it difficult to hide behind a democratic shroud. Hamilton addressed their ploy in the first Federalist paper. He argued that it is in the interest of a certain class of men in every state to resist all changes which would diminish their power, emolument, and control of office. Opposition to the Federalist Constitution came from local power elites, not their people. In turn, Hamilton accused many anti-Federalists of being big fish in little ponds bent on keeping their power by opposing ratification of the new constitution.

The political competition among ambitious men locally and nationally camouflaged a serious problem with the proposed constitution. The instructions given by the Continental Congress to delegates of the Constitutional Convention required that they bring their proposal back to the Continental Congress and the state legislatures for approval. This requirement derived from Article XIII of the Articles of Confederation:

> And the articles of this confederation shall inviolably be observed by every state, and the union shall be perpetual; nor shall any alteration at any time hereafter be made in any of them; unless such alteration be agreed to in a congress of the United States, and to be afterward confirmed by the legislatures of every State.

The draft accepted in the closed chambers of 1787 would not have gained the approval of either the Continental Congress or the states. The proposed ratification was in fact illegal under the existing Articles of Confederation. Madison had an answer for this as well. The state government, he reasoned, derived its authority directly from the people. To circumvent the existing Articles of Confederation, ratification of the new Constitution would have to derive its power directly from the people as well. In doing so, the state governments and the central government derived their authority from the same source. The old Articles of Confederation based their authority on the state legislatures, which were authorized actors for the state. That authorization, at least in theory, derived ultimately from the people of each state. No provision in the Articles of Confederation would bind ratification of the new Constitution if the ratification occurred in constitutional conventions around the various states, rather than within the state legislatures. In theory, the constitutional conventions had at least if not more authority than the state legislatures; the people directly elected members of the constitutional conventions. A Constitution derived directly from the people of the entire United States would have the same or greater sovereignty than the state legislatures within their bounds. The Federalists claimed that a majority of citizens in each of the states authorized the new union. A Constitution deriving from all the people would be superior to a constitution deriving from some of the people. Put differently, the very act of ratifying the new Constitution necessarily ended the sole sovereignty of each state.

Madison also answered the anti-Federalist claim that the states were more democratic. The only legislative chamber under the new Constitution that represented people was the House of Representatives. Madison had wanted the Senate similarly populated, except fewer in number and thus more people per constituency. A compromise at the Constitutional Convention had rendered Senate representation by state rather than by population. Although he cheerfully recommended the Constitution in the Federalist Papers, Madison considered the Senate compromise to be neither good political theory nor good political practice. (His prescience became increasingly apparent with the prolonged fight for control of the Senate. Would the new states enter free or slave?)

The problem of the new Senate aside, Madison turned previous democratic theory on its head. The states assumed, as had Pericles, Rousseau, and Montesquieu, that government must be close to the people to be democratic. Of course, the states were not particularly close to the people and, as Hamilton observed, they were largely in the hands of local and regional influentials. Madison went further. He argued that such governments would quickly dissolve into majority tyrannies.

Opinion, custom, and habit would replace knowledge and reasoning while undermining freedom as well. The tendency was an increasingly closed society. Madison saw factions as part of the fabric of society. Small governments simply gave one or another faction control over the rest. What one faction gained, the others would lose. The same would hold if there were a coalition of factions in control. Rather than favoring small, homogeneous societies, Madison argued for large, heterogeneous societies. The people could not present themselves at the seat of government in large societies, but the republican principle would allow representatives to perform that task. Representatives could hear the true interest of the people through the din of many, heterogeneous factions. The large societies, relying upon their representatives, would also benefit from the interaction between the republican principle and the size of constituency. The larger the constituency, the more influential people would be eligible for each representative position and this, in turn, would give the remainder of the people a talent pool from which to choose. In other words, the quality of representatives would rise to the top and these more qualified individuals will better hear and understand the true public interest. For Madison, democracy was not the victory of one faction or another but pursuit of the public interest. Large constituencies will better accomplish that pursuit.

When the anti-Federalists were not crowing the joys of Majoritarianism, they were arguing that small governments were better protective of freedom and liberty. If freedom and liberty add anything to majority rule, it presumably would be the removal of obstacles, the clearance of obstructions facing the individual and encumbering individual decision-making and choice. There are, of course, tensions between freedom and majority rule, clearly recognized in the dangers of majority tyranny. Some, like Jefferson, recognized the logical gap but simply insisted that, when confronted with choices depriving the minority of its freedoms, the majority would in good conscience not conclude such a choice (Jefferson 1801). Were the world so cognitive and compassionate! Taken on their own terms, the concepts of freedom and liberty were quite compelling. Rhetorically linking liberty and freedom with government closer to the people would give cover to the latter, but a rhetorical link is neither a logical nor experiential one.

Madison did not want to enumerate rights in the new Constitution for at least two reasons. First, the very conception of large constituencies and a heterogeneous society meant that there always would be multiple centers competing for power, that none could dominate the others, and that coalitions were at best temporary arrangements, until the very basis for the existence of coalescing factions melted away. Factions competing for power, while factions appeared and disappeared, transformed or divided, gave a negative liberty—freedom from—to the people of the United States. This could never happen in small constituencies, where majority tyrannies were the expected outcome. Second, Madison recognized the inherent difficulties in enumerating rights. Regardless of how exhaustive the list, what of those not on the list? Have we lost them? What of the tendency (certainly true of many Supreme Court justices), that anything not listed is something not granted? Madison attempted to avoid this conundrum by not providing a list at all.

BILL OF RIGHTS

The home-rule anti-Federalists would have none of the brilliance shown in Madison's reasoning, and instead demanded a Bill of Rights that would protect the individual by limiting the actions of government, especially big government. Rhetorically combining democracy, closeness to the people, and the concepts of freedom and liberty, the anti-Federalists built a political platform that might not stop the new Constitution but could at least force some modification. That accomplishment came in the form of a Bill of Rights which Madison promised to introduce in the first Congress under the new Constitution. The Bill of Rights does not share the political theory governing the Constitution itself. It rests on a different and inconsistent rhetorical platform. Ultimately, the logic for a Bill of Rights went back to the Deist view that divine principles were writ large in the universe, that some of these principles were unalienable rights given to man, and that each person had the ability to read nature and know natural rights. For the home rule anti-Federalist, equal people saw and understood equal things. Small governments were directly accountable to the people; a small government contained people who knew and understood the same vision of nature. The anti-Federalist papers reveal that these same people believed various conspiracy theories aimed at the Federalists.

Attachment of a Bill of Rights to the Constitution essentially worked as a limit on the power of the central government against individuals, but it did not protect individuals from the states. It had limited impact on state sovereignty or the larger struggle between national and state sovereignty under the Federal Constitution. It did create a wasteland where the states could step in and now do what the central government could not do. (Incorporation or absorption through the due process clauses of the Fifth and Fourteenth Amendments ended many of those forays.) The Ninth Amendment did address Madison's concern that an enumeration of rights would preclude later recognition of other rights. Madison's efforts to control the effects of enumeration through the Ninth Amendment were to prove relatively futile, in part because interpretations of the amendment might (see Black's dissent in *Griswold v. Connecticut*, 381 U.S. 479 (1965)) empower the people against government. It has enjoyed very limited use in the courts.

The Ninth Amendment's heyday occurred during Justice Arthur Goldberg's brief tenure on the Supreme Court (1962–1965). In his concurring opinion written for Griswold, Goldberg argues that liberty protects fundamental rights. The concept of liberty extends beyond the list of rights in the Bill of Rights to include such fundamentals as the right of marital privacy. Goldberg argued that the Constitution did not require SCOTUS to derive marital privacy from the right of privacy, itself a penumbra of the First Amendment. The due process clause of the Fourteenth Amendment protected fundamental personal rights and liberties against state abridgment. The Ninth Amendment protects fundamental personal liberties from federal or state abridgment. Goldberg cited the Ninth Amendment for the same purpose that Madison wrote it: "the enumeration in the Constitution of certain rights, shall not be construed to deny or disparage others retained by the people." Goldberg reaffirms Marshall's observation in *Marbury v. Madison*, 5 U.S. 1 Cranch 137 (1803) that the Court may not presume that clauses put into the Constitution are without effect.

The Tenth Amendment comes closest to the anti-Federalists' efforts to preserve state sovereignty, considering the new Federal Constitution. The Tenth Amendment reserves to the states or people any power neither given to the central government nor denied to the states. The set of powers in the remaining area are small indeed, focusing on police powers under ordered liberty, and made even smaller by the Civil War amendments. Despite the mention of the people in both the Ninth and Tenth Amendments, the Supreme Court used the Tenth Amendment during the Lochner Era to strike down most federal efforts at social legislation, such as number of children's working hours or time of children's working hours. When the Lochner Era ended in 1937, the Tenth Amendment went into dormancy for fifty years.

In the modern era, Rehnquist resurrected the Tenth Amendment in *National League of Cities v. Usery*, 426 U.S. 833 (1976). Focusing on the employment arena, Rehnquist sought to stop application of federal wage and hour standards on state employees. Without any discernable basis, Rehnquist attempted to rescue state sovereignty by announcing a "traditional governmental functions" standard and whether a federal Commerce Clause requirement would impair a state's ability to function effectively in a federal system (see also *Fry v. United States*, 421 U.S. 542 (1975)). In his dissent, Brennan described the newly found constitutional principle to be an abstraction without substance. Using the new principle, Rehnquist found unconstitutional the 1974 amendment to the Fair Labor Standards Act which broadened the definition of "employer" to include public agencies, and "enterprise" to include the activities of public agencies. In doing so, SCOTUS also overruled *Maryland v. Wirtz*, 392 U.S. 183 (1968). In an inconsistency often seen in his later decisions, Rehnquist upholds *Fry*, *supra*, which grants Congress commerce clause emergency powers to intervene on the wages of state and local appointees. The standards for such intervention include the existence of a problem that only the central government can solve, interference for a limited, specified time, and no real displacement on how state choices are structured, and no additional pressure on the state budgets. Notwithstanding these exceptions, it would thus appear that the states have some power over wages and hours of its employees and that the Congress does have some reach through the Commerce Clause.

Anti-Federalists were certain that the Tenth and Eleventh Amendments re-asserted state sovereignties. They would have welcomed the Rehnquist era to craft if not reassert state sovereignty. Neither amendment has such an assertion. The Tenth Amendment is a truism, intuitively obvious, or the leftovers amendment. The states or people have any power not delegated to the United States, nor prohibited by it to the states. There is here no positive grant of authority. The Tenth Amendment clearly had no impact when Marshall interpreted the necessary and proper clause to take a loose construction that any means to a constitutionally prescribed end would be an indirect but constitutional power of the national government. That interpretation created an entire class of indirect and hence unspecified powers for the national government that are, by implication, an extension of the delegated powers.

ELEVENTH AMENDMENT

Some who misinterpret the motivations for the Eleventh Amendment do so for political reasons, but the actual motivation is relatively straightforward. The colonies had borrowed considerable monies for their conduct of the Revolutionary War, and their creditors were now pressing for repayment. Under English common law, no one could sue the king (or sovereign) directly, but he would typically consent to a suit. Many of the new states lacked the grace of the king, or his integrity for that matter, and did not wish to respond to their creditors. Because creditors could not sue the state within its own courts, many creditors sued directly in federal court. *Chisholm v. Georgia*, 2 U.S. 419 (1793) gave victory to the plaintiff in a diversity suit, even though the state of Georgia refused to appear, asserting its sovereign immunity to such suits unless the state so consented. Consequently, the Eleventh Amendment removed federal court jurisdiction regarding such diversity suits (a citizen of one state could not sue another state) and regarding suits by foreign citizens upon a state. In practical terms, this meant that the holders of debt incurred during the Revolutionary War could not pursue the state-as-debtor by legal means in the state courts or in the federal courts. The sovereignty implied here is the estoppel of suits to recover state fiduciary obligations. The Eleventh Amendment re-established the common-law fiction that any sovereign, even if a semi-sovereign state, was immune from law suits without its consent.

The wording of the Eleventh Amendment is especially instructive: "The Judicial power of the United States shall not be construed to extend to any suit in law or equity, commenced or prosecuted against one of the United States by Citizens of another State, or by Citizens or Subjects of any Foreign State." This is a clear limit on the power or reach of the federal judiciary. It is not a positive grant of power to the states. It does not even reference the common law legal fiction of sovereign immunity. Like the Tenth Amendment, it can only be by political conjecture that either of these amendments provides the basis of state sovereignty in a Federal system. The Seventeenth Amendment (popular election of Senators, ratified in 1913) further undermines state legislatures as power intermediaries.

Hans v. Louisiana, 134 U.S. 1 (1890) added a restriction not textually found in the Eleventh Amendment. In addition to diversity cases, the Court decided that the Eleventh Amendment also included a suit against a state by one of its own citizens. The Court considered the decision a sensible extension that was consistent with the common-law principle that a sovereign must consent before a plaintiff may sue. The Court further argued that an earlier Court had wrongly decided the *Chisholm* case, an argument to which Justice Harlan took exception in his concurring opinion. Neither the Tenth Amendment nor the Eleventh Amendment nor the *Hans* case impair the Supremacy Clause or affect the ability of the U.S. government to sue individual states (*United States v. Texas*, 143 U.S. 621 (1892)). The states surrendered their sovereignty to the general government by joining the Union.

THE CIVIL WAR AMENDMENTS

The Civil War amendments, the Thirteenth, the Fourteenth, and the Fifteenth, especially the last two, further restricted state sovereignty. The Thirteenth Amendment reached individual behavior, while SCOTUS quickly limited the Fourteenth and Fifteenth Amendments to reach the state alone, under the state-action doctrine. Shortly after the Civil War, the court argued that the abolishment of slavery simultaneously meant the abolishment of the badges and incidences of slavery (The Civil Rights Cases, 109 U.S. 3 (1883)). Were this the case, the Thirteenth Amendment would lack any further reach, as the 1883 Court argued. Later Courts have distinguished slavery from its badges and incidences, the latter including things like prejudice, and thus reinvigorated the power of the Thirteenth Amendment. Section two of the Thirteenth and Fifteenth Amendments gave Congress the power to enforce the amendments' provisions. Section 5 of the Fourteenth Amendment similarly grants Congress the power to enforce the provisions of that amendment by appropriate legislation.

All three of the civil rights amendments have significantly altered the sovereign balance between the federal and state governments. Despite the post-civil war court's effort to limit the implication of the badges and incidences, SCOTUS eventually made the conceptual distinction between persistent traces of slavery and slavery itself. The amendment gave lasting civil power to the Federal government. The same applies to voting rights through the Fifteenth Amendment. It is the Fourteenth Amendment that has had the most far-reaching implications for the states. It provides the first constitutional definition of citizenship, it reiterates the privileges and immunities clause found in the Constitution, it adds a due process of law provision with almost the same wording as the Fifth Amendment provision, and, significantly, it adds the Equal Protection Clause.

In operative terms, when applying these amendments, the court distinguishes among strict scrutiny, intermediate scrutiny, and rational scrutiny. Strict scrutiny requires the state to have an interest that overwhelms a constitutional protection, including those incorporated against the states through the Due Process Clause of the Fourteenth Amendment. The burden of proof is on the state, and the initial presumption is against the state. Rational scrutiny, on the other hand, only requires the state to demonstrate that it has a legitimate interest in overcoming a supposed constitutional protection. Here the burden of proof lies with the plaintiff. Racial discrimination belongs in the strict scrutiny category, meaning that the burden is on the state to prove that legislation should overcome due process or equal protection. The plain result of this is that the Federal courts strongly disfavor racial discrimination. This federally protected constitutional interest reaches directly into the police powers of the states, once largely the domain of state control. Through the Fourteenth Amendment, SCOTUS has effectively incorporated against the states most of the protections in the Bill of Rights, and section 5 of that Amendment gives Congress the authority to enforce those protections. The story now comes full circle. The central government won the battle over state sovereignty, starting with the adoption of the Federal Constitution, even if the skirmishes continue. Whether secured by the Supremacy Clause or reinforced by the Fourteenth Amendment, the Federal government was sovereign over the states. It is against this pattern that we examine the Rehnquist Court.

STATES-RIGHTS VERSUS CIVIL RIGHTS

State sovereignty got its second wind after World War II. The 1948 Democratic convention nominated Harry Truman and included in its platform several planks addressed to life in the South. These included a proposed federal anti-lynching law, the ending of poll taxes for Federal elections, a plank against employment discrimination in Federal jobs, and desegregation of the armed forces. The Dixiecrat revolt led many Southern delegates to withdraw from the Democratic Convention, form a States-Rights Party, and nominate Strom Thurmond, governor of South Carolina, for President. The States-Rights Party won Mississippi, South Carolina, Alabama, and Louisiana. The focal point was civil rights. The Southern states sought to do politically what they failed to accomplish judicially.

Although the States-Rights Party was short lived, Southern Democratic Senators used Senate procedures, including the filibuster, to delay or derail Federal civil rights legislation. Congress still managed to pass some limited civil rights legislation until the blockbuster Civil Rights Act of 1964. That legislation goaded the South to move from the Democratic Party to the Republican Party. The solid Democratic South largely became the solid Republican South by the end of the 1960s. The core purpose of the states-rights, or better stated, the state sovereignty claim was the ability of state and local governments to undermine or ignore the Democratic push for Federal civil rights legislation. Nixon countered the Democrats with the appointment of William Rehnquist to the SCOTUS bench. Prior to that appointment, Rehnquist had served as Assistant Attorney General for the Office of Legal Counsel for President Nixon. Months after the Rehnquist appointment, Nixon himself was to face impeachment charges. Rehnquist, an obscure choice in a game of quid-pro-quo, saw himself as the judicial standard-bearer for state sovereignty and, of course, a check upon federal civil rights activities. Unlike the anti-Federalists, the Rehnquist formula largely ignored individual rights, thus ceding that protection to the Federal government. We examine the real follow-through below.

At Rehnquist's confirmation hearing for position of justice and then again for Chief Justice, several members of the Committee on the Judiciary asked Rehnquist about his legal brief supporting *Plessy v. Ferguson*, 163 U.S. 537 (1896), written while an intern for Justice Jackson. The committee also asked Rehnquist about his role in Operation Eagle Eye while practicing law in his native Arizona and serving as poll watcher. Operation Eagle Eye was a Republican Party effort to discourage minority voters in Arizona. Rehnquist tried to side-step his legal brief for *Terry v. Adams*, 345 U.S. 461 (1953), in which he had argued for the reaffirmation of *Plessy*. He claimed at his confirmation hearings that he wrote the brief to reflect Justice Jackson's own opinion. The actual *Terry* case itself decided against a whites-only pre-primary in Texas. Justice Jackson concurred with the Terry decision, and the next year Justice Jackson voted for *Brown v. Board of Education of Topeka*, 347 U.S. 483 (1954). Rehnquist distanced himself from the *Terry* brief and from Operation Eagle Eye, so far so that some members of the committee for his associate justice appointment, and then again, his Chief Justice appointment, accused him of outright perjury.

NOTES ON METHODOLOGY

The Warren tradition, examining cases by year of decision, is an illustration of the historicist method. We understand the state of decision-making by understanding the state of man, society, and state at that moment in history. The topic under discussion, the reasoning offered, and the decision reached give a portal into the problems, socio-legal construction of the issues, and the legal-political decisions encapsulated in the case opinion. Historicism is an ancient approach to understanding political thought and has easily emerged as a method of legal research (Llewelyn and Hoebel 1941), an epistemology of history (Popper, *The Poverty of Historicism* 1999), and even the structure of scientific revolutions (Kuhn 2012).

Another commonly recognized method is the idealist inquiry. The analyst assumes that there is an unimpeachable premise by means of which to analyze or assess a current case decision. The analyst may focus on fairness, equality, substantive due process, human rights, et cetera. Having articulated the proper instantiation of the principal, the analyst proceeds to contrast the decision, its application of the guiding principle, and the extent to which the decision flows from the proper construction of the principle. From whence these principles derive is another matter. We have journeyed far from the self-evident truths of Thomas Jefferson. We have had great difficulty attributing substantive insights to "Reasonable Men." Some, like Rehnquist, attribute these principles to the structure of the Constitution or suppose the implications of separation of powers, checks and balances, federalism, or state sovereignty. None of these implications are in the text of the Constitution. Some may turn into the historical construction of a concept or its original intent to establish current meaning. Now the method blurs the distinction between historicism and idealism. Divining original intent is a skill of dubious accomplishment.

Contemporary political science focuses on the individual decision-maker, rather than the Court. Methodological individualism assumes that we need to consider the motivations of each decision-maker and their coalition formation. Motivations may include self-interest, the public interest, ideology, policies or partisan preference, and even religious doctrine. Based on identifiable, individual preferences, the researcher then looks for combinations or possible coalitions of fellow judges in making judicial decisions. Political scientists are particularly interested in conservative versus liberal courts; attention to appointments and departures are crucial. Judges bring values and preferences to the court and are much less likely to acquire them while on the court. Coalitions and idiosyncrasies emerged against this background. The political science perspective diminishes the importance of *stare decisis*, and in so doing, may lose sight of the forest for the trees.

Each perspective has its value with findings unique to that perspective. We focus on case precedents or stare decisis. The unit of analysis ultimately becomes the Court, whether the ruling be unanimous, a majority, or even a plurality. Tracing topics, such as the Supremacy Cause or the Interstate Commerce Clause, assumes that the logic may disjoin, at least somewhat, from a given historical context or ideology. SCOTUS, or The Supreme Court of the United States, is our shorthand for Court decisions that will last at least for a time, serve as precedents. We examine continuities in case precedence and against these we identify change in direction or more subtle shifts in evolving case logic. Many causal forces are working in judicial decision-making, and we focus on the evolution of case logic for constitutional clauses. The governing opinion is the SCOTUS position, because this result determines the case precedent, whether the Court is unanimous, a majority, or even a plurality. If, as virtually all judges aver, stare decisis is the method of maintaining consistency in Court opinions, then a focus on this forgotten topic, as it unfolds in constitutional clause topics, is a worthy endeavor. There is no claim here to exhaust all the forces at work in judicial decision-making, and none of the more common perspectives purport to do so. The charge of a single-factor analysis is also misleading because we examine the interpretation of constitutional clauses over time and pay close attention to both change and continuity in case precedence. We do seek to add to the political science and law literature by reigniting the approach that Warren himself thought preferable to the approach he adopted.

CONCLUSION

The quest for state sovereignty eventually tied historically and practically with civil rights. Whether this tie is conservative or liberal depends upon the political timeline. The term "liberal," to liberate, to remove obstructions, associates with the coalition including individual rights. It is not helpful to ask whether Rehnquist meets some Talismanic ideal of "conservative" or even of "sexist." Our task, as we travel from the Marshall Court to the Rehnquist Court, is more difficult. What was Rehnquist's method? Was he consistent and, if not, why? Did he consistently support state sovereignty? What other themes did he use, and why? What of individual rights? Inconsistent decisions or those using ill-conceived formalisms produce what Justice Souter calls "unsustainable" case law. They are poor guides to the lower courts and smudge the value of *stare decisis*.

Rehnquist did not bring new theories to the Court, but old beliefs, sometimes in new packages. He introduced formalisms as a method of divide and conquer, but it often created unforeseen problems that required revision and sometimes stacking formalism on formalism. Even if largely unsuccessful, Rehnquist's struggles highlighted legal problems before the Court and nation as well as points of stress when he tried forcing new wine into older skins.

Rehnquist introduced some formal distinctions or exceptions that are as difficult to apply as it is to crack a gnat's back. The result is unsustainable case law. A good measure of unsustainable case law is a decision quickly overturned or a formalism accepted and then disavowed by a colleague. The struggle over formalisms often add to judicial confusion below.

In the chapters that follow, we examine judicial decision-making on separate topics of judicial decision-making across the eras from Marshall through Rehnquist. When Rehnquist comes onto the Court, the tides of state sovereignty are not on his side. How well did he navigate these waters? In chapter 2, we examine developments concerning the full faith and credit clause. In chapter 3, we do much the same for the privileges and immunities clause. In chapters 4 and 5, we focus on the interstate commerce clause. Chapters 6 and 7 review various strands of justiciability and habeas corpus cases across the eras, and chapter 8 provides an overview and conclusion.

NOTE

1. A small diversion on "home-rule" may be in order. When speaking of the imperial relation among nations, colonial home-rule would indicate that the imperial power has turned its colony loose. A small community with a closed society has a very different form of home-rule. Here, home-rule parallels the classic democratic idea of a small self-governing territory. The line between democracy and theocracy becomes dimmer and dimmer. Most of the colonies were far too large for this type of home-rule, as the federalists were quick to point out. Confusing small, closed societies with the larger, more diverse colonies might give the anti-Federalists a propaganda advantage, but it merely camouflaged the great heterogeneity of the many colonies compared to the small, homogeneous communities of Pericles, Rousseau, and later, Salem Village.

Chapter 2

Full Faith and Credit

The first paragraph of Article IV in the Constitution introduces a clause designed to govern how the formal citizenry records of one state incorporate those of another state. Section 1 reads:

> Full Faith and Credit shall be given in each State to the public Acts, Records, and judicial Proceedings of every other State. And the Congress may by general Laws prescribe the Manner in which such Acts, Records and Proceedings shall be proved, and the Effect thereof.

The Full Faith and Credit Clause essentially says that (a) public acts, (b) public records, and (c) judicial proceedings taking place in one state are recognizable as valid by any state into which the implicated citizen should move or travel. The clause in simple terms makes state differences in these three areas non-exclusive and of less consequence; it may even move the states toward some form of uniformity to avoid the inevitable clashes. Nothing of the sort has ever happened, suggesting that judicial interpretation of this clause has dramatically limited its reach.

The early SCOTUS decisions focused on whether international private law would govern the relation between judgements made in one state and recognized as such in another. Private international law would deny such recognition, making a debt (*nul debit*) or record (*nul tiel record*) concluded in one state essentially invisible in another. When the writers of the Constitution included the Full Faith and Credit Clause, the intention was to replace this international private law. The question then remained whether a principle of comity, of statute, or of constitutional stature required one state to recognize judicial decisions in another. Comity would simply require that the decisions of a foreign court are *prima facie* evidence in the instant court. Congress acted in 1790 to specify the method of authenticating state court records, thus giving judicial judgements, by statute, the effect of records under the Full Faith and Credit Clause. Justice Story relies heavily on this statute in *Mills v. Duryee*, 11 U.S. Cranch 481 (1813) when recognizing the decision of a New York case in a federal court. Justice Marshall restates the *Mills* decision in *Hampton v. McConnel*, 16 U.S. 234 (1818), but significantly adds the constitutional stature that results of a judicial decision by one court would have the same effect in any other court. Pleas available in the originating state court would be available in the host state court.

POST-MARSHALL

The unsettling *McElmoyle v. Cohen*, 38 U.S. 312 (1839) decision substantially modified the simpler *Hampton* decision. The heyday of the Marshall Court had passed with Marshall in 1835, and the newer decision tempered the meaning of the Full Faith and Credit Clause. The *McElmoyle* Court agreed that the decision of a court in a sister state was conclusive on its merits. At this point *McElmoyle* begins to diverge. Although the judgment of a court in one state is recognizable in a second state, the acknowledged judgment must follow the host state's laws and rules of execution (*lex fori*), not those of the originating state. The *McElmoyle* case also made it clear that any state could legislate on the remedy for suits from other states, except for the merit of the suit itself. Such legislation includes a statute of limitation. Any statute of limitation in the host state governs the judgment settled in the originating state.

The *McEmoyle* case goes even further. If someone dies in one state, having a judgment against him in a sister state, the administrator of the estate should treat the out-of-state judgment as a simple contract debt and handle it as other contract debts. If there are insufficient funds, the contracts divide the revenue. Thus, the execution in the host state of a judgment made in the originating state does not have the same rank or compulsion as judgment might have in the originating state. Despite later cases whose decisions wandered around *McEmoyle*, that case effectively set substantial limits on the Full Faith and Credit Clause for the remainder of the nineteenth century.

THE LOCHNER ERA

As SCOTUS moved into the twentieth century, it was in the grips of a laissez-faire Social Darwinism (1887–1937) generally labeled the *Lochner Era*. In *Lochner v. New York*, 198 U.S. 45 (1905) SCOTUS held that the Fourteenth Amendment guaranteed the right to purchase as well as sell labor. SCOTUS found that New York State interfered with individual liberty by using health regulations to limit the number of hours a baker could work each week or each day. Voiding the police power of the state as an interference with the right of contract complemented SCOTUS' use of the Tenth Amendment to put similar limits on federal efforts, however justified. Highlighted against the background of the *Lochner Era*, Justice Holmes announced a peculiar full faith and credit decision in *Fauntleroy v. Lum*, 210 U.S. 230 (1908).

Speculating on cotton futures was illegal in Mississippi but legal in Missouri. The *Fauntleroy* defendant lost and refused to pay for his speculation, but eventually both plaintiff and defendant agreed to arbitrate the debt in the state of Mississippi, even though the source of the debt was illegal under Mississippi law. The defendant then moved temporarily to Missouri, in whose courts the plaintiff sued to enforce the terms of arbitration reached in Mississippi. Missouri found the terms of arbitration enforceable and valid, entering judgment for the plaintiff. SCOTUS required, under the full faith and credit clause, that the award be binding in Mississippi. The Mississippi defendant, now turned appellant or plaintiff against the Missouri decision, argued in Mississippi courts that the original agreement was illegal under Mississippi law in the first place and hence unenforceable in any Mississippi court. SCOTUS applied Marshall's reasoning in *Hampton* that Mississippi could not look beyond the Missouri decision for an error in law.

The four dissenters in *Fauntleroy* argued that the decision unduly expanded the full faith and credit clause. The dissent held that the full faith and credit clause gave no new power to Missouri Courts, save to make obligatory the comity practice already recognized among sovereigns like Mississippi. The dissent took exception because the contract in question was illegal and prohibited in the enforcing state. In this case, the contract and the arbitration took place in Mississippi, where the contract and associated acts were illegal and unenforceable. Mississippi would favor the original defendant and thus no enforceable decision if it should ever come before its courts. To establish this, however, the Mississippi Court would have to look to the validity of the Missouri Court decision, allowing a decision that may or may not "have the same credit, validity, and effect as in the state where it was pronounced."[1] The Holmes majority in *Fauntleroy* had re-elevated the Story/Marshall interpretation in *Mills* and in *Hampton* over the *McEmoyle* modification.

In *Bradford Electric Light Co., Inc. v. Clapper*, 286 U.S. 145 (1932) SCOTUS reiterated that a state statute counted as a "public act" within the meaning of the Full Faith and Credit Clause. The cases discussed previously focused on judicial decisions, so *Clapper* was a significant reassertion of the Full Faith and Credit Clause. SCOTUS also held federal courts bound to this command. Just as the Supreme Court distinguished between a judgment (proper focus of the Full Faith and Credit Clause) and the cause of judgment, SCOTUS distinguished between a defense against an asserted liability and the cause of action prompting a suit. In the instant case, domicile Vermont employers and employees tacitly accepted the Vermont Workman's Compensation Act, whether working in Vermont or temporarily in another. Workers implicitly agreed to that Act's injury or death compensation provisions, which explicitly excluded actions based on tort. In *Bradford*, a Vermont employee died while on assignment in New Hampshire. Survivors filed a wrongful death suit in New Hampshire, even though barred by the Vermont statute for employees normally resident in Vermont. The federal court took diversity jurisdiction, but it accepted the Vermont statute as a defense. SCOTUS extended command of the Full Faith and Credit Clause to territorial statutes in *Alaska Packers Assn. v. Industrial Accident Commission*, 294 U.S. 532 (1935).

POST-LOCHNER

After the Lochner Era, *Titus v. Wallick*, 306 U.S. 282 (1939) continued the *Fauntleroy* logic. In *Titus*, SCOTUS ruled that the Ohio Supreme Court could not substitute its standards for a New York court judgment and, by having done so, Ohio raised a Federal question under the Full Faith and Credit Clause. SCOTUS held that Ohio had to enforce the New York judgment. A decade later, in *Union National Bank v. Lamb*, 337 U.S. 38 (1949), SCOTUS again claimed certiorari review of a state supreme court's refusal to honor a judgment valid in a sister state. A plaintiff revived in Colorado an old claim from 1927 and sought enforcement in a Missouri court, where the respondent then lived. The Missouri court refused to honor the Colorado claim, because the time limits of its own courts would not permit such a revival. SCOTUS found that decision erroneous, although SCOTUS did permit the Missouri Court to examine due process considerations upon remand. In both cases, the actions of one state's supreme court on the judgment of a sister state effectively created a Federal question, with the appeal papers in the lower courts serving as the petition for certiorari to SCOTUS.

The apparent rule since *Fauntleroy* has been that it is the judgment of a sister court that gets full faith and credit. The integrity of a sister court judgment cannot be impaired, except for attacks on whether the sister court had proper jurisdiction. We get a distinctively different result in *Pacific Employers Ins. Co. v. Industrial Accident Commission*, 306 U.S. 493 (1939).[2] Here SCOTUS reserves for itself to determine how compelling the Full Faith and Credit Clause is when the laws of one state conflict with those of another. Comparing California and Massachusetts employee compensation statutes, each of which gave its state complete and sole control over compensation for a worker injured while on assignment in the other, SCOTUS decided that the Full Faith and Credit Clause could not, in this instance, resolve in favor of the home state instead of the forum state where the injury occurred. California statute and court decisions argued that entertaining the compensation laws of another state for a temporary employee would be obnoxious to the California policy expressly providing for no exemption of any employer from California rules for compensation.

SCOTUS supports this new reading of the Full Faith and Credit Clause in *Watson v. Employers Liability Assurance Corp, Ltd.*, 348 U.S. 66 (1954). The motivation in this case results from a noted change in place of negotiation and issue of a liability policy, place where delivered, and where an injured person may reside. This "nationalization" of insurance contracting and coverage essentially made it more difficult and costly for an injured person to pursue a remedy if the Full Faith and Credit Clause required that the statute at point of origination or delivery were to govern in the injured party's home state and/or supersede specific contract provisions. SCOTUS found that, when a contract affects the people of several states, each state may have its own interests enforced by its own contract policies. Alternately, a state may require compliance with its own contract statues as a condition for the insurance company to do business in that state.

In *Carroll v. Lanza*, 349 U.S. 408 (1955), SCOTUS revisits *Pacific* and effectively reaffirms it. In the instant case, an injured employee of a subcontractor, both residents of Missouri, received weekly payments under the Missouri Compensation Act. The injury occurred in Arkansas. Both Missouri and Arkansas compensation acts disallowed common law suits between employee and general contractor. The subcontractor employee sued the general contractor for negligence damages in Arkansas. SCOTUS held that the Full Faith and Credit Clause did not allow the Missouri Workmen's Compensation Statute to bar a common-law suit in Arkansas, and that the Arkansas statute did not bar an employee suit against a third party, in this case the general contractor, in Federal court.

The dissent distinguished among precedent cases in commercial law, insurance cases, and workmen's compensation cases. Unlike other workmen's compensation decisions, Arkansas' sole interest was being the accident site. The general contractor operated out of Louisiana, and the employee and subcontractor were residents of Missouri. For Arkansas statute to prevail, the decision would cast doubt on the continued relevance of *Bradford v. Clapper*, but SCOTUS did not overrule that case. The dissent argued that favorability to the claimant is not a good court presupposition, but that logic appears to be the one used by the majority. The dissent favored exclusive use of the Missouri statute, giving full faith and credit to the state appearing to have the greatest interest in the controversy.

Congress entered the full faith and credit fray in 1946. What became the Federal Tort Claims Act[3] required federal courts to "look to the first instance of the law of the State where the acts of negligence took place." The Claims Act also removed U.S. sovereign immunity against claims based on the negligence of a U.S. employee working within the scope of the job. The states had their own "conflicts of law" guides to proper jurisdiction when multiple state torts were involved. The states also had their own liability laws. In *Richards v. United States*, 369 U.S. 1 (1962), mechanics failed to follow federal repair guidelines in the Civil Aeronautics Act. An airliner, negligently overhauled in Tulsa, crashed in Missouri while en route from Oklahoma to New York. The Oklahoma Wrongful Death Act set no limits on recovery, but the Missouri Wrongful Death Act set the maximum recovery per person at $15,000. The courts initially applied Missouri law, but representatives of the deceased passengers sued to use Oklahoma wrongful death law, which attorneys read as more consistent with the Federal Torts Claim requirement. SCOTUS rejected that claim as well as another, pointing simply to where the negligence had its operative effect. SCOTUS argued that the Federal tort guidelines required the court to use Oklahoma law but, in doing so, would use Missouri's wrongful death statute, because Oklahoma's laws of conflict (applying place of injury to the substantive rights of those injured or killed) would refer the case to Missouri law and that, in any event, Oklahoma law cannot operate extraterritorially.

STATE SOVEREIGNTY

The growing tensions over the Full Faith and Credit Clause became quite apparent in *Nevada v. Hall*, 440 U.S. 410 (1979). The case arose from a two-car crash on California highways involving a car owned by the state of Nevada, driven by a state (university) employee during his job, who died in the accident. California courts imposed a far greater liability on Nevada than Nevada law would permit. SCOTUS ruled that the sovereign courts of a sister state could sue a sovereign state, and that the Full Faith Credit and Clause did not require California to substitute Nevada's law for its own. Justice Rehnquist joined one dissent to this case and wrote a second. We look at the latter.

Rehnquist took exception to the majority's claim that there was no constitutional source for state sovereign immunity. Rehnquist argues that the assumption used by previous courts, express decisions by SCOTUS, and the structural logic of the Constitution, all point to a constitutional source for state sovereignty. He points nowhere in the Constitution, but rather conjures underlying postulates derived from shared experience and common understanding. The implicit constitutional plan that makes the Constitution workable, giving each provision full workable effect, requires state sovereignty. It is not clear whether justices from across time and across the political spectrum would agree on what these postulates are or what the underlying constitutional plan looks like. Rehnquist's interpretism, asserting some universality of postulates and plans, does not make it so. Rehnquist had carried forward his opinion in *National League of Cities v. Usery*, 426 U.S. 833 (1976), where he invalidated a federal minimum wage for state workers because it threatened a state's "ability to function effectively in a federal system." Rehnquist revealed his peculiar view of federalism and its effective functioning. In criticizing the literalism of the majority, Rehnquist substituted vague standards allowing multiple political interpretations.

There is no question that the pattern of SCOTUS decisions regarding full faith and credit versus state sovereignty have been quite mixed. In his dissent in *Carroll v. Lanza*, 349 U.S. 408 (1955), Justice Frankfurter cites twenty-one cases of state sovereignty conflict, with the forum state winning ten times and the sister state eleven times. Rehnquist, well after the Civil War amendments, had a particularly expansive view of state sovereignty, concluding that no state is subject to suit without its consent. Rehnquist further argues that this view of sovereignty is the foundation of the Eleventh Amendment. In other Rehnquist cases that we examine, the Justice dismisses as dicta considerable portions of previous SCOTUS opinions, yet in *Hall* Rehnquist complains that the Court will not accept dicta making the Eleventh Amendment the basis of state sovereignty/state immunity.

The Eleventh Amendment, by its text, removed the Federal courts from jurisdiction over citizens of one state suing another state or foreign subjects suing a state. There is nothing in this text that says a citizen of one state, in that state's court, may not sue that state. *Hans v. Louisiana*, 134 U.W. 1 (1890) protected, under aegis of the Eleventh Amendment, a state from suit by one of its own citizens in Federal court. The issue at the time of the Eleventh Amendment was Marshall's expansive Federal court reach when various state legislatures sought to ignore their Revolutionary War debts. Rehnquist wanted more; he sought the re-establishment of state sovereignty lost after the Civil War to the central government via the Civil Rights amendments. In his dissent in the *Nevada* case, Rehnquist makes fast and loose with previous case opinions and in some instances used comments quite out of context. Justice Rehnquist sought an even greater expansion of the Eleventh Amendment. For example, Rehnquist cites Frankfurter's dissent in *Great Northern Life Ins. v. Read*, 322 U.S. 47 (1944) as agreeing that the Eleventh Amendment constitutionalized state sovereignty/immunity from suit. In the same dissent, Frankfurter, who is not in broad agreement with Rehnquist's claim, writes:

> Whether this immunity is an absolute survival of monarchical privilege, or is a manifestation merely of power, or rests on abstract logical grounds, see *Kawananakoa v. Polybank*, 205 U.S. 349 (1907), it undoubtedly runs counter to modern democratic notions of the moral responsibility of the State.

Early Full Faith and Credit Clause promoters sought to reduce the parochialism then existing among the several states. That clause drove over considerably rougher terrain with the advent of industrialism and our movement into the administrative age. The relevance of the full faith and credit clause to workman's disability compensation is one example. *Magnolia Petroleum Company v. Hunt*, 320 U.S. 430 (1943) elevates that clause by arguing that a case adjudicated in one state is the *res judicata* of every other state. The court further argues that, when states refuse to recognize such a decision, it is a violation of a Federal right. In the instant case, a resident of Louisiana injured in Texas received compensation under a Texas statute which declared the Texas award final and prohibited further recovery anywhere, including sister states. The injured workmen sought further recovery in Louisiana, but the Texas law denied recovery and that state's law had finality under the Full Faith and Credit Clause.

Four years later, SCOTUS again considered the question regarding a worker residing and hired in one state but suffers a debilitating injury in another state. In the *Industrial Commission of Wisconsin v. McCartin*, 330 U.S. 622 (1947), Wisconsin agreed that the claimant would not lose any rights under its law, if Illinois was agreeable. Illinois made full payment under its compensation regulations, and after that, Wisconsin made its payment, minus the amount awarded in Illinois. Using a previous Illinois Supreme Court Ruling, SCOTUS held that the Illinois award was final only with respect to other Illinois provisions and statues; the Full Faith and Credit Clause would allow Wisconsin to award additional compensation in accordance with its own laws. Although an exclusive right proviso like that in the Texas statute is not in the Illinois regulations, this appears to be one of the few differences between *Magnolia* and *McCartin*, even though the SCOTUS decisions were opposite.

The Rehnquist Fog

Because a state could include finality language in its compensation statutes to trigger the Full Faith and Credit Clause, it was reasonably clear that SCOTUS should overturn either *Magnolia* or *McCartin*. This issue arises in *Thomas v. Washington Gas Light Company*, 448 U.S. 261 (1980). A deeply divided court, four signing the main opinion, three a concurring opinion, and two joining a dissenting position, held that the Full Faith and Credit clause did not preclude a second, supplementary compensation. In the instant case, a man residing and employed in Washington, D.C., suffered a work-related injury in Virginia and received compensation under a Virginia statute that forbade seeking further compensation anywhere (including Washington, D.C.). The plurality decision and overall majority judgment was against using Full Faith and Credit to require Washington, D.C., to honor the finality in Virginia's statute. The plurality overturned *Magnolia*, which had included a similar statute-based finality provision. The plurality argued that the legislature of one state should not legislate for the people of another, and that this extra-territorial control gave states, under the Full Faith and Credit Clause, a power they did not possess.

The concurrence questioned the reasoning of the plurality but pointed out that the fundamental purpose of the full faith and credit provision was to end litigation, so that the effects of adjudication in that state did not reopen in another. The concurrence argued that the plurality decision did not have such finality, nor act as a nationally unifying force, as the Full Faith and Credit Clause supposedly did. Neither the concurrence nor the dissent supported overruling Magnolia. Both the concurrence and dissent emphasized the difference between the status of statutes and adjudication decisions, with only the latter deserving full faith and credit.

Rehnquist, writing the dissent in *Thomas*, argued that the injured workman had an initial choice of state disability compensation plans. Once he made that choice, however, the Full Faith and Credit Clause should prevent any further adjudication in a sister state. Rehnquist goes on approvingly to quote the plurality observation that the *McCartin* rule was an unwarranted delegation of SCOTUS responsibility to the states for final arbitration on full faith and credit. Rehnquist then criticizes the plurality for invoking *stare decisis* as the reason for trying to find a new theoretical foundation for *McCartin*, even though five of the nine judges considered it weaker than Magnolia.

Rehnquist leaves us with the image of two distinct arenas of *res judicata*, and the injured workman may choose between either for adjudicative relief, but after that close the matter and may not open in a sister state. Unmistakable language in one state's compensation rules can effectively block any further action in another state. The surface problem may appear to be an injured party doing remedy shopping; however, *Magnolia*, the precedent preferred by Rehnquist, limited the choice between two plans and that is it. (*McCartin* would now be the law.) The problem is that when invoking Rehnquist's rule, you effectively have one legislature making decisions for another, as would appear authorized by the Full Faith and Credit Clause. The new industrial and administrative age has produced new forms of the general interstate problem that the Framers of the Constitution sought to resolve in favor of unifying the nation. Rehnquist, apparently inadvertently, embraced the anti-state sovereignty version of the Full Faith and Credit Clause. Rehnquist cites with approval the plurality's assessment in *Thomas* that the rule in *McCartin* "represents an unwarranted delegation to the States of this Court's responsibility for the final arbitration of full faith and credit questions." If anything, Rehnquist supports greater SCOTUS intervention in full faith and credit issues, assuming it does not apply the *Magnolia* rule. Rehnquist certainly knew that the plurality (and governing) decision in Thomas had overruled *Magnolia.*

Rehnquist also reveals a couple of judgment hot-spots that will appear and reappear over the course of his SCOTUS career. First, Rehnquist is sometimes hostile to law review articles that question former SCOTUS decisions and appears irked when his colleagues import the logic in those articles into their decision-making. Second, when SCOTUS attempts to balance competing interests, which Rehnquist rejects as an unauthorized exercise in balancing interests, he then generally favors business interests over personal welfare. These issues are little more than tale about Rehnquist's personality and personal values. We take notice now because both issues reappear, and both have causal influence on Rehnquist's judgment.

Five years later, Rehnquist delivers the majority decision in *Phillips Petroleum Co. v. Shutts*, 472 U.S. 797 (1985). Here appears another problem unique to the industrial and administrative era that was simply beyond the experience or imagination of the Founding Fathers. In *Phillips*, the respondent faced a class of 28,000 certified royalty holders from all fifty states, Washington, D.C., and some foreign countries. Phillips Petroleum had bought natural gas from eleven states during the 1970s. Ninety-nine percent of the gas leases and 97 percent of plaintiff class members lived outside Kansas, the state in which the trial occurred. Phillips had sold gas through interstate commerce, its price regulated by the Federal Power Commission, not the Federal Energy Regulatory Commission. A requested price increase could go into effect before final Commission approval, but if denied, Phillips would have to repay customers the difference between old and temporary new prices, plus interest. Phillips generally kept royalties earned on these higher price charges until the final approval of each price request. A small percentage did receive royalties on the higher prices, but only if they had executed a bond or indemnity in case of a price increase denial. These royalty owners received interest, set at the rate Phillips Petroleum would have to pay customers if the commission denied a price.

Phillips Petroleum eventually gained approval of all three requested price increases, so it paid the suspended royalties to royalty owners, without interest. Three royalty owners from other jurisdictions filed suit for the interest, and Phillips asked for and received permission to bring the suit before a Kansas court using Kansas law and to certify the suit as class action.

Phillips lost the suit and the court ordered it to pay interest on the royalties. The Kansas court set those interest rates at the same rate Phillips would have had to pay its customers if they had not received the price increase. The suit raised two issues: whether the Kansas court had jurisdiction over the 28,000 absent royalty owners, and whether Kansas law governed the interest rates paid to royalty owners in other states. The Kansas Supreme Court essentially affirmed jurisdiction and affirmed use of Kansas law in determining the interest rates that Phillips would pay royalty holders.

SCOTUS affirmed the jurisdiction question, making a distinction between defendant and plaintiff, with only the defendant able to prevent a court from imposing an undue burden on it. The class action was an exception to judgment *in personam*, because of the numerical size of those with the same complaint and the possibility of economic vulnerability if each person had to go it alone. Even if most absent members of the class had minimal contact with Kansas and thus would not have standing alone, the provision of some due process protections, including an opt-out option, would be sufficient to certify members of the class. An opt-in provision was not necessary for plaintiffs.

Whether Kansas law determines the interest rates on sequestered royalties is more of a problem. First, SCOTUS found a substantive difference between Kansas law-based interest rates and the rate due under Texas law or Oklahoma law. Second, using Kansas law alone would require a Kansas interest in the case, made through significant contact or significant aggregate contact with the plaintiffs. The use of Kansas law alone would otherwise appear arbitrary and unfair, as the plurality explains in *Allstate Insurance Co. v. Hague*, 449 U.S. 302 (1981). The dissent in *Allstate*, which included Rehnquist, stated that law only casually or slightly related to the case would not pass due process under the Fourteenth Amendment and that, under full faith and credit, the forum state must respect the laws and judgments of other states. It comes as no surprise, given that Rehnquist delivered the *Phillips* opinion, that the exclusive use of Kansas law was so arbitrary and unfair as to fail constitutional requirements. Because of the diversity of location for the royalty holders, the Kansas court has several choices of law besides its own.

The judgment on Kansas law is certainly not consistent with either the *Magnolia* or *McCartin* rule. Phillips creates an anomaly where the Kansas courts get jurisdiction over the plaintiff class, but its courts must use the laws of other states in setting the interest rates for its royalty holders. The SCOTUS decision also goes awry quickly. The practical consequence is that the defendant provides the court with interest rates under various state laws, in its effort to reduce its overall obligation to its royalty holders. The Kansas court receiving this information can either perform a parallel fact-finding investigation or request each implicated state to get involved in providing the Kansas court with the necessary information. Apart from states with large numbers of royalty holders, exactly how far down the list of fifty states, Washington, D.C., and some foreign countries need the Kansas court seek information before applying its own law? On the surface, this decision may appear to honor some form of state sovereignty, but it virtually stands the Full Faith and Credit Clause on its head. Rather than other states recognizing the judgment, the pronouncing court is responsible for using the law of at least some other states. Putting nation-wide law suits into the jurisdiction of state courts simultaneously illustrates the limits of the states qua sovereignties and illustrates the confusion when the forum state laws are inadequate to guide final judgment.

An odd combination results from the Phillips case. On the one hand, a state court may grant standing to a nation-wide class action suit, even though there are tenuous ties at best between the state and the plaintiff. On the other hand, the state court authorized to hear a nation-wide suit applies, not its own state laws, but those of the states most involved in the judgment. The implication is that state courts can appropriately estimate what laws or what legal results would obtain in a sister state, under their laws, even though those courts have not been party to the hearing and judgment process. This opened the doors, particularly for corporations like Phillips, to introduce its own favorable version of other state laws, as indeed it did. Interestingly, the Kansas court ultimately took recourse to the interest rates used by the Federal Power Commission to determine interest rates for customers, if denied a price increase. For all intents and purposes, therefore, the Kansas courts fell back upon Federal standards rather than its own law or that of other, more closely involved states.

While corporate lawyers found great promise in the Rehnquist decision, the doors opened resulted in a flood of nation-wide suits filed in state courts, and a host of new legal problems facing the state and Federal courts. It was with silent acumen that Justice Scalia engaged in a salvage operation three years later in *Sun Oil v. Wortman*, 486 U.S. 717 (1988). A set of related Sun Oil cases had been before the courts at roughly the same time as the Phillips cases. Both companies had filed cases in Kansas, and both involved royalty interest rates. The Sun case also questioned whether Kansas law should govern the statute of limitations on claims, or whether the substantive laws of a different state were germane here. Scalia had to tread tricky ground here to limit the reach of Phillips without directly overturning it. As we see below, Rehnquist joined part of the *Sun* decision but joined O'Conner in dissenting in part.

Sun Oil Company challenged whether the Kansas Supreme Court could make it liable for royalty interests on some older claims because, under the substantive law of the claimant's state, the statute of limitations had passed;

the more liberal Kansas statute of limitations would not govern under the new variant of the Full Faith and Credit Clause and the Due Process Clause of the Fourteenth Amendment. Sun Oil also challenged the Kansas Supreme Court decision regarding the interest owed on the withheld-as-suspended royalty payments. The gas producing properties were located primarily in Texas, Oklahoma, and Louisiana. The Kansas courts used the FPC rates for reimbursing customers in the event they denied a price increase request, because Sun Oil had already agreed to abide by the general terms set by the FPC. A remand from the U.S. Supreme Court required the Kansas courts to use the rates applicable in each of the states that were home to the gas producing properties. The Kansas trial courts, on remand, again used the FPC rates. Scalia argued in *Sun Oil* that the *Phillips* case had distinguished between substantive and procedural law, with only the former subject to the remand.

The statute of limitations issue revolved around whether these limitations were matters of procedural or substantive law. Sun Oil challenged the earlier decision in *M'Elmoyle* that limited application of international conflict law to the states by the Full Faith and Credit Clause. Consequently, application of a forum state's statute of limitations should be substantive and that the statute of limitations of the state in which the claim's merit arose should govern. Abstractly, the right to royalty interests derives from the original promise, and what is enforceable derives from a statute of limitations. To complicate matters further, SCOTUS held in *Erie R. Co. v. Tompkins*, 304 U.S. 64 (1938) and re-examined in *Guaranty Trust v. York*, 326 U.S. 99 (1945) that the procedure/substantive dichotomy should give way when necessary, such as the need to get consistent outcomes in Federal and state court trials on similar claims. Rather than the goal of consistency, Scalia argues that the Full Faith and Credit Clause guarantees that either of opposite state laws may be applicable, to delimit the spheres of state legislative competency. Each state has competency over its own procedural law. Thus, the Kansas courts may, but do not have to apply their own state's statute of limitations.

Rehnquist agrees with Scalia's analysis of applicable statutes of limitations, but parts ways on the same subject in *Phillips*, namely what law governs the interest rates on delayed royalty payments. Rehnquist's decision in *Phillips* clearly indicates that the forum state may not apply its own law to set these rates, but rather should use the interest rates required in the state of merit. The Kansas courts responded by using the FPC rates, because the existing laws in the merit states were not to the contrary. Sun Oil claimed that the Kansas courts had deliberately misconstrued these laws. Scalia responded that Sun Oil could establish a misconstruction only if it shows that the Kansas court decisions contradicted the laws of the merit states and that those contradictions are before the Kansas courts. Scalia pens that SCOTUS can find no misconstruction under this construction of the term. Scalia agreed with the Kansas courts that Texas and Oklahoma and Louisiana, albeit for slightly different reasons, had implicitly accepted the FPC rates when they complied with the other FPC regulations.

O'Conner and Rehnquist argued that the Kansas courts did violate the Full Faith and Credit Clause and the Due Process Clause by using the FPC rates. They argue that the general interest rates set by each of the merit states should prevail, rather than the SCOTUS holding that various exception clauses in the merit states' laws effectively allowed the FPC rates used for purposes of equity. O'Conner and Rehnquist essentially argue that the FPC rates are acceptable only if there is a positive action to that effect in each state in which merit has arisen. The Kansas courts' inference about what the merit states might do is insufficient to sustain use of the FPC interest rates. This is a reverse claim to the SCOTUS majority claim, that explicit decisions by sister court states would need introduction into Kansas courts before successfully challenging the use of FPC rates. The majority and the dissent each feel that their interpretation of the Full Faith and Credit Clause should govern.

Scalia seems to have understood how preposterous it would be to allow state courts to hear nation-wide class action suits and then rely on the defendant to introduce guiding cases or for the state court to interpret another state's laws in meting judgment. The Framers also understood that the Federal system did not allow states, where a claim has properly arisen, to commandeer the judiciary of another to do its bidding. A nation-wide claim such as royalty holders across fifty states is properly a national problem. Why stop at the interpreted judgment of the three largest gas producing states? Nearly ten percent of the gas producing properties involved here are located outside these three states.

CONCLUSION

The Full Faith and Credit Clause declares that the public acts, the public records, and the judicial proceedings in one state are recognizable as valid in another state. Like the Interstate Commerce Clause, Full Faith and Credit envisioned a single sovereignty and the demise of competing petty sovereignties. In *Hampton*, Chief justice Marshall had interpreted the phrase quite broadly, indicating that the results of a judicial decision by one court would have the same effect in any other court. The later *McElmoyle* decision added three important criteria. First, the target state must affirm the source state judgment. Second, the laws and rules of the second state governed the execution of that judgment. Third, any state could legislate on the remedy for suits arising in other states. It is *Hampton* that receives support from a majority

Court during the *Lochner Era* in *Fauntleroy*. *Bradford* elevates state statutes as defense in a diversity suit.

SCOTUS introduces a significant modification of the Hampton logic in *Pacific Employers Ins. Co.* Here SCOTUS injects itself as the arbiter of competing state laws. In *Pacific*, SCOTUS set aside *Clapper* as a special case where the home state does not have an exclusivity provision in its compensation act. Its conclusion, that a state statute from the home state may be a defense in the forum state, was unnecessary. Most important, SCOTUS set aside the requirement that the forum state follow the laws of the home state. States under the federal union have reserved some attributes of sovereignty. "Full faith and credit does not here enable one state to legislate for the other or to project its laws across state lines to preclude the other from prescribing for itself the legal consequences of acts within it."

The *Carroll* decision effectively supported *Pacific* and brought the continued relevance of *Clapper* into question. The dissent argued that the majority implicitly was assuming a position favorable to the claimant to determine which state's law would prevail. The dissent argued that the state with the greatest interest in the controversy should have its law determinant. The Federal Tort Claims Act in 1946 required the court to first look at the state laws where the negligence occurred. When claimants used that suggestion, SCOTUS answered that the place where the negligence chain started would be the state law used, with the exception that that state's laws of conflict would point to the wrongful death statute of the state where the negligence chain ended.

Justice Rehnquist enters an area of unsettled law in his dissent in *Nevada v. Hall*. Here, Justice Rehnquist attempted to argue that there was a constitutional basis for state sovereignty. He pointed to previous SCOTUS decisions and the structure of the Constitution, even in the absence of a specific constitutional clause supporting the view. Justice Rehnquist veers further into uncharted territory by arguing that the source of state sovereignty was shared experience and common understanding. In the earlier *Usery* decision, Justice Rehnquist cited a state's ability to function effectively in a Federal system. In a later decision Rehnquist uses the Eleventh Amendment as further evidence of state sovereignty.

The conflict between the *Magnolia* and *McCartin* decisions allowed the *Thomas* Court to overrule Magnolia with four votes, even though the three concurring votes and the two dissenting votes would overrule *McCartin*. Rehnquist cast one of the dissenting votes in the *Thomas* decision. Rehnquist supports the finality rule, which effectively allows one legislature to make law for another. Rehnquist would allow the injured worker choice between two sets of state rules, but after that, close the issue. Rehnquist wants the responsibility left with the Supreme Court to arbitrate full faith and credit questions, not allow the states to bargain, as *McCartin*.

In the *Phillips* case, Justice Rehnquist pens the majority decision. The controversy was the interest rate paid to some 28,000 bond holders across all fifty states and Washington, D.C. The court sequestered their royalty interest pending approval of a price increase. The trial occurs in Kansas, but most of the gas sold under the sequester arrangement came from states other than Kansas. Phillips got the price increase and paid the royalties but did not pay interest on the royalties. The Kansas courts claimed jurisdiction and claimed the use of Kansas law in setting the interest rates. SCOTUS approved the jurisdiction question but found the Texas or Oklahoma interest rates preferable to the lower Kansas rates. Kansas had to implement the laws of some other state, with the defendant providing information on those rates to the Kansas court, and then the Kansas court could either do parallel fact finding or ask the implicated states to get involved directly. In his attempt to honor the sovereignty of other states, Rehnquist renders the Kansas court their servant. Kansas ultimately fell back upon the FPC standards. Although Rehnquist dissented from the interest rate settlement part of the *Sun Oil* case, Scalia appears to have understood how preposterous the Rehnquist logic in *Phillips* would be when applied to class action suits involving plaintiffs in many, if not most states, each of which had its own unique solution to the interest rate issue. Using the FPC rates as the fallbacks position, unless explicitly disallowed by a state, allows Scalia to return some manageability to the Pandora's Box opened by Rehnquist.

NOTES

1. Marshall's view in *Hampton v. M'Connel* was subject of discussion by both the majority and the dissent in *Fauntleroy*. The dissent cited *Wisconsin v. Pelican Ins. Co.*, 127 U.S. 265 (1888) as good law governing *Fauntleroy*, but the Holmes majority found it effectively irrelevant. (Compare *Milwaukee County v. M. E. White Co.*, 296 U.S. 268 (1935).) Interestingly, both the majority and the dissent felt that the Marshall interpretation was guiding. In an Article IV case, *Anglo-American Provision Co. v. Davis Provision Co., No. 1*, 191 U.S. 373 (1903), the majority also found a jurisdiction control matter irrelevant to the *Fauntleroy* issue. (New York's courts could deny jurisdiction, and thus entry to its courts, to two Illinois corporations over a judgment rendered in an Illinois court.)

Wisconsin v. Pelican Ins. Co., 127 U.S. 265 (1888), discussed by the majority and minority, was an Article III and Article I issue, not a full faith and credit issue. The state of Wisconsin got a considerable judgment against a foreign corporation for failing to meet certain statutory requirements of corporations doing business in the state. Wisconsin sought enforcement in SCOTUS, and the question is whether the

U.S. courts, either through the Constitution or the Judiciary Acts, had power over penal, as opposed to civil disputes. The Wisconsin fines were penal, and thus beyond SCOTUS power.

2. Signs of the Hampton rule's disintegration are also in *Milwaukee County v. M. E. White Co.*, 296 U.S. 268 (1935).

3. The provisions of the Tort Claims Act: 28 U.S.C. §§ 1291, 1346, 1402, 1504, 2110, 2401, 2402, 2411, 2412, and 2671–2680.

Chapter 3

Privileges and Immunities

The Founding Fathers were extremely worried about the disarray introduced by competing states under the Articles of Confederation. Because the proposed Constitution would go to state conventions of the people rather than state legislatures, the Framers designed Article IV of the Constitution as a check upon state sovereignty. One of those checks, reviewed above, is the Full Faith and Credit Clause. The second check is in the second section of Article IV, the Privileges and Immunities Clause, or how to treat citizens from one state in another, either in traveling or relocating. Section 2, paragraph 1, of Article 4 reads:

> The Citizens of each State shall be entitled to all Privileges and Immunities of Citizens in the several States.

Taken literally, Full Faith and Credit and Privileges and Immunities Clauses appear as intended: border busters. The same applies to rendition of traitors and criminals (Article IV, Section 2, paragraph 2). Article IV, Section 2, paragraph 3 requires the return of run-away slaves, regardless of any differences in state laws governing slavery.

The Privileges and Immunities Clause reappears as the Privileges or Immunities Clause in the Fourteenth Amendment. Because the clauses are so similar in wording yet have generated different case law, we will refer to the original Privileges and Immunities Clause as the Comity Clause. That name, commonly used when referring to the Article IV version, clearly suggests more courtesy than compulsion. The literal wording requires treating the resident of one state, moving to or traveling through another state, the same as all other citizens of that state. Once again, judicial interpretation has limited the meaning and reach of this clause. On the one hand, courtesy is not legally binding. Second, if presence or residence in an area is sufficient to claim all the privileges and immunities of any other person in that area, state borders would have limited meaning for a mobile population.

There is an interesting difference in the progression of the Full Faith and Credit Clause and the Comity Clause. Full Faith and Credit starts as a strongly worded requirement, deliberately intended to replace old international law on the subject. If Privileges and Immunities are matters of comity, the Clause starts much weaker than Full Faith and Credit, but slowly gains strength in the first two-thirds of the twentieth century. If enforced strictly and swiftly, the two clauses would put enormous pressure for uniformity across the states and diminish importance of state boundaries, per se.

Over time, the Comity Clause faced three big questions. First, how do we tax an individual working in one state and living in another? Specifically, can state law distinguish between resident and non-resident in tax law? Second, how should a state conceive of its natural resources (wildlife, oil, minerals)? What effect does this have on privileges and immunities? Finally, what about labor and employment? Can a state preferentially favor residents over non-residents?

PRIVILEGES AND IMMUNITIES AS FUNDAMENTAL RIGHTS

The initial rules on privileges and immunities go back, not to a decision of the Supreme Court, but to Justice Washington's 1823 judicial circuit decision in *Corfield v. Coryell*, 6 Fed. Cas. 546, no. 3,230 C.C.E.D. Pa. 1823. Justice Washington made a narrow decision, based on the natural rights conception of the time, that limits privileges and immunities to fundamental rights belonging to citizens of all free governments. Although Justice Washington disavows an intention to list these fundamentals, he then names seven:

1) Protection by the Government
2) Enjoyment of Life and Liberty
   Acquire and possess property
   Pursue Happiness and Safety
3) Pass Through or Reside in any State
   Purposes of trade, agriculture, professions
4) Habeas Corpus
5) Institute and Maintain actions of any kind in Courts of the State
6) Hold and Dispose of Property (Real or Personal)
7) Exemptions from higher taxes or impositions than paid by its Citizens

Since these belonged to any citizen of a free (democratic) government, the Privileges and Immunities Clause adds little or simply repeats what "everyone knows." Justice Washington declined to extend the Clause further and, especially, to "public patrimony:" the rights or advantages that belong only to the citizens of a state. The state may exclude non-citizens or non-residents from the common property held by a state for its citizens. In the instant case, Justice Washington ruled that a state had the right to fisheries within its borders akin to property rights. The state holds property for its people only, and the state was under no obligation to grant co-tenancy with citizens of another state.

The Comity Clause fared no better when SCOTUS weighed in with *Conner v. Elliott*, 59 U.S. 591 (1855). A young Louisianan, with guardian's permission, married a Mississippi man and together they took up domicile in Mississippi. During the marriage, her husband had acquired property in Louisiana. By Louisiana law, a marriage in Louisiana created community property between husband and wife. Property acquired after a couple relocates to Louisiana would also be communal. Louisiana recognized no other communal rights, implicitly or explicitly. The wife in this case outlived her husband, but Louisiana denied any claim on property her husband acquired during their marriage, the couple having remained in Mississippi.

The appeal to SCOTUS centered on a single question: does a right attached to a contract, because of the place it occurs, also attach to a marriage domiciled elsewhere, as a right of U.S. citizenship? If so, the widow could make claim on her husband's Louisiana property as a property right. If not, the widow must forfeit all property acquired by the husband in the state of Louisiana, because at no point was the marriage domiciled in Louisiana. If the state of Louisiana were to extend to the widow all the rights and privileges of properly domiciled Louisianans, then the widow could claim her husband's property as a matter of property right. SCOTUS ruled that the widow had no rights in Louisiana other than those inhering in her being a citizen of a free government, as described by Justice Washington in *Corfield v. Coryell*. The husband's acquired property attached only to the contract and place of execution; it was blind to both husband's and wife's citizenship. Communal rights grafted onto a marriage contract made in Louisiana and domiciled in Louisiana were creatures of statute, only for those covered by the statute, regardless of citizenship. Any rules grafted to a Mississippi marriage were the business of that state and that state only. The law of the place where made and performed governs a contract.

CIVIL WAR AND THE CIVIL WAR AMENDMENTS

Corfield v. Coryell had effectively rendered the Comity Clause without real constitutional significance. The revival of that Clause was slow in coming. Adoption of the Thirteenth Amendment in 1865 effectively ended the impact of slavery on state sovereignty. It was also becoming clear that the Radical Republicans who controlled Congress after the Civil War were not about to allow readmission of the Confederate states to the Union without first guaranteeing that the Southern state governments could not *de facto* do what they could not do *de jure*. It is against this background that *Crandall v. State of Nevada*, 73 U.S. 35 (1867) stands out. The Fourteenth Amendment was in the ratification process, but the experience of the Civil War and the need to move troops hither and yon, plus of course ratification of the Thirteenth Amendment, had made SCOTUS sensitive to national needs and the deadly consequences of asserting state sovereignty.

The state of Nevada has imposed a passenger tax on railroad passengers leaving the state or passing through it. Nevada made little effort to camouflage the passenger tax as some form of tax on the railway itself, so there was little question this was a passenger tax similar in some ways to the *Passenger Cases*, 48 U.S. 283 (1849). *Crandall* maneuvers considerable constitutional terrain without explicitly using the Comity Clause, but the case implicitly expands the concept of immunities, and it foreshadows changes to come. The defense argued two constitutional principles: whether the Nevada tax was a forbidden impost or duty on exports (people) and whether this was interstate commerce. If rail travel fell under the latter, then is this an exclusive power reserved to Congress; alternately, may the states exercise that power until Congress passes superseding legislation? SCOTUS was uncomfortable extending "export" to people and differentiated the situation from the *Passenger Cases*. The logic of the latter option, eventually replaced by dormant commerce clause analysis, is that Congress may recognize local regulations in some areas as sufficient for the time being and chooses not to act further to supersede state action, as discussed in *Cooley v. Board of Wardens*, 53 U.S. 299 (1851). SCOTUS undertook the commerce clause analysis, but then declined to make it the basis of a decision.

SCOTUS raised the view that, absent an explicit constitutional clause, there are some powers that are essential to and inherent in being the central government. Reflecting on the troop movements during the Civil War, the Court pointed out that the central government needed an unimpeded vehicle for calling up troops, and that the Nevada tax could prove an essential bottleneck. What would happen, for example, if the late Southern governments were to impose an extremely high tax to prevent a troop call-up? Correlatively, the citizens of a national government needed unimpeded access to their government, and a tax like that of Nevada's would impede the ability of citizens to seek redress, contact legislators, and so forth. Nevada's taxing systems and others like it could impede the flow of citizens in a way that undermined the national government. Under these circumstances, the tax, however seemingly benign, was unconstitutional.

The privilege of leaving a state without penalty; the privileges of entering a state without penalty; and the immunity of cross-state passengers from the onerous taxes imposed by each state through which the railroad moved; all point to an underlying constitutional right. The *Crandall* Court inferred a right from the existence of a national government. Neither the comity privilege nor this inferred right required Justice Washington's conception of fundamental rights. SCOTUS was not yet ready, in the *Crandall* case, to give some real meaning to the Comity Clause, beyond the lip-service of Justice Washington. The logic for expansion of comity was there; the following year the states ratified the "Privileges or Immunities" Clause as part of the Fourteenth Amendment.

SCOTUS takes a step back in *Paul v. Virginia*, 75 U.S. 168 (1869). A Virginia statute required that any insurance company, not incorporated in Virginia, secure a license to carry on its business, and to deposit bonds with the state treasurer that would reflecting the capital employed. Sanctions would follow shortly in another bill. SCOTUS side-stepped the Virginia legislation using two arguments that we have already seen and another, perhaps more significant. First, SCOTUS accepted reasoning from *Conner v. Elliott* that the privileges and immunities clause only covered fundamental rights, and that this insurance legislation was simply a special privilege provided by a state to its citizens and not available to citizens of other states. Second, in keeping with its tepid interpretations of the Inter-State Commerce Clause, SCOTUS ruled that an insurance policy was not a matter of commerce. Finally, because at this point corporations had not benefitted from Fourteenth Amendment interpretations, SCOTUS argued that corporations were not citizens and hence not protected by the Privileges and Immunities Clause.

A year later, and in contrast to *Paul*, SCOTUS rules against a state statute requiring licensing of foreign vendors at a rate twice that of in-state vendors in *Ward v. Maryland*, 79 U.S. 418 (1870). The state of Maryland sought to control the sale of most goods in districts including Baltimore through yearly licensing, on criminal penalty for violation. SCOTUS knew the case came before them as a test case on the Maryland statute. After extensive commentary on the ability of both state and national government to tax, subject to constitutional limitations, SCOTUS then finds that, by whatever name, the tax violates the Privileges and Immunities clause of Article IV, Section

2. Like its predecessors, the Court makes no effort to define "privileges and immunities," except to remark on its comprehensiveness.

SCOTUS, in *Ward v. Maryland*, goes beyond Justice Washington's enumeration of fundamental rights and cites several specific components of privileges and immunities: engaging in lawful commerce, acquiring personal property, taking and holding real estate, entering actions in courts of the state, and exempting foreign state residents from higher taxes or excises than imposed on its own citizens. The last component, foreign resident exemption from taxes higher than on its own residents, clearly puts the Maryland statute in violation of the Comity Clause. In the earlier part of the decision, Justice Clifford defended the state's right to tax. After invoking the privileges and immunities constitutional prohibition, Justice Clifford then argues that, if a state indiscriminately imposed taxes against citizens of other states, it would eviscerate Congressional power to regulate interstate commerce. Thus, the Maryland statute violated both the Comity Clause and the Inter-State Commerce Clause. The Maryland statute was repugnant to the Constitution and invalid.

The *Slaughter House Cases*, 83 U.S. 16 Wall. 36 36 (1872) present the first clear confrontation between the Comity Clause in Article IV, Section 2, and the Privileges or Immunities Clause in the Fourteenth Amendment. SCOTUS makes several claims in this decision that do not survive historical scrutiny. What may be more interesting are the strange tangents onto which the Court finds itself. Louisiana granted a corporate monopoly over the landing, slaughter, and butchering of livestock. The Court found little controversy over landing controls, but control over the place of slaughter and butchering raised objections from butchers who typically cut their meat in local butcher shops. SCOTUS argued that corporations had had exclusive privileges for some time, and so any objection to the practice have appeared, if at all, only of late in the U.S. Constitution. The first twelve amendments were roughly coterminous with the Constitution itself. Thus, the focus would have to be on the Civil War amendments, or the Thirteenth, Fourteenth, and Fifteenth Amendments. These are the primary grounds pursued by the plaintiffs.

In its response, SCOTUS first argued that the three amendments in question involved black slavery. To be sure, the terms were general enough to proscribe other forms of slavery or outlaw certain forms of discrimination or to guarantee the vote, but taken in historical context, they grant few new powers to Congress but impose specific limitations on the states. Second, SCOTUS assumes that the definitions of citizenship—(1) born or naturalized in the country and subject to its laws; (2) resident of a state—created two separate statuses, rather than the latter being a subset of the former. Next the Court moves to the Privileges *or* Immunity Clause, but here introduces the difference just cited. Of considerable consequence was the distinction between "privileges and immunities," Article IV, Section 2, and "privileges or immunities," Fourteenth Amendment, Section 1. SCOTUS takes immense significance from the difference between "Citizens of each State," Article IV, Section 2, or "citizens of the United States," Fourteenth Amendment, Section 1. SCOTUS asserts that the Fourteenth Amendment protects only the privileges *or* immunities belonging to a citizen of the United States (Fourteenth Amendment), not a Citizen of a State (Constitution). Finally, it is the states that protect the class of rights elaborated in the Bill of Rights.

The distinctive take on the Fourteenth Amendment versus the Old Constitutional package (the Constitution plus the first twelve amendments) does not end here. SCOTUS claimed that Article IV, Section 2, gave the citizen of each state no added security of rights and did not control the States in their grant or refusal of rights to their citizens. The Comity Clause only provided a measure by which to judge the privileges due citizens from other states within your jurisdiction as each State has determined what is due to their own citizens. The only Federal-level impositions were those mentioned in the Constitution without the Bill of Rights: no ex post facto laws, no bills of attainder, no laws burdening contracts. The plaintiffs in The Slaughter House Cases, SCOTUS concluded, were in error because the Fourteenth Amendment neither made the Federal government the protector of civil rights in the various States nor granted Congress the power to do so. SCOTUS does admit that constructions of an argument drawn from its possible consequences are not the strongest, but in this case, the Court insists that its construction is correct, or else the Civil War amendments (a prescient observation) reversed the entire power relation between the central and state governments.

General Citizenship and Special Citizenship

In *McCready v. Virginia*, 94 U.S. 391 (1896) SCOTUS introduces a distinction between citizens, depending on circumstance. The issue was whether a resident of another state could, in a Virginia stream that would ebb and flow with the tide, "plant" oysters until the oysters fattened and were ready for harvest. SCOTUS agrees that the central government has constitutional control over navigation, but it excepts oyster planting and harvesting so long as it does not interfere with navigation. SCOTUS uses the narrow definition of interstate commerce such that commerce begins only when an article or product has entered the commerce stream. The oysters do not enter the commerce stream until harvested and sent to market, thus avoiding any central government control via interstate commerce. This leaves the stream bed itself and, although fed with tide waters, it remains the property of the state in which it is located. In this case, Virginia owns the stream bed and holds it as common property for its domiciled citizens only. Because SCOTUS concludes that access to the stream bed is based on a special citizenship defined by its locale, a state may prohibit use of the bed to foreign state residents without violating the Comity Clause.

Under the U.S. Constitution, the Federal courts had jurisdiction over common-law actions as well as suits in equity. The latter practice has deep roots in English jurisprudence, substituting principles of fairness for rules of law. In Federalist #83 Hamilton describes equity to include consideration of fraud, accident, trust, or hardship. Early Federal equity cases took no cognizance of state laws until the Supreme Court ordered, in 1839, that Federal courts sitting as equity courts must take into consideration whether the state law has created or removed a substantive law for its citizens. Equity case load began to rise after the Civil War and became increasingly frequent in the *Lochner Era* (*Lochner v. New York*, 98 U.S. 45 (1905) 1887–1937). During this Era, SCOTUS emphasized freedom of contract against state police powers and the Tenth Amendment against non-contract constitutional intervention. The Federal Rules of Civil Procedure (1938) eventually combined common law cases and equity cases into "civil actions."

Given the growth of cases in equity and the complications introduced by diversity, equity eventually touched upon two constitutional powers in Article IV: Full Faith and Credit (Section 1) and Privileges and Immunities (Section 2). SCOTUS had held in *Green v. Van Buskirk*, 72 U.S. 307 (1866) that the Full Faith and Credit Clause was applicable in equity suits with diversity. In that case, a citizen of New York (Bates) owed a debt to two other New York citizens (Van Buskirk and Green). Van Buskirk held a chattel mortgage on some iron safes owned by Bates but located in Illinois. Van Buskirk sued for possession of the safes in a New York Court, while Green sued in an Illinois court. Under Illinois law, Green gained ownership of the safes; he sold them, with the proceeds going to Green. Green brought his suit two days after Bates gave the chattel mortgage to Van Buskirk, but Van Buskirk had not filed those papers in New York before Green began proceedings in Illinois. Van Buskirk next successfully sued Green in a New York court to recover the proceedings from sale of the safes. Green then brought the case to SCOTUS, Messieurs seeking relief under the Full Faith and Credit Clause. SCOTUS concluded that filing and making public the Illinois proceedings occurred before the New York proceedings, and thus the New York courts would have to respect the Illinois court decision.

The conjunction of the Full Faith and Credit Clause and the Privileges *and* Immunities Clause appears in *Cole v. Cunningham*, 133 U.S. 107 (1890). Daniel Bird suspended payment due to Butler and Hayden of Butler, Hayden & Co. All three were residents of Massachusetts. Aaron Claflin & Co. of New York, in turn, owed Bird for goods previously consigned. The Butler, Hayden firm assigned their claims to one Fayerweather of New York who, in turn, filed suit against Bird, and another suit naming the Claflin firm as garnishees. Between the New York filings, Bird's creditors met in Massachusetts. The suits continued in New York courts while the estate of Bird moved toward insolvency in Massachusetts. Two people appointed as assignees for insolvency in Massachusetts filed an equity suit against Butler, Hayden in Massachusetts to have them stop attachment proceedings in New York, or to surrender their gains in New York to the Massachusetts' assignees. Insolvency proceedings continued, while the highest Court of Massachusetts granted the equity suit against Butler, Hayden, and its assignee, Fayerweather. The Massachusetts decree did not pretend to make law for New York; rather, it ordered citizens of its own state to abide by Massachusetts judicial proceedings rather than try to circumvent them.

Butler, Hayden argued both the Full Faith and Credit Clause and the Privileges and Immunities Clause against Massachusetts' enjoining them from continuing the New York suit. The Full Faith and Credit Clause rendered judicial decisions in one state's courts as cognizable evidence in the courts of another state. The Privileges and Immunities Clause entitled foreign (different states') citizens the same privileges and immunities extended to their own citizens. Both the majority and dissent address these two Article IV clauses, but neither makes a clear distinction between the effect of the Full Faith and Credit Clause and the Privileges and Immunities Clause.

Butler, Hayden insisted that, even if the Fayerweather assignment be invalid, the subsequent decision in New York courts was valid. Thus, either or both clauses trumped state equity rules. This is the conclusion reached by the dissenters. The Massachusetts decree ordering Butler, Hayden to discontinue the New York suit was *in personem*, in this case the partnership of Butler and Hayden. The insolvency assignees in Massachusetts urged that it was unclear whether the assignment of interests to Fayerweather, without his advance knowledge or approval, was legal. Further, the actions of Butler, Hayden were fraudulent because designed to circumvent the equity rules of Massachusetts. If the Constitution does not change normal equity rules, and instead pronounced only rules of comity, then Massachusetts should proceed. This is the majority position.

The SCOTUS majority pointed out that the Full Faith and Credit Clause required consideration of such decisions as credible evidence, not valid judgments, per se. Rules of comity were simply self-imposed rules on authority already possessed. New York courts could, by New York law, point foreigners back to their state of origin laws. Courts of equity, in contrast, could restrain suits on a judgment of law. The Privilege and Immunities Clause allowed, but did not demand, the courts in New York to put an end to the seizure of the money owed to Bird by Claflin. Thus, Butler, Hayden had the privilege of using New York courts, but those same courts could defer to the legal action in Massachusetts. Whatever New York courts chose to do did not prevent Massachusetts courts from exercising their jurisdiction over its own citizens. If a plaintiff voluntarily makes himself party to the proceedings in another state, they otherwise would bind him.

The *Cole* majority argued that their decision favoring the Massachusetts decree was consistent with the decision in *Green v. Van Buskirk*. Illinois law had made void mortgages not acknowledged and recorded, in contradistinction to the laws in New York. The Illinois ruling had been the governing one. The Cole dissent, on the other hand, argued that the assignment of Butler, Hayden interests to Fayerweather was sufficient to allow the New York courts to proceed and that Fayerweather's residency in New York rendered the Massachusetts' *in personam* action mute. And, just as *Green* found favor of the Illinois courts, so the dissent felt that *Cole* should find favor of the New York courts, even though the majority opinion supported Massachusetts.

Corporations and the Lochner Era

SCOTUS briefly revived Article IV Section 2 Privileges and Immunities Clause in *Blake v. McClung*, 172 U.S. 239 (1898), albeit with a twist. There are two opposite rulings in *Blake*, drawing more new distinctions that previously. As a background, recall that the Fourteenth Amendment first defined U.S. citizenship. SCOTUS took the term "persons" in that amendment to include corporations in a headnote added to *Santa Clara County v. Southern Pacific Railroad*, 118 U.S. 394 (1886). That inclusion was not adjudicated, per se. The *Slaughter House Cases* (1872) had already opined separate rather than coterminous spheres for U.S. versus state citizenship. In *Blake*, two more definitional exercises appear. First, the term "resident" is a "citizen," apparently because the Fourteenth Amendment simply defines residence in a state as the basis of state citizenship. Second, SCOTUS grants that corporations are citizens (not just persons) in the state of incorporation, but corporations are not citizens when it comes to constitutional protections such as Article IV Section 2 Comity Clause. Additionally, SCOTUS considerably strengthens the original Privileges and Immunities Clause. Article IV Section 2 now does more than suggest common courtesy, it requires it.

Tennessee had passed a statute imposing certain registration requirements on foreign corporations and subjected them to the same judicial proceedings as their own corporations as well as to the same taxation. In case of insolvency, the corporation is liable for its debts, but the debts of natural person residents of Tennessee take primacy over those of natural person nonresidents. A Tennessee court declared a British company engaged in mining, manufacturing and freight to be insolvent, and appointed a receiver to administer assets, giving resident holders of debt full priority. The receiver paid debts owed from the normal course of business, but U.S. citizens, not living in Tennessee, sued. A superior court accepted the distinction between residents and non-residents, but ruled that all non-residents, whether U.S. citizens or not, equal entitlement to a ratable portion of the remaining assets.

The suit before SCOTUS raised three constitutional grounds: Article IV Section 2, plus Due Process and Equal Protection Clauses of the Fourteenth Amendment. SCOTUS gives support for previous Court case-by-case approach to "privileges and immunities," plus Justice Washington's list of fundamentals. SCOTUS then proceeds to enumerate fundamental rights or the good of the whole: protection by government, life and liberty, the right to acquire property, and the right to pursue and obtain happiness and safety. More particular privileges and immunities include the right to reside in or pass through any state, habeas corpus, access to the state courts; the right to take, hold, or dispose of property; exemption from taxes higher than those paid by other citizens of the state, and the elective franchise. SCOTUS cites the famous justification for privileges and immunities found in the Articles of Confederation: "the better to secure and perpetuate mutual friendship and intercourse among the people of the different states of the Union."

SCOTUS cites *McCready* as confirming that the Privileges and Immunities Clause removes the disabilities of alienage in other states by giving them equality of privilege. Although some of its precedents had given exclusive privileges to citizens of a state, the same does not apply to trade or interstate commerce more generally. The Tennessee insolvency statute created an inequality between residents and non-residents of Tennessee when transacting business with the instant corporation. The non-resident transactions occurred under the cloud that an insolvency would first pay in full natural person obligations of residents. Doing so is repugnant to the Constitution under Article IV Section 2.

After this resounding reaffirmation of the original Privileges and Immunities Clause, SCOTUS applies an opposite decision to a corporation qua citizen of the state under whose laws organize it, but that derives from the legal assumption that members of the corporation are citizens of that state. The corporation *qua* citizen is not, however, a citizen within the meaning of Article IV Section 2. The corporation is a state "citizen" only under the Fourteenth Amendment, as asserted in *Santa Clara County*. SCOTUS goes on to conclude that the corporation is not a "citizen" within the meaning of the Due Process and Equal Protection Clauses in the Fourteenth. The Virginia corporation at issue had a claim upon the insolvent corporation, even if it did not have priority in asset distribution. It was not a citizen under Article IV Section 2 and thus cannot lose due process under the Fourteenth Amendment. It cannot claim equal protection of the laws because that clause requires the person be within the jurisdiction of the offending state. The Virginia company, not created by, nor doing business in Tennessee, is not within Tennessee jurisdiction.

SCOTUS continued working through the problem of what privileges and immunities to share across state lines and which would qualify as citizen privileges by location. Complaints based on both Article IV, Section 2 and the Fourteenth Amendment's Due Process and Equal Protection Clauses further exacerbated the problem. Taxation illuminates the confluence of principle and reality. Connecticut and its municipalities had various taxes meant to support the operations of government. The state taxed personal property, such as stock shares, held within the state, absent a deduction for real property, because the latter was subject to a property tax. Non-resident stock holders paid a standard millage, without real property tax credit. The complaint charged that the state taxed non-resident stock holders at a significantly higher rate than resident stock holders because the latter had the real property tax deduction on the property owned by the company in which they held shares. Clearly the tax discriminated between resident and non-resident stock holders, but the question was whether this discrimination rose to the level of prejudice violating privileges and immunities or equal protection. SCOTUS found neither, because the overall Connecticut tax system had municipal property taxes on resident stock holders qua property holders not paid by non-resident stock holders, so the difference was a washout. Variance in taxes paid, absent deliberate intention, is ultimately part of imperfect human nature on which to found human judgment.

The SCOTUS decision in *Chambers v. Baltimore & Ohio R. Co.*, 207 U.S. 142 (1907) is important, not because it decided that there was no violation of the privileges and immunities clause, but because of how it described that right. The case involved two citizens of Pennsylvania, the husband died because of a rail accident in Pennsylvania, and the widow sued in Ohio (corporate home of the railroad) for negligence in the death of her husband. The case worked its way to the highest court of Ohio, which dismissed the case for lack of statutory jurisdiction. The widow appealed to SCOTUS under Article IV Section 2. SCOTUS pointed out that the right to sue and defend in the courts is a fundamental right, a privilege of citizenship, and demands equality of treatment. The federal Constitution protects the right and it is not a matter of comity. The courts of Ohio are, however, closed to all plaintiffs on behalf of a non-citizen of Ohio, whether the plaintiff be a citizen of Ohio. Thus, Ohio courts treated citizens and non-citizens seeking access to Ohio courts equally. Only the Ohio citizenship of the deceased was the requirement for access to Ohio Courts that may be applying the negligence laws of another state. SCOTUS ultimately decided against a violation or Article IV Section 2, because the cause on which the widow sought relief was a special provision of Pennsylvania not cognizable by the Ohio courts. Three members of the Court filed a dissent, arguing that the Ohio statute and the Ohio Supreme Court violated the Privileges and Immunities Clause.

An important exception appears in *Hudson County Water Co. v. McCarter*, 209 U.S. 349 (1908). A New Jersey plaintiff laid mains and contracted for water to move from New Jersey to Staten Island. In response, New Jersey made it unlawful to transport, in any way, fresh water from New Jersey into any other state for use therein. The plaintiff then contracted with New York City to deliver fresh water for the Borough of Richmond. New Jersey then sought to enjoin the plaintiff from carrying daily waters for Richmond. The plaintiff sought SCOTUS relief from the New Jersey statute under several constitutional claims, including the obligations of contract, privileges and immunities, and equal protection of the laws. The defendant claimed residual rights in the bed of the stream and could prohibit title to the water on a large scale. SCOTUS chose to put the authority of the state on the police powers as limits on the rights of private property. The state, Justice Holmes reasoned for SCOTUS, represents the interests of the public and has standing in court to protect the atmosphere, water, forests, and game within its territory. Private property rights cannot trump the foundations of public welfare and health.

SCOTUS opened the proverbial Pandora's box with the conservation decision in *Hudson*. In *West v. Kansas Natural Gas Co.*, 221 U.S. 229 (1911), a couple years after the *Hudson* case, SCOTUS faced a state statute that treated natural gas and oil as objects of state conservation, even though the surface land owners had the right to take possession of the gas and oil below. SCOTUS argued that, in matters of interstate commerce, there are no state lines, and the welfare of all the states is at stake. Once in possession, gas and oil cannot stay for intrastate transport only. Thus, conservation for local commerce is not a justifiable use of police power, nor can the state deny appropriate right of way for interstate commerce.

The Court again assessed the interface between taxation and the privileges and immunities clause in *Shaffer v. Carter*, 252 U.S. 37 (1920). If a state law did not provide remedy for a claim against an unconstitutional tax lien, then SCOTUS has jurisdiction and available relief under equity. By now quite settled, a state may not rule beyond its borders, but the judiciary of one state can enforce state statutes *in personam* compared to *in rem*. In this case, a citizen and resident of a foreign state objected to the income tax imposed on a business owned and managed in the forum state. SCOTUS found that the tax depends for its constitutionality under the Privileges and Immunities Clause by how it operates, not its motivating theory. The statute in question allowed residents to deduct gross income losses within and without the state, while non-residents could only deduct gross income loss within the forum state. If the plaintiff suffered any such losses, because upon that principle it denies even the ability to raise the issue, the operation of the tax is not necessarily discriminatory because residents paid tax on all their income, earned inside and without the state, whereas the non-resident only paid taxes on income earned within the forum state. The forum state could also tax both real property and income taxes. For violating the tax provisions, the instant foreign citizens had a tax lien placed on all their properties, personal and real, within the forum state. SCOTUS ruled that because the plaintiff did not appear to have non-productive property in the state, and that therefore everything upon which the lien was productive property, the lien survives.

Yet another taxation versus privileges and immunities controversy occurs in *Travis v. Yale & Towne Mfg. Co.*, 252 U.S. 60 (1920). Once again, a state income tax came under fire, this one in New York. The state statute permitted residents a host of deductions from all gross income, while non-residents could take the deductions only with respect to income earned within the state. New York also grants residents exemptions for head of family, dependents, and so forth but grants credits to non-residents for the ratio of taxes payable to the forum state and total income but makes these credits provisional on the foreign state's credits being comparable to New York's. In addition, a withholding tax imposed on incomes earned in New York by non-residents but avoidable by petition for residents. SCOTUS found neither the withholding tax nor its effect upon the company accounting or its labor relations sufficient for relief. Exemptions granted to residents but not non-residents were, however, in violation of Article IV Section 2. SCOTUS again affirms the importance of the Privileges and Immunities Clause in making the citizens of the United States one people. Making credits dependent on other state's laws is equivalent to the state legislating beyond its borders; the forum state cannot bargain away the privileges and immunities of citizens of the United States. Retaliation cannot correct discrimination, and hence it offers no cure.

The conflict between conservation and commerce overshadowed the Privileges and Immunities Clause for a time, even though SCOTUS could have recast some of the cases as discrimination between residents and non-residents. In *Foster-Fountain Packing v. Haydel*, 278 U.S. 1 (1928), for example, the state of Louisiana used conservation as a vehicle for claiming that shrimp harvested in its waters were the property of the citizens of the state and that the meat could not enter commerce until removing the heads and hulls for use as a fertilizer and in chicken feed. Not surprisingly, only about 5 percent of the shrimp meat harvested in Louisiana went for Louisiana consumption. Most raw shrimp shipped to Biloxi, Mississippi, for processing and further shipment. This processor considered the head and hulls a nuisance, with most returned to the sea rather than fertilizer or chicken feed. The statute had the obvious effect of stopping shipment to the Biloxi plant, by far the largest processor of Louisiana shrimp, thus forcing the processing onto

Louisiana land, even though the Biloxi port was far more convenient. Clearly, the statute discriminated against the Biloxi processors.

SCOTUS settled the controversy on the conservation-commerce argument. As SCOTUS had done earlier, once extracting a product (netting shrimp, drilling natural gas), it has entered the commerce stream and hence governed by the Interstate Commerce Clause. The two large exceptions were conservation of water, forests, etc., but these become common property guarded by the state and could not be "taken" from the natural environment. The other exception was game, which had peculiar property characteristics, in that the game moved from location to location, per se, but the state could reserve their "taking" as a privilege of citizenship in that locale and held as a trust for its own people. Louisiana tried to use the game exception as a rouse for the shrimp act, but SCOTUS noted the greater similarity to natural resources "taken" for the welfare of all citizens of the United States. One of the justices cautioned against calling Louisiana out on its deception, because SCOTUS could reach a decision on shrimping with private ownership without looking to the shroud of fraud.

Another shrimping case could not avoid a constitutional appeal to the Privileges and Immunities Clause. South Carolina statutes regulated shrimping in the three-mile maritime belt off its coast, and an incorporated group of fishermen who were residents and citizens of Georgia sued in *Toomer v. Witsell*, 334 U.S. 385 (1948). SCOTUS failed to find standing for the association, but individual members faced fines and imprisonment for violating the statutes without relief except for litigation after heavy losses. SCOTUS found that South Carolina could use its police power to regulate the three-mile belt, absent any action of Congress. The shrimp in South Carolina waters were migratory, moving from the waters of North Carolina down to Florida waters later in the year. The effort to aid residents of each state as the shrimp moved South resulted in retaliatory measures among the affected states. SCOTUS found that the regulation does violate the Privileges and Immunities Clause by charging a nonresident license fee that was one-hundred times that charged resident shrimpers. South Carolina again raised the conservation-game exception allowing special privileges for residents ("citizens") of South Carolina per the *McCready* case. SCOTUS noted that the oysters in the McCready case stayed in inland waters until removed by man, while the shrimp were migratory and in open sea waters. Another regulation requiring non-residents to prepare shrimp for interstate shipping at a South Carolina dock, even if paying a stamp tax, violated the inter-state commerce clause.

The Rehnquist Sojourn

The confluence of state taxing versus Privileges and Immunities Clause reappears in the Rehnquist era in *Austin v. New Hampshire*, 420 U.S. 656 (1975), with Rehnquist joining the majority. New Hampshire adopted a Commuters Income Tax, which taxed foreigners' incomes earned in New Hampshire at a specific rate but would lower it if the home state had a lower income tax rate. New Hampshire did not tax earnings of residents, and ultimately it did not tax incomes derived out-of-state. No discernable offset reduced the discrimination between residents and non-residents. Nor can the statutes of one state depend upon the configuration of statutes in another. Retaliation was no cure as well, leaving the most affected without legislative voice. In short, SOCTUS found that the New Hampshire tax violated Article IV, Section 2.

We get renewed consideration of the conservation/gaming versus commerce in *Baldwin v. Fish & Game Comm'n of Montana*, 436 U.S. 372 (1978). In this case, Montana required non-residents to pay significantly higher for an elk hunting license than residents. Montana elk spend their summers up the mountains on Federal land. In winter, they wander down closer to civilization where farmers may give them an extra bale of hay. Big game is plentiful in Montana, and it has hundreds of outfitters who equip and guide hunting parties. Three quarters of all extracted elk occurred on Federal land. SCOTUS ruled, as it did in *Geer v. Connecticut*, 161 U.S. 519 (1896), that Montana owned and could regulate the elk population for conservation, that non-resident access to the elk was only recreational and not fundamental, and thus did not rise to the protection of the Privileges and Immunities Clause. Protection of wildlife is within Montana's policing authority. Rehnquist again joined the majority opinion.

A lengthy dissent penned by Brennan and joined by White and Marshall did find discrimination in licensing charges and would apply Article IV Section 2. They argued that Article IV Section 2 protects nonresidents from the unjustifiable discrimination by residents; this principle supersedes Justice Washington's outdated conception of fundamental rights underlying privileges and immunities. Citing *Toomer*, Brennan argued that there had to be a reasonable relationship between the dangers represented by nonresidents and the discrimination practiced upon them. Brennan, heralding the death of *McCready*, points out that the notion of a state owning game is a nineteenth century legal fiction. The lack of control over resident hunters is not conservation control, but an invitation by residents to destroy a natural resource while excluding nonresidents. Brennan thus finds no justification for the 7.5 difference in licensing costs and would apply the Privileges and Immunities Clause to find the statute unconstitutional.

In a rare unanimous court decision, SCOTUS found unconstitutional the Alaskan program giving residents preference over nonresidents for any job touching on the Alaskan oil and gas industry. Alaska argued that the discrimination was necessary to fight its unemployment, and besides, Alaska owned the oil and gas fields. Alaska would promote its interests through issuance of residency cards. The Alaskan Supreme Court already had struck down a one-year residency requirement. Instead of a toothless comity, SCOTUS cites the *Paul* reasoning that the Privileges and Immunities Clause removes the disabilities of alienage in other states, including discrimination. The *Toomer* case emphasized that there had to be a substantial reason for alleged discrimination, and one of those reasons had to be the dangers posed by nonresidents. Alaska's unemployment problem was insufficient to overcome the Privileges and Immunities Clause, because much of its unemployment traced back to lack of education and job training or geographic remoteness. SCOTUS again refuses to follow the *McReady* decision and argues that more recent law confirms that ownership as the basis of regulation is not absolute. The Alaskan program has enormous reach, including positions that have little or no relationship to Alaskan gas and oil. SCOTUS also pointed out the close relation between the Privileges and Immunities Clause and the Interstate Commerce Clause, and that the Alaskan program also had commerce clause infirmities.

A closely divided court adds a market participant exception while the dissent focuses on a commerce clause violation. *Reeves, Inc. v. Stake*, 447 U.S. 429 (1980) involves the refusal of a state-owned cement plant in South Dakota to sell cement to out-of-state buyers in times of shortages. Originally planned to fulfill only the needs of its residents, South Dakota soon found itself selling cement to as many as nine different states. Twenty years after it began supplying virtually all the cement needed by a Wyoming firm, plant difficulties and a construction boom combined to fulfill fewer orders than it received, threatening the Wyoming firm with its very existence. The South Dakota cement commission ordered South Dakota meet its own needs first, then all contract commitments. The plaintiff in this case had no pre-existing long-term supply contract, so its orders went to the bottom of the list.

SCOTUS, with Rehnquist in the majority, reasoned that the interstate commerce clause governed states as market regulators but not as market participants on behalf of their own people. These types of formalisms are typical of Rehnquist decision-making. It preserves, on the surface, *stare decisis*, while introducing a distinction that allows an opposite result. The SCOTUS majority also gave lip service to state sovereignty.

The dissent argued that the South Dakota policy of residents first generated exactly the type of economic protectionism that the commerce clause sought to overcome. Although not litigating the Privileges and Immunities Clause, it remains the silent partner of the Interstate Commerce Clause, especially in this case. The majority decision not only made it legal for South Dakota to treat residents very differently than non-residents, it also allowed residents with unlimited access to the cement resources to engage in interstate commerce competition against the very firms that could not get a cement supply. This effectively make South Dakota an accomplice, witting or not, to use one state's resources to monopolize business transactions in another. In this case, it meant that in-state companies could compete for customers in the very region served by the firm that South Dakota cement policy crippled. Being a market participant in the production of cement, South Dakota also gave its own concrete producers a monopoly within the state and a possible monopoly in other states or regions as well. This clearly raises constitutional issues under both the Privileges and Immunities Clause and the Interstate Commerce Clause.

SCOTUS continued to expand the market participation exception to the interstate commerce clause. Citing *Hughes v. Alexandria Scrap Corp.*, 426 U.S. 794 (1976), with Rehnquist voting with the majority, Maryland became a market participant for paying scrappers to dispose of abandoned automobiles. Maryland then amended the statute to favor in-state scrappers over out-of-state. Despite the obvious discrimination, SCOTUS found Maryland's amended statute constitutional because Maryland acted as a market participant and not a market regulator. SCOTUS used the same logic in *Reeves*. In *White v. Mass. Council of Constr. Employers*, 460 U.S. 204 (1983), SCOTUS allowed the mayor of Boston to require at least 50 percent of the workforce on projects funded in part or whole by the city be residents of Boston. Rehnquist, writing for the court, dismissed the commerce obstacle by rendering the city of Boston a market participant in these city projects and hence exempt from the strictures of the commerce clause. Rehnquist notes that the respondents no longer press the Privileges and Immunities Clause in support of their Commerce Clause argument. The dissent argued that *White* went far beyond *Hughes* or *Reeves*, because the mayor's order on city-only funded projects extended to the hiring practices of private firms. The power to dictate to private firms is the power to regulate.

The ostensible reason for the 50 percent Bostonian employment rule in *White* was to reduce unemployment in the city. It did not fully finance most of the projects affected. One year after White, with Rehnquist again writing for the Court, we get a very different decision in *Building Trades v. Mayor of Camden*, 465 U.S. 208 (1984). The City of Camden had, much like the Boston case, ordered that 40 percent of employees of contractors and subcontractors working on city construction projects be Camden residents. Here, subject to the Privileges and Immunities Clause, SCOTUS found the Camden rule unconstitutional. Municipalities, being agents of the state, cannot escape a constitutional rule applied to states such as privileges and immunities. The Camden ordinance received state approval under its affirmative action guidelines, so presumably hiring Camden residents would address both the unemployment and the minority employment issue. Camden claimed the market participant exception to commerce regulations. Interestingly, pending constitutional challenges, the city amended and adopted language very like that use in the successful *White* decision the year before. SCOTUS chose to construe the Camden ordinance as an extension of the state Treasurer's power to adopt affirmative action goals. SCOTUS then found the nonresident interest in employment sufficiently fundamental to trigger privileges and immunities. The market regulator/participant distinction is relevant to commerce clause challenges but not privilege and immunity challenges, where the livelihood of the Nation itself is at stake. To justify discrimination under the privileges and immunities requires showing that nonresidents are a species of the evil at which the statute aims. SCOTUS thus reversed the New Jersey court decision and remanded it for further fact finding. The dissent questioned whether the Privileges and Immunities Clause covered municipal discrimination.

The *White* and *Building Trades* cases present an obvious problem. The precedent in *White* supposedly is binding under the commerce clause, essentially foreclosing use of the commerce clause about city hiring decisions because the city is a market participant. On the other hand, the same practices may or may not clear Privileges and Immunities scrutiny, depending upon how fundamental the discrimination and whether the discriminated nonresident is part of the evil remedied by the relief. Clearly, this moves a class of cases away from the commerce clause and into the privileges and immunities analysis. The *Building Trades* case was probably a corrective on the implications of the *White* case, but now we resurrect the issue of "fundamental" discrimination and raise a host of questions regarding what evidence is sufficient to demonstrate that those discriminated against are part of the problem. The latter will certainly allow case-by-case decisions, but that at the cost of the wide swath cut by the market participant rule and the resurrection of what is "fundamentally" protected by the Privilege and Immunities Clause.

Another Privilege and Immunities case occurs the next year in *Supreme Court of New Hampshire v. Piper*, 470 U.S. 274 (1985), with seven justices in the majority, one concurring in the result, and Rehnquist dissenting. In the instant case, a resident of Vermont, a few hundred yards from the New Hampshire border, had taken and passed the New Hampshire bar exam. The New Hampshire Supreme Court denied her admittance to the New Hampshire bar, since the court limited bar admission to state residents. Suing under the Privileges and Immunities Clause, the Vermont resident overcame some less than substantial reasons why she must be a resident of New Hampshire. SCOTUS ordered her admission to the New Hampshire bar. SCOTUS repeated the logic that the Privileges and Immunities Clause demanded equal treatment between residents and non-residents if denying a fundamental right (e.g., employment), and equal treatment would contribute to the vitality of a single Nation.

Rehnquist argues that the principle of state sovereignty, that each state is free to establish its own laws for its citizens, should be just as important as the principle of forging a cohesive union. The states differ by locale, state laws differ accordingly, and law as a profession relates closely to these substantive differences across states. This, Rehnquist argues, the state has a right to expect. Rehnquist further rejects use of "the less restrictive means analysis," which would suggest that New Hampshire could accomplish its goals without going so far as refusing a non-resident entry to the local bar. Rehnquist supports the "substantive reasons" given by the New Hampshire Supreme Court for refusing to bar nonresidents. Rehnquist often elaborates his opinion using a general or hypothetical situation instead of the one before the court. For example, although Piper lived within 400 yards of New Hampshire, Rehnquist cited the procedural delays if counsel lived 1,000 miles away. Whether nonresident legal counsel is part of the problem addressed by New Hampshire's residency requirement surely cannot stand, because the court delays are occurring under the residency requirement. The distance to the court house is, in this example, more important than the distance to the border. Finally, the bar exam itself tests for knowledge of local law, and the extent of that knowledge is not dependent on residency, per se.

CONCLUSION

The Article IV, Section 2 privileges and immunities clause has had a sordid history in SCOTUS case law. This clause is among the most politicized in the Constitution, in significant part because it has the potential to reduce state sovereignty by requiring a state to treat residents and non-residents alike. The Clause itself soon earned the "Comity Clause" nickname, suggesting that the provision was more a rule of courtesy than a rule of constitutional law. The Clause does not enter serious SCOTUS jurisprudence until 1855. An 1823 Circuit Court interpretation guided its early use, although deeply mired in the Enlightenment view of natural rights, that essentially suggested that the Clause did little more than restate the laws common to all free governments. The Circuit Court did, however, introduce an important distinction between public and private property, the former being the province of a state serving as guardian of the common property of its residents.

The post-Civil War Courts clearly recognized the potential reach of the Clause and, the addition of the Civil War amendments, would dramatically change the balance of power between Federal and state sovereignty. The interpretive game was on. In addition to interpreting the Article IV, Section 2 Clause as a rule of comity, the reappearance of similar words in the Fourteenth Amendment led to the definitional and distinctional exercises that attempted to render one or both clauses impotent. Various renditions distinguished between person, citizen of the United States, citizen of the state, and residents only. Substantive differences get thicker, including capacities essential to a central government, those inherent in police powers, privileges created by states for their residents only, ordinary law versus principles of equity, and even a muddling of full faith and credit with privileges and immunities. The privileges issue adds chunks to the stew by including corporations as state creatures and then considers whether they have some or any of the protections of natural persons. The SCOTUS rulings also intermingled privileges and immunities with diversity, the taxing power, the interstate commerce power, the citizenship clauses of the Fourteenth Amendment, and its due process and equal protection clauses. SCOTUS further divided the terrain of state policy into conservation, regulation and use of natural resources, property used for public welfare and health, and even variances that result from imperfections in human nature and human judgment.

Rehnquist introduces his new-found constitutional basis for state sovereignty, and then uses the political and constitutional confusions toward that end. Rehnquist was the natural enemy of any clause that empowered the nation over the states. That attitude put him at odds generally with the privilege and immunities clause, and the Civil War amendments were particularly consternating. His introduction of market participant as opposed to market regulator introduces a broad avenue to cross interstate commerce, privilege and immunity precedents, and legislation on discrimination. His distinctions helped preserve the appearance of *stare decisis* while circumventing its use. On the surface, his SCOTUS votes seem to affirm all or more privilege and immunities premises at one time or another, but the key consistency throughout is the effort to support state sovereignty. His distinctions had much the same effect as those after the Civil War; the Court could secure decisions more politically acceptable by splitting the back of gnats, which does not make sustainable case logic.

Chapter 4

Interstate Commerce Clause

MARBURY AND MCCULLOCH

"Judicial review," pens Chief Justice Marshall, is the only legitimate means of constitutional interpretation (*Marbury v. Madison*, 5 U.S. 137 (1803)). Marshall cites the limited, but dispositive role, of the Supremacy Clause (*McCulloch v. Maryland*, 17 U.S. 316 (1819)). Together, the commerce clause and the Supremacy Clause give the central government exclusive power over inter-state commerce (*Gibbons v. Ogden*, 22 U.S. 1 (1824)). The states would maintain ordinary police powers, but the central government would control economic exchange among the states and resist efforts by the states to tax organs of the central government. When legitimate central power confronts state power in taxation, the central government would prevail.

The instant topic in *McCulloch* was a state tax on a branch of the Second Bank of the United States. Congress had approved a national bank in 1791 with a twenty year charter. It expired in 1811, with a tie breaking negative vote case by the Vice President in the Senate. The (first) Bank of the United States generated heated debate in Washington's first administration. Secretary of Treasury Hamilton wanted incorporation of a bank to provide a ready source of money if the nation needed to borrow when faced with war; to make it easier to assume Revolutionary War debts; to promote economic development such a concentration of capital would facilitate; to draw European capital to American shores; and finally, to keep the wealth of those few very rich Americans at home rather than deposited overseas. Secretary of State Jefferson and many others opposed the bank, using many of Hamilton's own arguments against it and, adding for good measure, that there was no constitutional power to incorporate, let alone to incorporate a bank. Jefferson advised President Washington that the bank would be unconstitutional.

The debate continued with the incorporation of the Second Bank of the United States in 1816. *McCulloch* finally ended that debate. In a far-reaching decision, using phrasing such as "the power to tax is the power to destroy" or "Let the end be legitimate, let it be within the scope of the Constitution, and all means which are appropriate, which are plainly adapted to that end, which are not prohibited, but consistent with the letter and spirit of the Constitution, are Constitutional." Justice Marshall (through judicial review) concluded that the incorporation was constitutional and that no state could tax a local branch of the national bank. "Though limited in its powers," the government of the Union "is supreme within its sphere of action." Of the Court and its duty, Marshall opines "we must never forget that it is a *Constitution* we are expounding." The means available to the central government, he avers, are adequate to its ends and do not depend for execution of its powers on the governments of the states. The general government creates laws for the whole people; a state cannot make laws for those outside its borders, over whom it has no control.

The anti-Federalists thought the bank was an unnecessary concentration of economic power in the hands of a few, that it undermined the sovereignty of the states, and that it challenged the fundamental principles of democratic government. When Jackson became president, he made it clear that he would not reauthorize the bank charter, set to expire later in his first term. Jackson then ordered the withdrawal of deposits of the Federal government and transferred them to the various state banks. There were state and federal currencies in circulation. The central government tax on state banking script (money) went into effect in 1866, leaving six variants of federal currency as an everyday exchange vehicle. This fell to three after the Great Depression and then to one after 1970.

The tendency toward centralization in the banking industry mirrored the centralization seen in other industries in the nineteenth century. The Sherman Anti-Trust Act of 1890 controlled the growing monopolies, trusts, and price-fixing schemes. The United States created the Federal Reserve System in 1913 to better coordinate money and credit across the national and state banks. Periodic financial panics made increasingly apparent the need for some form of central bank to control the monetary system. Agitation over the monetary system had been growing since the Civil War, and led to several political movements, including the Populist Party and its eventual fusion with the Democratic Party in 1896, with its platform to abandon the gold standard and add silver to increase the tight money supply. Substantial agreement emerged in the late nineteenth and early twentieth century to do something about the monetary system, but there was considerable disagreement about who should oversee monetary policy. In 1863, during the Civil War, a dual banking system emerged: banks were either chartered and supervised by the nation or chartered and supervised by the states. The national charters required a bank to buy U.S. Treasury securities as part of their capitalization, helping to pay for the Civil War. Following logic dating back to the Second Bank of the United States in *McCulloch*, the states could not tax national banks and SCOTUS generally shielded national banks from state laws. Private parties owned most of the various bank charters. In 1927, Congress passed the McFadden Act, a prohibition on interstate banking. Creative private capitalists began setting up bank holding companies that allowed them to hold independent banks in several states. Congress responded with the Bank Holding Act of 1956, restricting a bank holding company to banks and financial practices firms within a single state. A crucial amendment by Senator Douglas of Illinois required the Federal Reserve Board (FRB) to allow out-of-state bank holding companies to hold banks in another state only if given explicit statutory permission to do so by the target state. Consequent to the Douglas Amendment, there were no interstate banking acquisitions for the next fifteen years, at which time a patchwork of state statutes emerged permitting interstate banking, with some states permitting acquisitions from any other state to states allowing acquisitions in a designated region or with states that had reciprocity agreements. Some states had bans on interstate acquisitions.

These statutory enablements were the topic of *Northeast Bancorp, Inc. v. Governors, FRS*, 472 U.S. 159 (1985). Rehnquist, writing for all participating justices, finds no violation of the commerce clause, the Compact Clause, or the Equal Protection Clause, in state statutes limiting acquisitions to holding companies in a region of states. SCOTUS does not consider the constitutionality of the Douglas Amendment, as variously interpreted, but rather, whether the state statutes are consistent with the Amendment, and whether the state statutes are constitutional.

Here Rehnquist takes a curious turn. He affirms the Federal Reserve Board's interpretation of the Douglas Amendment "as a renunciation of federal interest in regulating the interstate acquisition of banks by bank holding companies." The FRB then claims that the renunciation eliminated any objection to the statutes under the Compact Clause or dormant commerce clause. The FRB concluded that restriction of acquisitions to regional states is a rational way to maintain a banking system responsive to regional needs. Rehnquist makes fast and loose with Senator Douglas' phrase "to the degree," interpreting it to permit a state to lift the federal ban entirely, keep it, or partially life it, as seen in the regional state statutes. He argues that the regional statutes would be unconstitutional if the regulation of commerce in this area had remained dormant, but Congress allowed the regional approach when it passed the Douglas Amendment. His stunning conclusion is that, when Congress so chooses, "state actions which it plainly authorizes are invulnerable to constitutional attack under the Commerce Clause." He also disposes of the Compact Clause challenge and the Equal Protection challenge.

GIBBONS

It is in *Gibbons*, the third case of the Marshall trilogy, where Marshall establishes the dispositive central government supremacy over inter-state and foreign commerce, freight and passengers, steam or sail, including coastal navigation. Justice Marshall explicitly rejects so-called "strict constructionism." There is nothing in the Constitution prescribing such a rule; the "necessary and proper" clause is an enumerated power, not in the constitutional section on the limitations of power. A narrow construction, designed to cripple the central government, has no propriety. Those who wrote the Constitution used words in their natural sense, not constrained in a way that meets the intentions of some theory not contained in the instrument itself. The power invested in the Constitution is for the general advantage, not for special interests.

Regulating commerce does not stop at the jurisdictional lines of the states. In *Gibbons*, Marshall argues:

> The deep streams which penetrate our country in every direction pass through the interior of almost every State in the Union, and furnish the means of exercising this right. If Congress has the power to regulate it, that power must be exercised whenever the subject exists. If it exists within the States, if a foreign voyage may commence or terminate at a port within a State, then the power of Congress may be exercised within a State.

The states have control over intrastate commerce, but a state must not affect other states and it must not affect the execution of any of the general powers of government. If commerce collides with state law, commerce regulation wins. Congress cannot delegate its power to the states but, Congress may adopt a state statute, for example pilotage. In this case Congress also acts prospectively; adopting legacy legislation presupposes the right in the maker to legislate on the subject.

Do not limit commerce to buying and selling, or the traffic of objects. It is, writes Marshall, "intercourse between nations, and parts of nations, in all its branches, and is regulated by prescribing rules for carrying on that intercourse." Commerce must include the rules of navigation and traffic as well as the rules prescribing the conduct of individuals in barter. An inhibition to action implies the existence of the general power. If the Constitution specifies that one port or another gets no preference, by regulation or revenue, then the

Founding Fathers must have intended or granted the general power of regulation and revenue. Marshall draws a similar inference from the granted power to impose embargoes. The embargo power extends to commerce among the states. That power continues the flow of foreign commerce, from outside the country, through the various states, or from one state through or to a point in another. Power granted in the Interstate Commerce Clause is complete; it is the power to regulate. Both the central and state governments have the power of taxation, subject to the supremacy of the central sovereign. Only the central sovereign has the power over inter-state commerce.

Marshall also addresses a problem that recurs over the next two centuries. Given that Congress has the power, if it does not regulate, may the states do so until the central government chooses to act? In *Gibbons*, counsel for the appellant argued that the power to regulate excludes the action of all others. Marshall found great force in the argument, that the defense had not refuted it, but then focused on state statutes that interfered with an act of Congress. For example, does the power to lay duties on imports or exports derive from the taxing power or the commerce power? The Constitution requires that all duties be uniform, making duties on imports or exports an exemption from the acknowledged taxing powers of the states. The prohibition on duties is an important limit because the duties may be for regulating commerce and for raising revenue. In the state case, the states may raise only revenues sufficient to pay for inspection laws, a part of the police powers of the state. Duties may imply regulation of commerce, raising of revenue, or simply paying for necessary inspection laws. An explicit constitutional prohibition makes it clear that states may not attempt to regulate commerce or raise general revenue through duties and imposts.

Inspection laws, deriving from the taxing powers of the state and reflecting only necessary police functions, operate on the article before it goes into or after it comes out of commerce. These laws are part of the mass of legislation said to be part of the police power of the state, where locally-tailored regulation better serves the public than general regulations. If Congress enacts a general inspection regulation, it pre-empts any police power-derived local inspection regulation. If Congress chooses to adopt state inspection regulations, albeit these derive from the concurrent but inferior police power, then both the unique commerce power of the central government and the usual police powers of the state support state regulation. If Congress sees fit to pass a general inspection regulation based on its commerce power, then any tailored regulation derived from local police power must give way. Exercise caution in judging the enabling source of power. A national statute may derive from either the tax power or the commerce power; the state statute can only derive from its taxing power, supporting the general police function of the state.

The mental gymnastics here are impressive. More than one general power may motivate a law. Both the central government and the states have the power of taxation. Only the central government has power over inter-state, foreign, and Indian commerce. Sometimes a state regulation may be a ruse for exercising the commerce power. The Constitution eliminates one of the key areas where this may occur, prohibiting state-imposed duties on exports or imports. The states have explicit limits to their taxing power; they may not impose duties; they may not interfere with inter-state, foreign, or Indian commerce; they must yield to Congress if conflict occurs. State inspection regulations may derive from the police powers, but the state tax may be no more than necessary to support the inspections. Inspection fees are not a silent means of revenue.

A special caveat needs attention. The new Congress could not do everything at once, but this in no way indicates an abdication of power. In the early days of the Republic, for example, Congress explicitly chose to adopt local pilotage regulations. It did so because it had the only power to do so, but it had yet to work out more general pilotage principles. The colonies had used their police powers to create these legacy pilotage regulations, but the states lost such power under the new Constitution. Congress adopted those legacy rules as a stop-gap measure until Congress chose to change them. These legacy rules were in force because Congress chose them, under its commerce powers, until it saw fit otherwise.

MISREADING THE MARSHALL LEGACY

Justice Marshall provided an elegant solution to the perplexing problem of when the police power begins and the commerce power ends: after sale. Little more would need elaboration, were it not for the ill-informed decision of Justice Barbour et al. in *New York v. Miln*, 36 U.S. 102 (1837). Assume that Justice Barbour tried to honor *stare decisis* when interpreting Marshall's ruling, he failed, as did many of his colleagues, except the dissenting opinion of Justice Story. All the justices recognized that *Gibbons* was one of two possible precedent cases. The fact that *Brown v. Maryland*, 25 U.S. 419 (1827) served as precedent may help us understand why Justice Barbour misread *Gibbons* and, in the process, reopened the boundary problem between the police power and the commerce power. Justice Marshall wrote the decision in *Brown*, so it behooves us to quickly examine that case. Marshall describes the question as whether a state may require an importer to take out a costly license before selling an imported item, even if in original packaging. The constitutional issue focuses on the exclusive Congressional rights to lay imposts or duties and to control interstate commerce. The import license required in the

Maryland statute was unconstitutional. The state taxing authority begins only when, by action of the importer, it becomes mixed with the mass property of the state by breaking-up the original package. The right of gathering reasonable inspection fees remains unabated.

The Maryland license tax is also unconstitutional under the commerce clause. The exclusive commerce power over its objects enters the interior of the state and authorizes the sale of these articles. Sale is an important ingredient of commercial intercourse, and exclusive control by Congress follows. "It has been observed that the powers remaining with the states may be so exercised as to come in conflict with those vested in Congress. When this happens, that which is not supreme must yield to that which is supreme." This line appears to have introduced a confusion that will surface again and again.

Four different options emerge. First, because the constitutional grant of commerce power to Congress is complete, inaction means that Congress decides to leave the area free of regulation. Second, in the absence of Congressional action, the states are free to exercise their police powers as commerce power until superseded by federal legislation. Third, if Congress has acted, the regulation is complete, and the states may exercise no commerce or other power that infringes on the Congressional legislation. Fourth, if Congress has acted, the states may also act in that area, so long as it does not interfere with the federal legislation. Marshall affirms the third option in both *Gibbons* and *Brown*, and he indicates probable support for the first option. He invokes the Supremacy Clause when states, acting in accord with powers left to the state, excluding commerce, produce an outcome that conflicts with federal commerce legislation. This is not co-administration of the commerce power. The state may exercise no commerce power, but if its taxing or police power lead to a collision of results, the state effort must give way.

Now we have better perspective on the *Miln* decision, which affirmed New York's power to require a ship's master, under penalty of law, to provide the name, place of birth, age, occupation, and last legal settlement of each passenger within twenty-four hours of arrival in port. Commerce has come to an end within a day of arrival. The U.S. Passenger Laws have performed their duties. The Court, over Justice Story's dissent, found the regulation an exercise of police power and not a regulation of commerce. Barbour has turned the issue around, asking whether the New York legislation is consistent with the police power. If so, it is not a state exercise of the commerce power and hence is constitutional. The Court ultimately dismisses the relevancy of *Brown* and draws its decision from *Gibbons*.

Barbour postulates that persons are not the subjects of commerce. In *Gibbons*, however, Marshall makes numerous statements to the contrary. Carrying persons or merchandise are indistinguishable. Marshall writes that the "provisions of the law respecting native seamen and respecting ownership are as applicable to vessels carrying men as to vessels carrying manufactures, and no reason is perceived why the power over the subject should not be placed in the same hands." Marshall even uses the "proof by exception" argument to show that the constitutional provision to prevent regulation on the import of slaves until 1808 demonstrates the existence of a more general power to regulate voluntary or involuntary migration. Toward the end of his decision, however, Marshall points out that the focus of the New York legislation is on the ship's powering, wind or steam. Thus, the person versus merchandise is not the decisive issue.

Despite Marshall's clear discussion of passengers in *Gibbons*, Barbour decides in *Miln* that New York has the power to require passenger information from the ship master, because it had such power *before* the Constitution, even though similar information already must go to the U.S. Department of State. Justice Barbour, writing for the Court, affirms the remark in *Gibbons* that the inspection laws of the several states form a portion of the immense mass of legislation which embraces everything within the territory of a state not surrendered to the general government. In *Gibbons*, however, Marshall cites necessary inspection laws as an exception to the duties on exports and imports clause in the Constitution.

Balbour diminishes Marshall's reasoning chain, from commerce to navigation to navigable waters to passenger vessels, used by the Marshall Court to justify Congressional licensing of coastal steam ships. Because U.S. law would be supreme under the commerce clause, New York's exclusive navigation grant was a constitutional violation. Justice Balbour continues by placing passengers outside of commerce and under the rights and privileges of whatever state territory they happen to be. Because the national commerce power derives from a different source than the state police power, and if there is no collision, Barbour concludes that both may legislate on the same topic.

Justice Balbour then dismisses *Gibbons* and *Brown* and claims to settle the New York reporting requirement as resting on the impregnable grounds of state sovereignty over its police power. That power is neither surrendered or restrained, but rather, the police power is complete, unqualified, and exclusive. All members of the ship's crew, at voyage end, are thus subject to New York's laws. The same, he says, applies to the vessel itself as forfeitable under New York's laws. Besides, the passengers cease their connection with the vessel when the voyage ends, and thus become people subject to New York law.

There are two lengthy concurrent opinions in the *Miln* case, but it is Justice Story's dissenting opinion that helps illuminate the problems with the *Miln* decision. The New York law has more than the simple registration section for those debarking in New York as well as others who debarked before the ship's arrival in a New York port. The second section may require a $300 bond for each non-citizen to indemnify the city to provide for poverty. Section three requires, at the mayor's request, the relocation to last place of residence of anyone thought likely to become a burden on the city. Section four requires each non-citizen to make a report to the mayor if they intend to reside in New York. The fifth section spells out recovery of penalties. The sixth makes the ship liable to seizure and attachment. The seventh section repeals earlier laws, and the eighth section makes a false affirmation a punishable perjury. Story focuses on the entire act; Balbour chose to focus on the first section.

Given Marshall's explicit inclusion of passengers in trade and commerce, Story concludes immediately that the New York act interferes with interstate commerce. The states do not have the authority to enact laws which operate on subjects beyond their jurisdiction or trench upon powers reserved for Congress to regulate commerce: "If the act is a regulation of commerce and that subject belongs exclusively to Congress, it is a means cut off from the range of state sovereignty and state legislation. . . . The power given to Congress to regulate commerce with foreign nations and among the states has been deemed exclusive from the nature and objects of the power and the necessary implications growing out of its exercise." There should not be double operations on commerce. The exclusive Congressional power over commerce produces a uniform whole rather than the fragmented system that would emerge if we allow states to concurrently exercise state powers, invading the commerce power, subject only to Congressional supremacy in case of conflict. Saddest of all, Justice Marshall heard the oral arguments in the *Miln* case, agreed with Justice Story, but died before SCOTUS wrote the opinion.

Navigation

Justice Balbour dimmed the clear line Marshall had drawn between state police power and national commerce in *Gibbons*. The Taney decision in the *License Cases*, 46 U.S. 504 (1847) dimmed Marshall's bright line between the "general mass of goods and services" at the state level and "selling," the end of the commerce process controlled by the national government. Justice Taney begins by problematizing the line between foreign and domestic commerce, the latter falling entirely under state jurisdiction. Citing *Brown*, Justice Taney traces foreign commerce into the state to the point of sale, as did Marshall. The state could impose no burden while the import was in its original package until broken up for retail. Once sold by the importer, foreign commerce ends.

Justice Taney asserts that the licensing laws do not operate on foreign commerce but on retail or domestic traffic. In one case, Taney argues that the liquor was in inter-state commerce, where Congress had not exercised its power, instead of foreign commerce, where Congress had legislated. Taney concludes, in finding for the states, that the grant of power to the central government is not an absolute prohibition on the exercise of power over the same subjects by the states. When in conflict, SCOTUS reaffirms the central government supremacy. Taney erroneously asserts that "*Gibbons v. Ogden* unquestionably affirms that such regulations may be made by a state, subject to the controlling power of Congress." Taney uses the decision in *Willson v. Black Bird Creek Marsh Co.*, 27 U.S. 245 (1829) to buttress his interpretation of *Gibbons*. *Willson* was the last decision written by Justice Marshall. It supported a state act permitting the building of a dam over a navigable stream affected by the ebb and flow of the tide. Taney interprets the case to say that, if Congress does not exercise its commerce powers, the states are free to do so unless and until Congress acts. It is unclear why Marshall did not consider this stream to be part of the navigable waters automatically controlled by Congress, but Taney's interpretation misses a key point. It is Marshall himself in the Gibbons case who introduces the idea of a dormant commerce clause, and before the Civil War, dormant commerce meant an arena exclusive to Congress in which it has not acted and thus interpreted as Congress not wanting any regulation in that area, at least until Congress acts to the contrary. In *Willson*, Marshall remarks "We do not think that the Act empowering the Black Bird Creek Marsh Company to place a dam across the creek can, under all the circumstances of the case, be considered as repugnant to the power to regulate commerce in its dormant State, or as conflicting with any law passed on the subject."

The peculiarity of the *Willson* case may be instructive. Marshall points out that the act of the Delaware assembly authorized the construction of a dam across one of those many creeks, passing through a deep level marsh adjoining the Delaware, into which the tide flows. The state interests here include enhancing the value of the banks along the creek by controlling the marsh and improving the health of the inhabitants. (This was an area of extreme mosquito infestation that affected the life expectancy of inhabitants, even though the legislature did not know the connection between mosquitoes and disease at that time. The shortened life expectancy, especially among males, was well known.) Marshall likely concluded that keeping every one of these creeks navigable by forbidding improvement such as this dam was an unnecessary (as opposed to unjustified) intrusion on state police power. Marshall preferred that these be an issue between the government of Delaware and its citizens. In no sense, however, does this case change Marshall's conception that a dormant commerce existed.

A carelessly written decision by Justice Curtis in *Cooley v. Board of Wardens*, 53 U.S. 299 (1851) is a clear departure from Marshall's concept of dormant commerce. The concurring opinion of Justice McLean restores the interpretation first offered in *Gibbons*. Curtis' logic is straightforward. The regulation of navigation is part of the power to regulate commerce. The regulation of pilots is a regulation of navigation. Thus, the power to regulate commerce extends to the in-port pilots. Congress chose to adopt local pilot legislation as its own. At this point Curtis introduces what he takes to be a logical conundrum: if Congress adopts local laws as its own, then the states must first have a constitutional power of their own to legislate. Thus, the commerce power cannot be exclusive to Congress, but available to the states. Marshall's original interpretation, that the older, local pilotage laws derive from a police power different from the constitutional commerce power, and after the adoption of the Constitution, Congress must adopt to take effect. Once stated, there is no reasoned basis for a concurrent commerce power.

Fortunately, Justice McLean addresses the logical leap in the Curtis decision in *Cooley*. McLean quotes the relevant solution from *Gibbons*, that the states once had the police power under which they legislated on this subject, but it is the formal adoption of these local systems by Congress that make them part of inter-state, foreign, and Indian commerce regulation. McLean points out that, regarding commerce, Congress may adopt the laws of a state, but it cannot enable a state to legislate. If the states had concurrent commerce power, they could make minor changes to their regulations every time Congress legislates, in a form of one-ups-man ship. "Congress, to whom the subject peculiarly belongs, should have been applied to, and no doubt it would have adopted the act of the state." Unfortunately, several cases adopted the Cooley logic, such as *Veazie v. Moor*, 55 U.S. 568 (1852), *Pennsylvania v. Wheeling & Belmont Bridge Company*, 59 U.S. 421 (1855), *Almy v. California*, 65 U.S. 169 (1860), *Crandall v. State of Nevada*, 73 U.S. 35 (1867), and *Woodruff v. Parham*, 75 U.S. 123 (1868).

The navigable water problem has deep roots in English common law. Bodies of water affected by changing tides were effectively the property of the king. These bodies of water were potentially navigable. Riparian interests only extend to submerged lands not affected by the changing seas. Potentially navigable areas in the United States are the property of the people. Since there were no riparian rights to navigable waters, the government could take without compensation. In *United States v. Rands*, 389 U.S. 121 (1967), SCOTUS ruled that the state pay compensation for the value of the taken land before navigable improvements, rather than the value of the land after improvements were in place. Congress followed by amending the Rivers and Harbors Act to require, as a matter of legislative grace, compensation for the value of land after improvements were in place.

The commerce clause gave strength to the government's claim to navigable waters. In *Kaiser Aetna v. United States*, 444 U.S. 164 (1979), petitioners had developed a shallow lagoon in Hawaii for a marina and dredged a channel across a barrier beach to join the marina with a navigable bay and the Pacific Ocean. The owners sought to restrict access to the marina from navigable water, because it was a private development. Connecting the lagoon to open water made it subject to navigational servitude (common law conception where the waters were the property of the king) under the Commerce Clause. Its connection to navigable waters made the marina subject to the Army Corps of Engineers. SCOTUS, citing *Gibbons*, found that Congress had the power to open the marina to public use; because of the significant private investment, it would need a riparian condemnation with just compensation, as required under the Fifth Amendment. The right to exclude, Rehnquist writes for the majority, is a fundamental element of the property right and the state must pay just compensation. The dissent points out that, under the ebb and flow test, whether affected by the changing tides, the pond was never private property. The central government also has authority under navigable servitude because the waters are now navigable water and navigable in fact. Thus, the marina meets all the tests used to define navigable servitude and hence under the regulation of the United States Government. In a disagreement over whether compensation was due, Rehnquist opts for full compensation by creating yet another new rule, in this case whether private hands establish navigability. If so, the government had to use its power of eminent domain to take the marina with just compensation to open it to the public.

Post-Civil War Confusions

SCOTUS returns to the *Gibbons* logic in *Welton v. State of Missouri*, 91 U.S. 275 (1875). Justice Field delivered the opinion for the Court. A state of Missouri statute discriminated against traveling dealers selling wares from other states by requiring these to obtain a license, compared to merchants of goods and wares produced in Missouri. The license tax is an indirect tax on goods; a tax on the "occupation" of the importer is a tax on importation. Assessing whether the license was permissible under the Constitution, SCOTUS ruled that the power to regulate commerce is one without limitation, and to regulate commerce is to prescribe the rules governing it. SCOTUS recognized its previous holding that the states may regulate until Congress acts, "but where the subject to which the power applies is national in its character or of such a nature as to admit of uniformity of regulation, the power is exclusive of all state authority." The transportation and exchanges of commodities is of national importance and hence requires uniform national regulation.

SCOTUS held in *Welton* that the commerce power continues until the commodity has ceased to be the subject of discriminating legislation. Thus, the commerce power continues even after commerce enters a state until there is no longer a burden reflecting the nature of its origin. Congressional inaction on the subject is to be equivalent to a declaration that the commerce shall be free and untrammeled, or dormant commerce in the precise sense Marshall used the concept in *Gibbons*. Even if unintended, the operation of a law having such discriminatory impact is repugnant to the Constitution and hence void.

SCOTUS takes a side-step toward state sovereignty in *Munn v. Illinois*, 94 U.S. 113 (1876). The Court introduces the concept of "affected with a public interest" to give the state of Illinois statutory control over the rates charged by a privately-owned grain elevator, even though the receiving, mixing, and storing of grain appears one part of a continuing inter-state commerce system. SCOTUS argued that private property, devoted to a public use, is subject to public regulation. It also observed, however, that "the largest traffic between the citizens of the country north and west of Chicago and the citizens of the country lying on the Atlantic coast north of Washington is in grain which passes through the elevators of Chicago." The Court reasons that the grain elevators may relate to interstate commerce, but not necessarily so. The state may thus regulate the elevators, unless Congress acts, even though the state may, in so doing, operate on commerce outside its jurisdiction. Interestingly, the dissent focused on the invasion of private property rights.

A year later, SCOTUS begins back-peddling the *Munn* logic in *Railroad Company v. Husen*, 95 U.S. 465 (1877). Here SCOTUS found against a Missouri statute prohibiting Texan, Mexican, or Indian cattle driven or conveyed into that state between March 1 and November 1 of each year. Missouri argued that this exercise of police power was necessary to prevent diseases carried into the state's cattle population. SCOTUS found this to be an unreasonable exercise of police power and that the effective quarantine violated the inter-state commerce clause. An exercise of state power, no matter the supposed category of enabling power, cannot invade a domain of power exclusively given to Congress. The Missouri statute forbid the conveyance of cattle by rail through the state, even if never unloaded. This regulation to the point of prohibition is not a power available to the states. "it is the duty of the court to guard vigilantly against any needless intrusion."

SCOTUS disavows itself of any untoward implications of the *Munn* decision in *Wabash, St. Louis & Pacific Railway Company v. Illinois*, 118 U.S. 557 (1886). An Illinois statute prevented discrimination in pricing for railroad carriage while within the state, even though the transit continued to its destination in another state. The Court points out that the commerce clause is in the Constitution precisely because of the confusion that likely would follow if each state was at liberty to regulate the conduct of carriers while within its jurisdiction. Action on any commerce that is within a state but that crosses state lines is not permissible. In a clearly worded rebuff of

Munn, Justice Miller for the majority writes: “We must, therefore, hold that it is not and never has been the deliberate opinion of a majority of this Court that a statute of a state which attempts to regulate the fares and charges by railroad companies within its limits, for a transportation which constitutes a part of commerce among the states, is a valid law.” The national character of commerce, following the general rules and principles only set by Congress under the commerce clause, is the basis to evaluate the Illinois regulation of commerce crossing state lines. SCOTUS supported this position in *Bowman v. Chicago & Northwestern Railway Co.*, 125 U.S. 465 (1888) and *Leisy v. Hardin*, 135 U.S. 100 (1890).

The Wabash case re-establishes the clarity behind Marshall’s reasoning. First, Congress has plenary power over inter-state commerce. Second, Congress may adopt legacy pilotage rules if it chooses, but it must explicitly adopt them as its own. Third, if Congress does not legislate in this area, SCOTUS will assume that Congress wants no rules, thus leaving the arena dormant. Fourth, Congress may change pilotage rules as it sees fit. And finally, the states may not use their power of taxation to encroach upon the commerce powers of the national government.

Brennan v. Titusville, 153 U.S. 289 (1894) reinforces Marshall’s position. *Brennan* is one of several licensing cases SCOTUS decided after the Civil War, where cash-strapped states sought new revenue sources. *Brennan* was a traveling salesman selling picture frames door to door. He sent solicited orders to Chicago for manufacturing the frames, and then shipped back to the salesman. The city held him in violation of an ordinance requiring hawkers, peddlers, and merchants to take out a license at rates varying with the amount of time doing such business in Titusville. Justice Brewer, writing for SCOTUS, reversed the conviction and took the opportunity to further clarify inter-state commerce rules. Whether justification for the ordinance be under the police powers of the state or the taxing powers of the state, neither claim could trump Congress’ plenary power over inter-state commerce. Brewer cites decisions drawn from several previous cases that clearly state that the police power or the taxation power cannot in any way limit powers given to the national government. The state cannot stop the Congressional plenary power over inter-state commerce, foreign commerce, and commerce with Indians at the border of a state, until the item loses the character of its point of origin and subsides into the common mass of property of the state. “[I]t is settled that nothing which is a direct burden upon interstate commerce can be imposed by the state without the assent of Congress, and that the silence of Congress in respect to any matter of interstate commerce is equivalent to a declaration on its part that it should be absolutely free.”

Rehnquist's Inter-State Commerce

Rehnquist's dissent in *Allenberg Cotton Co., Inc. v. Pittman*, 419 U.S. 20 (1974) resurrects the "what is interstate" commerce problem. Allenberg contracted with many Mississippi farmers, from seed to harvest, to deliver their cotton to Allenberg. The company would transport the cotton to its Mississippi warehouses for sorting and baling, and then hold cotton as needed for a revolving inventory available for future shipment orders. One of the farmers failed to perform his side of the contract, so Allenberg sued in state court. The Mississippi state court found that Allenberg did not have access to the Mississippi courts because it had not gotten a required certificate of authority to do business, which would involve a paid license fee to the state. SCOTUS found the cotton to be in the interstate commerce stream from the moment of contract, and hence Mississippi could not demand a business license before using its courts. Rehnquist, in his dissent, wanted "interstate commerce" to begin with shipping the cotton from the Allengberg warehouse. Thus, Allenberg would need the foreign correspondent license. Rehnquist also questioned whether a "mutual exclusivity" rule should preclude both the nation and state operating on the same stream of commerce at the same time.

Rehnquist's dissent in *Healy v. Beer Institute, Inc.*, 491 U.S. 324 (1989) raises serious doubts whether Rehnquist understands the plenary power given to Congress via the Commerce Clause. A Connecticut statute required beer shippers to affirm that, as of the posting, prices asked of Connecticut wholesalers are no higher than that asked of wholesalers in bordering states. There are no brewers in Connecticut, so it is entirely dependent upon out-of-state shippers, and Connecticut officials believed that the brewers charged Connecticut wholesalers higher prices than charged in other states. Connecticut officials worried that the price differential would drive residents near bordering states to cross the border for beer purchases. Under commerce clause analysis, the Connecticut regulation was an interference with interstate commerce and interpretable by bordering states as an effort to affect their prices as well. SCOTUS overruled an older decision based on the Twenty-First Amendment, *Joseph E. Seagram & Sons, Inc. v. Hostetter*, 384 U. S. 35 (1966). This decision had proliferated the use of affirmance laws across the states. Further, any brewer premiums offered to other state wholesalers must have price-matching by lowering prices to Connecticut wholesalers. Under quid-pro-quo state regulations, states could drive the interstate wholesale price to the lowest denominator of any state, regardless of variations in local conditions. All brewers affected by the Connecticut regulation sold in other states as well, but not all brewers sold in Connecticut. The Connecticut affirmance regulation could be discriminatory as well. Rehnquist countered by continuing to assume that the Twenty-First Amendment makes or should make a difference in commerce clause analysis. Because Connecticut had no breweries, it could not be protectionist; it just wants its citizens treated as favorably as those in other states. Rehnquist says that this motive is insufficient to constitute a violation of the Interstate Commerce Clause, but then commerce clause reasoning does not depend on motive. Rehnquist goes on to say that absent any proof that Connecticut's affirmation law will affect the price of beer charged in other states, there is no commerce violation. Perhaps, Rehnquist speculates, there is some sort of market imperfection that the Connecticut affirmation regulation can correct.

ADJUSTING TO TECHNOLOGY

During the last decade of the nineteenth century and the first two decades of the twentieth century, SCOTUS faced a rash of commerce cases involving three technologically emergent areas: railroad, telegraph, and regulatory administrative agencies. None of these technological advances were known to or contemplated by the Founding Fathers, but the ability to "expound a Constitution" allowed SCOTUS to adjudicate the impacts of these technological changes into constitutional law. These advances reflect streams of technological change that unfolded throughout the twentieth century: transportation, information, and administration.

The compromised evolution of constitutional law during this period was serious; its timeframe: the *Lochner Era* (1887–1937). The dominant logic at that time did not favor among individual rights (save the right-to-contract), state sovereignty, or national sovereignty. It imported two popular but ultimately discredited views: laissez-faire and social Darwinism. A significant segment of the population still accepts one or both views, but their logics have not withstood the challenges of evidence. Laissez-faire could not continue without state intervention to preserve competition, because the trend of laissez-faire was the destruction of competition in favor of trusts and monopolies. Government intervention in the economic order saved capitalist economic competition. Social Darwinism was always a perversion of Darwinism, per se. For Darwin, the process of adaptation was never at an end. Changes in environments would create new favors and new challenges that "selected" different forms, even within species. Social Darwinism, with its strong racial component, stopped the process of evolution, only to announce that adaptive change was at an end, and that the best had won the challenges of survival. An empirical marker of the "best," in turn, was power, social position, and the color of skin.

The legal corollary to these points of view was limiting the use of government power generally. The Tenth Amendment would check national action;

the· right-of-contract checked state action; and the right-of-contract was the basic expression of any other individual right. Because of the grossly different bargaining positions of the individual laborer and the corporations, this legal theory, although on the surface seemingly friendly to individual rights, elevated the Contract Clause well above other guarantees in the Constitution. The beneficiaries, in the final analysis, were corporations. Thus, even though the right-of-contract gave great advantage to corporations, they heralded it as the victory of freedom. In consequence, the tension between Federalists and anti-Federalists, national sovereignty and state sovereignty, dissolved into a hideous parody on anarchism: that government is best which governs least, because nature will do what government should not even try to do. The resulting case history becomes increasingly *ad hoc* in this period, with precedents reinterpreted through the skewed lens of an automatic harmony of interests. SCOTUS announced new principles in one arena, then contradicted them in another. The most grievous misadventure occurs when flawed ideas map onto the changing technological conditions of the late nineteenth and early twentieth centuries.

RAILROADS

The railways served cross-national transportation of general goods and growing military needs. Nonetheless, the judicial decision-making pattern does reflect an odd marriage between the new technology and the *Lochner* mindset: right-of-contract, limited national sovereignty, and limited state sovereignty. The fit between a *Lochner* logic and an inter-state technology is tenuous, except for private corporations. The enormous expansion of the railroad system before and after the Civil War made shipment and travel in all directions simpler, faster, and inexpensive. Railroad expansion quickly highlighted the issue of inter-state versus intra-state services.

Constitutionally, national sovereignty ruled inter-state commerce; the states asserted state sovereignty when they sought control over a variety of transportation issues through their police powers. SCOTUS initially used the inter-state commerce clause to limit state sovereignty. Cross-country coordination quickly became imperative for the physical rail infrastructure, such as fixing railroad track gauge; equipping railroad cars to run on, and exchange among, one or another rail system; scheduling trains to avoid frontal or rear-end collisions with another train; and the switching of cars, off-loading and re-loading. States cannot rule beyond their own borders, but an interconnected railway system surely did. Big capital focused on main or trunk lines, state and localities sought branch lines. Local demand, coupled with the deep investment railroads required, plus the lack of high risk capital for branch line development, inevitably tapped state and local treasuries for financial support.

SCOTUS recognized the supremacy of Congress in interstate commerce generally, but relaxed its position on dormant commerce, that is, areas in which Congress had not acted. Did Congress pre-empt any state legislation, or were the states free to legislate until displaced by Congressional legislation? SCOTUS would soon add yet another layer of confusion: the states could legislate in an area previously considered preempted, so long as the national and local statutes do not conflict. This effort to expand state sovereignty at the cost of national sovereignty had a relatively short shelf-life.

Despite a dominant belief in spontaneous economic coordination, capitalists did not provide what local government should not provide; towns and counties issued bonds to pay for privately-owned branches of rail service. The sheer economies of scale involved in the railroad industry, and a lack of adequate return from a branch line, led a significant number of small rail systems to declare bankruptcy, leaving these towns and counties holding worthless bonds. Larger rail lines typically bought the small bankrupt lines at close-out prices. The spiral of failures from branch to trunk lines continued, with old mortgages assumed under new mortgages, until many of these larger railroad lines also declared bankruptcy. Some states forbade issuing bonds by towns and counties (*Barnum v. Okolona*, 148 U.S. 393 (1893)). Illinois put a prohibition in its Constitution in 1870, but SCOTUS ruled that the earlier Cairo, Illinois bond offering in 1867 remained constitutional and in force (*Cairo v. Zane*, 149 U.S. 122 (1893)). The Federal government and some state governments generously gave public lands for trunk lines, major branch lines, and depot construction.

Intra-State and Inter-State Ping Pong

Not until the *Wabash, St. Louis & Pacific Railway Company v. Illinois*, 118 U.S. 557 (1886) case had SCOTUS reaffirmed that lack of regulation in interstate commerce is the wish of Congress, thus forbidding state forays into inter-state commerce under aegis of police power. Congress could keep the area free of legislation or dormant; Congress could adopt local legacy (pre-constitutional) statutes as its own; or Congress could pass a law that would trump all other laws. The distinction between intra-state and inter-state commerce power now became the focus; SCOTUS allowed the states control of intra-state commerce under their police powers, regardless whether Congress had acted.

Shortly after the *Wabash* case, SCOTUS sways back toward state sovereignty. In *Joy v. St. Louis*, 138 U.S. 1 (1891), park officials, in charge of a large acreage set aside for a driving park, did not want railroads to cross the park and destroy the scenery; similarly, they did not want side tracks, other paraphernalia, and depots crowding public lands, inconveniencing the public, and destroying the park's scenery. The railroads, on the other hand, needed a route through the park as well as access to a passenger depot. Two railroads and the park officials reached an agreement: the park would permit one through right-of-way, subject to several restrictions; the two railroads would share costs of the common rail-bed and separately bear different supporting expenses. Each completed their separate tasks, but one of the railroads failed to pay its share of the rail-bed, thereby nullifying the tri-party agreement. The park officials, and by implication the city of St. Louis, did not want the park burdened by another right-of-way; earlier contracts had included the expectation that other railroads would have access to the single right-of-way.

This created two problems: what would be the terms of access to the rail-bed for railroads other than the original two railroads, and whether the railroad that failed to pay its share of the roadbed should have access. SCOTUS found the St. Louis public interest to govern the situation, and thus honor the single-track route through the park, even though this created a commercial bottleneck. Railroads generally had access, subject to the owning railroad's rules and priorities, plus compensation. The second railroad involved in the original tri-party contract would be as any other railroad, subject to the rules and regulations and routine use-compensation to the owning railroad.

SCOTUS continues its state sovereignty furlough in *Minneapolis & St. Louis Ry. Co. v. Emmons*, 149 U.S. 364 (1893). The Court found it consistent with the police powers for a state to require fencing of railroad tracks, and to award treble damages on accidents and inconveniences, should the railroad failed to comply. Without comment on the costs put upon an interstate carrier to build the intra-state fences, the Court approved the state requirement. Similarly, in *New York & New England R. Co. v. Bristol*, 151 U.S. 556 (1894), SCOTUS claimed jurisdiction but then allowed the Connecticut legislature to order serial changes in grade crossings, largely at the railroads' expense. Much the same occurred in *New York, N. H. & H. R. Co. v. New York*, 165 U.S. 628 (1897). In the absence of Congressional legislation, SCOTUS held constitutional the requirements imposed by New York, such as steam heating passenger cars and guards and guard-posts on railroad trestles and bridges, even though these have some bearing on interstate commerce.

SCOTUS previously had set up a roadblock to certain forms of state taxation on corporations. In *New York, L. E. & W. Railroad Company v. Pennsylvania*, 153 U.S. 628 (1894), SCOTUS found Pennsylvania's effort to add additional tax to a portion of a New York railway running through its state, as a violation of the contract (right-to-contract) establishing the original obligations between the railroad and state. In the same year *Cleveland, C. C., and St. Louis Railway Company v. Backus*, 154 U. S. 439 (1894), however,

SCOTUS allowed the tax assessor of the home state to consider the value of the entire line, even though part of it be in another state, and then pro-rate the tax base on the number of miles within the home state.

Congress once again asserted its control; SCOTUS returned to its national sovereignty work and found congressional legislation to dominate state legislation. In the *Lake Shore and M. S. Railway Company v. Ohio*, 165 U.S. 365 (1897), Congress conferred upon the Secretary of War authority concerning the bridges over navigable waterways. If a bridge is an unreasonable obstruction to the free navigation of waters beneath it, the Secretary of War shall give notice of the necessary changes and a reasonable time within which to make them. The Secretary of War must approve of new construction proposed to it. SCOTUS also held that the United States could exercise eminent domain for construction of a railroad through Cherokee Nation land (*Cherokee Nation v. Southern Kansas Ry. Co.*, 135 U.S. 641 (1890)).

SCOTUS often gave favor to the states, as in *Hennington v. Georgia*, 163 U.S. 299 (1896). Here, the Court accepted Georgia's use of its police power for preventing the running of freight trains on Sunday. SCOTUS concluded that preventing Sunday rail freight traffic had little impact on interstate commerce, but that it did promote the general welfare of the citizens of Georgia. In the same year, however, *Illinois Central R. Co. v. Illinois*, 163 U.S. 142 (1896) SCOTUS found unconstitutional a state statute requiring trains to make brief stops at all county seats in the state. SCOTUS based that ruling on a violation of the interstate commerce clause and obstructing the U.S. mails.

A year later, involving only intra-state passenger service, *Gladson v. Minnesota*, 166 U.S. 427 (1897) approved a state statute requiring regular passenger trains, running wholly within the state, to stop at all county seats to take on and discharge passengers. SCOTUS found this permissible, even if the passenger trains connect with another of the same company but ran into another state and carried interstate passengers and U.S. mails. SCOTUS reaffirmed this position in *Lake Shore & Michigan Southern Ry. Co. v. Ohio*, 173 U.S. 285 (1899), where an Ohio statute requiring regular passenger trains both ways, except Sundays, to stop thrice daily in towns of 3,000 or more with enough time to debark and embark passengers. SCOTUS held that the statute would apply to interstate trains carrying interstate commerce as well, until Congress acted upon the subject. SCOTUS had now shifted to the position that, in the absence of Congressional action, the states were free to legislate in the so-called dormant zone until Congress enacted its own legislation.

LIABILITY AND TRUSTS

Railroad accident liability added a particularly vexing problem for local, state, and national government. SCOTUS eventually presents the alternatives in *Baltimore & Ohio R. C. v. Baugh*, 149 368 (1893). SCOTUS had previously given considerable deference to decisions reached in lower courts, because liability decisions were local matters. Baugh argued that a general law was necessary that distinguished itself from the master-servant rule in *Chicago, Milwaukee & St. Paul Railway v. Ross*, 112 U.S. 377 (1884). The Baugh rule rejected both the master-servant and servant-servant rules and announced general law based on the nature of the act itself. Baugh argued that each employee accepts a certain amount of risk when taking the job, and that his salary presumably reflected the risk. Regardless of level in the supervisory hierarchy, each employee had a set of tasks that defined due diligence for that job. Following the rules, even the fellow servant may escape liability. If it be the rules rather than the judgment of individuals that is at fault, then there is liability; if not, then there is no liability. The result of this reasoning protected the company from most liabilities.

Thirteen years after nationalizing railroad liability through the Baugh rule, SCOTUS brought inter-railroad trade agreements under the national control of the Sherman Anti-Trust Act. In *United States v. Trans-Missouri Freight Ass'n.*, 166 U.S. 290 (1897), the railroad argued that the Sherman Anti-Trust Act did not even cover railroad common carriers, and by the time the case made it to the Supreme Court, members had dissolved the association. SCOTUS took the position that the prohibitory provision in the 1890 act applied to all contracts in restraint of interstate or foreign commerce without exception or limitation. Responding to the dissolution of the association, Scotus pointed out that the railroads had discovered a way around the act: to dissolve one association under scrutiny and replace it with a similar association under a different name.

The United States Government filed against the Trans-Missouri Freight Association in 1892 and named its eighteen participating railroads. When filing their answer to the charges in the Circuit Court for Kansas, most of the carriers initially denied even being a member of the association. The circuit court dismissed the case because one of the defendants had successfully moved that the association dissolved itself by November 19, 1892. At the same meeting dissolving the Trans-Missouri Freight Association, the old association members established a committee to set up a new agreement for discussion at a meeting on December 6, 1892. The defendants objected to a government appeal to the U.S. Supreme Court, but the U.S. Supreme Court agreed to hear the suit anyway.

The original Association formed in 1889, but SCOTUS argued that it became illegal with the passage of the 1890 bill. The association owners' guidelines made it clear it was an effort to restrain competition. A designated chairman controlled rate setting, under the direction of a committee appointed to establish rates, rules, and regulations on traffic. Great disagreements went to arbitration. Members of the association were free to meet the competitive rates of lines not members of the association, but to give such notice to the chairperson. Violations within the association went to investigation and, if necessary, fines imposed. Cheating, such as under-billing in weight or billing of freight under the wrong classification, would also be subject to penalties.

In that same year, SCOTUS ruled against the thirty-one railroad companies comprising the Joint Traffic Association in *United States v. Joint Traffic Association*, 171 U.S. 505 (1898). The association claimed jurisdiction over competitive traffic, fixing rates and fares, and the course pursued with connecting companies. The Association gave lip service to the Interstate Commerce Commission and pledged its cooperation. SCOTUS took special exception to the establishment of rates and fares. Citing Congress' power over interstate commerce, SCOTUS objected to restraint of trade that shut out the operation of the general law of competition. This is very much in line with the SCOTUS objection to establishing rates, rules, and regulations found in the Trans-Missouri freight association case. Clearly national sovereignty, understood to encourage competition, trumped both the right-of-contract and state sovereignty, highlighting the tension among freedom of association, right-to-contract, and interstate commerce. In *United States v. Reading Co.*, 253 U.S. 26 (1920), SCOTUS cited the Sherman Antitrust Act in finding unconstitutional the setting up of a holding company that dominated competing interstate railroads and great competing coal companies. SCOTUS ordered the holding Company dissolved and the railroads and coal companies returned to independent competing activity.

In *Northern Pacific R. Co. v. Egeland*, 163 U.S. 93 (1896) SCOTUS affirmed the use of the jury to determine questions of fact, leaving questions of law to the judges. SCOTUS was moving, however, toward inter-state sovereignty in liability cases. Setting aside various state laws and disclaimers on bills of lading, SCOTUS points out that items received for interstate shipment are in interstate commerce from beginning to agreed end and require a contract covering the whole; state contracts under state statutes are no substitute (*Richmond & A. R. Co. v. Patterson Tobacco Co.*, 169 U.S. 311 (1898)). The carrier at the initial end carries liability throughout, and it may of course seek liability from carriers down the line, even though the original shipper need only seek relief from the initial carrier. SCOTUS found a Missouri statute to the same effect constitutional in *Missouri, Kansas & Texas Ry. Co. v. McCann*, 174 U.S. 580 (1899).

SCOTUS upheld Federal law, the Carmack Amendment, on inter-carrier liability in *Atlantic Coast Line R. Co. v. Riverside Mills*, 219 U.S. 186 (1911). Companies had used a bill of lading to declare non-assumption of the liability of others, but this condition is inconsistent with Federal law. If the initial receiver contracts to carry beyond its line, it bears the common-law liability throughout, but it may then recover from the responsible line along the contracted route. A carrier may have chosen to end transit at its warehouse, and thus ending any further liability by effectively making the next carrier the "originator." Although the arrangement may abridge freedom of contract, Congress may do so because freedom of right-to-contract is not absolute, and the Constitution authorizes Congress to do so.

Bankruptcy

SCOTUS was much slower in adopting a national bankruptcy plan for the interstate railroads. The inter-state consequences of financing and mortgaging became worse with large, consolidated lines. Often, the conglomerates, having previously absorbed the mortgages of their parts, declared bankruptcy (*Quincy, Missouri & Pacific R. Co. v. Humphreys*, 145 U.S. 82 (1892)). Bonds and stocks were pay for private firms, but the economy could never meet the face value of the stocks, especially under bankruptcies (*Fogg v. Blair*, 139 U.S. 118 (1891)). Resolving interstate bankruptcies required federal action.

In *Ashley v. Ryan*, 153 U.S. 436 (1894), SCOTUS faced the continued consolidation of railroads, including the lands they held as part of the original land grant agreements. These conglomerations operated across state lines but were still subject to the taxing power of the states, the taxing power of the national government, and the national control of inter-state commerce. The *Ashley* court allowed the states to adopt incorporation fees based on the proportion of the entire conglomeration's authorized stock for the privilege of incorporating in that state, without violating the interstate commerce clause. If the main conglomeration failed in financial responsibilities and went into bankruptcy, *Ashley* permitted the dissolution into corporations established within each affected state for the pro-rated stock of the dissolving company. Incorporation fees could consider property held out-of-state as well as property within the state.

Clipping Police and Taxing Powers

In *Flint v. Stone Tracy Co.*, 220 U.S. 107 (1911), SCOTUS confirmed that Congress had the power under its commerce powers to tax corporations as an excise tax for doing business. In *Railroad Commission of Ohio v. Worthington*, 225 U.S. 101 (1912) what constitutes Interstate carriage becomes further national. Even when merchandise billing extends only to a point within the state where a vessel is located, it is a burden on interstate commerce to place a rate on that part of the interstate carriage which includes the loading into vessels ready to go beyond state borders. The Interstate Commerce Commission regulates so-called lake cargo, which reaffirms that the national government has exclusive authority over interstate commerce as well as the right to set interstate commerce rates. Transferring the coal intended for transportation beyond state borders, even though coming to rest for a time before loading into vessels, is part of the process of moving coal from the mine to the port and beyond. It is interstate commerce.

The large number of personal injuries led Congress to legislate the required height of draw bars on fully loaded freight cars and their maximum variation when unloaded or partly loaded (*St. Louis, I. M. & S. Ry. Co. v. Taylor*, 210 U.S. 281 (1908)). Following a deference to national legislative acts, even those it considered unwise, SCOTUS supported the requirement; automatic couplers reduced the chance of accidents when compared to the link and pin coupler. In *Southern Railway Co. v. United States*, 222 U.S. 20 (1911), SCOTUS upheld a federal requirement that all locomotives, cars, and similar vehicles, whether in interstate commerce or not, had to have the automatic coupler safety appliance. Congress has plenary power over commerce, the Court pointed out, so it had no objection that avoidable dangers arose whole or in part out of matters connected with intra-state commerce. Interstate and intra-state commerce typically used the same rail lines. "Speaking only of railroads which are highways of both interstate and intrastate commerce, these things are of common knowledge: both classes of traffic are at times carried in the same car, and when this is not the case, the cars in which they are carried are frequently commingled in the same train and in the switching and other movements at terminals."

SCOTUS continues its efforts to clip police power in *Kansas City Sou. Ry. Co. v. Kaw Valley Drainage Dist.*, 233 U.S. 75 (1914). A state's direct interference with inter-state commerce is not justifiable. The state may not destroy a bridge, across which an interstate railroad line necessarily passes, even if it would help the drainage of the district. Similarly, in *Illinois Central R. Co. v. Behrens*, 233 U.S. 473 (1914), SCOTUS ruled that the Federal Employers Liability Act applied to those engaging in intrastate commercial activities as well as interstate commercial activities. Because the railroad is a highway for both intrastate and interstate commerce, and the two classes of traffic are interdependent, Congress may regulate the liability of the carrier for employee injuries when engaged in general work pertaining to both classes of commerce. Considered in isolation, it may be interstate or intrastate commerce. An employee engaging in switching several cars loaded for intrastate freight, however, is not under the employers' liability act, nor does this change if the employee later goes into interstate activities on the same line.

SCOTUS did allow the states to move beyond the FELA rules. *Mountain Timber Co. v. Washington*, 243 U.S. 219 (1917) found the Washington State Workmen's Compensation Act constitutional; this act established a state fund into which both employee and employer paid to provide compensation for workers injured on the job or the dependents of workmen killed. The provisions of this act precluded other civil actions for personal injuries. A similar compensation system is in *New York Central R. Co. v. White*, 243 U.S. 188 (1917).

Wilson v. New, 243 U.S. 332 (1917) approved the eight-hour work day for employees of carriers engaged in interstate and foreign commerce, but it did not permit setting of wages. A minimum may be set for the latter; it also may be set for a minimal time during crises,

> If the act which, if done, would interrupt, if not destroy interstate commerce, may be by anticipation legislatively prevented, by the same token, the power to regulate may be exercise to guard against the cessation of interstate commerce, threatened by a failure of employers and employees to agree as to the standard of wages, standard being an essential prerequisite to the uninterrupted flow of interstate commerce.

The dissent found the reach of the Wilson ruling arbitrary and capricious and hence in violation of the due process clause. The railroads are private property, even if they engage in a public service. They cannot be subject to government control. The wage and hour bill is a taking of private property and in violation of the due process clause. Another of the dissenters argued that the doctrine affirmed in this case gave Congress the power to fix a maximum as well as a minimum wage; to compel arbitration of labor disputes, which may jeopardize the movement of the interstate traffic; and that to take measures, effectively to protect that free flow against any "combination," whether of operatives, owners, or strangers.

The tensions of right-to-contract and government efforts to keep commerce moving, was a key problem that the *Lochner Era* Court generally decided in favor of right-to-contract, with exceptions like *Wilson* and some ICC regulations reviewed below. In *Railroad Retirement Board v. Alton Railroad Co.*, 295 U.S. 330 (1935), a *Lochner Era* swan-song found the Railroad Retirement Act of 1934 unconstitutional, despite its earlier findings for state programs like Mountain Times and New York Central. SCOTUS held that the federal program violated due process, particularly in the taking of property or money of one interstate carrier and transferring it to another without compensation. Like many previous state-level retirement systems, the Railroad Retirement Act had to enforce contributions from both carriers and employees. SCOTUS objected to what it called un-severable sections, such as making all persons in carrier service, within one year prior to the passage of the act, entitled under its pensions, whether reemployed or not. Reemployment during the previous year would add all prior service to the count in computing annual payables. Those sixty-five years old and over who had ever been in the carrier service, regardless of whether discharged for gross negligence, are eligible for a pension.

SCOTUS reasoned that the regulation was not justifiable on the theory that greater contentment and personal security induced more efficient service. The retirement fund aided railroads with superannuated employees, compared with railroads with few of them. Legislation that clearly imposed arbitrary liability, to pay again for services long since rendered and at that time fully compensated, was not permissible. The Railroad Retirement Board case concluded that "the provisions of the act which disregard the private and separate ownership of the several respondents, treat them all as a single employer, and pool all their assets, regardless of their individual obligations and that varying conditions found in their respective enterprises, cannot be justified as consistent with due process."

Collective Bargaining

Virginian Railway Co. v. Railway Employees, 300 U.S. 515 (1937) is a post-*Lochner* decision regarding the amended Railway Labor Act. To avoid interruptions of interstate commerce for labor reasons, the act encourages labor to use collective bargaining between the carrier and authorized representatives, and mediation and arbitration when the bargaining does not result in agreement. Employees have the right to organize and bargain collectively through their representative. SCOTUS affirmed that the peaceable settlement of labor controversies that may seriously impair the ability of an interstate carrier to perform is a matter of public concern. An election among competing unions determined union certification as the official bargaining unit, results of which certify what union will represent the workers. SCOTUS found that the act mandating negotiation as constitutional within the interstate commerce clause and found it legally enforceable that employer meet with the duly-elected representative of labor or employees. The act does not require employers and employees to reach an agreement.

Easements

More than a century ago, railroads got land grants in a checkerboard system allocating half the land in odd tracks within ten (later twenty) miles of the track on either side, reserving the even tracks for the United States government to sell for homesteading. Several controversies developed at that time, such as two railroads coming close enough to claim the same land, or where replacement lands would come from if a previous deed granted part of the lot elsewhere. The issue before the court a century later was the issue of easements. Because of the checkboard pattern, access to even lots generally meant crossing odd lots, many of were in private hands.

The common-law solution was an easement-by-necessity, where access to one's land could require an easement over private property, without compensation. Rehnquist, a native of these lands and now writing for the Court, dismissed easement-by-necessity as a method for right of access. The bills passed to award the odd sections made scant or no mention of access. Governments now had the power of eminent domain, taking land in exchange for its fair market value.

In *Leo Sheep Co. v. United States*, 440 U.S. 668 (1979), the U.S. government had built an access road to a popular recreational area but made no agreement and gave no compensation to the owner of the property crossed by the access road. SCOTUS ruled that the easement involved in the road it built would require title to and compensation for the land. Rehnquist put the Court on the road to a solution favorable to the landowner, except for the expressed intentions of Congress, which of course were in the hands of SCOTUS to interpret. Because the government has an interest in settled expectations, certainty, and predictability of private titles, the eminent domain route, with appropriate compensation, would be Rehnquist's guiding principle for easements.

Wages

SCOTUS delivers an extraordinary rebuff to Rehnquist in *Garcia v. San Antonio Transit Auth.*, 469 U.S. 528 (1985). The Department of Labor found that the San Antonio Metropolitan Transit Authority, the major provider of transportation in San Antonio and a major recipient of federal assistance, is subject to minimum wage and overtime requirements specified in the Fair Labor Standards Act. A previous SCOTUS decision, *National League of Cities v. Usery*, 426 U.S. 833 (1976), authored by Rehnquist, had found that Congress does not have the power, under the Commerce Clause, to enforce these requirements in "areas of traditional government functions." Rehnquist conjured that traditional government functions argument as the formalistic dividing line between state and federal regulatory control. In a sharply worded decision, SCOTUS overturned *National League of Cities*, nine years after SCOTUS handed it down, arguing that the traditional functions distinction was not only unworkable but inconsistent with established principles of

Federalism. The limits of Federal sovereignty are not in bloated principles such as traditional government function, because the Constitution specifies limits of state sovereignty. SCOTUS points out that Article I, § 10 and § 8, Article III curtail the powers of state judiciaries. The Bill of Rights through the Fourteenth Amendment sharply contracts state sovereignty. The constitutional restraint on the Commerce Clause is one of process, not one of result.

TELEGRAPHS AND INFORMATION

Development of the electro-magnetic telegraph and proliferation of seaboard railways occur contemporaneously. Samuel Morse patented his telegraph invention in 1838 but sought a delay of the release of the sketch design until he could seek patents in Britain and France. A different telegraph system patented in England in 1837 and the general telegraph idea allegedly published in London Magazine meant that Morse failed to get a British patent, even though Morse had filed a caveat with the U.S. Patent and Trademark Office in 1837, giving him a year to apply for the patent while protecting his invention. He did get approval in France, but he could not get installation started within the two-year time frame required to keep the patent.

SCOTUS reviewed Morse's technology and competing patents from England and France. In *O'Reilly v. Morse*, 56 U.S. 15 How. 62 62 (1853), SCOTUS traced Morse's first design from 1832 to a proof-of-concept demonstration in 1937. Attracting private capital proved futile, until Congress funded a successful forty-mile experiment from Baltimore to Washington in 1843. That success garnered private funding to extend the line to Philadelphia and New York. Smaller corporations began installing lines in the East, South, and Midwest. One of the installers, Henry O'Reilly, refused to recognize the Morse patent, finally issued in 1840, and did not pay patent royalties. The Morse company sued O'Reilly, leading to an extensive SCOTUS review of the technology and timing, concluding that Morse was indeed the first inventor and that his invention was superior to any other telegraph patent.

In an 1848 follow-up patent, Morse had essentially claimed to be the inventor of any subsequent technology using electro-magnetism. Morse could not patent the principle itself; nor could the claim get a patent. Still, the claim gave O'Reilly an additional ground against Morse. Morse had not disavowed that claim and therefore the entire patent application should fall. SCOTUS found a disavowal necessary, but that the rest of the patent did not fall because Morse waited for the high court's decision before disavowing that claim. O'Reilly had been using the system patented by Alexander Bain in 1849. SCOTUS found that the Bain system was an infringement on Morse's patent. SCOTUS also found that, because the disavowal remained unfiled;

each side would have to bear their own court costs. Morse got the injunction against O'Reilly and the Morse systems absorbed existing Bain systems.

Although the Bain system was a violation of Morse's patent, a patent taken out by Royal Earl House in 1846 survived the patent scrutiny. The House system did not use Morse code. It required more bulky equipment and heftier lines. What it could do was transmit synchronously letter by letter as commands to a piano-style keyboard. In a twist of irony, Hiram Sibley recapitalized the House system in 1854 but then bought the Midwest rights to the Morse system in 1855. Sibley quickly converted the House system to Morse and hired one of the people from whom he bought the Midwest rights, Jeptha Wade, as manager. Morse and Wade then wrested control of the remaining House systems in the upper Midwest and renamed the entire entity as the Western Union Telegraph System in 1856. Regional consolidations took place elsewhere, leaving six firms owning most of the telegraph industry in the United States by 1857.

Trans-Continental Telegraph

In 1860 the push for a transcontinental telegraph led to a contract-bid offering by the U.S. Treasury, as authorized by the Pacific Telegraph Act of 1860. Sibley, the financier of the Western Union Telegraph conglomeration, became the only bidder and got the contract. He completed the line in October 1861, and shortly thereafter the new line consolidated within the Western Union Telegraph Company. During the Civil War, Western Union lost considerable property in the South, but at the same time the U.S. Government (North) had built some 15,000 miles of telegraph line in aid of the war effort. All 15,000 miles went to Western Union after the war. A new player entered the telegraph industry, the U.S. Telegraph Company, itself made possible by the expiration of the Morse patents. Two others survived the war: the American Telegraph Company and Western Union. Under terms of stock swap, Western Union absorbed the other two players and became a telegraph monopoly.

In addition to seeking entry into the international telegraph business, Western Union also tried to take over Bell Telephone. Because Jay Gould was trying a hostile takeover of Western Union, the company reached an agreement with Bell that each would respect the other's turf and not attempt to enter that business. Bell became AT&T, and it entered direct competition with smaller telephone companies. In 1908, AT&T also got control of Western Union. In the face of potential anti-trust activity and complaints of a new rival, the Postal Telegraph Company, AT&T divested itself of Western Union. In 1945, Western Union took control of the Postal Telegraph Company. Back in 1851, the promise and performance of the telegraph was widely known; some seventy-five companies were providing telegraph services. Morse had once tried to sell the telegraph patent to the United States government, and then telegraph services could become part of the U.S. Postal Service. Congress would have none of it, and it also later refused to buy telephone rights from AT&T. The immediate result was a piecemeal sale of royalty rights, with increasingly fragmented ownership. As seen above, the fragmentation was a moment on the sojourn toward trusts or monopolies.

Although the U.S. government had declined to buy either telegraph or telephone patents to become part of the U.S. Postal Service, the U.S. government did for the telegraph industry much as it had done for the railroad industry. In 1860, a year before the Civil War, Congress passed, and President Buchanan signed, The Pacific Telegraph Act. Besides the bidding noted above, the act granted right-of-way over public lands, priority use for the government and connections, as needed, with military posts, and non-discriminatory access by citizens. The awardee also would get permanent right-of-way for a branch line to Oregon. Dispatch of messages were in the order received, without discrimination, save the priority for government messages. The Coast Survey, Smithsonian Institution, and National Observatory would have access free of cost. The act also imposed message charge limits.

Under Lincoln and during the Civil War, with the Southern states no longer participating in Congress, the Union Pacific Railroad and Telegraph Company incorporated in 1862 with the charge of building a continuous railroad and telegraph line to the West. It would have a capital stock of $100,000,000 (100,000 shares at $1,000 each, later further split to $100 a share and 1,000,000 shares), with a limit of 200 shares per person. Right-of-way was granted through public lands, 200 feet on either side of the railroad, plus access to surface resources from the adjoining lands, plus land needed for workshops, depots, stations, buildings, machine shops, switches, side tracks, turn-tables, and water stations. The U.S. government would extinguish Indian titles to all lands under the operation of the act. In exchange for transportation of the mails, troops, munitions of war, and public stores, the corporation shall receive every alternate section of public land (odd numbers), up to five alternate sections on each side of the railroad per mile (10 per mile, later 20), up to ten miles distant to accommodate sold, reserved, or disposed of lands.

The corporation has access to all timber on these lands, but not minerals. The corporation had three years to dispose of the lands once completing the line, and the remainder subject to settlement and pre-emption, at a price no more than $1.25 an acre. The company would get ownership of the lands adjacent to every 40 (later 20) miles of completed roadway. The Treasury would also issue $16,000 (16 at $1,000, later increased to 32 and 48) for each mile of completed roadway at 6 percent per annum and maturity at 30 years, considered the first mortgage on the railway and all rolling stock (later modified to allow issuing corporation bonds as first lien). The government had priority use at a compensation rate no higher than that charged to private parties. After completing the roadway, the corporation must devote at least 5 percent of its earnings annually toward the retirement of these bonds. The government authorized the Central Pacific R. R. Co. of California under the same terms, to build eastward from San Francisco, to connect with the Leavenworth, Pawnee and Western Railroad Company of Kansas, which shall, in turn, connect with the Union Pacific (more companies add later). Difficult mountainous portions got triple bonds. The act also authorized branch roads, and the quick transfer of existing telegraph lines onto the railroad right-of-way. By the 1870s, Congress was authorizing suits in equity against the Union Pacific Railroad Company and other railroad companies for numerous failure-to-pay and contract infractions.

Inter-State Commerce

The very effort to establish continuous rail and telegraph lines from coast-to-coast raised inter-state commerce issues and permanently changed the relation between intra-state and inter-state commerce. Federal monies and lands underwrote the development, and Federal law required that the main trunk lines allow connections with smaller branch lines developed with state or local support. The amazing transfer of capital from public to private hands had largely been complete before the advent of the Lochner Era (1887–1937), where laissez-faire and social Darwinism governed SCOTUS reasoning and decision-making. Apostles of the self-made man got rich at the public trough; the source of enormous private capital accumulations at work in the Lochner Era: the transfer of public resources to private hands, and the haphazard enforcement of contract terms when violated. The telegraph lines, and later telephone lines, benefited from the federal investment in railway easements and the Congressional determination to keep these technological developments in private hands, rather than transfer their ownership to the U.S. Postal System.

The peculiar separation of fact and reality generated another confrontation between the taxing power of the states and the inter-state commerce power of the central government. SCOTUS made it clear, as early as *McCulloch v. Maryland*, 17 U.S. 4 Wheat. 316 (1819), that states could not tax organs of the Federal government, because the power to tax is the power to destroy. Cities and towns found the new technologies tempting sources of new income and began taxing the number of poles and length of wire in each jurisdiction. It was clear that localities exercising police powers had the right to recover from these industries the costs of police protection and other police functions. Beyond that, the local taxation could not go. But where does the line between reasonable and unreasonable tax rates begin, and who is to make that decision? By the end of the nineteenth century, SCOTUS once again separated the state-level police power from the national-level commerce powers.

SCOTUS confronted the issues in a trilogy of cases in 1903–1904. In the first of these, *Western Union Tel. Co. v. New Hope*, 187 U.S. 419 (1903), when New Hope, Pennsylvania implemented an annual licensing fee covering poles and lines in the city. SCOTUS held the fee as recovery of cost for local government supervision, and thus did not find the tax to be a property or transmission tax. The state courts could decide whether the license fee was reasonable. Western Union argued, to no avail, that the town had expended nothing on the poles or wires, leaving the maintenance and repair to the company. SCOTUS found no undue burden on inter-state commerce. SCOTUS continued this reasoning in *Atlantic & Pacific Tel. Co. v. Philadelphia*, 190 U.S. 160 (1903). SCOTUS again confirmed that the states could not tax inter-state commerce but could collect ordinary property taxes and a franchise tax. SCOTUS did permit taxes that recover costs of local supervision of the telegraph infrastructure. Juries decided whether a given supervision rate was reasonable. SCOTUS did not permit a license fee for revenue, but a license fee recovering costs of local supervision was constitutional.

Allowing local juries to determine the reasonableness of license fees for local supervision of telegraph lines was very problematic. Juries allowed exorbitant license fees that companies found to be confiscatory. Equally important, there were few or no services rendered for the license. SCOTUS faces the dilemma the next year in *Postal Telegraph-Cable Co. v. Taylor*, 192 U.S. 64 (1904). SCOTUS scolded communities that passed license fees to raise revenue rather than pay for rendered or expected services, but then attempt to camouflage their true intentions by labeling the license an inspection fee. The telegraph company claimed that the licensing fee was twenty times more than it would cost itself to inspect, supervise, and regulate its poles and lines running through the borough, even though the borough had spent no money on these services. The company further pointed out that, if every borough were to do the same, the license cost would render the telegraph company insolvent. No greater threat to inter-state commerce could there be than local tax or taxes that would end the inter-state commerce itself. In this case, the telegraph company provided proof of its own costs in maintaining, inspecting, supervising, and regulating its poles and lines in this borough. A municipality cannot include in its licensing fees the costs it might incur for recovering liability when the supervision itself supposedly reduces this risk. SCOTUS thus found the license fee exorbitant, despite the decision of several state courts to the contrary.

Information Technology

Information technology and the state resource problem reappear in *Reno v. Condon*, 528 U.S. 141 (2000). Departments of motor vehicles across the nation collect some personal information, including name and address, social security number, physical description, and vehicle description. States had been selling this information until Congress imposed restrictions on the sale and distribution of this information. Rehnquist held that the Commerce Clause did enable Congressional action, and that Federalism or the Tenth Amendment was not a barrier. Information is an article of commerce. SCOTUS distinguishes between statutes that regulate states and those requiring states to regulate their citizens. The first he finds constitutional under the Commerce Clause; the latter violates the Tenth Amendment. Under the Congressional statute, a driver must consent before the state releases the information. Penalties for violation include criminal fines and civil liabilities. Rehnquist argues that the decision here has precedence in *South Carolina v. Baker*, 485 U.S. 505 (1988), which would allow the Congressional legislation, rather than *New York v. United States*, 505 U.S. 144 (1992), and *Printz v. United States*, 521 U.S. 898 (1997), which would not. The Baker case resulted from The Tax Equity and Fiscal Responsibility Act of 1982. Congress removed the tax exemption from interest earned on state and local bonds unless the bonds are in "registered" form rather than "bearer." Unregistered bonds left no paper trail, making federal income tax evasion possible. Allowing Congress to tax the interest on unregistered bonds required, in turn, the overruling of *Pollock v. Farmers' Loan & Trust Co.*, 157 U.S. 429 (1895). *New York* focused on Low-Level Radioactivity Waste Policy, which SCOTUS held unconstitutional. *Printz* focused on Brady Handgun Violence Prevention Act, provisions of which SCOTUS found unconstitutional.

CONCLUSION

Justice Marshall drew a sharp line between the police powers of the states and the necessary and proper powers of the central government exercising supreme control over inter-state commerce. The general government, he counsels, makes laws for the whole people, while each state attends only to those within its borders. In an arena that has concerned the Court from the outset, Rehnquist plays fast and loose with cross-state controls on the banking industry, one of the very first forces confronting the Supremacy Clause and the Interstate Commerce Clause. Questionable distinctions like people and cargo, general mass of goods and services versus selling, help obfuscate Marshall's bright line between the central government and state power in matters of commerce. The quest for state sovereignty under a national Constitution inevitably stokes confusion and instability in case precedent.

The position Rehnquist takes in the *Kaiser* case illustrates both the underlying confusions and the roads opened to irrelevant considerations piggybacked into the inter-state commerce issue. In *Kaiser*, a private developer used publicly owned navigable waters and land to give a private marina exclusive access to the sea. The very act connecting the marina to the sea made it public property, but the private owners wanted to restrict access from the sea into the marina. The size of the private investment required condemnation with just compensation, and Rehnquist decided that just compensation meant not just the value of the property before improvement, but the value of property after improvement. Rehnquist defends the compensation of private value stacked on public lands by a new rule basing compensation on whether private hands established navigability in fact.

After the Civil War, SCOTUS attempts to put some continuity in its decisions by severing the holding that SCOTUS governs interstate commerce, silent or not, and SCOTUS sharing some interstate power with the states, when it is silent. In *Welton*, interstate commerce follows goods to their destination, but that the states may regulate until Congress acts. The Munn decision further clouds the convenient distinction between whether Congressional dormancy is action. Munn increases the police powers of the state via the "affected by a public interest logic," and then SCOTUS restricted police powers the following year in *Husen*, ruling against the use of quarantine as an invasion of a dormant Congressional power.

Rehnquist adds another confusion to interstate commerce. In *Allenberg*, the Court found that the Mississippi cotton entered inter-state commerce once the comprehensive contract was in place, from seed to harvest and beyond. Rehnquist tries to turn the clock back and start interstate commerce when the cotton ships *from* the warehouse. Rehnquist once again questioned the mutual exclusivity rule. Rehnquist then violates a second principle, suggesting that two errors may fairly cancel each other out, such as where the Connecticut regulation on beer pricing might correct some (unidentified) market imperfection.

SCOTUS faced a daunting task when it began expounding a Constitution for the new industrial era. Railroads, telegraphs, and the new administrative state (e.g., Interstate Commerce Commission) dramatically expanded interstate commerce. The dominant belief systems at the end of the nineteenth century had their own impact on interstate commerce and how SCOTUS applied Marshall's dormant commerce idea. The effort to limit government intervention under laissez-faire had the consequence of empowering large corporations at the expense of government.

Laissez-faire and powerful railroads left little to national or state government control over commerce. The emphasis on that-government-is-best-which-governs-least led to a natural erosion of dormant commerce, further complicating a separation between interstate commerce powers and state police powers. At one point, SCOTUS compounded dormant commerce when both national and state governments could act, so long as there was no conflict. If so, the Supremacy Clause decided. The unbridled investment of state and local funds into branch lines slowly cascaded into larger and larger bankruptcies while railroads demanded intrusive access to parks and other public lands under state and local control. The railroads had already won that battle at the national level.

SCOTUS found itself in the odd position where corporations benefited from the dormant commerce clause, until SCOTUS began permitting local police powers an expanded role in safety and liability requirements, from fenced-in railroad lines to liability for accidents and inconveniences to the public. Reassertion of national power was the assured result of the checkerboard application of state and local police powers to a national phenomenon. The early reassertions energize through national war powers. Still, the state exercised invigorated police powers by mandating intra-state routes and stops and days of rest. The impact on interstate commerce becomes increasingly burdensome, checked only by national war powers.

The common law and thus local police power failed in the areas of liability and trusts. SCOTUS introduced the Baugh rule that effectively replaced the older master-servant or servant-servant common law. Congress added the Sherman Anti-Trust Act, giving SCOTUS the power to control associations engaged in the restriction of foreign or inter-state trade. Free competition created voluntary associations that effectively controlled interstate commerce; SCOTUS saves competition by publicly regulating private regulators. Interstate bankruptcies created new problems that SCOTUS could not side-step.

The growth of extraction industries presented a new challenge to an old problem: when does inter-state commerce begin. The exercise of police powers and state taxing authority required SCOTUS to standardize the relation between extraction industries and inter-state commerce. The latter begins when the extraction beings, even if stockpiled before loading on a vessel for further transport. Standardization of all railroad cars with automatic couplers illustrated the renewed central government footprint on interstate commerce. This extended to matters like workmen's compensation and work conditions, such as the eight-hour day. The tension between Lochner-era beliefs and interstate commerce needs persisted for decades. The recognition of labor and its interests in collective bargaining helps move the SCOTUS focus into the post-Lochner era.

As population density rose throughout the United States, a problem as simple as easements now assumes dramatic relevance. The common law dictated easement-by-necessity. Under Rehnquist, the common law rule gave way to eminent domain, with proper compensation. Rehnquist goes further. In the now infamous *National League of Cities*, Rehnquist posits that traditional government functions are immune from interstate commerce requirements. *National League* overrules *Maryland v. Wirtz*. *Garcia v. San Antonio* overrules *National League* nine years later.

A similar problem arises with telegraphs and electromagnetic communication generally. These do not stop for a border pass, so it is certainly going to involve interstate commerce. Where the line poles are, and who pays for them, is another matter. Congress paid for the proof-of-concept implementation, with a forty-mile line from Baltimore to Washington. Private capital followed. SCOTUS settled the patent battles. War contracts extended the line trans-continentally, and Congress transferred ownership of 15,000 miles of line to the builders in exchange for lines lost in the Civil War. The U.S. Post Office would not buy the industry, even though Congress dedicated railroad bed lines for pole distribution and the United States extinguished Indian title to lands as needed. Private owners assumed monopoly ownership of the entire telegraph system. SCOTUS allowed local taxation only for cost recovery.

The states wished to capitalize financially on the technological revolutions. Whether they lacked interstate commerce powers, they certainly had the powers of taxation. One area which many states sought to exploit was the information gathered for driver licenses. Some of the information was particularly sensitive, including address and social security number. After a celebrity murder made possible by the simple purchase of driver license information, Congress sought to legislate its sale. SCOTUS eventually reviewed the Congressional effort to control the availability of that information. The constitutional issue focused on whether the Tenth Amendment could block that regulation. Rehnquist agreed that the Tenth Amendment was not a restriction on the application of interstate commerce control, because the regulation targeted states rather than requiring states to regulate their citizens. The subtlety of practicalities aside, SCOTUS ruled that Congress could prevent the casual dissemination of sensitive information gathered by the states.

Chapter 5

The Administrative State

THE INTERSTATE COMMERCE COMMISSION

Congress created the Interstate Commerce Commission in 1887, a delegation of Congressional authority, to promote commerce and help rectify rate or carriage discrimination among railroads. In *Texas and Pacific Ry. Co. v. ICC*, 162 U.S. 197 (1896) SCOTUS confirmed the legal standing of the ICC. It also took close note of the general impact of ICC rules. Congress did not initially grant legislative power to the ICC (e.g., it could not set rates). The ICC was an investigating or fact-finding agency charged with soliciting and digesting all available information and differences in circumstances that might have led to alleged discrimination on rate charges and access. SCOTUS then required that the ICC also receive information from the contending parties, and to consider all circumstances that might underlie rate differences, from start to end, including the use of railroad rates to influence foreign water cartage into one or another U.S. port.

Before creation of the ICC, which would extend Congressional legislation into some of its dormant commerce areas, SCOTUS had approved state statutes that posted carrier rates or that put rates on the bill-of-lading, even if involving interstate commerce. SCOTUS had argued that state statutes rested on police power, not the commerce power, and these could control until Congress acted (*Railroad Company v. Fuller*, 84 U.S. 560 (1873)). In *Chicago, M. & St. P. Ry. Co. v. Solan*, 169 U.S. 133 (1898). SCOTUS described these police power rules, not in themselves regulations of interstate commerce, but until Congress acts: "they are to be regarded as legislation in aid of such commerce." SCOTUS held valid rulings of the Interstate Commerce Commission that published carrier rates, rather than state statutes relying on bills-of-lading (*Gulf, Colorado & Santa Fe Ry. Co. v. Hefley*, 158

U.S. 98 (1895)). This supposedly would make commerce more transparent and help illuminate points of discrimination or favoritism more thoroughly before issuing a cease-and-desist order. The federal order itself displaced any state statute in an area that might produce a conflict of duties expected of carriers, even if the federal and state legislation could normally co-exist.

The Interstate Commerce Commission did much to reduce the SCOTUS workload involving railroads. Although the court was slightly deferential, it occasionally sets standards for the ICC. In *East Tennessee, V. & G. Ry. Co. v. ICC*, 181 U.S. 1 (1901), SCOTUS insisted on an important exception to the general rule that carriers charge a lesser rate for a shorter haul. Dissimilarity of circumstances sometimes require an exception. When competition is real and substantial, and not a product of constraint-of-trade agreements, when that competition exercises a potential influence and it triggers the dissimilarity of circumstance and conditions provided by the enabling statute, then the rule permits a lesser charge made for a haul to a more distant and competitive point. Lower rates had initially been necessary, for example, because the railroads were in competition with water cartage. The lower rate structure continued after competition from water cartage had largely disappeared (see also *Interstate Commerce Commission v. Alabama Midland Railway Company*, 168 U.S. 144 (1897)).

RESTRAINT OF TRADE

In *Addyston Pipe & Steel Co. v. United States*, 175 U.S. 211 (1899) SCOTUS concluded that when Congress chose to act under its interstate commerce power, it may declare void and prohibit the performance of any contract that directly regulated interstate or foreign commerce, whatever the extent. SCOTUS similarly decided that if tile makers without a state agree to sell only to certain tile dealers within another state, then the entire arrangement became a restraint on interstate trade (*Montague & Co. v. Lowry*, 193 U.S. 38 (1904)). When the direct, immediate, and intended effect of a contract is to restrain trade, any contract to buy at the enhanced price is null and void. This decision did more than effectively end a pipe price-fixing conspiracy. The pipe companies had asserted a right of contract. Now, the right-to-contract, if it interfered with interstate commerce, took a back seat.

The more expansive view of interstate commerce power is clearly apparent in *Baltimore & Ohio R. Co. v. ICC*, 221 U.S. 612 (1911). Here, the Interstate Commerce Commission attempted to regulate the labor hours of railway employees engaged in interstate commerce. Carriers had to make reports. SCOTUS reasoned that time-employed had a direct relation to efficiency as well as safety. The regulation extended to intra-state commerce as well.

Monitoring required reporting, and neither the corporation nor its officers may plead the fifth regarding the required reports. The court differentiated this case from the Employers Liability Cases because here both employee and carrier were involved in interstate commerce, and because of the intertwining of intrastate and interstate commerce. Reducing the stress and danger to interstate employees automatically implicates intra-state employees as well. Thus, the commission had not acted outside its granted authority.

In *Houston E. & W. Tex. Ry. Co. v. United States*, 234 U.S. 342 (1914), SCOTUS again ruled that whenever interstate and intrastate transactions of carriers were so related that the governing of the one involved the control of the other, it is Congress, and not the state, prescribing the final and dominant rule. Congress has delegated to the Interstate Commerce Commission the power to prevent all discrimination against interstate commerce. When, after investigation, it determines there is unjust discrimination against localities, the commission has the power to correct it. When there is discrimination between interstate and intrastate rate, the railroad was as free to lower one of them as it was to raise the other but match them it must.

Stockyards

The Packers and Stockyards Act of 1921 c. 64, § 316, 42 Stat. 159 argued that the dealers at the stockyards were part of interstate commerce. From the point of shipping cattle, all the way to the point receiving the meat, it is one interstate commerce, with the Chicago Stock yards being the throat (*Stafford v. Wallace*, 258 U.S. 495 (1922)). Conceived this way, Congress has the power to regulate and monitor activity at the stockyards through it power over interstate commerce. The act allowed Congress to monitor the big five meatpackers who got arbitrarily lower prices from animal commissioners and the stockyard management; packers and dealers eventually would increase the price facing the consumer. The stockyards became great national public utilities to promote the flow of commerce from the ranges and fields of the west to the consumers in the east. This general concept continues in *Lemke v. Farmers Grain Co.*, 258 U.S. 50 (1922). A North Dakota association bought grain in that state, placed it in its elevator, and promptly loaded it onto cars for shipping, typically out-of-state. SCOTUS found an unconstitutional burden on interstate commerce a state statute requiring a license and license fee for the purchasers of grain for grading, inspection, and weighing.

Passengers

Wisconsin R. Co. Commission v. C., B. & Q. R. Co., 257 U. S. 563 (1922) made it clear that raising intrastate rates is related to the effective control of the interstate system. These so-called Wisconsin Passenger Rate Cases protected interstate travelers by making the cost of intra-state passenger carriage match the equivalent rate for interstate passengers while moving through Wisconsin. *Dayton-Goose Creek Ry. Co. v. ICC*, 263 U.S. 456 (1924) approved the provision of the transportation act of 1920 which required carriers to contribute one half of their excess earnings to a revolving fund used by the Interstate Commerce Commission for making loans to carriers to meet capital expenditures, to refund maturing obligations, or to purchase equipment and facilities. SCOTUS upheld this provision because it guaranteed to each railroad a fair return on their property, it maintained an adequate national railroad capacity, and it provided for the necessity of enlarging transportation facilities. SCOTUS had pointed out in the *Texas and Pacific Railway Company* that the very nature of the railroad industry, its capital-intensive infrastructure and its trans-continental reach, made it all but unavoidable that the industry would be a monopoly. The ICC, it reasoned, was a proper government balance for that set of monopolies. Compare this result to *Allgeyer v. Louisiana*, 165 U.S. 578 (1897) where SCOTUS warned that freedom of contract must be wary of legislative control, and more so when contracts are voluntary.

Rehnquist

An early Rehnquist decision, writing for the Court, touches upon both the railroad industry and the administrative state (*United States v. Florida East Coast Ry. Co.*, 410 U.S. 224 (1973)). The American railroad infrastructure had faced severe challenges with the trucking industry since the end of the Second World War. During certain times of the year, and in different geographical regions, there was an acute shortage of railroad cars needed to ship grain, etc. Congress wanted railroads to invest some of their profits in new rail cars, but in the meantime, asked the Interstate Commerce Commission to ease the car shortage while encouraging new rolling stock investment. At the time of the Rehnquist decision, there were more than twenty railroads operating within the United States. The railroads shared cars across railroad lines, but some lines were tardy in returning borrowed cars, thereby increasing the shortage on lines that needed them. After three years of inaction, plus a renewed prodding by Congress, the ICC issues per diem rates for the use of cars owned by other railroads. The interim rule, then made permanent, effectively encouraged lines to return unused rail cars and to invest in additional cars of its own. Congress had given the ICC such rule-making authority in a 1966 amendment.

The railroads challenged the ICC rule on the basis that it had not conducted a trial-like (oral) hearing, as required by a couple provisions in the Interstate

Commerce Act and the Administrative Procedures Act. Although the ICC had received written submissions from the appellees, the district court ruled that failure to hold oral hearings prejudiced the railroads and it set aside the ICC rule. The Supreme Court reversed, arguing that only one section of the Administrative Procedures Act governed the ICC ruling in this case; it required no oral hearing.

Rehnquist's dissent to *Sporhase v. Nebraska ex rel. Douglas*, 458 U.S. 941 (1982) seriously tests his position on state sovereignty. The management of surface waters in the West had been matters of national concern for some time, but this case brings up the problem of groundwater in vast areas of the Southwest where irrigation was necessary for agriculture. The states had a checkerboard system of laws regarding groundwater. Some considered water to be an item of commerce, some did not. Some states allow wells to draw whatever water they could, other states controlled the yearly usage on designated areas of the state. The owners of adjacent tracts of land in Nebraska and Colorado brought the court case. The owners drew waters from a well in Nebraska to irrigate lands on both the Nebraska and Colorado tracts. Nebraska law forbade the inter-state movement of water unless the receiving state had a reciprocal water transfer agreement. Colorado refused all interstate transfer of ground water. Taken together, there could be no legal transfer of water across their common state line, so the land owners had to stop using water drawn in Nebraska for irrigation on their adjacent tract in Colorado.

SCOTUS found groundwater to be an item of commerce and thus the problem was subject to the Interstate Commerce Clause. SCOTUS found many of the Nebraska regulations reasonable, except the provision requiring a reciprocal agreement. Such an act would attempt to legislate for another state. In this case, the collision of state statutes effectively prevented any interstate exchange. By its inaction and toleration of state legislation, Congress has not consented to unilateral impositions of burdens on state commerce.

Rehnquist wanted the question limited to whether the commerce clause, absent any action by Congress in this area, would invalidate some or all the relevant Nebraska groundwater statutes. He argued that the SCOTUS majority changed the question to whether the commerce clause would enable Congress to regulate groundwater "overdraft." The key difference being, of course, that Congress had not exercised any authority in this area. Rehnquist again asserts that the sovereign states have an interest in its earth and air behind the titles of its citizens. As such, for example, the Nebraska regulations trump any property interests of the adjacent tract owners in ground water use.

The SCOTUS majority takes notice of the interstate aquifer, but Rehnquist does not address that point. Like rivers, the waters of which flow across or along state lines, the ground water in question comes from an aquifer that underlay several states. So curiously, while Nebraska simply allows use of the water, Texas, under which the same aquifer extends, allows unrestricted individual ownership.

Three years before *Sporhase*, the overturn of the *Geer v. Connecticut*, 161 U.S. 519 (1896) decision abandoned the state ownership theory of such natural resources. The SCOTUS majority held that states may protect and preserve its wildlife, but the pertinent economic unit is the nation, not the state. Any statute that overtly or covertly discriminates against another state is unconstitutional. In *Hughes v. Oklahoma*, 441 U.S. 322 (1979) SCOTUS found unconstitutional an Oklahoma statute preventing the transport of natural minnows procured from its waters for sale out-of-state. Commercial hatcheries in the state may ship minnows out-of-state. The state claimed the ownership of the natural minnows and held for the benefit of its people. On that ground, the state argued it may regulate, control, and assert its property rights.

Oklahoma used *Geer* as its justification. *Geer* allowed a state to prohibit the transport across state lines of game birds legally killed within the state. The problem focused upon ownership, because SCOTUS used the commerce clause to give the national government control over inter-state commerce. Forbidding the taking across state lines clearly involves inter-state commerce. Rejecting the ownership theory, the SCOTUS majority overruled *Geer*.

SCOTUS underscores the notion that when an animal, lawfully killed, becomes an article of commerce, the citizens of one state, to the exclusion of citizens of other states, cannot limit the animal's use. Oklahoma had, in *West v. Kansas Natural Gas Co.*, 221 U.S. 229 (1911), tried to prevent the transportation of its natural gas across state lines, but lost. Game, like gas, is now as any other natural resource that states cannot exclude from interstate commerce.

State discrimination against interstate commerce requires strict scrutiny. Rehnquist reaffirmed his belief in *Geer* but would justify it on grounds other than "ownership." The state is a conservator of wildlife for the benefit of its citizens. Rehnquist rejects as unimportant the Balkanized appearance such commercial activity might create. Each state, Rehnquist avers, has an interest in conserving and regulating the exploitation of its wildlife (in this case, minnows).

Rehnquist wrote for the majority in a case involving fish migrating upstream to spawn and downstream to the ocean to live out their maturity (*Idaho ex rel. Evans v. Oregon*, 444 U.S. 380 (1980)). The rivers involved three states and Amerindian tribes who, by treaty, held entitlement to 50 percent of each of three yearly runs of different species. Two of the states and the Amerindian tribes agreed to a division of the fish runs under auspices of a Special Master appointed by the district court, but the agreement left the third state and the United States out of the agreement. The United States had refused to join. If the third state pressed a diversity suit, SCOTUS would take jurisdiction from the district court. The third state, where most of the spawning occurred, could try direct negotiations with the other two states. It wanted a greater share of the fish moving upstream over eight dams.

Three options were possible. If the third state sued, the district court would automatically lose supervision of the diversity suit. If the United States joined in the agreement, it could represent the third state's concerns as well as Amerindian treaty rights. Besides, the United States operated the dams. The third option would allow the third state to enter the two-party agreement, even though its update was ready for implementation. SCOTUS opted for the third option and instructed the Special Master to rule accordingly. The preferred solution kept the national government from participating in the agreement, except that SCOTUS could still hear problems. The chosen option was neither consistent with agreements in which the United States was a participant, nor efficient or sure. The U.S. government stood in the shadows, even though its footprint was on the dams, the treaty rights, the estimate of fish flows, and ultimately the enforcement. The two parties in the original agreement, in conjunction with the Amerindian tribes, did not want the third party admitted to the agreement. The convoluted solution preserved some appearance of state sovereignty, but the reality of the situation painted a different picture. In typical twists and turns of Rehnquist, he argued that, when a state's claim is indistinguishable from that of a private consumer, it is insufficient to invoke SCOTUS' original jurisdiction. A state advancing sovereign or quasi-sovereign interest deserves original jurisdiction, but not so for states suing to promote the interests of their citizens.

FEDERAL POWER COMMISSION AND FEDERAL ENERGY REGULATORY COMMISSION

When Congress established the Federal Power Commission in 1938, the states apparently welcomed the inter-state regulatory partner. Thirty-six years later, in *Corp. Commission of Oklahoma v. Federal Power Commission*, 415 U.S. 961 (1974), the Court allowed the FPC to sue a state natural gas regulatory agency and enjoin state agency orders violating either FPC rules or the Commerce Clause. To the contrary, Rehnquist denied that the word "person" included the state regulatory agencies, despite parallel interpretations in other federal legislation. He also argued against this construction because it undermines notions of comity between state and federal bodies.

Among the late nineteenth and early twentieth century developments were the extraction and distribution of oil and coal, and the production and distribution of electricity. These are national resources and thus subject to the

Commerce clause. In *Arizona Pub. Svc. Co. v. Snead*, 441 U.S. 141 (1979), New Mexico imposed a tax on the privilege of generating electricity. New Mexico also had a gross receipts tax, and the energy tax was applicable against the gross receipts tax. Other states receiving New Mexico-generated electricity did not have an offset for the energy tax. Thus, in-state electricity users got a benefit that was unavailable to those out-of-state. The state courts found the energy tax valid, but SCOTUS invalidated the tax because it violated a federal statute forbidding such discrimination. The Supremacy Clause in the Constitution settles any battle between state and federal statute. Rehnquist concurred in the SCOTUS decision, but argued that the federal statute outlawing the New Mexico tax may be a sterile law, doing no more than the commerce clause itself, in which case the New Mexico tax is valid. Giving the federal statute the benefit of doubt, that the statute was not sterile, Rehnquist finds the New Mexico tax invalid.

Louisiana imposed a "first use" tax on natural gas coming into Louisiana that previously had not been subject to taxation (*Maryland v. Louisiana*, 451 U.S. 725 (1981)). Exemptions and credits to Louisiana users ultimately put the entire tax burden on out-of-state users. A special master's report recommended holding further evidentiary hearings, but Louisiana filed a motion to dismiss on jurisdictional grounds. SCOTUS denied Louisiana's motion to dismiss. SCOTUS found that Louisiana legislation violated the Supremacy Clause, giving power over costs associated with natural gas pipelines to the Federal Energy Resources Commission (FERC). The "first use" tax was then unconstitutional under the commerce clause. The gas originated on federally owned property in the outer continental shelf. Although SCOTUS has original or concurrent jurisdiction on several grounds, the dissenting Justice Rehnquist does not want the Court to invoke original jurisdiction.

EPA

Few issues demonstrate both the need for national policy and the need for an administrative agency than does environmental protection. Just as coal-burning plants in Canada contributed to acid rain in the United States, dirty air in one city cannot have local effects only. The Environmental Protection Agency, nemesis of state sovereignty everywhere, was charged with implementing ambient clean air standards quickly (*U.S. Steel Corp. v. U.S. E.P.A.*, 444 U.S. 1035 (1980)). Once the states identified areas as non-attainable, the EPA tried to implement procedural safeguards for the states while placing stringent restrictions on industries in the non-attainment areas. EPA took some procedural shortcuts to meet its own timeline set by Congress. Industries facing rules, without going through the announce and comment phase, sued to have designations as non-attainment areas set aside, because it did not follow strict administrative procedures. The court of appeals accepted the argument that EPA had good cause for dispensing with usual procedures, and that there was little chance that the rules would reverse in the more protracted procedures. SCOTUS rejected a petition for *writ of certiorari*, but Rehnquist wanted the full court to hear the complaint, because SCOTUS had the discretionary jurisdiction to resolve conflicts among the courts of appeal.

No state may ban the importation from another state of "value—less material" such as solid or liquid waste (*City of Philadelphia v. New Jersey*, 437 U.S. 617 (1978)). Rehnquist objects that the commerce clause leaves New Jersey with the choices of closing all its landfills or keeping them open to extra-state users. He opposes the use of the commerce clause to open state landfills to out-of-state users. Quarantine laws ought to break this requirement of importing valueless material. Rehnquist goes back to a series of late nineteenth and early twentieth century cases for the "dispositive" cases, including *Bowman v. Chicago Northwestern R. Co.*, 125 U.S. 465, 125 U.S. 489 (1888) and *Asbell v. Kansas*, 209 U.S. 251 (1908). Each state must attend to its own sanitary problems but should not expose its citizen's health and safety to waste imported from another state.

Rehnquist finds himself in a peculiar situation in *City of Milwaukee v. Illinois*, 451 U.S. 304 (1981). Milwaukee has been dumping considerable raw sewage into Lake Michigan. The state of Illinois sued for an abatement, and the federal court found what it called a "federal common law" that would allow addressing the nuisance, but SCOTUS did not want to take original jurisdiction, given the availability of lower courts. Illinois, then joined by Michigan, sued in district court. This "federal common law" was not an invasion of dormant commerce, but a few months later Congress passed the Federal Water Pollution Act. EPA then established effluent regulations. The Wisconsin Department of Natural Resources, the issuer of the permit for the Milwaukee sewer system, sued in state court to compel compliance with the permit's requirements.

Meanwhile, the district court found a federal common law violation, and issued effluent limitations and timetable for the construction necessary to eliminate the sewage overflows. The court of appeals found that the Federal Water Pollution Act did not pre-empt the common-law nuisance, but that the district court's more stringent conditions would give way to the permit and EPA regulations. SCOTUS ruled that the exercise of "federal common law" was no longer necessary because Congress had acted. No finding under the common-law principle was any longer available. Rehnquist, writing for the majority, argued that the intervening Congressional action removed the court-created "federal common law" cause for action. Rehnquist observes: "The enactment of a federal rule in an area of national concern, and the decision whether to displace state law in doing so, is generally made not by the federal judiciary, purposefully insulated from democratic pressures, but by the people through their elected representatives in Congress." Rehnquist then argues that when Congress has not spoken on an issue that is a significant conflict between federal interests or policies and the use of state law, then SCOTUS has found it necessary, in a "few and restricted" instances, to develop federal common law.

Oregon Waste Systems, Inc. v. Department of Environmental Quality of Ore., 511 U.S. 93 (1994) is yet another sanitary landfill case in which Rehnquist dissented from the court majority. Oregon imposed one rate for the disposal of solid waste for in-state and another rate for out-of-state waste disposal. The out-of-state surcharge captured the additional costs of the inter-state transfer. Out-of-state haulers thus paid $3.10 a ton, and the question is whether there is a justifiable cost recovery in the additional $2.25 surcharge. The state of Oregon tried to price the out-of-state surcharge to meet a cost-based fee that might pass SCOTUS scrutiny. The components in the surcharge included $0.58 a ton for state-wide activities for reducing environmental risks and improving waste management, $0.66 to reimburse tax credits and subsidies, $0.05 for review and certification of waste reduction plans, $0.72 for increased environmental liability, $0.20 for lost disposal capacity, $0.03 for public supported infrastructure, and $0.01 for nuisance impacts. SCOTUS examined the breakdown and found the Oregon surcharge facially discriminatory. The cost per ton for out-of-state disposal was more than three times that for in-state disposal, leading SCOTUS to conclude that a cost fee system must be within reason, and the Oregon charge was not, under negative commerce clause analysis. The Oregon charge was facially discriminatory; it does not even get to the assessment of whether the charge, in relation to putative local benefits, was a case for a nondiscriminatory regulation. Oregon failed because its cost analysis was based on a comparison between waste disposal and state income taxes as a relative equivalent of intrastate burden. Resource protectionism is not acceptable. Oregon apparently would rebate the $0.85 fee out of the $3.10 if permitted the surcharge. Even this way, the out-of-state charge is nearly three times that of the in-state charge. Degree of discrimination in any event is just a measure of the extent of discrimination. Strict scrutiny applies, meaning that there are simply no other alternatives available to reach a pressing state interest. In this case, the state meets neither condition. If the surcharge is a compensatory tax, there must be some demonstrated relation between compensation and the burden imposed. Again, Oregon failed. The base rate charged for in-state disposal would be the baseline for a compensatory tax.

Rehnquist's effort to reprieve the Oregon surcharge used many of his earlier arguments. He does cite two precedents as ways Oregon might side-step the commerce limitation: become a market participant (*SouthCentral Timber*

Development, Inc. v. Wunnicke, 467 U.S. 82, 93 (1984)), using *Reeves, Inc. v. Stake*, 447 U. S. 429 (1980); and being an owner (*Baldwin v. Fish and Game Comm'n of Mont.*, 436 U.S. 371 (1978)). Writing for the majority, Justice Thomas again warned about economic Balkanization among the states, but Rehnquist is unmoved. Rehnquist again complains that Oregon's responsibility regarding waste management now allows other states to exploit it by shipping their waste across state borders. Rehnquist prefers to consider "clean and safe environment" like SCOTUS considers water resources.

FTC

Parker v. Brown, 317 U.S. 3451 (1943) created a morass of interstate commerce problems when it ruled that states could effectively violate anti-trust laws and still have them constitutional because "state-action" would trump the Sherman Act, the Agricultural Marketing Agreement of 1937, and the inter-state commerce clause. The state plan restricted competition among agricultural product growers to maintain price. Most of the produce was for exportation out-of-state. SCOTUS argued that nowhere in the Sherman Act did Congress impose restrictions upon the states. Absent explicit Congressional action, the states were free to restrict commerce. The federal Agricultural Marketing Agreement had some overlap with the state program, but because the state had not activated the federal act through its prescribed procedures, the state is free to enact its own program, technically meeting the federal requirements. SCOTUS then reasons that the Agricultural Marketing Agreement does not occupy the same legislative space and does not preempt the state plan. SCOTUS then resurrects the manufacture-commerce distinction and finds the state plan does not violate the commerce clause, because the state plan focuses on manufacturing and does not operate in inter-state commerce. To the extent that the state plan affects inter-state commerce, the state legislation either coincides with the federal or falls within an accommodation of interests between state and nation.

Parker strained, to say the least, to reach the conclusions SCOTUS did reach. SCOTUS revisits the idea of state action immunity in *California Retail Liquor Dealers Assn. v. Midcal Aluminum, Inc.*, 445 U. S. 97 (1980). As a nod toward federalism, the state action immunity test requires the state to have a clear and affirmative policy allowing the anti-competitive conduct and to provide active supervision of the permitted conduct. The states under examination in this case met the policy criterion but failed the supervision criterion. SCOTUS, as did 34 state *amici curiae* and the state of Wisconsin, argued against this broad immunity rule under Sherman Antitrust activity. States can regulate without approving anticompetitive conduct, and thus affirm the benefits of competition within the framework of the anti-trust laws. The petitioners sought protection behind the state action screen. SCOTUS ruled that there had been no active supervision over these prices. This closed the state action option. Anti-trust laws apply to the price fixing scheme. Rehnquist's dissent objects to this strong active supervision requirement, and thus would allow price-fixing by private hands, with state approval, behind the shield of state-action. Rehnquist traces his opinion to *Parker*, that he felt authorized state officials to administer a regulatory program without being liable to anti-trust laws, because the Sherman Anti-Trust Act did not aim at the states. In *FTC v. Ticor Title Ins. Co.*, 504 U.S. 621 (1992) the Federal Trade Commission filed against six of the top title insurance companies, alleging horizontal price fixing for title searches and examinations. One company signed a consent decree, but the others entered litigation arguing state-action immunity from antitrust prosecution. SCOTUS found that, to claim state-action immunity, the state must maintain active supervision of its permitted price fixing. Rehnquist's dissent argues against requiring the second standard, state supervision, before claiming the state-action doctrine. The principles of federalism are enough.

Adjusting to Lochner

The Lochner Era escalated the right-of-contact to SCOTUS' top priority. Its first and foremost enemy was labor. SCOTUS saw the contract between labor and corporation as two parties agreeing to an exchange on equal grounds. Substituting labor union negotiation not only violated right-of-contract but it also elevated labor into a bargaining position that was unfair and placed undue stress upon corporations. Labor also tended to emphasize equality, but SCOTUS saw the right-to-contract as a vehicle for individuals to exchange their specific talents and abilities for wages. The right-to-contract also carries forth the Baugh rule, which emphasized that each laborer assumed risks relevant to his specific position in exchange for wage consideration. The Court similarly finds in favor of rights-of-contract over state's sovereignty after using the Tenth Amendment to banish national sovereignty. The changing technological environments, and thus the changing landscape for fraud and deceit, eventually led SCOTUS to reaffirm Congress' interstate commerce control.

SCOTUS restricted the objects reached by the interstate commerce clause in *Employers' Liability Cases*, 207 U.S. 463 (1908). Congress could regulate the relation of master/servant in liability, so long as confining the regulations solely to interstate commerce. Congress could not, however, reach the liability of common carriers in favor of the workman when not engaged in interstate commerce at the time of injury. When blending non-constitutional powers with constitutional ones, the entire statute must fall.

SCOTUS continued its restrictions on the reach of the commerce clause in *Adair v. United States*, 208 U.S. 161 (1908). This labor act provided for arbitration, but also sought to protect employees and future employees who were, are, or could become affiliated with a labor union. Employers asserted the right to fire a labor union member under their freedom of contract. The Court approvingly cited *Lochner v. New York*, 198 U.S. 45 (1905) in asserting the right to do business with whom anyone pleases, and of course, the right to refuse such business. The right includes the purchasing and selling of labor. An employer may use the fact of labor union membership to release of an employee. The interstate commerce clause provides no cover here. SCOTUS thus severs such a provision from the rest of the Act.

The now infamous *Hammer v. Dagenhart*, 247 U.S. 251 (1918) limited the range of federal power over interstate commerce. Here, the attempt was to control the shipping of goods made in a factory employing children. SCOTUS fell back on the distinction between manufacturing and commerce. SCOTUS also argued that the right to regulate is not the right to exclude, save in cases where the item is evil or immoral. Congress had no power to require the states to exercise their police powers.

In *Adkins v. Children's Hosp.*, 261 U.S. 525 (1923) SCOTUS reiterated a theme that has appeared through much of the *Lochner Era*. First, the right-to-contract about one's affairs is part of the liberty of the individual protected by the Fifth Amendment. Second, this liberty-of-contract includes the employment of labor. The parties have equal rights to obtain from each other the best terms they can by private bargaining. The court then found the minimum wage act of 1918 unconstitutional. This was an effort to fix the number of hours of work considering the difference between men and women, but it rejects the distinctions between the sexes regarding the liberty of contact. Thus, the federal attempt to set minimum wages for women in the District of Columbia was an unconstitutional interference with the liberty of contract.

Carter v. Carter Coal Co., 298 U.S. 238 (1936) is another gasp in the late Lochner Era. In 1935 Congress passed the bituminous coal conservation act, arguing that a national public interest affects the coal distributed, and it thus relates to the general welfare as to require regulation of that industry. These regulations would include collective bargaining for wages, hours of labor, and working conditions. The aim was to prevent the obstructions to the commerce that arise over labor disputes. SCOTUS found that an excise tax on the market value of the coal was a substantial drawback for those who agreed to the price-fixing and labor terms. It was not a tax but a penalty to coerce submission. Even in times of emergency, Congress cannot exercise a power not given. The central government is one of enumerated powers and those inherent in those enumerated. SCOTUS repeated the decision that production and manufacture of commodities are not commerce, even when done with the intent to sell or transport out-of-state. SCOTUS argued that the bill threatened to allow the commerce power to swallow the police power.

Morehead v. New York ex rel. Tipaldo, 298 U.S. 587 (1936) ruled against a New York law guaranteeing a fair wage to women. The state was without power by any form of legislation to prohibit, change, or nullify contracts between payers and adult women workers. SCOTUS used the due process clause in *Morehead* as it used the due process clause in *Adkins*. The sequence is clear: the national government's commerce power does not extend into the state's police powers, and the state's police power cannot violate the individual right of contract.

Lochner Has Passed Away

NLRB v. Jones & Laughlin Steel Corp., 301 U.S. 1 (1937) is the benchmark case in the post *Lochner Era*. The Court had been quite unfavorable to labor during the *Lochner Era*, with palpable hostility toward labor unions, picketing, or strikes. In *NLRB*, SCOTUS affirmed a fundamental right to organize and select representative of labor's own choosing for collective bargaining. Congress used its interstate commerce authority, coupled with the threat of labor strife and need for industrial peace, to safeguard the rights of employees, health organization, and free choice of collective bargaining representatives. The National Labor Relations Act established standards to which national labor relations must conform. Jones and Laughlin had fired men for union activity to discourage unionism. The board ordered reinstatement and payment of back wages. Business opposed the law on the basis that it invaded the reserved powers of the states to attend to their own local concerns. Quite important, in view of the previous decisions, SCOTUS held that Congressional authority to protect interstate commerce from burdens and obstructions is not just for transactions deemed an essential part of the flow of interstate or foreign commerce. Burdens and obstructions may be due to injurious action springing from other sources.

There were four dissenters to the *NLRB* decision. They clearly recognized that the Court had departed from its previous rulings. The dissenters approvingly cited the *Schechter* case as well as the *Carter* case. The NLRB rules applied to companies engaged in production, not interstate commerce per se, but the companies still had to reinstate with pay men dismissed for union activities. Any effect on interstate commerce by the discharge of employees is indirect and remote in the highest degree. The Tenth Amendment, they argued, protected the states and their sovereignty.

West Coast Hotel Co. v. Parrish, 300 U.S. 379 (1937) continues the abrupt shift from the Lochner Era. Depriving liberty of contract requires due process. If, however, the statute aims to protect the community against menaces to health, safety, morals, or welfare, it is due process. The case focused on the constitutionality of the state of Washington's minimum wages for women act. In that act, the welfare of the state of Washington protected women and minors from conditions of labor that affect their health and morals. The power given to its administrative board included the setting of a minimum wage to meet the cost-of-living and maintain the workers in health. The liberty safe-guarded by the Constitution is not necessarily the liberty of the contract, which is not even in the Constitution, but liberty in a social organization which required the protection of law against the evil which menace the health, safety, morals, and welfare of the people. This logic resurrects the fundamental-laws-of-peoples that are constitutional even if not mentioned in the Constitution, because they are fundamental to social order itself. In any event, inequality in the footing of the parties undermines the liberty of contract. SCOTUS overruled *Adkins v. Children's Hosp.*, 261 U.S. 525 (1923), which had ruled against minimum wages for women in Washington, D.C., *Morehead v. New York ex rel. Tipaldo*, 298 U.S. 587 (1936) had ruled against minimum wages for women in New York state but differed from the *Atkins* case because it accounted for the value of the service rendered.

The four dissenters argued that the decisions in the *Adkins* and *Morehead* were sufficient to cover this case. We cannot consider an old issue just because of the economic conditions which have supervened. The meaning of the Constitution does not change. This law asked the employee or employer to make an arbitrary payment for a purpose and upon a basis having no causal relation with his business, or the contract, or the work of the employee. The declarative base is not the value of the service rendered but the extraneous circumstance that the employee needed to get a prescribed amount of money to ensure her subsistence, health, and morals.

United States v. Darby, 312 U.S. 100 (1941) found the Fair Labor Standards Act of 1938 constitutional. This act fixed minimum wages, maximum hours, and compensation for overtime, all at the pain of fine and imprisonment and the prohibition of shipping goods manufactured at that facility. Congressional conception of public policy is that interstate commerce is not an instrument of competition under substandard labor conditions. SCOTUS overruled *Hammer v. Dagenhardt*, and limited *Carter v. Coal*. SCOTUS also found that the Tenth Amendment was not a limitation upon the authority of the national government to use all means for the exercise of a granted power which are appropriate and plainly adapted to the permitted end. Keeping appropriate records is a requirement on the employer. Articles which in themselves have harmful or deleterious property are not the only domain of interstate commerce. SCOTUS declared that the authority of the federal government over interstate commerce is not different in extent or character from that retained by the state over intra-state commerce. SCOTUS overruled *Hammer v. Dagenhardt* because it was a departure from prevalent principles.

State Sovereignty Reasserted

Rehnquist worked for greater state sovereignty in a pair of related cases: *Windward Shipping v. American Radio Assn.*, 415 U.S. 104 (1974) and *American Radio Assn. v. Mobile S. S. Assn.*, 419 U.S. 215 (1974). U.S. unions picketed two foreign ships for paying below scale wages and, by implication, had been responsible for loss of U.S. merchant seaman jobs. The foreign ships sued for an injunction in state court, but the state court argued that the National Labor Relations Act preempted its jurisdiction. SCOTUS ruled the picketing non-commercial and hence not covered by the NLRA and its Labor Management Relations Act (LMR) amendment. Thus, there was nothing barring state court jurisdiction, despite the request by unions to set aside state court decisions for lack of jurisdiction. Again, SCOTUS found the picketing non-commercial and that there were no first or Fourteenth Amendment rights violated when Alabama courts issued an injunction against the picketers.

An interesting confrontation of national and state sovereignty occurs in *Fry v. United States*, 421 U.S. 542 (1975). The majority affirmed the application of the Economic Stabilization Act of 1970 to state employee wages, to control inflation, prices, rents, wages, salaries, dividends, and interests. A state of Ohio statute mandated wage increases for state employees, but SCOTUS found the U.S. statute to govern state employee wages. Rehnquist dissented by repeating Justice Chase's declaration in 1869 that the Constitution looks to an indestructible Union, composed on indestructible states. Rehnquist admits the reasonableness of the wage stabilization but, coupled with some earlier precedents, *United States v. California*, 297 U.S. 175 (1936) and *Maryland v. Wirtz*, 392 U.S. 183 (1968), he cites a danger to our federal system. Rehnquist would use the Tenth Amendment to block the application of the ESA to the state wage statutes. Rehnquist finds an "affirmative constitutional right," inherent in its capacity as a state, to be free from asserted Congressional authority. The *California* case required a railroad wholly contained within the state of California to implement automatic couplers, under authority of the Interstate Commerce Clause. The *Wirtz* case allowed imposition of provisions of the Fair Labor Standards Act upon the states. Taken together, Rehnquist fears these cases would devour the essentials of state sovereignty. Rehnquist distinguishes between individuals attacking a Congressional act, individuals claiming violation of a constitutional right via the Congressional act, and a state asserting its "inherent capacity as a state."

Rehnquist then goes on to blur the case precedent history on taxing authority (shared by national and state governments) and commerce authority (reserved for national authority only). In arguing the overturning of the *Wirtz* decision, Rehnquist claims that the principle of *stare decisis* applies more to cases involving statutory authority than to cases involving constitutional law.

The Fair Labor Standards Act, as amended in 1974, applies to most employees, including those of state and local governments. Rehnquist tries to delineate an area of state employer-employee relations in areas of "traditional governmental functions," that are exempt from the power of Congress under the Commerce Clause. Rehnquist reasons that the FLSA would impair the states' ability to function effectively in a federal system. He cites a footnote in *Fry v. United States*, 421 U.S. 542 (1975), a case in which he was the lone dissenter. Rehnquist also takes this opportunity to overrule *Wirtz*, a case that he felt jeopardized state functions. Rehnquist states that the 1974 amendments may be within the scope of the Commerce Clause, but their impact on states qua sovereigns is severe. The Tenth Amendment functions as an affirmative check on Congress's Commerce power.

Rehnquist invented a principle of federal comity that he felt should increasingly dominate national policy. In *Fair Assessment in Real Estate Assn. v. McNary*, 454 U.S. 100 (1981), Rehnquist asserted that this principle of comity barred taxpayers' damage actions in federal court for an alleged unconstitutional administration of a state tax system. Thus, he argued, SCOTUS did not need to determine whether the Tax Injunction Act of 1937 barred the state system, because comity kept federal courts from granting damages. Rehnquist gets particularly assertive in *United Credit Bureau of America INC. v. N. L. R. B.*, 454 U.S. 994 (1981) when he took exception to an authorized act of the National Labor Relations Board ordering an employer to dismiss its state court action against an employee after the employee filed an unfair labor practice complaint. Rehnquist argued that the principle of federalism and comity (as he inferred them), did not allow the National Labor Relations Act to empower the NLRB to enjoin this state court damage action. SCOTUS denied certiorari, but Rehnquist filed a dissent nonetheless. A probationary employee sought new benefits from her employer a couple days after her hiring. The employer released her because her attitude toward the job had changed and that she no longer would be able to do the work required. She filed the unfair labor practice charge with the NLRB, but a day before that hearing the employer filed damage action in state court. The employer alleged that the employee had engaged in a fraudulent scheme to obtain a paid vacation with her new husband. The NLRB found against the employer solely because the employer filed the state damage action in retaliation and to discourage future NLRB filings. NLRB ordered the state action withdrawn and the employer to pay the employee's legal expenses. The court of appeals supported the NLRB decision, although the employers argued that federal labor law did not pre-empt the state court action. Rehnquist preferred that the state court hear the retaliation defense where she filed the damage action, and if the finding was unfavorable, the employee could appeal through the state court system, to the state supreme court, and then to SCOTUS. Rehnquist presumably felt that, despite the protracted court battle any employer could wage against an employee, the employer would not be deterring the NLRB grievance.

Limiting National Reach in Interstate Commerce: Lochner at Work

Congress passed the monopoly and restraint act in 1890 (26 Stat. 209, c. 647; Supp. Rev. St. p. 726), designed to protect trade and commerce against unlawful restraints and monopolies. Sharply divided courts took different positions regarding the reach of this act. In *United States v. Eaton*, 144 U.S. 677 (1892) SCOTUS ruled that a regulation by the Commissioner of Internal Revenue, approved by the Secretary of Treasury, imposing a penalty on an oleomargarine wholesaler for not keeping book and making revenue return, was unconstitutional. The Court, reminding that there are no common law offenses against the United States, found that the penalty and reporting requirements were without basis in statutory law. *Schollenberger v. Pennsylvania*, 171 U.S. 1 (1898), focusing on a state statute exercising police powers, ruled that oleomargarine was a food, that it was free to cross state lines in its original package, but that coloring oleomargarine may be a fraud. A state may not prohibit the introduction or sale of oleomargarine, but a state may regulate coloring for fraud or deception. SCOTUS follows a similar line of reasoning for the interstate transportation of liquor (*Bowman v. Chicago & Northwestern Ry. Co.*, 125 U.S. 465 (1888); *Leisy v. Hardin*, 135 U.S. 100 (1890); *Rhodes v. Iowa*, 170 U.S. 412 (1898)).

In *Hopkins v. United States*, 171 U.S. 578 (1898) SCOTUS let stand the Kansas City Live Exchange as a volunteer association of men having nothing to do with interstate commerce and not covered by the "restraints and monopolies" act of 1890. Exchange members received cattle and hogs that they would feed and prepare for market, and they set sale commissions; exchange members could not do business with anyone violating the rules and regulations of the exchange.

The same year, in *Anderson v. United States*, 171 U. S. 604 (1898), SCOTUS continued its support for the Trader's Livestock Exchange, the successor to the Kansas City live stock exchange. Unlike the Kansas City exchange, the Traders Exchange allowed cattle purchasers to join. Apparently impressed by the standards of courteous and ethical conduct toward one another, SCOTUS gave the Traders' Exchange considerably greater benefit of the doubt when it came to restraint in trade. As before, the exchange would only recognize a member of the exchange as a trader. SCOTUS argued, as did the traders, that they did not engage in interstate commerce.

The attorney general of the United States painted a much a darker picture. Members receiving stock unloaded at the Kansas City market might load them again for sale in Chicago, if the prices prevailing in the Kansas City market were too low. In one particular affidavit supporting the traders' exchange, the president of the exchange claimed that about 99 percent of the transactions by the defendants were with persons not members of the exchange. The affidavits provided by the government appeared to have less support on the court. In fact, SCOTUS claimed that there was no evidence of collusion. The court found "no feature of monopoly in the whole transaction." SCOTUS approvingly refers to *Allgeyer v. Louisiana*, 165 U.S. 578 (1897) that freedom of contract must be wary of legislative control, and more so when contracts are voluntary associations.

Rate fixing was a restraint on interstate commerce, sufficient for judicial intervention. A different form of restraint is the "ship it, hold it" process. If an interruption occurs in the commerce process, it may be the end of the first process, submersion into the mass property of the state where it comes to rest, and then a new commercial process begins. In *Diamond Match Co. v. Ontonagon*, 188 U.S. 82 (1903), the interruption or hold allowed a state to tax lumber left in the River of transit because not all of it shipped in the year cut. SCOTUS argued that there may be an interior movement of property which does not constitute an interstate commerce, because the interstate demand establishes the number of logs needed in any given year, leaving the rest saved, protected, and preserved. SCOTUS held that the constitutional provision requiring the consent of Congress to lay imposts or duties on imports or exports did not apply in this instance, even though the lumber shipped by rail from one state to another. The basic issue becomes whether commerce begins when the product moves within the state or when the product is on its final leg of movement, perhaps following some lull in activity, when it begins the journey of leaving one state and going into another for sale.

SCOTUS shifts to the co-administration narrative of interstate commerce reached in *Crossman v. Lurman*, 192 U.S. 189 (1904). The central government had, by this time, legislated on adulterated foods through the Interstate Commerce Clause. Before the Congressional statute, the arena was free of state action. After Congressional action, SCOTUS held constitutional a New York statute on adulterated foods as an exercise of police power, protecting the health and safety of its citizens, and similarly protecting them from fraud and deceit. The statute did not claim to reach beyond the borders of New York, per se, but rather exercised the protections the state affirms to its citizens.

American Steel & Wire Co. v. Speed, 192 U.S. 500 (1904) continues state control when commerce stops. Scotus argues that goods brought into a state in their original packages, once arriving at their destination and at rest within the state, effectively enjoyed the protection that that state affords and hence are taxable. Imports put into a warehouse for sorting and shipping are taxable. Putting imports into the hands of jobbers for sorting and then shipping is effectively the end of interstate commerce in the first instance and has not yet begun commerce in the second instance. *General Oil Co. v. Crain*, 209 U.S. 211 (1908) maintains the SCOTUS argument that merchandise may cease to be in interstate commerce at some intermediate point before its ultimate destination, if for the use and profit of owners, while under the protection of laws of the state. This would include the changing of shipping containers to make the product more saleable.

SCOTUS also allowed states to require inspection of cattle brought into a state and not intended for slaughter (*Asbell v. Kansas*, 209 U.S. 251 (1908)). Scotus considered this a proper exercise of the police function, even though it is also a direct regulation of interstate commerce. Congress had yet not chosen to intervene on the inspection of cattle. A similar story emerges regarding game (*New York ex. Rel. Silz v. Hesterberg*, 211 U.S. 31 (1908)). A state may exercise its police power to control the possession of game during off-season, even though imported from another country or state. SCOTUS refers to the latter qualifier as an incidental and remote effect upon interstate commerce.

SCOTUS had begun minimizing the federal reach of commerce, whether interstate or foreign. In *Keller v. United States*, 213 U.S. 138 (1909) the Court rejected a federal penal statute aimed at the use of aliens brought into the country. The federal government controls the rules of admission, but the police powers of the state have control once they arrive.

The case of *Savage v. Jones*, 225 U.S. 501 (1912) further blurred the line between interstate commerce and the police power of the states. Sales made in one state, but delivered to consumers in the original unbroken packages, agreeably constituted interstate commerce. Under its police powers, however, the state may require vendors of such items as dog food to disclose the minimum percentage of fat, fiber and protein, plus ingredients. State requirements, including certification stamps for sale, may not contradict those set by the Federal Food and Drug Act of 1906, which aimed to prevent the adulteration and the misbranding of articles in interstate commerce. Using the police powers of the state to prevent fraud is nevertheless constitutional if its effects upon interstate commerce are indirect and incidental.

Bacon v. Illinois, 227 U.S. 504 (1913) considered grain that stops in transit at an elevator for cleaning, weighing, sacking, etc., before sending on the next leg of its journey. SCOTUS found that once the grain begins its journey it is in interstate commerce but when it comes to rest at the elevator for further processing, it has entered the general mass of property in the state and remains there until sent upon the leg of its next journey, at which time it again becomes part of interstate commerce. That means Congress cannot use the commerce clause to regulate elevators.

Minnesota v. Blasius, 290 U.S. 1 (1933), in contrast to the *Stafford* case, considered cattle to have come to rest when shipped from one state to a stock market in another state. Even though they are a held in stockyard pens while the owner offers them for resale, they are taxable while in the stockyard pen. SCOTUS considered the cattle to have come to rest in a state and held there at the pleasure of their owner prior to disposal. SCOTUS admits that the crucial question is the continuity of transit. While the owner is holding the cattle, they become part of the mass property of the State. SCOTUS argues much the same about buying and selling cotton in *Chassaniol v. City of Greenwood*, 291 U.S. 584 (1934).

Congress Tries to Intervene: Lochner Wins

Congress had passed an act to protect trade and commerce against unlawful restraints and monopolies in 1890. In its lawsuit, *United States v. E. C. Knight Co.*, 156 U.S. 1 (1895), the government had asked that the American Sugar Refining Company restrain from any further conspiring, agreeing, combining, or acting together to maintain rules and regulations and rates. SCOTUS agreed that the central government had the exclusive power to regulate commerce, but that a monopoly in production is not under that power but rather under the police power, unless the monopoly acts to restrain commerce. The government asked that the agreements be null and void, that those receiving shares return them, and restore the status quo before the transfer of property. The government acts as a trustee of the public rights, replies SCOTUS, and private associations also have access to those rights. SCOTUS even argued the manufacturing trusts might be better because they could achieve the economies of scale that smaller, competing companies could not achieve.

In concurring with the *Sonneborn Brothers v. Cureton*, 262 U.S. 506 (1923) majority decision, Justice McReynolds pointed out that logic and taxation were not always the best of friends. There are three issues of interest here: whether the logic of out-of-country imports in the *Brown* decision also applies to imports from one state to another; whether sale in the original packaging is the end of commerce or is it coming to "rest and hold;" and whether an occupation tax on warehouse goods applies to all goods, imported or not.

Some precedent cases, but certainly not all, followed the *Brown* logic that commerce ends after sale in the original packaging, whether the source be a foreign import or an inter-state import. *Sonneborn* departs from this standard, in part by questioning whether it is even applicable to inter-state imports, and in part by suggesting that that the problem is neither a question of regulating nor burdening interstate commerce. *Sonneborn*'s second twist is that goods in original packages from inter-state commerce sold before entering the state, are not subject to an occupation tax, but goods brought into the warehouse through interstate commerce not sold before arrival, are subject to an occupation tax. This is a variant of the "rest and hold" alternative to sale as the end of the commercial stream.

Finally, SCOTUS argues that the proper test for an occupational tax on goods imported before concluding a sale, even if they remain in the original shipping package, is whether the same equivalent tax applies to all goods in the warehouse, regardless of source. *Brown* provided a crisp idea of sale as the end of commerce. The state may not interfere with protected imported goods, from whatever source, until sale, if they remain in their original packages. The *Sonneborn* decision clouds both principles to make room for greater mixed sovereignty. One year before *Sonneborn*, however, *Bailey v. Drexel Furniture Co.*, 259 U.S. 20 (1922) found the tax on employment of child labor unconstitutional. The bill attempted to impose a 10 percent excise tax on the entire net profit if the firm in question violated any of the bill's child labor provisions.

Empowering both the states and monopolies at the cost of the Interstate Commerce Clause extended the Court's assault on federal commerce power. Absent its *Lochner Era* faith in the right-to-contract, SCOTUS' decision in *Knight* would be out-of-place. SCOTUS found the American Sugar Refining Company not constrainable even if controlling 90-plus percent of sugar refining in the United States, because sugar manufacture bears no direct relation to commerce among the states or with foreign nations, and that in any event the combination did not occur through a conspiracy. SCOTUS effectively passes the responsibility to Congress because it assuredly exercises exclusive powers over interstate commerce and that absent an action by Congress regarding trusts, the subject shall be free from restrictions. SCOTUS then returns to the refrain that commerce follows manufacture, but it is not part of it. The manufacture of sugar falls under the police powers of the states. In his dissent, Justice Harlan argued that the gist of conspiracy is the tendency to prejudice the public by unjustly subjecting them to combined powers taking trade out of competition, even if the combined powers were all located in the same state.

LOCHNER V. THE NATIONAL INTEREST

A contrary movement toward nationalization occurs in *Standard Oil Co. of New Jersey v. United States*, 221 U.S. 1 (1910). In this case, SCOTUS gave breadth and depth to the Restraint of Trade Act passed in 1890. The concern here is the use of the freedom-of-contract to effectively restrain trade and commerce. Before passage of the antitrust act, the trustees of the Standard Oil Companies controlled the stock and ownership of corporations and limited partnerships engaged in the purchase, the transportation, the refining, the selling, and shipping of oil. The many charges against the Standard Oil Company of New Jersey included discriminatory practices by railroads, control of a pipeline, unfair methods of competition, local price cutting to suppress competition, and the virtual elimination of the sale of petroleum products to competitor corporations. SCOTUS held that restraint of trade impaired freedom of contract. The remedy stopped action of the combination and then dissolved it. The core injustice to avoid was doing wrong to the public or limiting the rights of individuals.

The difficulties of applying the antitrust act to the types of combinations and monopolies created by a standard oil reoccurred in the case of the American Tobacco Company (*United States v. American Tobacco Co.*, 221 U.S. 106 (1911)). *American* restrained competition through buying companies and putting their facilities out of the business or buying interest in the stock such that one company exercises ultimate control. It is clearly guilty of restraint of trade, as specified in the Anti-Trust Act. Imposing a remedy in situations like this is extremely difficult because it may have dire effect upon the public or upon other innocent stockholders. Upon remand, SCOTUS instructed the district court to dissolve the combination in no more than eight months, using injunction or receivership if necessary.

Congress amended its act to regulate commerce with the Hepburn Act, designed to incorporate oil pipe line carriers within the provisions of the act, and subjected pipelines to the Interstate Commerce Commission. In *Pipe Line Cases*, 234 U.S. 548 (1914), SCOTUS pointed out that no pipe line business must continue after the Hepburn act, but if they chose to do so, they must be common carriers. The act aimed at Standard Oil Company, which owned its own pipelines and dedicated those pipelines to the transport of its own oil. In *Eureka Pipe Line Co. v. Hallanan*, 257 U.S. 265 (1921), SCOTUS ruled that oil moving through a pipeline, even if gathered and stored for a brief time, is interstate commerce, not intrastate commerce. The Court suggested a conception of the storage tank as just a larger pipe. The same applies to natural gas (*United Fuel Gas Co. v. Hallanan*, 257 U.S. 277 (1921)).

In *International Textbook Co. v. Pigg*, 217 U.S. 91 (1910), SCOTUS expands further the reach of the Interstate Commerce Clause by striking down a state licensing system. When an out-of-state company engages in education by correspondence, the states may not burden the interstate transportation of textbooks. Six years later, in *Seven Cases v. United States*, 239 U.S. 510 (1916), SCOTUS again reinforces Congressional authority over interstate commerce, even when the enforcement appears to be a police regulation. Under the Sherley Amendment to the Food and Drug Act, Congress could condemn certain articles as branded or being false and fraudulent, such as preventive or curative power of drugs, whether in the original or broken packet is of little concern; when making claims, whether on package or on label, is also of no concern.

United States v. Ferger, 250 U.S. 199 (1919) establishes that a bill of lading is an instrumentality of interstate commerce. Congress does have the power to prohibit and punish the forgery and utterance of bills of lading for fictitious shipments. Thus, fabricated bills of lading cannot secure loans on goods supposedly but never shipped. SCOTUS has distinguished things in interstate transmission, or about to enter it, and control of the transmission process itself. The line between these two foci became increasingly dim. The process cases generally focused upon rate setting. The non-rate setting, restraint of trade rules of *Trans-Missouri* or *Anderson* more closely paralleled the treatment of oleomargarine (*Schollenberger*), before it entered and after it passed through the interstate commerce process, or the treatment of liquor, before it entered and as it was emerging from the interstate commerce process (*Bowman*, *Leisy*, then *Rhodes*).

Some barristers used the *Knight* case on sugar refining as a permit for monopolies. SCOTUS made it clear in a couple cases that there was no permit for monopoly. In *Swift & Co. v. United States*, 196 U.S. 375 (1905), several corporations were involved in restraining the trade in fresh meats. Agents would bid up livestock at stockyards that they controlled, convincing farmers and ranchers to send their livestock to the association stockyard, but then let the prices drop to the disadvantage of the farmers and ranchers. Agents kept fresh meat prices kept above market prices, pushed cartage charges to the dealers, and arranged to receive rebates to lower railroad costs below lawful rates. SCOTUS concluded that this was an illegal combination. SCOTUS also held that states, under the Fourteenth Amendment, *Carroll v. Greenwich Ins. Co. of New York*, 199 U.S. 401 (1905) could interfere with the right of association (insurance companies) when used to manipulate competition. The auditor of Iowa was free to apply a state prohibition of rate settings without running afoul of the Fourteenth Amendment.

SCOTUS stretches its distinction between “things” and “procedures” in *Loewe v. Lawlor*, 208 U.S. 274 (1908). SCOTUS found that unions and their leverage activities are restraints of trade and thus violate the Anti-Trust Act. Why do boycotts affect things but sugar trusts merely procedure? Boycotts are not all dissimilar to sugar trusts. If a sugar trust is a process for shipping sugar, why are not boycotts on hats shipped after production and before the wearing of the same category? The control over manufacturing is not simply an esoteric exercise; it affects the price of sugar. Strikes and boycotts on hats drive up their prices to better pay labor. It should matter little who is to profit, labor or industry. For both sugar and hats, a process exercised control over supply, not its transfer. After *Loewe*, it is increasingly difficult to see why SCOTUS left *Knight* good law.

In assessing new federal statutes, SCOTUS rejected the use of debate in Congress as a vehicle for discovering the meaning of a statute's language. Debate contains inherent uncertainties: some speak, some do not. Rehnquist (also Scalia) did the opposite; he used such debate records when he needed support for his position and, when it turned the table, Rehnquist rejected such debate and interpretation.

SCOTUS clarifies the *Lochner Era* approach to interstate commerce In the *Minnesota Rate Case*, 230 U.S. 352 (1913). The Court faced the issue of dormant commerce: did Congress intend to keep this area free from regulation, or were the states free to regulate in the absence of Congressional legislation? SCOTUS took the view that, if a federal power derived from a constitutional provision, the state could never legislate, whether the federal government had legislated. If the federal power derived from a statute, then the state may legislate in the absence of federal legislation. Once federally legislated, whether constitutionally-sourced or statute-sourced, the federal law trumped state law.

In a profound application of distributional logic, *Wickard v. Filburn*, 317 U.S. 111 (1942) implicitly used a" tragedy of the commons" logic in its interstate commerce decision-making, dramatically expanding nationalization. The Agricultural Adjustment Act of 1938 established a mechanism where a marketing quota might reduce the excess wheat available for marketing. Farmers voted to adopt wheat quotas, limiting the number of acres each person could produce to buoy the market price of wheat. The acreage quota assigned to each farmer included both wheat planted for markets and wheat planned for use on the homestead. The secretary of agriculture did have the power to set quotas under the Interstate Commerce Clause. Whether the subject of the regulation is production, consumption, or marketing was not material for deciding the question of federal power. Growing wheat for domestic use essentially took the farmer off the market for that amount of wheat produced; thus, the quota given each farmer included both the wheat grown for commercial purposes and the wheat grown for domestic purposes. The amount of excess wheat in this case was trivial; the farmer grew a few acres extra wheat for his farm's consumption. The court recognized that if every farmer were to do something like this, it would undermine the entire purpose of the wheat crop quota project. Thus, in typical "tragedy of the commons" logic, the quota system invited individual farmers to cheat, and severe penalties need application to such cheating for the quota system to work. The distributed nature of this type of problem definition has had enormous impact on later cases.

THROUGH THE EYES OF REHNQUIST

In *Armco, Inc. v. Hardesty*, 467 U.S. 638 (1984), West Virginia imposed a gross receipts tax on businesses selling at wholesale. The statute excepted local manufactures because they were subject to a higher manufacturing tax. A state tax may not burden commerce across state lines, and a compensating tax scheme, where out-of-state businesses are subject to one tax and local businesses another, is unconstitutional as well. These are the principles well understood since the end of the Lochner Era, so Rehnquist's dissenting opinion In *Armco* is of some interest.

Rehnquist argues that it is the appellant's responsibility to show that other states also impose a manufacturing tax to complain about the burden on interstate commerce imposed by West Virginia. Thus, one type of tax (a manufacturing tax on West Virginia businesses) may "off-set" an interstate tax on businesses. Rehnquist rejects the notion that a checkerboard among states would discriminate against a state with a manufacturing tax when paying the West Virginia wholesale tax, but a state without one would not face discrimination. It may also be necessary to calculate the burdens of the various taxes to determine if discrimination exists.

SCOTUS points out the motive for a low or non-existing manufacturing tax would be to encourage interstate commerce in its goods, but the West Virginia wholesale tax would operate against another state's encouragement of interstate business. Rehnquist proposes, then rejects, the type of analysis used in net income tax cases but asserts "Where a State's taxes are linked exactly to the activities taxed, it should be unnecessary to examine a hypothetical taxing scheme to see if interstate commerce would be unduly burdened." Rehnquist appears to dislike the facially discriminatory claim. In his effort to support state sovereignty here, Rehnquist undermines the "sovereign" decisions of other states that wish to make their goods more competitive by reducing or eliminating the manufacturing tax. Rehnquist also falls back into the conundrum of "quid-pro-quo," where another state may impose a wholesale tax on interstate commerce to off-set the disadvantages created by the West Virginia tax.

Rehnquist raises another set of problems in his dissent to *Kraft Gen. Foods, Inc. v. Iowa Dept. of Revenue and Finance*, 505 U.S. 71 (1992). Iowa sought to tax corporations' net income but, following the federal tax code, allowed deductions for dividends from domestic but not foreign subsidiaries. The Iowa scheme differs from the federal scheme in that it did not permit the deduction of taxes paid to other countries. The Iowa Supreme Court rules against Kraft, finding that Kraft failed to demonstrate that the taxing scheme gave Iowa businesses a commercial advantage over foreign businesses. SCOTUS found the Iowa statute facially discriminatory against foreign commerce in violation of the Foreign Commerce Clause.

The Iowa Supreme Court did find the taxing scheme rationally related to administrative efficiency. The only subsidiary dividend taxed by Iowa are those reflecting the foreign business activity of foreign subsidiaries. SCOTUS rejects Iowa's argument that a business could change its organization to avoid the Iowa tax and dismisses as insufficient the claim that Iowa subsidiaries do not have an unfair advantage. Administrative convenience is not a justifiable reason. The Iowa law effectively favors domestic commerce over foreign commerce, but foreign commerce, like interstate commerce, is a plenary power of Congress. The Iowa statute is discriminatory taxation. Rehnquist argues that a facial challenge must prove that there are no circumstances under which the Act would be valid. He finds no evidence suggesting that the Iowa tax systematically acts to discourage foreign commerce.

Rehnquist provides a good glimpse of how he would "Balkanize" the states using his view of federalism in *Chemical Waste Management, Inc. v. Hunt*, 504 U.S. 334 (1992). Alabama imposed a fee on the operator of a facility for hazardous waste disposed in the state, and an extra fee for hazardous waste brought into Alabama for disposal. SCOTUS has long opposed these efforts to separate one state from problems common to itself and other states. For Alabama to prevail on the extra fee, it would have to show that no nondiscriminatory alternatives were available before it could protect local interests. If Alabama wants to protect the health and safety of its citizens, it cannot do it by allowing treatment of its own hazardous waste but not that from another state. Rehnquist would allow a state to protect itself from hazardous or noxious materials brought across its borders. Taxes, he says, are fair ways for discouraging the consumption of scarce commodities, in this case, a safe environment.

A similar issue arises in *Fort Gratiot Sanitary Landfill, Inc. v. Michigan Department of Natural Resources et al.*, No. 91-636 (1992). Michigan requires a receiving county's plan to list its sources. If not listed in the sources, the source cannot use that waste facility, whether it be in-state or out-of-state. SCOTUS found that the county plan system unambiguously discriminates against interstate commerce. Michigan's system allows its individual counties effectively to disjoin the national economy. SCOTUS cites its earlier opinion in *Philadelphia v. New Jersey*, 437 U.S. 617, 618 (1978) where New Jersey's attempt to prohibit the import of solid or liquid waste from out-of-state violates the Interstate Commerce Clause. Michigan attempts to do roughly the same with its county plan system. Once again, SCOTUS points out that parochial legislation attempting to raise boundaries on another state is unconstitutional. Rehnquist, in contrast, denies that the Michigan plan is protectionist. He concludes that it focuses on legitimate concerns of the state: environmental, aesthetic, health, and safety. Michigan has attended to its own waste disposal, and allowing imported wastes destroys the incentive for other states to do their job.

Rehnquist values his conception of state sovereignty over the constitutional specifications of plenary inter-state commerce power given to Congress. The tension between SCOTUS and Rehnquist on landfill access furthers in *West Lynn Creamery, Inc. v. Healy*, 512 U.S. 186 (1994). Milk has generated several cases that ultimately have come before the Court, so it is not unusual that the West Lynn Creamery Case emerges. Massachusetts adopted a milk pricing order that placed a special assessment on milk sold by dealers to retailers. Whether the milk come from out-of-state or in-state producers, Massachusetts subjected all milk to the special assessment. The state distributed money raised by the across-the-board assessment back to Massachusetts dairy farmers only. Thus, the assessment itself was even-handed, but its purpose was explicitly to support in-state dairy farmers. Although the state courts found in favor of the assessment, SCOTUS found the pricing order unconstitutional. The assessment economically advantaged local dairy producers and effectively made out-of-state milk costlier.

Although the assessment and the subsidy, taken separately, would likely be constitutional, it is the combination of the tax and incentive that functions to disadvantage out-of-state producers by advantaging in-state producers. The pricing order functions as a protective tariff. The constitutional principle is that all the people must swim or sink together. Rehnquist feels that *Milk Control Bd. v. Eisenberg Farm Products*, 306 U.S. 346 (1939) is the controlling case, which established minimum prices for Pennsylvania dairy farmers. The price support affected the interstate commerce of a dealer who bought all his milk in Pennsylvania but sold it in New York. Rehnquist would affirm the Massachusetts assessment as an experiment where the state is a laboratory trying novel experiments without risk to the rest of the country (Brandeis raises this defense in dissenting from *New State Ice Co. v. Liebmann*, 285 U.S. 262, 311 (1932)). Rehnquist further accuses the Court's majority of insisting on laissez-faire economics.

Rehnquist pens *United States v. Lopez*, 514 U.S. 549 (1995) for a deeply divided court. At issue was Congress's Gun-Free School Zones Act, passed as an exercise of Congress's Commerce Power. The act makes it illegal to possess a firearm at a place known as a school zone. A gun is not an economic activity that "might, through repetition elsewhere, have such a substantial effect on interstate commerce." To infer a nexus with interstate commerce "would require this Court to pile inference upon inference." Guns (things), Rehnquist avers, do not substantially affect interstate commerce. Rehnquist rejects the "costs of crime" analysis and the "national productivity" analysis used to support the gun-free zones. He further rejects the "adversely affects the learning environment" argument. All these, he argues, provide no limit to the police power. Evidence linking gun and drug distribution already had emerged, but to no avail.

Rehnquist again struck at the Commerce Clause in *United States v. Morrison*, 529 U.S. 598 (2000). A student raped at Virginia Tech sought a federal remedy for gender-motivated violence, after what most would agree was an unsuccessful appeal through VT procedures. Respondents questioned the constitutionality of the federal remedy, and SCOTUS, with Rehnquist writing for a deeply split court, agreed that neither the Commerce Clause nor section five of the Fourteenth Amendment would provide support for the federal remedy. Rehnquist uses *Lopez* to support his decision in *Morrison*. The incident, he argued, was noneconomic and criminal; no jurisdictional element linked to the regulation of commerce; and using "but-for" causal chains from the incidence to its impact on interstate commerce are not acceptable.

Rehnquist rejects the "but-for" reasoning as opening virtually all areas to federal regulation. "Congress therefore may not regulate noneconomic, violent criminal conduct based solely on the conduct's aggregate effect on interstate commerce." Rehnquist rejects use of the Fourteenth Amendment when addressing discriminatory conduct because the Amendment addresses state action, not private individuals. Rehnquist admits that Congress normally does not have to establish the interstate commerce burden but doing so would enable SCOTUS to evaluate the legislation. Rehnquist once again repeats that he rejects "cost of crime" analysis and "national productivity" analysis, because they would permit Congress to regulate all violent crime and activities leading to crime. Rehnquist rejects Souter's dissent by asserting his view of federalism that the sovereignty of the states is in the structure of the Constitution. Here Rehnquist's reasoning comes full circle: there must be some state sovereignty in the structure of the constitution; because there is state sovereignty in the structure of the Constitution, proofs like "costs of crime" or "national productivity" are unacceptable.

Souter points out that this legislation comes with years of documentation that SCOTUS could use to assess and understand the connection between rape and commerce. Rehnquist rejects it on the basis that everything would connect, but for his finding this legislation unconstitutional. The legislature had a rational basis for its legislation, and the court can only deny that by refusing to accept the method presenting the reasoning. Reviving the long defunct distinction between commerce and non-commerce also revives problems the Court faced leading up to 1937. The causes of commercial effects need not be commercial; only under Rehnquist's vision of federalism is this dismissed. Federalism serves for Rehnquist what laissez-faire served for the pre-1937 Court.

Souter also points out that Rehnquist seems to think there are two separate spheres in which power exercises and that they never or seldom crossed: commerce and the state police powers. Souter points out that there is no such principle in the Constitution and, over the years, SCOTUS has rejected it time and again, including the short-lived "traditional government function." In responding to the "spirit" of the Tenth Amendment, Souter labels it as Justice Holmes had labeled it: invisible radiation emanating from the terms of the Tenth Amendment. Breyer points out that even the distinction between economic and non-economic is at best blurry. Breyer responds to the Rehnquist complaint that there would be little left for the states to regulate, or that there would be no limit to federal power. The observation is not a judicial defect but a practical reality of an intertwined nation. It is for Congress, not the Courts, to strike the balance between state and nation.

Rehnquist's final observations were especially troubling. He felt that the lady in question did not need a federal remedy, because no civilized judicial system would deny her relief. The problem is, that is exactly what occurred. Virginia Tech, an organ of the state, had managed to reduce multiple rape allegations to the use of bad language. Administrative error there be, but relief, there be not.

CONCLUSION

The political debate between the Federalists and the Anti-Federalists rested upon a deeper economic tension: industrialization versus agriculture. Whether the American civilization ever had political control over such a decision, the Civil War rendered the issue moot. The South needed enormous monetary resources to buy war materiel, and the sheer needs for heavy equipment prompted industrialization in parts of the rural South. The more industrial North was also more able to produce its own war materiel. If Birmingham, Alabama was the Pittsburgh of the South, the economic question proceeded to "how much" from "whether." The explosive growth of railroads and telegraph during and after the Civil War, with the main trunk lines built by private financiers but ultimately funded by the government, made it clear that the advantages of technology had an irresistible call of their own, prompting even counties and towns to mortgage their futures to make sure local branch lines could keep their town competitive with their neighbors.

The pre-Civil War vacillation between national sovereignty and state sovereignty became an increasingly futile exercise in the age of transportation, communication, and the growth of the administrative state. State's rights became the booty call of Jim Crowe. The intellectual division of labor made it very difficult to revive the reach of antiquated legislatures, which once could choose policy and direct its implementation. The administrative state was not just a federal compensation, but a compensation of governments generally, from the federal departments down to state and local departments. The intellectual division of labor made it difficult to produce a Renaissance man or woman; it was equally unlikely to produce a Renaissance government. Specialization was the key.

The facts-on-the-ground did not end myopic efforts to recover ancient principles eclipsed by new realities. The importance of national versus state sovereignties went the way of horse-and-buggy and sails, as steam conquered both land and sea. The Civil War amendments added a new dimension, with equality becoming an increasingly important component of both liberty and due process. Interpretations of the facts-on-the-ground were sometimes flights of fancy that diverged from emerging realities. That laissez-faire would produce a spontaneous harmony of interests, that capitalist competition would not destroy capitalism through monopolies and trusts, were two of these flights. The Social Darwinism interpretation, which sought to combine competition and inequality, was yet another. Social Darwinism was always a bastardization of Darwinism; adaptation was an on-going process for Darwin, and thus what we see is a temporary survival of the fittest in a temporary world. Social Darwinism replaced an on-going process with a metaphysical adaptation that had reached the end of its journey, that the differences among us were permanent and God-given absolutes, and that "equality" was a demand against Nature herself, especially on race and sex.

The SCOTUS decisions during the Lochner Era were anachronous, patterned, and relatively consistent, not with the society and economy, but with the flights of fancy that came to dominate the minds of people at the turn of the century. Science elevated us to fellow-travelers of Plato's philosopher-king. If the harshness of the series of depressions after the Civil War were not enough of a reality check, the Great Depression dispelled distortions of all but true-believers. It is to the latter class of citizens that we owe Justice Rehnquist. He rallied forth the principle of state sovereignty in a world where it meant less and less. More important, state sovereignty is not in the Constitution and certainly not in the Civil War amendments. No strict interpretation could exercise a principle never given. Ignoring the Ninth Amendment and embracing the Tenth Amendment, Rehnquist argued that somehow, somewhere, state sovereignty was endogenous to the structure of the Constitution. You could not read it, but it was there. The metaphysic of state sovereignty could take on a life of its own, the evidence be damned. The Rehnquist legacy was an industrial diamond ground to its core. Some of the Rehnquist claims about interstate commerce were possible, some improbable, and some simply preposterous. A review of Rehnquist's interstate commerce legacy helps bring some sorry stories to the big screen.

An ideologue has a peculiar view of evidence. The ideologue may question information, or, in Rehnquist's case, refuse to accept evidence that does not lead to his conclusion. The ideologue typically makes decisions in search of facts. The ideologue champions "I'll know it when I see it" over any effort to lay down rules of evidence. An ideologue makes short work of syllogistic reasoning. Rehnquist argued that something is true (or false) unless you can prove that it can ever be false (or true). That is roughly equivalent to claiming that the Christian view of Armageddon is true unless you can prove that it can never happen. An ideologue has difficulty differentiating descriptive, prescriptive, and prospective. If I say, the wages of sin are death, am I being descriptive, prescriptive, or prospective? It is true, so it must be all of them. The ideologue knows he/she has the truth; those who disagree are wrong. They gain nothing by prolonged debate or being "Brandeis-briefed" to death. The jury is the finder of fact, the lower courts the finders of law, and the Supreme Court the maker of law and, by extension, reality.

Three Justice Marshall decisions set the horizons for the Federalist Court: *Marbury v. Madison*, *McCulloch v. Maryland*, and *Gibbons v. Ogden*. SCOTUS was the only legitimate interpreter of the Constitution. Federal sovereignty trumps state sovereignty under any of the enumerated powers, broadly interpreted. Inter-state commerce, again broadly defined, is the exclusive province of the national government. The debate over the banking industry, as an illustration, closely paralleled the unfolding problems of transportation, communication, and administration. Rehnquist enters this picture in 1985, allowing bank holding companies to limit acquisitions to certain regions of the country. Limiting to region increased the holding company's footstep. Each state, by Rehnquist's reading of the national statutes, could allow any holding company to acquire their banks, to confine acquisitions to regional holding companies, or ban out-of-state bank holdings. What the state does, under his interpretation of the relevant national statutes, are "invulnerable to Constitutional attack" under the Interstate Commerce Clause, the Contract Clause, the Supremacy Clause, and the Equal Protection Clause.

Marshall offers support for two propositions regarding the commerce clause. If Congress has not acted, that area of commerce is dormant and closed to state action. If Congress has acted, it is the exclusive authority. Two other propositions appear in subsequent (non-Marshall) Courts. If Congress has not acted, the states are free to act. If Congress has acted, the state may also act, but must bow to federal legislation in case of collision. Marshall takes commerce to include merchandise and people. Some later Courts drop people from the equation. Finally, two views are most common regarding the end of the commerce process. For Marshall, the end is "sale." For some later Courts, the end is "ship it, hold it."

One of the oldest areas of national over state control is navigable waters, the focus of the *Gibbons* case. Rehnquist enters this arena with the *Kaiser Aetna* case. Although developed into a private marina, a body of water was legally the property of the federal government and could be open to the public. The private firm had developed federal land. The dissent points out that the developers took the risk, and the firm deserved compensation for the value-added. Rehnquist compensates the private developer by requiring eminent domain instead of a claim under the commerce clause. To make this switch, Rehnquist creates a rule that, if private hands link a public water to the sea, it deserves full compensation under eminent domain condemnation. This ad hoc rule has serious implications itself but postulating a private end-run to the commerce clause appears close to "the end justifies the means."

The *Allenberg* decision is an application of Marshall's logic in *Gibbons*; once Congress acts the states may not act. Rehnquist's dissent is early in his career on the Court, but he uses an antiquated argument. He argues that commerce starts, not with the contract, but with the shipment of cotton from Allenberg's warehouse. Rehnquist also questions the Marshall rule, preferring instead both state and nation operating on the same stream of commerce. Rehnquist's dissent in *Healy*, long after he joined the Court, seemed to ignore that, when a state's action affects the choices of other states, it is an interference with interstate commerce. The main SCOTUS decision overruled a precedent case allowing the use of state "affirmation" statutes, which essentially required private distributors to affirm that the price they charged was no higher than that they charge in other states.

Affirmation statutes allow one state to reach the regulation of another state and may set up a quid-pro-quo activity among states. Rehnquist again tries to turn attention away from commerce clause precedent by arguing that the Twenty-First Amendment should count for something. Rehnquist wants to look at the motivation of the Connecticut statute and, on that basis, determine whether it was sufficient to constitute a violation of the commerce clause. Finally, Rehnquist makes one of his syllogistic summersaults by arguing that there has been no proof submitted that Connecticut's affirmation law affects the price of beer in other states. If no proof, then no commerce violation. Rehnquist ends with his odd assertion that perhaps there is some correction of a market imperfection by the affirmation statute (no proof required).

Some Rehnquist decisions invoke principles long laid to rest, typically without knowledge of why the Court abandoned them in the first place, and without thought of what would happen if they return in a blaze of glory, and even whether he accomplishes the greater state sovereignty he wants. Rehnquist applies ad hoc special rules to twist a situation into his desired outcome. This practice Justice Souter condemned as unsustainable case law, but an ideologue is not a good chess player. There is no development, no thinking ahead of how one step may lead to others that create even worse scenarios than the conquered one. There is nothing that says stacked up ad hoc rules, or what Rehnquist projected upon others as stacking inference upon inference, will create a consistent body of logic sufficient to guide future decisions and mold the Court one way or another. Rehnquist is no Marshall.

When Rehnquist joined SCOTUS, the railroad industry was in disarray and decline. Just as steam superseded horse and sail, trucks and container cargo became technological threats to the dominance of the railway system. Settlement had grown apace with technology, so the modern Court faced problems that were legacies of the dominant rail corridor. One of these is the problem of easements. The way Congress gave alternate sections of land to underwrite railroad construction left access to the even sectors through the railroad right-of-way. The advent of cars and trucks meant the need for new and different easements.

The common-law approach was easement-through-necessity, without compensation. Rehnquist wanted this rule changed to the procedures of eminent domain. A court could condemn land for public purposes, but the state must pay fair compensation. The continued use of eminent domain essentially elevated the importance of private property, allowing the government to intervene only by condemning and compensating for the property.

In addition to extending private rights well beyond the limits of English common law, Rehnquist sought to do the same for local and state governments. In *National League of Cities*, Rehnquist introduces yet another new rule postulating the existence of "traditional government functions" which were immune to national control through the Commerce Clause. That effort failed within nine years. The SCOTUS majority lectured Rehnquist about the unworkability of the "traditional government functions" rule. The majority also pointed out that his approach was inconsistent with established principles of federalism. The use of formalisms to create exceptions to established rules often leads to forays without perpetuity or purpose.

Although the telegraph had become a relic of the early communications revolution, the revolution continued to unfold. The mass collection and dissemination of private information came before the Court in *Reno v. Condon*. The states had been selling driver's license information until Congress stepped in to stop it. Rehnquist agreed with the Congressional action, finding it consistent with his principles of federalism and not a violation of the Tenth Amendment. Information was an article (thing) of commerce. A national statute may regulate the states, but it may not require the states to regulate its citizens. Here, Rehnquist reverts to the old theory of state action, where the Fourteenth and Fifteenth Amendments operate on state action, not the behavior of individuals. Reliance on the state action principle seems at odds with his position on state affirmation laws.

Under a series of natural resource cases, from game to gas, SCOTUS had ruled that these were items of commerce and thus under national interstate commerce control. There could be little disagreement that there was state action involved here, so the question at best would be whether any of these were not items of commerce. Rehnquist supported an overturned case that allowed states to prevent the transport of their game over state lines. Under the *Geer* logic, these were natural resources owned by the state, and hence the state could withhold them from commerce. SCOTUS moved to strict scrutiny of any effort to keep these natural resources out of commerce and thus denied to people of other states. Rehnquist support the overturned case law, although he wanted to replace its ownership theory with the state-as-conservator theory of natural resources. Rehnquist's state action principle should trigger here because national enforcement aimed at state policies and agreements. Rehnquist rescued the state action theory while finding in favor of the states by arguing that, when the state claim is indistinguishable from private claims, state action cannot activate SCOTUS's original jurisdiction under diversity claims. We have another ad hoc Rehnquist principle, this one to restrict a diversity suit to uphold an inter-state agreement that excluded the national government.

Another interaction of Rehnquist with the administrative state might leave you speechless. The Congress had established the Federal Power Commission, later the Federal Energy Regulatory Commission, to regulate matters of interstate power. In the *Corp. Commission of Oklahoma* case, SCOTUS allowed the FPC to sue a state administrative agency. In a hail Mary grasp, Rehnquist argued that the state agency was not a "person" and thus the FPC could not sue the state. He added that to interpret the word "person" broadly would violate comity between state and federal bodies.

Rehnquist had become increasingly more political and less judicial. Perhaps a talented jurist like Marshall might have navigated the mine field to establish a legal foundation for his political views, but that option was not open to Rehnquist. Instead, we resurrect old principles applied in different situations, create ad hoc exceptions as needed, and stand true to a conception of federalism, itself poorly developed and ahistorical, that elevated comity between state and nation to a constitutional principle.

The saga does not end. States were seeking energy breaks for their own citizens but placing extra costs on out-of-state users. A federal statute invalidated such discriminatory state policies, and SCOTUS agreed. Rehnquist gave an empty concurrence to the SCOTUS decision, warning, however, that the federal statute might be sterile, that is, add nothing not already found in the commerce clause. If sterile, then the state policies would meet constitutional muster. In another case involving discrimination on power charges, Rehnquist argues that SCOTUS should not invoke its original jurisdiction. If all else fails, keep the Supreme Court out of it. When invoking Supreme Court jurisdiction was to his advantage, such as the U.S. Steel Corp. request for a *writ of certiorari*, Rehnquist wanted that alternative.

In a case where a city allowed raw sewage into public waters, Rehnquist invents a stop gap "federal common law" that governs when Congress has yet to act. SCOTUS then turned the case back to the lower courts, but meanwhile Congress passed the Federal Water Pollution Act. The lower courts used the "federal common law" standard until their decisions reached SCOTUS for review, at which time SCOTUS found that the "federal common law" was no longer available because Congress had acted.

The issue of waste disposal again divided Rehnquist from the majority. The appropriate commerce rule was that states could not ban the import of "value-less" material, just as the state could not ban imports or exports of other materials (except things like liquor, obscenity, and items of gambling), or engage in facial discrimination. Rehnquist wanted to allow states to close their waste facilities. He argued that quarantine laws were more appropriate than commerce laws. He elevates "clean and safe environments" as a consideration a state may use in banning wastes. Rehnquist then argues that, if all else fails, the state could become a market participant under market participant rules (giving the states considerably greater control) or taking ownership entirely. Even Justice Thomas warned about the effects of economically Balkanizing the states.

Rehnquist took comfort from the 1943 *Parker* case. This case allowed states to engage in trust-like behavior without violating the Sherman Act. *Parker* also defined manufacturing as outside the reach of inter-state commerce. This state-action immunity required a clear policy allowing anti-competitive conduct and provide active supervision. *California Retail Liquors v. Midcal Aluminum* failed the supervision test and stripped the anti-competitive shield. Rehnquist objected to the strong supervision requirement and thus he would allow price fixing with state approval.

After decades of anti-labor and anti-social legislation, the post-Lochner Court allowed collective bargaining and worker health and safety legislation. The Economic Stabilization Act of 1970 allowed federal and state wage control. Rehnquist objected that state wage control was a threat to the federal system, as he understood it. Rehnquist invents an "affirmative constitutional right" of the state to be free from asserted Congressional authority. He also revives, now with effect, his federal comity principle. When SCOTUS ruled against so-called compensation schemes when taxing out-of-state business, it was using principles in effect at least since the end of the Lochner Court. Rehnquist concocted a switch-22, where it was the appellant's job to provide evidence that other states impose a manufacturing tax, thus rendering some compensating scheme unworkable. One had to demonstrate discrimination before even a checkerboard of state taxes was discriminatory. A facially discriminatory finding is not dispositive. The interesting mistake here was that, in protecting one states taxing scheme, Rehnquist in effect undermined the ability of another state to make its goods more marketable. In yet another switch-22, Rehnquist argues that other states can use quid-pro-quo countermoves against the taxing scheme of another state, and apparently, balance each other. This is what the colonies were doing under the Articles of Confederation, and the Founding Fathers explicitly wanted to end this intramural rivalry.

In another case, the state imposed an income tax that burdened firms with overseas sales. SCOTUS found this facially discriminatory, and that "administrative convenience" was insufficient to justify such discrimination. In a syllogistic twist, Rehnquist argued that the facial challenge must prove that there are no circumstances under which the tax would not be discriminatory. In another dissent, Rehnquist argued that a state tax on out-of-state waste was a fair way for one state to discourage another from consuming scarce commodities, in this case a safe environment. At this point Rehnquist either does not understand the Founding Father's motivation for the Interstate Commerce Clause, or he does not care. Rehnquist is favorable to parochial legislation, despite the Founder's explicit concerns against this type of legislation. In yet another dissent, Rehnquist argues that these parochial statutes are just novel experiments tried by states instead of bringing risk to the rest of the country. Rehnquist then labels the SCOTUS concern over facial discrimination as an example of laissez-faire economics.

Three cases from Rehnquist's last decade on the Court deserve final attention: the *Lopez* case in 1995, *Boy Scouts of America v. Dale* 530 U.S. 640 (2000), and *Morrison* in 2000. We will not review the *Boy Scouts* case here. Both the Lopez and Morrison cases involved claims under the Interstate Commerce Clause. Rehnquist wrote for a divided Court in both instances. In Lopez, guns are not items of interstate commerce, and hence federal law invoking that clause is unconstitutional. To reach this conclusion, despite connections between drug and gun trafficking, Rehnquist rejected both economics-of-crime analysis and national productivity analyses. They proved "too much" according to Rehnquist. He rejected the national productivity argument in the Morrison decision, involving a college rape ultimately reduced to the use of bad language by her college administration. The woman in question dropped out of college, but no application of the *Wickard* logic could save Morrison's appeal. "But for" logic, used in the Wickard case, was not acceptable because it too "proved too much." Rehnquist then dismisses the Morrison case because the state action doctrine did not apply to the behavior of individuals, matter not the federal resources the college had received, or that the college was a state corporation. Rehnquist ends as he began, that there must be state sovereignty in the Constitution.

Chapter 6

Justiciability and Habeas Corpus

Justiciability is the 800-pound gorilla hiding behind judicial review. If judicial review expanded the role of the Supreme Court, it is justiciability that helped corral that power. Justice Marshall states the case for judicial review: it is emphatically the providence and duty of the judicial department to say what the law is. If a statutory law be in opposition to the Constitution, the law or the offending section is null and void. Justiciability plays a critical but silent role in *Marbury v. Madison* 5 U.S. 137 (1803). The Judiciary Act of 1789 gave SCOTUS the jurisdiction to issue writs of mandamus to public officers. Marshall found that grant unconstitutional; the writ is possible only under appellate, not original, review. Marbury went to the wrong court. The constitutional distinction between original jurisdiction (ambassadors, public ministers and consuls, a state) and appellate authority (all other cases) limits what SCOTUS can hear and do. Marbury came before the Court on the jurisdictional authority that Marshall found unconstitutional. It is the combination of both judicial review and justiciability that make the Marbury case so significant.

SCOTUS claims the duty of judicial review, then limits that power through justiciability rules. SCOTUS promulgates these rules; they are not in the Constitution. The justiciability rules are many and far-reaching. Some derive from the Court's interpretation of the "Cases and Controversies" clause from Article III of the Constitution. Other rules derived from what the Court sees as wise avoidance. These rules, discussed in this and subsequent chapters, include the prohibition against "advisory opinions"; "standing," particularly as it relates to "Cases and Controversies"; "ripeness and mootness," with special reference to the causal and remedial components of "Cases and Controversies"; "separation of powers," expressed as political questions; and "federal questions" deriving from the federal structure of the Constitution and the Eleventh Amendment. SCOTUS applies justiciability rules inconsistently across and within policy issue areas. This gives the Court considerable latitude in decision-making, leading to temporal variations as different constellations of Justices decide whether to wax or wane the Court's power. The court often breathes life into "state sovereignty."

ADVISORY OPINIONS

The doctrine of justiciability was not unique to the Marshall court. It should not be surprising that problems of justiciability arose soon after the Constitution took effect, even before the Court heard its first case. The first two incidents focused on whether the Supreme Court should make advisory opinions, despite the" Case or Controversy" clause in the Constitution. The first of these involved a request by Hamilton. The state of Virginia vehemently opposed Hamilton's debt assumption and redemption program. He considered Virginia's attack on his proposed policies as destructive of the new constitutional order. Hamilton sought advice on how to proceed against the Virginia claim that the assumption bill presumed powers not granted by the Constitution. Hamilton's requested advisory goes far beyond a political conflict; he wanted to introduce into Congress a set of resolutions that condemned the anti-Federalist line of reasoning generally. Chief Justice Jay, the first Chief Justice of the Court, responded with advice, albeit a bit paternal. Hamilton had described his thought on the question as undigested and sudden. Jay cautioned Hamilton to weather the storm. Reacting to Virginia's resolutions would increase their visibility and importance. Simply ignoring them might condemn the resolutions to disgrace and reduce the importance of such resolutions in the future.

Several states in the Union and countries around the world have adopted the advisory opinion practice. The practice has deep roots in English common-law history, as Lords, and then the people, wrestled power from the king. Many at the Constitutional Convention favored advisory opinions, but the practice ultimately fell to the checks-and-balances logic within the Constitution's separation of powers. There is no explicit provision for or against advisory opinions in the text of the Constitution. In 1893, in the second instance requesting an advisory opinion, the anti-Federalist Secretary of State Thomas Jefferson prodded the Federalist President George Washington to ask the Court whether it would provide advisory opinions on some questions of law. This time, Chief Justice Jay, responding for the entire Court, politely but firmly rejected advisory opinions as beyond the power of the Court under the new Constitution.

A new advisory twist occurs in *Hayburn's Case*, 2 U.S. 2 Dall. 409 (1792). Congress passed a bill for the relief of Revolutionary War pensioners while rejecting invalid claims. The bill wanted the federal justices to serve as hearing examiners. Atty. Gen. Randolph asked the Supreme Court to issue a writ of mandamus to the circuit court, requiring the judges to serve as requested. In the initial hearing, SCOTUS asked Randolph why he thought he could act *ex officio* without a request from an affected individual. Randolph answered as to his powers, but the Court rejected the *ex officio* motion. Randolph next moved on behalf of petitioner Hayburn. SCOTUS took this motion under advisement, but never posted a decision.

In a letter to the President, the justices of the Pennsylvania district court declined to proceed. They cited numerous objections, starting with the observation that the assigned tasks were not judicial in nature. Second, the request lacked constitutional justification. Third, under a checks-and-balance system the courts are independent of the other two branches of government, but this bill would subject their judgment to both executive and legislative intervention. The circuit court for the North Carolina district also declined the assignment, pointing out that the constitutional branches of government are separate, that the issue is not judicial, or if so, not up to constitutional muster. These justices also asserted that no decision of any court of the United States is liable to revision or suspension by the legislature itself. The justices volunteered to serve as commissioners, but they expressed concern about a Congressional bill on the subject. The bill focused on the Court, but it was questionable whether Congress could give individual judges the power to serve as commissioners. The justices also realized that the letter they sent to the President may appear as if it is an advisory opinion, but the justices felt this exception necessary because of the potential distress to meritorious individuals deserving relief.

Chief Justice Jay also served on the circuit court for the district of New York. In that circuit court's opinion, each branch of government had the duty to oppose encroachments of the other. Neither the executive nor the legislature could assign duties to the court. The requested pension decisions were not of a judicial nature, because the executive and legislature could revise the decisions. The justices concluded that they could serve as commissioners. The Congress extended the Court term by five days, so the Court would meet, handle any business for that day, adjourn, and then serve as commissioners for the pension cases.[1]

Congress repealed three relevant sections of the Veterans' Relief Act in 1793, substituting instead a new mechanism for hearing veterans' claims. Congress also passed a savings clause, maintaining the hearings and findings in the cases that justices qua commissioners had decided the previous year. Congress asked the Secretary of War and Atty. General to obtain an adjudication from the Supreme Court on the validity of the pensions granted by the so-called commissioners. Congress gave SCOTUS original jurisdiction to make this determination in the case of *Yale Todd* in 1794. Amicable action docketed the case. SCOTUS found that the act of 1792 could not legally ask judges to serve as court commissioners, because the legislature could exercise review of their decisions and give those decisions a construction that would be unjustified. Thus, the offending sections of the 1792 act were unconstitutional, and the state could recover any money so awarded. At that time, it was not unusual for Congress to give SCOTUS special original jurisdiction in certain cases not enumerated in the Constitution, but Congress has long since discontinued that practice.

No one filed a record of the *Yale Todd* case at the time, so the Chief Justice inserted a note into *United States v. Ferreira*, 54 U.S. 13 How. 40 (1851). Here, Congress asked the justices to sit as hearing examiners for claims made by Spanish individuals arising from military hostilities in Florida, as specified by the peace treaties of 1812 and 1813, and given effect by laws of 1823, 1834, and 1849, the year Florida became a state. The Secretary of Treasury would review the awards and he had final authority over awards. In the instant case, the district court awarded Ferreira a judgment. SCOTUS made clear that such awards were not judicial, and that the justices were acting merely as commissioners. SCOTUS questioned how this case came to the Supreme Court. There were no proceedings of record. The district court legally should transmit the case to the Secretary of Treasury. Further, the Constitution requires the President to appoint all government officers, with the advice and consent of the Senate. Congress cannot fill such offices on its own accord. SCOTUS then dismissed the case for want of jurisdiction.

Cases and Controversies

The pre-Marshall court seemingly rejected advisory positions as an oracle of legal judgment. SCOTUS instead adhered to the Cases and Controversies Clause in the Constitution. SCOTUS would not answer a list of questions as a court, even though the individual justices would continue socializing with the very people who sought official answers. It was a small social circle. The Federalists, those who ardently supported the new Constitution, had been involved in the country's fate from the Declaration of Independence through the Constitutional Convention, and now occupied various positions in the new government order. What the judges would not do *en banc* the individual justices could do privately. Emphasis on the Cases and Controversies Clause focused the Court on concrete matters rather than abstract principles. Still, the Court knowingly accepted cases contrived to get a constitutional judgment, as in *Hylton v. United States*, 3 U.S. 3 Dall. 171 (1796). This case ultimately focused on whether a uniform carriage tax was constitutional. SCOTUS issued a writ of error to the circuit court bringing forth the *Hylton* file. Hylton had refused to pay the federal carriage tax. He originally argued that the 125 carriages he possessed were for his own personal use. A divided SCOTUS sent the case back to the circuit court. Hylton pled guilty on the failure to pay the charge; then SCOTUS issued a new writ of error. Now, the sole issue before SCOTUS was the constitutionality of the carriage tax: Congress must apportion a direct tax among the states, as it apportions representatives; Congress may use the uniformity rule if the tax is indirect. A direct tax includes a capitation tax and a tax on land in the state. An indirect tax operates on individuals and is blind to state boundaries. SCOTUS found the carriage tax constitutional, an indirect tax uniformly applied to an object or service.

In a series of congressional decisions in 1902, 1904, and twice in 1906, Congress passed laws regarding the allotment of lands and funds to Cherokee Indians. Historically, the Indian tribes owned the land collectively, but Congress felt that allocating lands to each Amerindian facilitated demise of the larger society. The statute would prohibit Amerindians from alienating, selling, disposing of, or encumbering their lands for a quarter century. In the first act, Congress allocated land to adults enrolled in the tribe. Subsequent acts added children of enrolled adults to the list of land grantees. Doing so would reduce the allocation of land promised in the 1902 law by increasing the number of recipients in 1906. In 1907 Congress authorized a suit against the United States by Amerindians displeased with the allocation changes between the 1902 and 1906 act, legal fees payable from Amerindian funds.

Court of Claims

In a sharp rebuke to Congress, SCOTUS restated the principal in *Heyburn*'s case that neither the legislative nor executive branch could assign to the Court functions not properly judicial. Congress cannot contrive a controversy to test the constitutionality of prior acts of Congress, as in *Muskrat v. United States*, 219 U.S. 346 (1911). Absent a true case or controversy, that is, absent true adversaries, the court will not pronounce on the constitutionality of acts of Congress. In the *Muskrat* case, the Congress gave original jurisdiction to the court of claims over the Cherokee cases, with appeals to the Supreme Court. SCOTUS rejected jurisdiction.

The court of claims heard claims against the federal government that previously would be private bills in Congress. Congress provided appellate jurisdiction to the Supreme Court, with all court costs and legal fees drawn from the beneficiary fund held by the U.S. treasury. The court of claims would forward its findings to Congress for appropriation. Under subsequent legislation, the court of claims sent its results to the Department of Treasury and Congress would appropriate the required monies to the Department of Treasury. SCOTUS ruled in *Gordon v. United States*, 69 U.S. 2 Wall. 561 (1864) at 117 U.S. Appx. 698 that its appellate jurisdiction did not reach to cases from the court of claims. Presumably, these are not the types of cases specified in the Constitution; Congress cannot enlarge it. SCOTUS reviewed the slip note of the recently deceased Justice Taney for *Gordon*. SCOTUS will not review the administrative proceedings of the court of claims nor entertain appeals from its decrees. Taney held that SCOTUS could never review a decision from the final judgment of the court of claims.

De Groot v. United States, 72 U.S. 419 (1866) took a judicial decision or question of law on appeal from the court of claims. Thus, a judicial question is an exception and meets appellate jurisdiction. In *Gordon*, the Court of Claims had denied a review petition for damages done by U.S. troops in the war of 1812 with Britain. A majority of the Supreme Court denied the appeal because it had no jurisdiction over appeals from that court. The formal record stated little else, in part because Justice Taney had drafted a longer analysis but suddenly died.

In the longer Taney brief, legislative courts do not meet the requirements specified in Article III. Taney read his brief but did not record it. SCOTUS concluded that it could exercise no jurisdiction. Discovered among Taney's papers, SCOTUS had the longer manuscript published as a standalone appendix to the *U.S. Reports* in 1886. Taney points out that a legislative act of 1863 asked the court of claims and SCOTUS to do no more than certify their opinion to the U.S. Secretary of Treasury for estimation and submission back to Congress for appropriations. Up to this time, the court of claims did not possess a judicial power mentioned in the Constitution. Whether the Supreme Court can hear an appeal without the power of pronouncing judgment is another matter. If the Constitution does not judicially impose a power, Congress cannot require SCOTUS to exercise it. There are no appeals from the decisions of the U.S. Supreme Court. Congress cannot extend the appellate power beyond that prescribed in the Constitution. As early as the Heyburn case, SCOTUS held unconstitutional and void a law subjecting the decision of the court to revision by a Secretary or Congress. The Court can constitutionally take the jurisdiction of any decision only if made by an inferior court exercising an independent judicial power granted in the United States Constitution. SCOTUS uniformly refuses to take jurisdiction, absent a court of the United States possessing the original record and to which the Constitution authorized SCOTUS to send a mandate carrying its judgment into effect. Without such a lower court, SCOTUS only expresses an opinion which is not a legal judgment. Whether an act of Congress is within its delegated powers is a judicial decision of the courts, but clearly confided to it by the Constitution. After *De Groot*, the court will abstain from exercising any power that is not judicial in nature.

The seemingly forceful rejection of all advisory opinions may not be as complete as the Court claims. The Declaratory Judgment Act of 1934 gave SCOTUS a new and powerful tool. The act allowed the court to end a case or controversy, without specific relief, by declaring the rules settling the matter. There is no mandatory requirement, but there is general agreement that others will abide by the ruling. There are also indirect paths to an advisory opinion. Dicta in a court decision may provide guidance far afield from the instant case. Much the same applies to concurring and dissenting opinions. Sometimes the signal is quite loud, such as the predicate for statements like "to avoid constitutional problems." An injunction reaches beyond available facts to anticipate the likely court ruling. Slightly less clear signals derived from negative court decisions or the decisions to place a case on the docket and not take up others. Rehnquist attempts signaling when it is of advantage to him but rejects prior signaling to which he takes issue.

There are important historical incidents as well. President Monroe wrote a pamphlet on the limits of federal power and had it distributed to member of the Supreme Court. The Court issued individual opinions and a joint opinion on the pamphlet. In a clear violation of their own principles, five Supreme Court justices served on the Electoral Commission set up by Congress to resolve the Hayes/Tilden presidential election in 1876. Tilden, with the support of a consolidating Democratic South, won the election by a quarter-million votes. Fraud and corruption charges disrupted the Electoral College vote, so Congress created the Electoral Commission to decide contested slates from Florida, Louisiana, South Carolina, and Oregon. The first three challenged slates came from the only deep South states yet to join the solid Democratic South in a long-lasting rejection of Lincoln's Republican Party. Although Tilden started with 184 Electoral College votes and Hayes 165, The Electoral Commission, along strict party lines, gave the 20 challenged electoral seats to Hayes, who then won a contentious Senate (Republican) and House (Democratic) struggle 185 to 184. The five Supreme Court Justices on the Commission, along with five Representatives and five Senators, voted along strict party lines.

One of the strangest advisory opinion cases occurs in *Chicago & Grand Trunk Ry. Co. v. Wellman*, 143 U.S. 339 (1892). What makes it particularly interesting is that SCOTUS and several courts below issued an opinion, despite the collateral holding that friendly suits did not qualify as a case or controversy. Justice Brewer presented the SCOTUS opinion. When the case arrived at the Supreme Court, the writ presented a single question: whether the original trial court erred when it refused to instruct that a Michigan 1889 law was unconstitutional. The state of Michigan passed a law in 1889 fixing the per mile charge for passengers. The law did not address freight rates, nor was there an analysis whether the railroad might increase its revenues through freight rather than passenger charges. Indeed, the amount of discovery needed to make such a decision was woefully inadequate. Two witnesses argued that freight rates in a competitive environment would not work an increase in revenue. No matter, because the court did not submit the question to the jury, whether reducing passenger rates might increase the number of passengers and therefore increase railroad revenues. The focus was on whether a law could fix passenger rates generally.

The railroad wanted the passenger rate law declared unconstitutional; the reduced freight and passenger rates would not only eliminate profits but drive the railroad toward bankruptcy. Congress by this time had passed several laws regarding railroad rates; the Supreme Court had heard several cases involving railroad rates. The general layout of laws made it quite clear that the legislature and judiciary might be involved in railroad issues. The legislature has power to fix rates; legislative intervention in railroad matters is not unconstitutional. Judicial intervention only protects against unreasonable rates.

The Michigan Supreme Court described the case as a friendly suit, designed to test the constitutionality of the Michigan law of 1889. The Attorney General had to secure counsel for the public interest when the case went before the Michigan Supreme Court. No one represented the public interest in the first two courts. The railroad confirmed it was a friendly suit, but since without fraud or trickery, it did not matter. The Michigan Supreme Court ruled against the railroad. SCOTUS described the railroad's operative theory in a slightly different way. The plaintiffs wanted a direct appeal from the legislature to the courts, so that if they lost in the first arena they may seek victory in the second. The friendly suit effectively undermines the Cases or Controversies Clause. On the very day the law went into effect, antagonists tested the rate, the suit commenced, and within two months the trial court had an answer. An agreement between the two parties settled questions of fact, which then precluded further inquiry. SCOTUS raised the possibility, for example, that the railroad would conceal excessive executive salaries within the category of operating expenses. Justice Brewer concludes the opinion by lecturing the lower courts that the two friendly parties may have misled them into doing wrong to the public. The courts must seek full disclosure of the facts, not agreements and general theories. SCOTUS then affirmed the judgment of the Michigan Supreme Court.

Texas struck a familiar chord in *Texas v. Interstate Commerce Comm'n*, 258 U.S. 158 (1921). The state of Texas filed a very long brief against both the Interstate Commerce Commission and the Railroad Labor Board. Texas wanted two titles of the Transportation Act of 1920 declared unconstitutional and void; an annulment of all action taken under those two titles; an injunction restraining the defendants from any further action. Texas classified both the ICC and the Railroad Labor Board as citizens of states other than Texas. Using this diversity jurisdiction, Texas argued that SCOTUS had original jurisdiction. SCOTUS responded that the two corporations were creatures of the United States government and hence were not citizens of any state. Texas could not invoke original jurisdiction, and Texas offered no other claim. Congress passed both objectionable titles under its interstate commerce powers. Plaintiffs could challenge these powers in the district courts. Much of the Texas bill dealt with abstract issues of state versus national sovereignties. SCOTUS responded that this part of the bill did not present a case or controversy. Neither the United States nor the carriers are parties to this suit and proceeding without their representation is inadmissible. The limits of original jurisdiction of the U.S. Supreme Court prevents it from entertaining the Texas bill. SCOTUS dismissed it.

Congress renewed its interest in advisory opinions during the first term of Franklin Roosevelt, given how the Court systematically dismantled the National Industrial Relations Act: live poultry (sick chicken) (*A. L. A. Schechter Poultry Corp. v. United States*, 295 U.S. 495 (1935)); railroad retirement (*Railroad Retirement Board v. Alton Railroad Co.*, 295 U.S. 330 (1935)); bituminous coal conservation (*Carter v. Carter Coal Co.*, 298 U.S. 238 (1936)). The beginning efforts to craft a constitutional amendment allowing advisory opinions did not survive the Court change in 1937 (switch in time saves nine), after Roosevelt's proposal to add an additional justice for each one on the Court over eighty years of age (Court packing bill). It is Congress, not the Constitution, which governs the number of Justices on the Supreme Court. After the switch of a single vote on the Court, it no longer thwarted Congress and the President in their industrial recovery efforts.

Declaratory Judgments

The problem of advisory positions got considerably more complex when Congress passed the Declaratory Judgment Act of 1934. The Act supposedly provided a new remedy, short of an injunction or class action. It further allowed some relaxation of the cases and controversies and available relief requirements. Some of the core issues of the new federal court power unfold in *Public Service Comm'n v. Wycoff Co., Inc.*, 344 U.S. 237 (1952). In the instant case, a plaintiff requested the federal district court to declare the movements of motion picture films and newsreels between points in Utah to be in interstate commerce and to issue an injunction against the state's interference with such movements. The district court dismissed the complaint because no interference had yet occurred. The appeals court reversed, and SCOTUS in turn reversed with instructions to dismiss. SCOTUS held that the injunction was at best premature and that there was no basis to consider a declaratory judgment. An injunction would require proof of probable action by the state and that, in doing so, it would cause irreparable injury. The complaint met neither requirement.

The Declaratory Judgment Act confers an option on the Court, not a litigant right. Again, *Wycoff* is lacking as an actual controversy, and a declaratory act would preempt established administrative procedures. If the case were right for determination, the disagreement could not be nebulous or contingent, and the court must understand the legal issues at stake, what its effect would be upon the adversaries, and what purpose it serves. Justice Jackson, writing for the court, argued that federal declaratory proceedings against state officials must consider implications for the federal system of government. Anticipatory judgment by a federal court to interfere with state administrative procedures is not tolerable. A plaintiff cannot use a federal declaratory judgment to ward off possible state action. It is a characteristic of that action which determines whether there is a federal question.

In his dissent, Justice Douglas points out that the movement of films in Utah is interstate commerce because it is a continuation of a stream into and back out of the state. The state administrative agency defines it, and the district court accepted, as the movement between points in the state, or intrastate commerce, and hence subject to state police powers. Utah requires a state permit to do business already covered by federal permit. The complaint is proper because it arises under the Constitution and laws of the United States. It is a federal court that must protect the federal right.

An interesting shift occurs in the Warren, Burger, and Rehnquist Courts. We find increased cautions against policies that "would raise constitutional problems." Using the codes of "raising Constitutional issues" or "possible Constitutional problems" are not qualitatively different from advisory opinions, except that the Court may offer that observation even if not asked by Congress or the President. It does not avoid the forward-looking advisories that the earlier Courts sought to avoid. The use of dicta to deliver otherwise advisory opinions raises the question, why?

In *Ellis v. Dyson*, 421 U.S. 426 (1975), the district court dismissed a request asking for declaratory judgment on the constitutionality of a loitering ordinance and for injunction expunging the records of arrest and conviction. A municipal court convicted plaintiffs of violating the loitering ordinance. Plaintiffs did not appeal to the county court, fearing an even heavier fine. The federal district court argued that a declaratory judgment and injunction against future criminal prosecutions was not available as a relief unless the plaintiffs had alleged bad faith prosecution, harassment, or likelihood of irreparable injury. The court of appeals affirmed, but SCOTUS remanded the case to district court to incorporate its findings in *Steffel v. Thompson*, 415

U.S. 452 (1974). SCOTUS counselled that injunction requests are separate from declaratory judgment requests. The plaintiffs abandoned the injunction request; SCOTUS repeated that Congress intended the declaratory relief as a milder alternative to injunction.

The plaintiff in *Steffel* faced criminal trespass charges if he continued passing out handbills (against the Vietnam War) on an exterior sidewalk along a shopping center. Plaintiff claimed a violation of First and Fourteenth Amendment rights, backed by the Civil Rights Act. SCOTUS affirmed that threatened prosecution is sufficient evidence of a case or controversy and that the plaintiff need not further expose himself for arrest to meet case or controversy thresholds. The district court on remand should decide whether the controversy continued, given the wind-down of the Vietnam War. *Steffel* overturned the core precedent on which the lower court dismissed the *Ellis* complaint. Federal declaratory relief is possible under threat of prosecution alone. In *Ellis*, the Court ruled that the constitutional considerations such as harassment or bad faith prosecution are no longer the test for a declaratory judgment, and the plaintiff need not exhaust all state or administrative remedies. SCOTUS did express doubt whether the *Ellis* controversy still existed.

MOOTNESS

The lower courts, as with the Supreme Court, should take judicial notice of matters like the constitution and laws of the state. This includes notice of the days for legislative elections, conventions to revise a constitution, when seating for the convention commences, and when its acts take effect. Sometimes local events cross the finish line before a case winds its way through the judicial process. If, in the appellate process, the appellate court decides for the defendant, but the timing of decision has passed the occurrence of events, then no effective relief is possible. The appellate court should not proceed to a decision but instead it should dismiss the appeal.

In *Mills v. Green*, 159 U.S. 651 (1895), South Carolina called an 1894 convention to revise its constitution. Voters were to elect delegates to the convention, but the commencing statute allowed the supervisor of registration for each county to give new regulations regarding the registration of voters and the certificates of registration. The plaintiff claims that these regulations violated both the constitution of South Carolina and the Constitution of the United States. He claims that the new regulations abridged and destroyed the suffrage of certain citizens of the state. The plaintiff could not register to vote because he could not comply with the unreasonable and burdensome regulations. Unless registered, a citizen could not vote for delegates to the constitutional convention. The regulations removed the plaintiff and citizens in similar circumstances from the voter rolls, resulting in a convention that would work grievous and irreparable wrong.

The circuit court, aware of the time deadlines, issued a temporary injunction on behalf of the plaintiff. The circuit court of appeals reversed the judgment of the lower court and dissolved the injunction. The plaintiff appealed to the Supreme Court, but the defendant moved to dismiss the case on grounds that there no longer was an actual controversy. SCOTUS agreed. The court would not issue opinions on moot questions or simply abstract propositions. If SCOTUS could not provide effective relief, it can provide no judgment and it will dismiss the case. The Court stays its hand if there is an intervening event, owed neither to the plaintiff nor the defendant, and beyond their control. If the plaintiff died, the Court would abate the writ of error. The same would occur if Congress passed a new law relevant to the controversy. If the event were due to the defendant, the court would look to the rights of the plaintiff before the event occurred. In this case, the defendant simply exercised his duties as statutorily required, surrendering the registration book to the election managers.

Changing Conditions in the World

Mootness also arises when changing conditions in the world make various contracts and clauses in contracts inoperative. In *United States v. Hamburg-Amerikanische Co.*, 239 U.S. 466 (1916), World War I interrupted several questions seeking legal resolution. The government pressed an anti-trust case against several steamship lines that had agreed among each other to parcel out a certain proportion of passengers to each. The respondents claimed that Congress never intended to put such steamship lines under the anti-trust act. Although a decision may set a case precedent, this does not empower a court to make decisions without a concrete case or controversy before it. These cases are moot. SCOTUS took notice of the European war and its impact on American shipping. The case or controversy has disappeared, and to pursue the case would be to use a decision to predict future conduct. If the court below has decided against the government regarding its antitrust charges, SCOTUS would reverse the lower court decision and direct that court to dismiss the bill without prejudice. The Court ruled a similar result in *United States v. American-Asiatic S.S. Co.*, 242 U.S. 537 (1917), where the government accused American, British, and German steamship companies of violating the U.S. Antitrust Act; the lower court found against the government's claim that the anti-trust act covered ocean carriage. The Supreme Court could not reach the merits of the act because the agreement had become a casualty of the European war. Like the Hamburg-American agreement, SCOTUS reversed this case and remanded to the court below for dismissal without prejudice.

A different reason for mootness occurs in *Atherton Mills v. Johnston*, 259 U.S. 13 (1922). A father and son sought an injunction against the federal child labor tax law. The father added the son's wages to the family income but, when the child labor laws took effect, the employer would dismiss the child from his job because he was between fourteen and sixteen years old. The lower court issued an injunction preventing the son's employer from dismissing him. By the time this case got to the Supreme Court, the son was older than sixteen, and hence the child labor law no longer covered him. SCOTUS declared the case moot. It reversed the lower court ruling and sent the complaint back to the lower court for dismissal without costs to either party. SCOTUS did not consider the merits of the child labor tax act. The Court did not raise the question whether this suit met the terms of a case or controversy.

SCOTUS bluntly decrees mootness in *Barker Painting Co. v. Painters Union*, 281 U.S. 462 (1930). A trial judge issued a preliminary injunction against a Union's wage rules that led to a job walk out about a third of the way into the work. The plaintiff invoked legal arguments under common law, the Sherman Act, and the Fourteenth Amendment. The company completed the work before the district court could consider a decision on the merits, so it dismissed the bill. The circuit court similarly refused to consider the bill on its merits, although it raised analogies with a similar case, but then affirmed the dismissal. Both sides wanted the court to continue examining the merits of the case, but SCOTUS ruled that the court should go no further afield then its duty compels. SCOTUS found no need to continue examining general propositions or issuing prophetic statements. The Court affirmed, dismissing the bill as moot.

Bible Reading, Adam Clayton Powell, Abortion

The Court also dismissed one of the petitioners in *Doremus v. Board of Education*, 342 U.S. 429 (1952) for mootness, because she had graduated from the school requiring the reading of five verses of the Old Testament daily. A second taxpayer, ineligible as a federal taxpayer but potentially eligible as a municipal taxpayer, also petitioned for the end of Bible reading. The facts provided qua municipal taxpayer were insufficient to link with the school or the Bible reading statute. The New Jersey Supreme Court allowed the case to go forward on its merits, despite the shortcomings as a case or controversy. It issues a declaratory judgment, finding the Bible reading constitutional, admittedly attempting to test its constitutionality in SCOTUS.

The Supreme Court pointed out that the New Jersey Court had held no trial, made no findings of fact, but did do a pretrial conference and pleadings. The New Jersey Supreme Court lamented in its decision that it probably lacked jurisdiction and used the declaratory judgment improperly, absent a case or controversy. SCOTUS reaffirmed the mootness, suggesting that it would not decide arguments after events had put them to rest. The judgment involved a religious difference, not a taxpayer action linked to the cost of the Bible reading. No injury has occurred other than the feigned taxpayer issue, so SCOTUS dismissed the appeal as neither case nor controversy. Justice Douglas felt that the taxpayer alleged a real mismanagement of the schools and deserved a decision on the merits.

The Warren Court took big steps toward justiciability in *Powell v. McCormack*, 395 U.S. 486 (1969). In this decision, SCOTUS made decisions regarding mootness and political questions, among others. His constituents elected Adam Clayton Powell to serve in the House of Representatives for the 90th Congress, but Congress voted to exclude him (not expel him) for misappropriating public funds and misusing the New York courts during the previous session. Powell sought injunctive, mandatory, and declaratory relief. Congress denied Powell services, entry, and salary. The appellants got the District Court to dismiss the complaint for want of jurisdiction. While the case was pending before SCOTUS, the 90th Congress ended; his constituents elected Powell to the 91st Congress and it seated him. The respondents argued the case moot, that the Speech and Debate Clause in the Constitution precluded judicial review, that the expulsion power given to each house by the Constitution supported the exclusion, and finally that the court lacked jurisdiction over the subject matter or that it was not justiciable because it involves a political question. SCOTUS ruled that the case was not moot because the back-salary issue stood unresolved, even though the 90th Congress had adjourned. It further ruled that Powell should get declaratory relief; that the Speech and Debate Clause applied to other Congressmen but not to House employees; that expulsion had to be separated from exclusion; that SCOTUS had subject matter jurisdiction; that the case was justiciable because it could be judicially determined; that the case was not a political question because the House exercised powers it did not have and that it did not conjure a potentially embarrassing confrontation between two co-equal branches of government; and that Congress is limited to the standing requirements expressly prescribed by the Constitution.

The District Court and the Court of Appeals had dismissed the complaint, but SCOTUS found that to be an error. His exclusion from the 90th Congress entitled petitioner Powell to the declaratory judgment. SCOTUS dropped the Congressmen from the suit, but the employees of the House remained on the bill. The case raises not a political question but a federal question under the Constitution. If there is a live dispute between the parties, the courts may consider declaratory relief whether other forms of relief are available. Declaratory relief is not available if: (1) there is a textually demonstrable constitutional commitment to another power under the separation of powers; (2) there is a lack of judicially discoverable and manageable standards; (3) a decision cannot be made without a prior policy determination; (4) the court action expresses disrespect for coordinate branches of government; (5) there is an unusual need for unquestioning adherence to a political decision; or (6) there is the possibility of embarrassment if different departments make multifarious pronouncements on the same question.

The abortion controversy masks a very important decision about justiciability in *Roe v. Wade*, 410 U.S. 113 (1973). The central question was whether matters capable of repetition, but evading review, were justiciable. There are three justiciability decisions in *Roe v. Wade*: all plaintiffs established a personal stake in the outcome; the case was being adjudicated in an adversary context; and it was capable of judicial resolution. Roe was pregnant when she filed the suit and still pregnant when she filed an alias affidavit. She had standing when she filed the original petitions. Her pregnancy was directly related to the claim she brought to court. It was unclear whether she was still pregnant when the district court held its hearing. When the district court filed its findings, the respondent claimed mootness. The typical federal rule requires that the controversy exist at each stage of the appellate process. The human gestation period is shorter than the time it would take to complete an appellate process. The pregnancy status would not survive much beyond the original hearing. This also means that the court would deny a pregnant plaintiff appellate review. SCOTUS held that pregnancy was capable of repetition, but evading review; the case was not moot. The Roe plaintiff had established justiciability.

SCOTUS dropped the other plaintiffs. A doctor was one of the plaintiffs. Texas courts convicted him under the Texas abortion statute, and he faced further charges under that statute. The doctor challenged in federal court the very statute under which the prosecutor charged him in state court. SCOTUS held that if the doctor claimed a violation of constitutional rights, he could make that case in state court. SCOTUS decided that the three-Justice district court had erred in providing declaratory relief and that it should have dismissed the request for injunction, even though the district court did not grant it. Another set of plaintiffs, the Does, generally asserted the claims of Roe, but SCOTUS held that the chance of harm to their marital happiness was simply speculative. The harm is remote, and their claim is not justiciable.

Now Justice Rehnquist enters the justiciability field with a dissenting opinion. Roe could have been in her last trimester when she filed this suit. Even in the framework of the SCOTUS decision, Texas would have been able to regulate the pregnancy as the case moved forward. The Court, he argued, is deciding a hypothetical lawsuit. The Court has long followed the rule that a decision should never be broader then the conflict requires. Rehnquist even questioned whether Roe had any protection under privacy. A licensed physician would be involved, so as such the operation is hardly private. Further, even if there were a deprivation, it is not an absolute; the requirement is that no deprivation can occur without due process. The medical judgment made by the majority is more appropriate to the legislative than the judicial department. The Court has found, within the meaning of the Fourteenth Amendment, powers unknown to the drafters. Most of the states have had laws restricting abortion for at least a century. In his dissent on *Doe v. Bolton*, 410 U.S. 179 (1973), Rehnquist also rejects the use of strict scrutiny when assessing the constitutionality of state abortion laws.

PROCEDURAL: CASES AND CONTROVERSIES, INJURY, REMEDY

The Constitution requires that the federal courts hear cases or controversies. SCOTUS has interpreted, *inter alia*, that the interests of the plaintiff must differ from those of the defendant. If this does not appear to be the case, then there can be no controversy. If so, SCOTUS will throw the case out, as it did with *Lord v. Veazie*, 49 U.S. 8 How. 251 (1850). The judgment of the circuit court will be null and void, and no writ of error issued upon it. Plaintiffs brought the instant fictitious case over river navigation rights before the Court to get a judicial decision without properly hearing from those whose interests were decidedly different from that of either the defendant or plaintiff, but directly affected by any decision on navigation rights. The feigned case was reprehensible and possibly treated as a punishable contempt of court. SCOTUS dismissed the case and then remanded it to the district court for further proceedings, presumably on the question of contempt.

In *Williams v. Hagood*, 98 U.S. 72 (1878), South Carolina had guaranteed railroad bonds for $4,000,000, but in 1872 it legislatively recalled those bonds for destruction in exchange for revenue bond script of $1,800,000. The plaintiff had purchased $417,000 of the original bonds and had to exchange them for $166,000 in treasury certificates. The next year, the state legislatively tried to cancel the revenue bond script as well as the tax passed to retire that script. The plaintiff sought the 1873 laws declared unconstitutional because they impair the 1872 contracts but failed to specify his own injury or threat of imminent injury. Lacking a threat, there is no remedy. The bill effectively asked SCOTUS to rule on an abstract question touching on the statute's constitutionality. SCOTUS dismissed the case, although without prejudice so the complainant might press another suit in equity for himself.

A different procedural issue arises in *Smith v. Adams*, 130 U.S. 167 (1889). The Dakota territory organized counties under various county seats. The law here was somewhat convoluted but appointed a temporary county seat until the first general election occurred. If half of the general election voters chose the current county seat, the vote settled the county seat location. Otherwise, upon petition of two thirds of the qualified voters in that county, there would be a designation on the next ballot. In 1886, Congress passed several guidelines governing special laws in the territories of the United States, ranging from divorce, roads, and changing the county seat. Those acts of territorial legislatures in conflict with the congressional statute were null and void. The county seat of Brown County was Columbia, but in 1887 the county held an election for the specific purpose of moving the county seat to Aberdeen. The city of Aberdeen has sweetened the pie by guaranteeing $5,000 worth of well-located property for the county courthouse if the move succeeded. The territorial law appeared to target Brown County, and the territorial legislation collided with federal legislation on the same topic.

A person challenged the county elections before the district court. The territorial court dismissed the challenge, but the supreme court of the territory reversed and remanded. Its decision was therefore not a final appeal; the case could not come before the U.S. Supreme Court, so SCOTUS could not dismiss it. The amount of money involved in the case did not meet minimum standards for docketing at the Supreme Court, and the Abilene offer of land could not count as part of the money involved. The Congressional act of 1885 required that the amount of the decree be greater than $5,000, so SCOTUS dismissed the case. Because there is no treaty or specific Congressional statute under attack, the financial minimum was critical. A third person's promise of lands, or a donation for successful prosecution, will not add to the value of money at stake. SCOTUS declined to accept the case because the territorial supreme court had not entered a final decision, but simply remanded it.

Procedural errors can get a case dismissed for want of jurisdiction, but *Lambert Run Coal Co. v. Baltimore & Ohio R. Co.*, 258 U.S. 377 (1922) adds a new twist. The ICC assumed management of railroad cars to facilitate their availability in areas of need. There were two sets of rules, one governing ordinary times and the second governing emergencies. At the time, the ICC was operating under the emergency rules. The coal company sued in state court, which has no jurisdiction over matters involving the ICC. The plaintiff moved the case to district court, but cases of this type needed a three-judge panel. The company claimed that the railroad had ignored the ICC rules and, instead, followed its own set of rules. The so-called private rules were the emergency rules. The coal company sought an injunction against the ICC through its deceptive representation to the district court, but that court could not exercise jurisdiction because the case began in state court. Nevertheless, the district court issued an injunction and the circuit court of appeals reversed that order and instructed the district court to dismiss the bill for want of jurisdiction.

The court of appeals ruled that only a three-judge panel could issue an injunction, and that the railroad was using the ICC emergency rules, and by deception the coal company wanted to stop them. SCOTUS added that the district court derived jurisdiction from the state court's jurisdiction. Since the latter did not exist, neither did the former. A frivolous claim or fictitious situation cannot confer jurisdiction on the court. SCOTUS ruled that the district court should have dismissed the bill for lack of jurisdiction as soon as it became apparent that the suit really asked to set aside an order of the ICC. The United States must join a case against an agency like the ICC, but the United States had not consented to a state court suit, so the case could not go forward anyway. In addition to the order having the district court dismiss the bill, the circuit court of appeals should have dismissed for want of jurisdiction and without prejudice.

Pendleton and ICC

The Pendleton Act of 1883 and the birth of the ICC in 1887 were watershed moments in the growth of the administrative state or, as preferred by some, the rationalization of society or the bloating of bureaucracy. The proliferation of administrative rules, and their judicial status, significantly increased the caseload in the courts. The explosive growth of the extraction industries, such as natural gas and oil, and the necessary transportation systems (railroads and pipelines), created interstate nightmares for the court system. One particularly troublesome issue was a review of evaluation, rates, and rules, and whether the courts have the power to amend them. Congress had given the Washington, D.C. courts amendment powers, but these powers are legislative in the usual federal court system. In *Keller v. Potomac Elec. Power Co.*, 261 U.S. 428 (1923), a public utility brought action against the D.C. Public Utilities Commission. Under the federal pact creating the commission, SCOTUS had final review. SCOTUS pointed out, however, that the Constitution created the Supreme Court, not an act of Congress, and therefore Congress could not give legislative authority to SCOTUS. Because of the savings clause included in the act, SCOTUS struck the paragraph legislatively giving it final review without affecting the remaining parts. SCOTUS dismissed an appeal from the D.C. Court of Appeals for lack of jurisdiction.

Congress charged the D.C. utility commission to evaluate the property of all public utilities within the district. The Potomac Electric Power Company objected to its evaluation and filed an appeal. The case moved through the D.C. courts and eventually came before the Supreme Court. SCOTUS would not hear the merits of the case, but instead requested briefs on whether Congress had the constitutional power to vest the district courts and the Supreme Court with the power to review proceedings of the commission. The plaintiff had the burden of proof.

Chief Justice Taft repeated a general rule that legislation looks to the future, while a judicial inquiry looks to the present or past. Still, Congress has the same power as the states to vest the judicial power of the District of Columbia with additional legislative powers, excepting that of the Supreme Court and other courts created under Article III of the Constitution. The judicial process requires a case or controversy and it cannot provide an advisory opinion. The appeal to SCOTUS could not stand.

The same line of reasoning, albeit a state-authorized declaratory judgment, occurs in *Liberty Warehouse Co. v. Grannis*, 273 U.S. 70 (1927). Kentucky has a declaratory judgment law. The question is whether the Federal Conformity Act requires the federal courts to respect state law. SCOTUS, consistent with its prior position, argued that no Article III court could issue a declaratory judgment, because the Constitution limits jurisdiction to cases and controversies where relief is possible. The *Grannis* case involved a suit against the state's attorney general to determine whether a law governing the sale of tobacco leaf at public auction could pass constitutional muster. The federal district court dismissed the suit for lack of jurisdiction. The Kentucky law allowed a declaratory judgment of rights, whether relief was possible. Plaintiff brought a diversity suit, claiming possible violation of the constitution of Kentucky, the Commerce Clause of the U.S. Constitution, the Due Process and Equal Protection Clauses of the Fourteenth Amendment, and Sherman Anti-Trust Law. The warehouse corporation claimed that the 1924 Kentucky auction law would seriously affect their business and confiscate their rights, business, and property. The plaintiff wanted the federal court to apply the Kentucky declaratory judgment law under the Federal Conformity Statute. SCOTUS found no adverse litigation, no actual violation of the new auction law, and no allegation that the commonwealth attorney had or contemplated taking action against the plaintiff. SCOTUS refused jurisdiction over abstract questions or advisory opinions and ruled that the Federal Conformity Statute did not indirectly authorize a declaratory judgment.

Jurisdiction

Lack of jurisdiction because a bill failed the case or controversy test occurred quite often in cases where the state complained about the exercise of federal power. In *Willing v. Chicago Auditorium Association*, 277 U.S. 274 (1928), the plaintiff sought federal court help. This suit originated when the Chicago Auditorium Association sought to remove a cloud from the land title it derived from a long-term lease. Plaintiff removed the bill from state court to federal district court where the court dismissed it, followed by a circuit court of appeals reversal, which was in turn reversed by SCOTUS. Most of the parties were citizens of Illinois, except a few who, through diversity, got the suit removed to federal court.

The Auditorium Association self-organized in 1886 to construct a large auditorium, galleries, facilities for conventions, and more, all for profit. The city granted five leases for ninety-nine years and extended three of these through 2085. Lessees built a monumental auditorium before 1889, containing an auditorium, recital halls, a hotel, and business offices. The association partly financed the structure by the issue of stocks and bonds. The structure was never financially remunerative to the stockholders, who desired to replace it with a tall, modern commercial building. The leases appeared to require that the lessees maintain the original building. After unsuccessful talks with one of the lessors, lessees pressed a suit for the right to tear down the original structure and build a new one, with appropriate securities provided in the interim. The cloud upon the title made the structure unmarketable. Apart from an oral conversation with one of these lessors restraining the lessees from its plans, the defendants had taken no hostile action. The plaintiff was essentially seeking a declaratory judgment, which the federal court could not provide. The bill did not establish a case or controversy within the meaning of Article III.

In *Ex parte Bakelite Corp.*, 279 U.S. 438 (1929), SCOTUS distinguished between constitutional courts and legislative courts. The latter could have powers and jurisdiction assigned through Congressional statute. Article III limited the constitutional courts; they required a case or controversy and possible relief to establish jurisdiction. The constitutional courts give justices life tenure during good behavior. Congress sets the service terms for judges in the legislative courts. Constitutional courts cannot issue advisory opinions. Legislative courts, such as the court of customs appeals, may issue opinions on cases that do not meet case and controversy requirement, as Congress provides. The customs court of appeals may hear appeals from decisions of the tariff commission. SCOTUS denied the request to issue a writ of prohibition to the court of customs appeals but did not rule on whether it had that power in the first place.

A quick and unexpected turn occurs in *Nashville, C. & St. Louis Ry. Co. v. Wallace*, 288 U.S. 249 (1933). Tennessee had adopted a uniform declaratory judgments act. It passed an act to tax stored and withdrawn gasoline from facilities build on Tennessee's soil. A railroad argued that the declaratory act violated both the Commerce Clause and the Fourteenth Amendment. The bill comes before SCOTUS from the Tennessee Supreme Court. The railroad only challenged whether there was a case and controversy. The Tennessee declaratory judgment act permitted its court to declare a right, even if it offered no further relief. The defendant wanted the entire act invalidated, even though adverse parties sought a declaration of their legal rights under the bill. SCOTUS ruled that the defendant did not seek an abstract opinion, because this decision went directly to whether it would pay the assessed taxes on its storage and use. SCOTUS ruled that relief was not an indispensable component of a judicial judgment. Here, a case or controversy was necessary under the declaratory judgment act, but not the prayer for relief. SCOTUS ruled that once the railroad brought gasoline into Tennessee, unloaded and stored it, the gasoline ceased to be a subject of transportation in interstate commerce, and thus lost its immunity from state taxation. Relief by injunction is not a prerequisite to the exercise of judicial power.

The Federal Declaratory Act also becomes part of the deliberations in *Ashwander v. Tennessee Valley Auth.*, 297 U.S. 288 (1936). Although the act provided for declaratory judgment in the federal courts, SCOTUS ruled that the act in no way changes the case and controversy requirement of all constitutional courts. In the *Ashwander* case, SCOTUS ruled that the declaratory judgment act did not permit advisory opinions, or abstract questions based on hypothetical facts. Congress enabled the construction of Wilson dam, part of the Tennessee Valley Authority (TVA), under its war and commerce powers. The generation of electricity was simply derivative to navigability, and that its disposal was under congressional control. The TVA bought transmission lines within fifty miles of the dam for distribution of power generated at the dam. TVA also agreed to sell surplus power to the Alabama Power Company. Stockholders of the power company, having failed to get the board of directors to annul the contract, sued in federal court to have the contract declared invalid and to enjoin its performance. The district court agreed and set aside the contract; the circuit court of appeals reversed. SCOTUS affirmed that reversal.

SCOTUS ruled that the plaintiffs had standing. The plaintiffs also sought a decree against the policies and programs of the TVA. The policies and programs of the TVA did not present a justiciable controversy. In his concurring opinion, Justice Brandeis argued that SCOTUS should simply have affirmed the circuit court without further commentary, because ordinary stockholders have no standing to interfere with management. The Court should not pass judgment on a constitutional issue before necessary. Brandeis cites seven rules that the Court has adopted to accomplish this goal. (1) the Court will not pass upon the constitutionality of legislation in a friendly, non-adversary, proceeding; (2) the Court will not anticipate a question of constitutional law before it is necessary to decided it; (3) the Court will not formulate a constitutional rule broader than required; (4) the Court will not pass upon a constitutional question if the case may be dispose of on other grounds; (5) the Court will not rule on the constitutionality of a statute unless the plaintiff clearly demonstrates injury; (6) the Court will not rule on the constitutionality of a statute when the plaintiff has availed himself of the benefits; (7) the Court will construct or construe a statute, if possible, in order to avoid a constitutional decision.

Congress made a significant change in lower federal court procedure when it introduced the Federal Declaratory Judgment in 1934. SCOTUS found the act constitutional in *Aetna Life Ins. Co. v. Haworth*, 300 U.S. 227 (1937). Chief Justice Hughes described the act as procedural; it provides remedies and procedures regarding controversies, taken to be less comprehensive than cases, that are actual, not hypothetical. The declaratory law does focus on actual controversies, but it contains both procedural and substantive implications. On the procedural side, pleadings may include petitions, declarations, or complaint asking for a declaration, which would have the effect of being final and hence reviewable. It also reaffirms that the adverse party must be in the proceedings as an adversarial party. A court may submit issues of fact to a jury in the form interrogatories, with judicial instructions, instead of a general verdict. The substantive side has considerable reach. A judicial decision may declare sides and other legal relations, whether further relief is possible. It is this last clause that is of special relevance, because it broadens what is justiciable from cases and controversies where relief is possible, to a much more general definition of relief that goes to a declaration of rights and other legal relations. The Federal Declaratory Act does not distinguish between constitutional rights and those created by statute. The act also permits controversies of fact.

Using the Federal Judiciary Act, SCOTUS overruled both lower courts to hold the controversy between Aetna and Hayworth justiciable. Aetna issued Hayworth five policies on his life, with disability benefits. Heyworth received payments from the first policy, but Aetna held that premiums on the remaining policies had lapsed and therefore no disability payments were in order. Hayworth argued that the disability occurred before non-payment of the premiums, and thus the disability extinguished the premium liability in all remaining policies; one of the remaining policies required additional disability payments. The plaintiff wanted the last four policies declared null and void. SCOTUS only ruled that the case met the standard of cases and controversies; the Federal Declaratory Act was consistent with the constitutional powers given Congress to legislate on the formal powers of the lower federal courts. SCOTUS did not limit relief to award of process or the payment of damages; the claimant need not seek an injunction; demonstration of irreparable injury was also unnecessary. The disputes need to be susceptible to judicial determination, but neither an advisory nor hypothetical opinion was in order. Legal resolution would follow determination of the facts in this case. The legal interest lay in the preservation of contracts. The suit meets diversity requirements.

SCOTUS faced several cases involving the declaratory judgment thus made possible. In *Altvater v. Freeman*, 319 U.S. 359 (1943), SCOTUS made yet another foray in establishing underpinnings for a declaratory judgment. The holder of a patent for cutting out the upper part of shoes, and the owners of machines implementing the design led to a suit and countersuit. The lower court found infringement of the original patent but non-infringement under patents reissued after surrender of the original, which ended that license. The lower courts did not lift the original injunction and respondents were paying royalties for other articles at pain of triple damages. The fact that royalty payments continued did not prevent the counterclaim of invalidity but rendered the dispute real and not hypothetical or abstract; a declaratory judgment was the reasonable alternative to continued payments or risk of non-payment damages. Validity claims required the same level of case or controversy under the declaratory judgment act as required under regular judicial proceedings. SCOTUS ruled that the counterclaim was still alive and remanded to the circuit court for further consideration.

Two decades after its passage, the Federal Declaratory Act still raises problems of justiciability. The specter of ideological judgment becomes increasingly apparent deciding whether a declaration is in order. In *Longshoremen's Union v. Boyd*, 347 U.S. 222 (1954), an immigration official threatened to apply an ambiguous clause in a new federal law that would cause all residents in California and Washington going to Alaska for seasonal employment to go through alien entry procedures instead of alien resident procedures. Disqualifications were more severe for alien entry then alien resident re-entry, so the union asks for a declaratory judgment before the seasonal work began that would guarantee re-entry as alien residents. The Court found that the issue was too hypothetical or abstract to merit a declaratory judgment and ordered the district court to dismiss the complaint. In his dissent, Justice Black provided details not found in the main SCOTUS decision, and pointed out that this was exactly the type of case or controversy that would merit a declaratory judgment. While the facts appeared to support Justice Black's assessment, the Court majority apparently sought to avoid taking issue with laws motivated by the communist or red scare of the early 1950s. It is interesting to note that the controversial law focused on any alien seeking re-entry to the mainland United States from Hawaii, Alaska, Guam, Puerto Rico, or the Virgin Islands. Congress thought that the new law would help arrest Communist infiltration.

Four years later, *Evers v. Dwyer*, 358 U.S. 202 (1958) presents a different result. A Tennessee statute required that blacks, riding on public transportation, sit in a segregated area. The plaintiff refused seating in the segregated area, so two policemen confronted him with three choices: move to the segregated area, get off the bus, or face arrest. The plaintiff filed suit against the city of Memphis, the railway company, and one of the company's employees, seeking a declaratory judgment and injunction for himself and all others similarly situated, to enforce a constitutional right. A three-judge panel for the district court found that the complaint lacked a controversy; that the defendant had deliberately challenged the segregation command to instigate litigation; and that the defendant was not representative of colored citizens using public transportation. SCOTUS ruled that there indeed was a controversy meriting a declaratory judgment. SCOTUS did observe that the line between an abstract question and a controversy was necessarily one of degree. The defendants made it clear that they intended to enforce the segregation statutes unless they were unconstitutional. Although the plaintiff got off the bus, SCOTUS ruled that it was not necessary to proceed to arrest before challenging the statute in court. Interestingly, SCOTUS also found that whether the defendant purposefully instigated the confrontation was not significant. The district court had refused to consider the complaint on its merits, but SCOTUS remanded the case for a hearing on the merits.

We get another ideological twist in *Poe v. Ullman*, 367 U.S. 497 (1961). Two married women and a doctor had their request for a declaratory judgment in Connecticut's Supreme Court of errors dismissed. SCOTUS heard the case because of constitutional claims under the Fourteenth Amendment. The married women sought advice on the use of contraceptive devices from a doctor who could provide such advice. Both women had medical cause for using contraception. A Connecticut statute passed in 1879 made illegal the use of and advice on contraceptive devices. The state charged two doctors and a nurse with operating a birth control clinic, and the Connecticut Supreme Court sustained the law in 1940. The state subsequently dropped charges against the two doctors and the nurse, but the legal action seems to have resulted in the closing of all birth control clinics in Connecticut. In the present quest for a declaratory judgment, the state's attorney intended to prosecute such violations of Connecticut law. SCOTUS argued that the state's attorney had not attested directly to this intention, and that this supposed intention arose simply from the state's attorney's public duty. The lack of immediacy of harm raised questions of justiciability. SCOTUS further observed that the plaintiffs' own attorney revealed that drug stores openly sold contraceptive devices. There was no immediate antagonism, so the complaint did not meet the case or controversy requirement for a declaratory judgment. In its decision, SCOTUS referred to the seven rules identified by Justice Brandeis as the Court's own limitation regarding claims of constitutional rights. SCOTUS deferred to the judgment of the state legislature and its enforcement officers. SCOTUS also declined to pronounce an abstract decision.

In his dissent, Justice Douglas argued that the court went outside the record, using a novel power to claim that a tacit agreement not to prosecute effectively removed justiciability. Douglas argued that the Court's decision was transparent vis-à-vis the birth control issue. Douglas highlights the rules for a federal declaratory judgment: (1) case or controversy; (2) appropriate for judicial determination; (3) not hypothetical, abstract, academic, or moot; (4) adverse legal interests; (5) real and substantial; (6) admit a specific relief; (7) award of damages not essential; (8) irreparable damage irrelevant. The Senate report leading to adoption of the Federal Declaratory Act pointed out that, without a declaratory judgment procedure, it would often be necessary to violate or purport to violate a statute to seek judicial determination. The instant case is a classical candidate for a declaratory judgment. A tacit agreement bound neither the state's attorney nor the police. Douglas also points out that SCOTUS chose to ignore contraceptive criminal prosecutions in the minor courts. Douglas argued that the Court should have incorporated all the Bill of Rights through the due process clause of the Fourteenth Amendment, not just parts of them. This controversy certainly denies due process. The Connecticut statute denies, not sale nor manufacturing, but use. With full enforcement, the state will be in the bedroom to guarantee proper procedure.

Justice Harlan, in his dissent, argues that SCOTUS had just done violence to the concept of justiciability. The Court leaves the plaintiffs with the threat of unconstitutional prosecution. The statute deprives the plaintiffs of life liberty or property without the due process of law. Harlan cites four strands of declaratory power: (1) the court's power derives from its duty to decide; (2) recognizable interests require immediate resolution; (3) the controversy is the litigant's controversy; (4) other means of redress are unavailable. The 1940 test case of the Connecticut statutes changed defiance into compliance. The plaintiffs have no legally recognized right against prosecution in state court. The prosecutor will succeed, if by whim he chooses to prosecute. The supreme court of Connecticut has already given its approval. There is no justification for the failure to decide in this Court on that case. SCOTUS owes plaintiffs anticipatory relief; these plaintiffs wait for actual prosecution. SCOTUS leaves a controversy on constitutional claims to the discretion of the prosecutor. Nothing limits the Due Process Clause of the Fourteenth Amendment to the rights enumerated in the first eight amendments; it includes the fundamental rights of any citizen in a free society. The Due Process Clause balances the rights of individuals within the bounds of an organized society. The Connecticut statute violates the right to privacy for marital couples, one of the basic guarantees of ordered liberty.

A case is not justiciable if the statute's language is so ambiguous it is inapplicable. In *United States v. Evans*, 333 U.S. 483 (1948), plaintiff challenged section 8 of the 1917 immigration act for lack of clarity. That section sought to criminalize the harboring or hiding of illegal aliens. When a statute admits three or four interpretations, the matter is legislative, not judicial. To save the statute, the court would need to expand the meaning of its penal language but remain blind to the reach of the statute. This it should not do; case dismissed.

Race issues increase the chance that a case is justiciable (*Dombrowski v. Pfister*, 380 U.S. 479 (1965)). The doctrine of unconstitutional uncertainty, or void-for-vagueness, refers to the statutes that are so overly broad that rational people likely would come to different conclusions as to what it meant. If the statute be federal, SCOTUS would attempt to interpret it narrowly enough to pass constitutional muster. If it be a state statute, SCOTUS would normally allow the state supreme court to narrow its interpretation before adjudging constitutional uncertainty. If the prognosis for such action is slim and the potential injury severe, SCOTUS might strike the statute down immediately. In the *Dombroski* case, Louisiana passed a subversive activities and communist control law, plus a communist propaganda control law. The plaintiff, a black civil rights organization, argued that these control laws were so overbroad that the state could apply them in abridging black civil rights through harassment and threats of prosecution to discourage blacks from asserting constitutional rights. A three-Judge district court panel dismissed the suit for failure to state a claim upon which to grant relief. Two of the three-judge panel argued for federal abstention while the state courts sought to narrow the statute's interpretation to preserve the last of vestiges of state sovereignty.

The plaintiff argued that state action impaired both the freedom of expression and the Fourteenth Amendment. SCOTUS considered First Amendment rights so basic that an overly broad statute would bring irreparable harm to the plaintiffs while the case moved through the state courts. Louisiana accused the black civil rights organization as subversive or a communist front organization, using the statute to seize documents and records even though prosecution to final judgment was unlikely. SCOTUS found that the abstention doctrine was inappropriate when statutes facially violate constitutional rights or have a chilling effect upon their exercise. When the abstention doctrine is at war with the vagueness doctrine, the vagueness doctrine applies, and plaintiff may seek an injunction, although the federal court may modify if subsequent state court action clarifies the statute.

In this case, Justice Harlan finds himself among two dissenters. Harlan argues that, as a matter of comity, the abstention doctrine should hold until the case winds its way through the state courts. Harlan points out that the instant judgment supersedes the abstention doctrine whenever a plaintiff raises claims in federal court regarding violations of the First and Fourteenth Amendments. The SCOTUS majority seems to assume that state courts are less apt to vindicate constitutional rights. Further, rather than an orderly progression of cases, the current holding encourages a race to the forum of its choice in determining standing and criminality.

The abstention versus vagueness issue reappears two years later in another First Amendment case, *Zwickler v. Koota*, 389 U.S. 241 (1967). The federal plaintiff was guilty of violating a state statute on the distribution of the anonymous political handbills. The state supreme court overturned his conviction. The federal bill requested a declaratory judgment against the state statute and an injunction barring further prosecution under an overly broad statute that violated the Civil Rights Act. A three-judge panel for the district court applied the abstention doctrine and dismissed the complaint from federal courts. SCOTUS considered two issues: (1) whether abstention be appropriate without the injunction; (2) whether abstention be appropriate with the injunction. SCOTUS observed that the powers of federal courts dramatically increased consequent to the Civil War. Both the federal courts and the state courts could hear federal constitutional claims. The plaintiff thus had choice of forum. The doctrine of abstention was a judicial rule created in 1941 and, under specific circumstances, the federal courts would stay their hand pending a state court clarification of an overly broad or vague statute. The rule does not cover cases where the plaintiff claims that the overly broad statute necessarily offends certain constitutional rights. SCOTUS ruled that the plaintiff could seek a declaratory judgment in federal court.

The district court wanted a showing of special circumstances justifying the injunction before it would rule on the declaratory request. SCOTUS ruled that the question of declaratory relief was different from the request for an injunction. SCOTUS asked the district court three-judge panel to reconsider the request for a declaratory judgment and, separately, the request for an injunction. The latter may simply be unnecessary because of the comity between federal and state courts. Justice Harlan concurred in this judgment but raised an issue on the abstention doctrine. An abstention would be appropriate to avoid a premature and perhaps unnecessary decision on a federal constitutional matter, or to avoid unsettling delicate federal-state relationships. Harlan argued that neither rule applied in the *Zwickler* case and that the district court should proceed to the merits. Harlan does object to the use of over-breadth or vagueness to overcome the abstention doctrine. First, the Court has delimited neither doctrine. Second, the bill complaining of over-breath or vagueness does not make abstention inappropriate. Third, if assumed to do so, it would reduce the abstention argument to a pleader's option. Foresight to claim over-breadth would then automatically take the case to a hearing on the merits.

Two years later, in an ironical twist, this case reappears as *Golden v. Zwickler*, 394 U.S. 103 (1969). SCOTUS remanded the *Zwickler* case so that the district court could consider issuing a declaratory statement about the plaintiff's alleged violation of a New York statute for distributing anonymous fliers supporting his candidate for Congressional office. That candidate eventually won a spot on the New York Supreme Court, but the plaintiff pressed on, claiming that he intended future political work under much the same terms as those that got him arrested in the first place. The district court took no further testimony on the declaratory issue in *Zwickler* but found that the case originally met the terms for a declaratory judgment and issued it.

SCOTUS argued in the *Golden* case that the bill no longer met the cases and controversies requirement, and that the hand bill issue now was irrelevant because the candidate was unlikely to seek that seat in the future. SCOTUS held that the plaintiff had an interest in the election of a Congressman unlikely to run again. Lacking a solid case and lacking immediacy and reality, SCOTUS found against issuing a declaratory judgment and remanded *Golden* back to the district court. SCOTUS also ruled that a proper check for a declaratory judgment is not whether the controversy exists at the time of the hearing on remand. The original controversy had passed. The district court must dismiss the bill.

Justice White, with Rehnquist among the majority, delivered an opinion that reached far beyond the case at hand (*CSC v. Letter Carriers*, 413 U.S. 548 (1973)). The plaintiff, a mix of federal employees, their union, and political committees of both parties, asks a three-judge district court panel to rule unconstitutional a provision in the Hatch Act preventing political activity by federal employees. A majority of the panel found that clause unconstitutional for being vague and overbroad. SCOTUS reversed. For decades, the Hatch Act had barred certain federal employees from political campaigning or political management. The Pendleton Act, the statute creating the Civil Service Commission, barred use of office and limited political action by civil servants. Civil Service Rule One spells out limitations on political management and political campaigning. The Hatch Act extended rules from the classified service to all civil servants. The rule specifically permitted the expression of opinion, but Congress sought to balance freedom of expression and opinion with interference on the efficiency of the civil service.

The Roosevelt administration extended these prohibitions to state civil servants. The Civil Service Commission, developing a body of rules on a case-by-case basis, elaborated the prohibitions under rule number one. Senator Hatch placed these rules in the Congressional record in 1940. Rule updates occur using the case-by-case method. SCOTUS updated the 1970 body of commission rules and affirmed them as law for both federal and state. The *CSC* opinion is particularly important because it affirms actions of the administrative state that provide meaning to terms used in the legislative acts. That is, the growth of administrative rules improves the efficacy of vague and over-broad doctrines in court proceedings. The three dissenters considered the Civil Service Commission rules merely a gloss on the Hatch Act.

The civil rights era quickly unwound with the exit of Chief Justice Earl Warren. In *O'Shea v. Littleton*, 414 U.S. 488 (1974), Rehnquist voting with the majority, seventeen black residents and two white residents filed a civil rights class action suit against a state magistrate and state circuit judge, arguing a pattern of illegal bond-setting, sentences, jury fees and unfavorable practices in criminal trials. The plaintiffs, and others similarly situated, claimed that these practices systematically deprived them of their rights under the Constitution. The district court dismissed the bill, pointing to judicial immunity for state officials. The court of appeals reversed. Not only was an injunction against state judicial officers not forbidden, but absent sufficient remedy at law, the plaintiffs could ask the district court to fashion appropriate relief. SCOTUS reversed; the plaintiff had not made a claim that constituted a case or controversy. None of the plaintiffs claim they had suffered personal injury and the complaint was in most general terms. A speculation that any of the plaintiffs would suffer the deprivation is too remote. Even if there were a case or controversy, adequate relief would not be available. The intrusion of federal power into daily state court operations would conflict with recognized principles of equitable restraint. There is no showing or threat of imminent injury.

The complaint does contain specific examples of prior injury done to some of the plaintiffs by the state's attorney and his investigator. The plaintiffs claim that non-white persons charged with violations of city ordinances must pay for a trial by jury if they do not pay the fine. The plaintiffs asked that the court enjoin such practices, but they offered no examples directly attributable to one of the respondents. SCOTUS found the claim conjectural, and not real or immediate. SCOTUS also assumed that the original plaintiff would not violate a valid statute, and thus not face prosecution, conviction, or exposure to any of the alleged discriminatory behaviors. As a consolation prize, a federal writ of habeas corpus is available if city officials arrest one of the original plaintiffs and the judicial officials behave prejudicially to the administration of justice. In his concurring opinion, Justice Blackmun agrees that the bill failed the case or controversy test, but he thought the court should have stopped there, rather than moving into a discussion of equitable relief.

The dissenters took a different view. Justice Douglas pointedly remarks that the accusations were numerous, including setting bond without regard to the cases and as a punishment, higher jail and monetary sentences on black citizens, and required black violators of city ordinances to pay for a jury trial if they could not pay the ordinance fine. Neither the district nor the court of appeals cited failure to state a case or controversy; SCOTUS did. Douglas also observed that the amended complaint cited harassment without violation of ordinances and harsher charges when something did occur. The charges are not about individuals but about classes of the individuals, or guilt by race. Discriminatory patterns establish clear violations of equal protection. Douglas agrees with Blackmun, who wrote a concurring opinion, that the court foray into the discussion of relief is an advisory opinion, forbidden to the court.

The refocus of the SCOTUS majority continues. A three-judge federal district court declared unconstitutional five provisions of Arizona's farm labor statute, and finding this inseparable from the whole statute, declared it unconstitutional, enjoining its enforcement. SCOTUS found three of the five provisions presented a case or controversy, but the remaining two were nonjusticiable as failing to present a case or controversy and thus would be merely advisory (*Babbitt v. United Farm Workers Nat'l Union*, 442 U.S. 289 (1979)). SCOTUS would have preferred the district court wait until the Arizona courts had construed two of the three justiciable provisions. SCOTUS reversed the district court, with Justice Rehnquist joining the majority. Justice Brennan, dissenting in part, objected to waiting for a constitutional adjudication until after the state courts ruled. He cites the doctrine of abstention from exercising federal jurisdiction as the exception, not the rule. The doctrine involves issues where state court interpretation might change the underlying constitutional issue. The criminalizing provision remanded to the district court does not meet the abstention requirement; this is a case of equity. The provision is plain and unambiguous. Because this provision covers the others, it impacts on certain First Amendment rights. The threatened criminal liability might go so far as chill the words used in a new round of litigation. Abstention is inappropriate, and the First Amendment should prevail, absent a compelling state reason.

Rehnquist parts ways with the majority in *ASARCO v. Kadish*, 490 U.S. 605 (1989). In 1910, Congress granted federal lands to certain Western States, excluding mineral lands, for the support of public schools. These lands had strict provisions for sale, including advertising, bidding, and appraisal. SCOTUS limited the mineral lands to those known at the time of the grant (*Wyoming v. United States*, 255 U.S. 489 (1921)), but Congress then extended terms of the grant to include all mineral lands under the Jones Act of 1927. A further amendment in 1951 removed advertising, appraisal, and lease value restrictions on lands with hydrocarbons. Arizona had included the original lease requirements in its constitution, but not the statute related to hydrocarbon lands. Individual taxpayers and a teachers' association sued the hydrocarbon statute as violating the Arizona constitution. Mineral lessees of state school lands were the defendants. The trial court defined the defendants as a class action for all present and future mineral land lessees, and then upheld the statute. The Arizona high court reversed and remanded to the trial court to declare the statute unconstitutional and to consider what further relief might be appropriate. SCOTUS affirmed.

Before reviewing the merits of the case, SCOTUS faced three issues of justiciability. The Arizona Supreme Court sent the case back to the trial court with instructions to see what additional relief was appropriate, raising the question whether the Arizona Supreme Court had made a final decision. When this case reached the Arizona Supreme Court, the plaintiff asked the court to declare the state statute invalid and to provide an injunction against further leases. SCOTUS found that the Arizona Supreme Court judgment was the final judgment, because there were no remaining federal issues for the trial judge to consider. The second issue was a claim of non-justiciability because the plaintiff had no standing to sue. This problem focuses on the interests shared with millions of others and that individually they are minute and undeterminable. Federal tax payers would have no standing, but the same does not always hold for municipal tax payers, school trust funds and general revenue fund schools in Arizona. It is unclear whether money to the school trust fund would affect state taxes because school support still relies upon some general funding from the state. The economic chain from trust fund to school, general revenue to school, and general revenue to taxpayer relief is tenuous. The case may not meet redressability requirements for a hearing in federal court. Courts using federal rules would dismiss this case at the outset.

Article III of the U.S. Constitution does not bind state courts, given the American federal system. Thus, the state courts may consider a constitutional issue or a federal statute issue using rules that differentiate it from the federal system. Once the trial court makes a decision, the plaintiffs may allege injury from the state court decision itself, which rests on federal law. The original defendants bring this lawsuit; the state court decision has injured them, and now for the first time they seek entry to the federal courts. These plaintiffs hold invalidated mineral leases. Petitioners allege that the declaratory judgment issued, and the relief given, violate federal statutes. They have standing; granting relief in this court would remove the invalidation of their leases. The petitioners have met federal standing requirements: a real injury, the injury traceable to a cause, and relief is possible.

The third issue of justiciability is the true presence of a case or controversy. The parties to this suit began adverse and remain adverse. Valuable legal rights are at stake. The possible invalidation of the mineral leases, a question of law, certainly makes the decision specific and substantial. This is not an advisory opinion or a hypothetical ruling; nor is the ruling abstract. It would be inappropriate to dismiss at this stage. The court then offered a specific rule:" when a state court has issued a judgment in a case where plaintiffs in the original action had no standing to sue under the principles governing the federal courts, we may exercise our jurisdiction on certiorari if the judgment of the state court causes direct, specific, and concrete injury to the parties who petition for our review, where the requisites of a case or controversy are also met." The case meets requirements of justiciability. There are no specific and independent grounds on which the state courts could make the final decision without reference to federal statute because it was a federal act that established the school trust fund. The court can proceed to the merits. SCOTUS then affirmed the Arizona Supreme Court judgment that the challenged Arizona statute was invalid.

Rehnquist felt that SCOTUS should dismiss the *Wyoming* case for lack of standing. He further takes issue with the rule enunciated by the Court, requiring at least a very persuasive justification. Contrary to the Court's majority, Rehnquist does not believe that dismissing the present appeal will leave a legal landscape in which the Supreme Court cannot review many important decisions.

Justice Rehnquist writes the opinion in *Parratt v. Taylor*, 451 U.S. 527 (1981), dismissing the case for lack of stating a claim. A defendant ordered a hobby package lost within prison mail distribution while the defendant served time in segregation. Upon release the prisoner sought his package but it had disappeared from prison custody in clear violation of prison mail policy. The plaintiff filed a deprivation of property without due process of law in violation of the Fourteenth. The lower courts found the negligence complaint actionable, but SCOTUS reversed. Rehnquist argued that the action had to contain two elements: conduct committed by a person acting under color of state law; the conduct deprived a person of rights, privileges, or immunities secured by the U.S. Constitution. Rehnquist found the second point lacking. The state has tort procedures that will allow full recovery for the plaintiff. No intention required; simple negligence will do. There is no federal common law. The instant case makes no reference to a right deprived other than the Fourteenth Amendment. Appeal under this amendment requires a deprivation without due process of law. Rehnquist then repeats the premise that where only property rights are involved the postponement of judicial enquiry is not a denial of due process if opportunity exists for judicial determination of liability. The loss does not occur as the result of a state procedure, but its failure.

Rehnquist further restricts use of the Fourteenth Amendment's due process clause in *Daniels v. Williams*, 474 U.S. 327 (1986). We find a relatively minor case with considerable review consequences. A sheriff's deputy left a pillow on a staircase, and the prisoner qua plaintiff slipped and suffered bodily injury. The plaintiff sued for deprivation of liberty without due process. The plaintiff won in the lower courts, and SCOTUS reversed. Negligence by an official does not trigger the Due Process Clause of the Fourteenth Amendment. The negligence here was a failure of reasonable conduct, not a gross abuse of official power. Rehnquist then overrules his own five-year-old *Parratt* decision to the extent that it is inconsistent with the *Daniels* decision. Relief must be through tort law. In this case, the respondent claimed sovereign immunity and thus insulation from tort law. Variously, the lower courts argued that the Fourteenth Amendment protected property but not liberty; that state-of-mind did matter; and that gross indifference rather than simple negligence was necessary to trigger Fourteenth Amendment due process. The federal judiciary deals with large concerns, not traditional tort law. Finally, the difference between negligence, on one end of the continuum, and intent, on the other, is abundantly clear. In a concurring opinion, Justice Stevens make it clear that, even if the state refuses prisoner recovery in state tort court, it does not trigger a federal concern.

CONCLUSION

There is a Janus-faced consequence to Marshall claiming the sole right of judicial review. What gets reviewed? The answer lies, in large part, in the non-constitutional rules of justiciability. These rules are many in number, and as we have seen from the Rehnquist materials, subject to refined and restated caricatures. The rules start simply: there must be a case or controversy. SCOTUS, in turn, makes strict distinction between its original jurisdiction and appellate jurisdiction. The Court must further keep a wary eye on what to avoid, the separation of powers, and federalism; the Court earns its legitimacy through its decisions. The people do not elect the Court; nor can they hold justices popularly accountable. The plaintiff must have a direct or highly likely injury. The case must be current when it finally rises through the appellate chain. There must be a close connection between the relief requested and the injury suffered. It must be within the Court's power and influence to provide that relief.

The justiciability rules give ample leeway in determining what the Court will hear. Requests for advisory opinions it will not honor. Courts around the world permit advisory opinions, but the specific American objection is that the Court decision is final, and what comes before it is the final judgment of lower courts. When justices served as commissioners for hearing and awarding veteran claims, a subsequent SCOTUS judgment declared the enabling legislation unconstitutional and justice-commissioner awards recoverable by the state.

SCOTUS found itself chiding the government for contriving conflicts. The Court also rejected, except in a special circumstance, any appeal from a legislative court such as the Court of Claims to the Supreme Court. The Court reminded Congress that the Constitution sets its appellate jurisdiction and the legislature cannot change that. A Congress from the Great Depression era gave the Court a new tool that softened the boundary between decisions and advisory opinions: the declaratory judgment. Congress meant the new power as an alternative to class actions or injunctions. The Court subsequently separated the injunction and declaratory judgment so that the courts might use either singly. Federal declaratory relief is possible under threat of prosecution, but the plaintiff need not exhaust all available state or administrative remedies.

SCOTUS was very aware that a case following the slow appellate procedure may have lost its timeliness and be moot. The death of a defendant would typically terminate a case, as would a deadline long past. SCOTUS will dismiss a case if it cannot provide effective relief. Equally interesting is the impact of changing world orders on contracts made under one world order but before the court during the succeeding world order. SCOTUS dismissed anti-trust cases involving shipping, for example. SCOTUS also dismissed cases where the changing age status of the plaintiff disqualifies standing. It also dismissed a labor case where the work project in question was over. In yet another case, a complaint about school procedures lost its currency with the graduation of the plaintiff. In these four examples, the case became moot.

Different decisions on mootness are also possible. Congress excluded one of its members from taking his seat in one term as punishment for behavior in a previous term. By the time the case reached SCOTUS, the Congressman had returned to office for yet another term, but this time Congress seated the Congressman. The constitutional issue focused the difference between "exclusion" and "expulsion," with only the latter power in the Constitution. Because Congress denied salary to the Congressman during the "exclusion" term, the case was not moot. One of the most important mootness cases occurred when a pregnant lady sued for the right to abortion. When the pregnancy terminated is not clear, but pregnancy in general is a condition that would never reach Court review because the gestation term is much shorter than the appellate term. SCOTUS announced the principle of "capable of repetition, but evading review." Situations of this nature escape dismissal for mootness.

SCOTUS avoided many cases on grounds such as fiction or deceit, failure to state a crisp injury, the amount of value at stake before docketing the case, lack of diversity, and failure to state a case or controversy. With the growth of the administrative state, Congress at first gave the Supreme Court final review of rate decisions, and so forth. SCOTUS again pointed out that the Constitution created the Supreme Court and that it did not have a legislative function. Congress could vest considerable powers in the Washington, D.C. Courts, but that could not include an appeal to SCOTUS.

Congress passed the Declaratory Judgment Act in 1934, giving new powers to the federal courts. SCOTUS found the grant constitutional; the judgement lacked the remedy typically associated with court decisions, but it did maintain the requirement that a real controversy exist. Article III created the Supreme Court; Congress had near-plenary power over the lower federal courts. The declaratory judgment was not and could not issue an advisory opinion. Congress gave the federal courts the ability to declare sides and other legal relations, which effectively broadened the definition of relief to include a declaration of rights and other legal relations.

The Court created the federal abstention judicial rule in 1941 as a vehicle for standing back and allowing state courts to first address state statutes of constitutional uncertainty, typically because they are overly broad. Sometimes, the courts can save a statute by interpreting its offending sections in such a way to narrow their meaning and thus pass constitutional muster. The typical federal court response to these statutes is to declare them void for vagueness. Allowing the state courts to tailor a statute through interpretation avoids the constitutional uncertainties that would trigger void for vagueness. SCOTUS would abstain pending state action unless the issue involves constitutional rights. SCOTUS appears to favor the lower federal courts issuing a declaratory judgment rather than an injunction, because the former gives the states more leeway and is more consistent with the comity rule.

Rehnquist votes with the majority in a case that allows civil servants the right to opinion but not the right to political activity. The prohibition on political activity was a confluence of restrictions in the Pendleton Act, the Hatch Act, rules produced by the Civil Service Commission and read into the Congressional Record, and finally the extension of these prohibitions to state civil service. The plaintiffs wanted to engage in party activities and political management, but SCOTUS upheld the Civil Service Commission rule. An interesting component of this case is that, case by case, the Civil Service Commission filled in the meaning of words and requirements in these various acts, codified them, and then Congress adopted its interpretation.

The federal attention to race protection drops after the Warren Court. When a state magistrate and circuit judge used bonds, sentencing, and trial charges against a group of black men, SCOTUS, with Rehnquist voting in the majority, decided that the plaintiffs had not made a claim that constituted a case or controversy. The plaintiffs' complaint was too general and did not indicate actual personal injury. SCOTUS did counsel that if any of the plaintiffs found himself in the situation they were complaining about, the writ of habeas corpus would always be available. The dissent in this case pointed out that none of the lower courts had found the case lacking in case or controversy. Further, the Court's foray into the equity problem constituted an advisory opinion.

Congress granted lands to several Western states, excluding mineral lands, that the states could sell, under strict conditions, to support school trusts for public education. Congress limited the mineral land exception to those known at the time, but Congress eventually extended this exception to all mineral lands. A later law allowed easy sale of hydrocarbon lands, prompting a suit between individual taxpayers and a teachers' association, on the one hand, and mineral and lessees, on the other. SCOTUS affirmed a state court decision that the removal of restrictions on hydrocarbon lands was unconstitutional. Rehnquist took issue with the majority on several grounds, starting with the standing of the original plaintiffs. Rehnquist also took issue when SCOTUS ruled that, even though the original plaintiffs would have no standing in federal court, the decision could come for review if the state court decision itself created direct and concrete injury to the party asking for SCOTUS review.

Rehnquist writes the decision in *Parratt*. The plaintiff files for deprivation of property without due process; SCOTUS reversed the lower court finding, requiring instead that a person must act under color of state law to deprive the person of rights. Rehnquist argued that there were no rights deprived in the prisoner's claim, and that the prisoner should pursue state tort procedures. The hidden assumption was, of course, that the state permits the prisoner to sue it or the state's subsidiary prison. A second prisoner case affirmed the same claim in the lower court and SCOTUS overturned. Rehnquist feels that he did not handle the problem of negligence well in his own *Parratt* decision six years earlier and overrules that part inconsistent with his decisions in this case, *Daniels*. Negligence that is the product of reasonable conduct is not a gross abuse of power. Once again, the prisoner must seek relief through tort law. It is simply unfortunate if the respondent had claimed insulation from tort law. SCOTUS requires intent, such as gross indifference, not simple negligence. A concurring note from Stevens makes it clear that, even if the prisoner may not gain recovery in state court, it still does not trigger a federal concern.

NOTE

1. The Advisory Opinion and the United States Supreme Court, 5 Fordham L. Rev. 94 (1936). Available at: h p://ir.lawnet.fordham.edu/ r/vol5/iss1/7.

Chapter 7

Standing, Ripeness, Political Question

STANDING

Restricting access to the federal courts results from a rule of justiciability called standing. One of the most egregious decisions of Court history occurs under an early assertion of non-standing. The Cherokee expected protection from the federal government against the intrusion of Georgia, but the President refused to provide assistance. An act of Congress in 1830 provided for an exchange of the lands west of the Mississippi for Indians residing east of the Mississippi, but only by voluntary approval. Georgia then passed a law to survey and dispose of lands within the limits of Georgia and occupied by the Cherokee. The state cancelled Cherokee contracts, then scheduled Cherokee improvements and possessions for disposal. The state further forbade anyone to act under pretense of authority of Cherokee laws. Georgia also sought to protect the gold mines and other valuable minerals for its own use.

The Cherokee formally sent a bill to the Supreme Court asking that it provide relief from these Georgia measures (*Cherokee Nation v. Georgia*, 30 U.S. 5 Pet. 1 (1831)). There is no question that Marshall understood what was happening:

> This bill is brought by the Cherokee Nation, praying an injunction to restrain the State of Georgia from the execution of certain laws of that State which, as is alleged, go directly to annihilate the Cherokees as a political society and to seize, for the use of Georgia, the lands of the Nation which have been assured to them by the United States in solemn treaties repeatedly made and still in force.

The Cherokee could seek remedy only if the Supreme Court had jurisdiction. While SCOTUS recognized the Cherokee as a state, they were not like the other states in the union. SCOTUS rejected the notion that the Cherokee were a foreign state. Marshall then labels them as domestic dependent nations; hence they are not giving standing before SCOTUS as a foreign nation or a state and they cannot maintain an action before the court. SCOTUS, Marshall concludes, is not the proper forum for the requested redress.

The concurrence written by Justice Johnson exacerbates the problem. The Cherokee have surrendered their sovereignty. The Hopewell treaty granted only hunting rights. The advancement of their interests beyond the hunter state cannot threaten the unquestioned rights of a state of the United States over that territory. Society in the hunter state bore the promise of vacating the territory when game ceased. A fixed state of society ties the Cherokee permanently to the soil and that amounts to a permanent destruction of Georgia's preemptive rights. No Indian tribe is a state, domestic or foreign. Johnson would reject the bill as a political question that lies outside the jurisdiction of the court. Georgia has the status of a sovereign state under the Constitution and has jurisdiction over the Indian Territory within her boundaries. The Indian assertion that they have rights is without foundation.

The Marshall court split on the Cherokee case decision. Justice Thompson, with the support of Justice Story, dissented. Much of the complaint, and the relief there desired, lies in the hands of the executive because these involve political power and thus it is a political question before the court. Nevertheless, if Georgia has infringed rights of person and property, the Court can grant partial relief. The Cherokee people are a sovereign state. They govern by their own laws, usages, and customs. The Cherokee had control of the land before the Europeans arrived. These were foreign nations to the Europeans. The Cherokee may sell land only to the United States under terms of various treaties, but they continue self-government and are in enjoyment of their land. As such, the Cherokee nation is not within the jurisdiction of Georgia laws. Our treaties give the Cherokee exclusive right of occupancy, and the United States legally must guarantee and protect that nation. The Court can interpose relief involving rights of person or property presented under judicial proceedings. They have not surrendered rights to their mines, so the Cherokee enjoy a full use and deployment of those resources. The Georgia act is repugnant to our treaties with the Cherokees and Georgia has infringed on the Cherokee rights of property.

In the second Cherokee case, *Worcester v. Georgia*, 31 U.S. 6 Pet. 515 (1832), also written by Marshall, Worcester was a missionary to the Cherokee Nation in Georgia and failed to vacate that part of Cherokee land attached by the state of Georgia. The state indicted and prosecuted him. Worcester claimed, in turn, that the laws of Georgia were repugnant to U.S. treaties with the Cherokee and thus were unconstitutional and void. The Superior Court of Gwinnet County, Georgia sentenced Worcester to prison for four years of hard labor. SCOTUS agreed that the Judicial Act of 1789 gave the Court jurisdiction by writ of error. In *Worcester*, SCOTUS argues that Georgia understood, as did other states, the federal government, and foreign powers that

> the universal conviction that the Indian nations possessed a full right to the lands they occupied until that right should be extinguished by the United States with their consent; that their territory was separated from that of any State within whose chartered limits they might reside by a boundary line established by treaties; that, within their boundary, they possessed rights with which no state could interfere; and that the whole power of regulating the intercourse with them was vested in the United States.

In *Worcester*, SCOTUS reviews its jurisdiction under the twenty-fifth section of the Judiciary Act, then confirms that the Cherokees are a distinct community, occupying their own territory, in which the laws of Georgia can have no force, and Georgians may not enter but by the consent of the Cherokees themselves. The intercourse with the Cherokees is between their nation and the federal government under our Constitution. The Georgia act convicting Worcester is null and void. Marshall further points out that protection does not imply the destruction of the protected. The Indian nations are distinct political communities. The Executive branch supported Georgia; the Worcester decision did not save the Cherokee nation.

Standing as Taxpayer

The struggles SCOTUS had with Cherokee standing appear in several areas of concern and, like the Cherokees, access to the Court is systematically restricted. SCOTUS eliminates an enormous constituency when it restricts or denies standing as a taxpayer of federal income tax, a direct tax made possible by the Sixteenth Amendment in 1913. For decades, the *Frothingham v. Mellon* case, combined with *Commonwealth of Massachusetts v. Mellon*, 262 U.S. 447 (1923), determined the standing, or perhaps better to say non-standing, of the taxpayer in federal lawsuits. Its initial focus was on the relation between federal and state sovereignty. Federal taxation fell on the individual, not on the state. At root there is an abstract question of political power and sovereignty, but that is far outside judicial cognizance.

A state may not wish to participate as *parens patriae* in a federal program. Under modern interpretations of the Fourteenth Amendment, citizenship lies in the United States; state citizenship derives from residence. In the instant case, a federal statute offered maternity care support to the states, but any state could choose not to participate. The maternity statute required nothing of the individual, except through taxation. SCOTUS finds that the plaintiff has failed to show that she has sustained or is in imminent danger of sustaining direct injury. Both lower courts had rejected the challenge. Millions of Americans share the relation of the taxpayer to monies in the federal treasury. Any individual relation is comparatively minute and indeterminable. Future taxation or payment of funds is remote, fluctuating, and uncertain. SCOTUS has no general authority over the acts of another branch of government under the separation of powers.

Flast v. Cohen, 392 U.S. 83 (1968) introduced a complication in the *Frothingham* rule. Plaintiffs sought a declaratory judgment that certain expenditures made under a federal statute violated the Establishment and Free Exercise Clauses of the First Amendment. The use of funding was either improperly authorized or else unconstitutionally permitted by an education act. The suit focused specifically on funds used in New York City. SCOTUS ruled that the Constitution did not automatically deny standing to taxpayers if they have the requisite personal stake. The taxpayers must first establish a logical link between that status and the statute under attack. They must also establish a nexus between taxpayer status and the alleged constitutional infringement of the taxing and spending power.

These taxpayers have standing because they alleged violation of a constitutional protection against the abuse of legislative power. If, as the respondent argued, the three-judge district court panel convened improperly because the plaintiffs focused only on New York City programs, then the entire effort would fail because the taxpayer would have to make a remote connection to the expenditures generally. SCOTUS ruled that the concentration on local programs simply gives specificity and focus to the issues; the relief sought would apply to a program that had the same unconstitutional features as that under challenge in New York City. Congress had passed legislation preventing a single federal judge from issuing a broad injunction. Had convening the three-judge panel been inappropriate, a sole district judge would not be able to act either. SCOTUS thus argued through a maze of restrictions designed to keep such a case off the Supreme Court agenda.

Now the question focuses on the *Frothingham* rule: Constitutional rule or judicial self-restraint? SCOTUS had previously granted standing for tax payers in municipalities, but the federal funding focused on the indeterminate nature of the relationship between taxpayer and program. *Frothingham* claimed that giving a federal tax payer standing would inundate the courts. SCOTUS argued in *Flast* that the existence of class action suits already mitigated that concern. Justiciability melds two concerns: the need for an adversary and an issue capable of resolution; keeping the federal courts from intruding on other branches of government. Political questions, advisory opinions, mootness, and standing are all possible limits on justiciability, but it is not a legal concept with fixed content. It cannot easily distinguish policy concerns from constitutional ones.

SCOTUS speaks of a two-prong nexus for federal tax payers to gain standing: there must be a logical link between taxpayer status and the type of legislative enactment under challenge; there must be a logical link between taxpayer status and the precise nature of the constitutional infringement claimed. SCOTUS interprets the first challenge to mean challenges of unconstitutionality of Congressional power under the Taxing and Spending Clause of Article I. In his concurring opinion, Justice Douglas calls for the overturning of *Frothingham*. Most state courts grant standing as taxpayers. Justice Fortas wants to limit standing for taxpayers only to claims on the Establishment Clause. In his dissent, Justice Harlan argues that the majority seems to have made a distinction between rights that are specific limitations and rights that are not. The simple solution is for Congress to give individual litigants the standing to represent the public interest in the authorization of the statute.

Standing and Campaigning

The *Frothingham* developments aside, there is a notable interaction between declaratory judgments and standing in *United Public Workers v. Mitchell*, 330 U.S. 75 (1947). This is a direct appeal from a three-judge district court panel denying an injunction. SCOTUS took jurisdiction even though not docketed in a timely manner. One set of plaintiffs were employees in the executive branch who wanted the Civil Service Commission stopped from enforcing certain articles of the Hatch Act taking away their right to engage in political management and political campaigns, and to issue a declaratory judgment against that section of the Hatch Act.

One of the complaints did not present a justiciable case or controversy because plaintiffs admitted no violation of the act or threat of removal. In another complaint, the plaintiff-employees had violated the Hatch Act and another faced removal. That complaint was justiciable. The Act made removal mandatory without administrative or statutory review or no prior court proceedings, so a declaratory judgment does lie within jurisdiction, but SCOTUS decided against taking it because the breach was subject to disciplinary action without violating the Constitution. The Hatch Act does not prohibit participation at the ballot box, only activity the government finds offensive to efficiency.

SCOTUS also lectures that the judicial power is most effective and respective of separation of powers if it refuses to get involved in ill-defined controversies. When sufficiently defined, the issue becomes whether the political sovereign can impair the rights of individual classified employees, even if not absolute, for protection of a democratic society against the evils of political partisanship in undermining efficiency and management. Justice Jackson would have dismissed the sole qualifying plaintiff for untimely appeal. In his dissent, Justice Black reveals that the Hatch Act affects approximately three million federal jobs alone, with permanent bar against reemployment in that position, to say nothing of the thousands of state workers so affected. The prohibition against political management and campaigns joins a long list of other acts forbidden, such as expressing views at a party caucus, soliciting votes, participating in a political parade, or even publishing a letter, signed or unsigned, pro or con, involving a party, candidate, or faction. The challenged provision should be unconstitutional on its face. The prohibitions are vague, broad, ambiguous, and uncertain in their consequences. Justice Douglas similarly questions whether our laws should insulate government employees from American political life?

Standing and the Environment

The mismatch between cases and controversies versus appeals for the public interest becomes quite clear about standing for environmental concerns in *Sierra Club v. Morton*, 405 U.S. 727 (1972). An early leader of the modern environmental movement, the Sierra Club requested an injunction stopping a federal agency from approving a ski development in a federally protected-area and a declaratory judgment protecting national parks, game refuges, and the forests of the country. The Administrative Procedures Act gave court standing to a person suffering legal wrong because of an agency action. The decision must adversely affect or aggrieve the plaintiff person within the meaning of the statute.

The issue here is whether a corporation could act on behalf of the public, and whether adverse effects on aesthetics and ecology fall within the affected or aggrieved requirement. The district court issued a preliminary injunction and the court of appeals reversed. SCOTUS ruled that a person or corporation must demonstrate personal injury or imminent injury but added aesthetic and environmental well-being to economic well-being as injuries-in-fact. SCOTUS ruled that the Sierra Club did not have standing. The Sierra Club brief did not claim that any member of the organization had used the development site. Allowing the Sierra Club to claim a special interest as grounds for standing would eviscerate the standing limitation. Finding a lack of standing, SCOTUS did not consider the case on its merits. It would not take environmental groups long to realize that they could get standing in court simply by having some of their members claim that they use or have visited the area in question. Rehnquist did not to participate in the deliberations.

Justice Douglas' dissent would grant the Sierra their preservation. Giving standing to an inanimate object is like a ship with a fictional personality in Maritime Law. Judicial processes already consider a corporation as a person. Congress may claim to act in the public interest, but it often becomes captive of those it seeks to regulate. Much the same applies to regulatory agencies. Inarticulate members of an ecological group cannot speak for themselves; they need someone to speak for them. There is a case or controversy here. In his dissent, Justice Blackmun points out that a rigid and inflexible response to problems that challenge present methods and concepts leaves an emergent problem to irreparable harm and the bell tolls for all of us.

In two back-to-back cases, *Vermont Yankee Nuclear Power Corp. v. NRDC*, 435 U.S. 519 (1978) and *Duke Power Co. v. Carolina Env. Study Group*, 438 U.S. 59 (1978), Rehnquist opposes district court oversight of the Atomic Energy Commission or Nuclear Regulatory Commission. Rehnquist pens the decision in *Vermont Yankee* and writes a concurrence in *Duke*. In both instances, Rehnquist argues that the case is not justiciable and that the court of appeals and/or the district court has gone too far. In *Vermont Yankee*, two issues ultimately focused the suit: how the AEC handled environmental impact and how it handled energy conservation. The appeals court argued that the AEC used inadequate rulemaking procedures regarding environmental impact and then licensing. During the process, the Council on Environmental Quality added energy conservation to the issues considered under environmental impact. The SCOTUS majority held that the courts were not free to impose additional procedural rights than those specified by Congress. SCOTUS scolded the court of appeals for going beyond its simple review powers and exploring "best procedures" as it saw fit. The Administrative Procedures Act sets standards and Congress has given considerable discretion to agencies charged with substantive judgments.

In *Duke Power*, Congress imposed liability limits in the event of a nuclear accident. The plaintiff wanted this law declared unconstitutional, because the corporation would not have built the nuclear plant but for a limitation on liability. SCOTUS found that the plaintiffs had standing, that there was sufficient evidence of imminent harm, and that the "but for" argument satisfied the relief prong of the constitutional requirement for cases and controversies. Judging the case on its merits, SCOTUS declined any constitutional relief under the Fifth Amendment and Due Process and Equal Protection Clauses of the Fourteenth Amendment. SCOTUS therefore overturned the district court decision. In his concurrent decision, Rehnquist agreed in reversing the district court decision and sending the case back for dismissal for lack of justiciability. In later cases, Rehnquist will take great issue with "but for" arguments and eventually try to forbid their use. The logic here is invidious: if the cause of the injury is a law, removing the law may not constitute relief.

Standing and Civil Rights

While the court was denying standing to environmental groups, it also denied standing to citizens complaining of a violation of their constitutional rights. The domineering relation between the British military and American colonists led to a deep suspicion of the military in civilian life, reflected even in making the President of the United States the Commander in Chief of the Armed Forces. After the urban riots in 1968, the Pentagon had the army conduct surveillance on citizens through various electronic means, and so forth. Civilian citizens complained that such surveillance chilled their constitutional rights to free speech as well as the fundamental understanding that the military should have no role in civilian life. The case came before SCOTUS in *Laird v. Tatum*, 408 U.S. 1 (1972). The court majority, including Rehnquist, concluded that this type of data gathering, and surveillance, had too distant a relation with constitutional rights, and that therefore the plaintiffs could not demonstrate objective harm or immediate harm, so the issue was non-justiciable. The army surveillance covered a variety of groups and individuals. Army intelligence agents attended public meetings and wrote field reports. The district court dismissed the quest for a preliminary injunction and decided that the citizens had not demonstrated any injury or realistic threats growing from the army action. The court of appeals reversed, citing

> the *present existence of this system* of gathering and distributing information, allegedly far beyond the mission requirements of the army, constitutes an impermissible burden on [respondents] and other persons similarly situated which exercises a *present inhibiting effect* on their full expression and utilization of their First Amendment rights.

SCOTUS reversed the court of appeals; it felt that the lower court had properly identified the issue, whether a complainant argued a chilling effect by existence of a governmental investigating and data-gathering activity, perhaps broader in scope than necessary but nevertheless a valid governmental goal, has met the requirements needed to invoke jurisdiction of the federal court. Unlike the court of appeals, the Court majority found that the situation did not merit jurisdiction. The majority further argued that the complaint distilled to a simple disagreement with the judgment of the executive branch.

Justices Douglas and Marshall vehemently disagreed. There is no law granting such power to the military and there is no constitutional basis for it. The American tradition favors civilian supremacy over the military power. The army allegedly has files on membership, ideology, programs, and practices of activist political groups, even including the Southern Christian Leadership Conference. The complainants charge that this intelligence gathering system harasses, intimidates, and deters citizens from exercising their constitutional rights. The dissenting justices found this to be a constitutional intrusion. The present controversy is neither remote nor imaginary. The army intelligence reports were massive and widely distributed. Civilian surveillance is not the constitutional business of the army, and Congress has not entrusted that business to them. Justice Douglas refers to it as a cancer in our body politic. Ours is a history of rebellion, not of submission.

Ideological differences are often quite apparent when SCOTUS invokes a problem of justiciability. Just after the bitterly divisible Vietnam War, an association of four armed forces reserves opposed to the Vietnam War, plus some members of self-described taxpayers, filed an Incompatibility Clause bill against members of Congress who were also members of the reserve in *Schlesinger v. Reservists Committee*, 418 U.S. 208 (1974). That clause, in Article I, forbids anyone holding an office under the United States from being a member of either house of Congress. Both the district court and the appellate court found that the taxpayers had no standing, but both courts held that the former members of the armed forces reserve did have standing.

SCOTUS denied standing to both. The taxpayer finding was not surprising, because it is very difficult to establish a connection between the status of tax payer and the claims being adjudicated. For the former members of the Armed Forces reserve, SCOTUS called the violation of the Incompatibility Clause an abstract injury, locating only the generalized interest of all citizens, and hence the suit fails to rise to the level of a case or controversy. SCOTUS reasoned that none of the plaintiffs had a judicially cognizable injury. The Constitution leaves many questions to the political process; it does not matter if no one would have a standing to sue on this topic. Rehnquist joined the majority decision. The plaintiffs sought dismissal of members of Congress from the armed forces reserve and recovery of back-pay, an injunction against enrolling anyone in the armed forces reserve while serving in Congress, and a declaration that membership in the reserves is an officer under the United States. Application of the Incompatibility Clause in this case focused on potential undue pressure from the executive because a congressperson also served in the reserve, or a conflict of interest and obligation between duties as a member of Congress and duties as a member of the armed forces reserve. The lower courts found members of Congress ineligible to hold a commission in the reserve but denied relief on the other components of the request.

The dissenting opinions constructed the problem quite differently. Justice Douglas cited three ends that the judicially created instrument of justiciability might serve: the first two of these we have heard often, namely, that it is a political question and best left to another branch of government or that it clears court dockets of abstract questions or questions involving no case or controversy. It is the third, however, that makes justiciability itself political: protecting the status quo by reducing the challenges to its institutions and greatly restricting the classes of people who may challenge administrative action. The original statement against taxpayers' standing is *Commonwealth of Massachusetts v. Mellon*, 262 U.S. 447 (1923) (and *Frothingham v. Mellon*). The liability of any tax payer for the costs of the statute is indefinite regarding direct injury and constantly changing; it belongs to the political branches of government.

Forty-five years later, in *Flast v. Cohen*, 392 U.S. 83 (1968), the tax payer does have standing: here, the tax payer is challenging Congressional power under the Taxing and Spending Clause of Article I, rather than the incidental expenditure in the administration of a regulatory statute; further, the challenge focuses on an enactment exceeding Congress' taxing and spending power. In the *Flast* case, the taxpayer had the required personal stake, and the Establishment Clause imposed a specific limitation on the taxing and spending power of Congress.

The *Schlesinger* case rested on both the Taxing and Spending Clause and the Incompatibility Clause. This is not against members of Congress but rather against the Secretary of Defense and the armed services members of Congress who hold commissions as reservists. Whatever be the reason, the Constitution establishes barriers against certain types of affiliations and certain types of appropriations, freeing the federal bureaucracy from an entitlement with the legislative branch. It must be a personal stake. SCOTUS cannot deny standing simply because many people suffer the same injury. Justice Brennan repeats an observation that standing focuses on the status of the plaintiff, not whether the issue is justiciable. Justice Marshall argues that members of the armed forces reserve may be of different opinions, but each side deserves to have their arguments considered by Congress members, free of conflict of interest. One side risks their freedom of expression compromised by the entanglement of the other side. This is a direct and concrete injury.

Standing and Zoning

The ideological use of standing to narrow the pathway into court continues in *Warth v. Seldin*, 422 U.S. 490 (1975). SCOTUS agreed with both lower courts. Five sets of plaintiffs lacked standing, three on the original bill and two trying to join it. The complaint holds that zoning ordinances and their application discriminated against low and moderate-income families, keeping these out of town. The plaintiffs on the original action include a nonprofit organization aimed at alleviating the housing shortage for low and moderate income people in the larger metropolitan area, several individual taxpayers, several area residents with low and moderate incomes who were also members of minority and ethnic groups, and two attempted to join the complaint, one an association of home builders in the area and the other a county organization representing a number of organizations interested in housing problems. SCOTUS found that none of these plaintiffs or potential plaintiffs met the requirement of standing, either because there was no case or controversy or because the grievance was too general. Plaintiffs against exclusionary zoning practices must allege concrete harm that would benefit by court intervention. The court also argued that the line of causation was too attenuated, or that some plaintiffs were advocating relief for people other than themselves. Of the two who seek addition to the complaint, one alleged no monetary injury to itself and the other demonstrated no or little record of involvement with the respondents. Rehnquist joined with the majority.

Standing and Taxes

SCOTUS extends its taxation bar to standing in *Simon v. Eastern Kentucky Welf. Rights. Org.*, 426 U.S. 26 (1976). Rehnquist again voted with the majority. Several low-income individuals and organizations brought action against the Secretary of the Treasury and the Commissioner of the Internal Revenue for giving favorable tax treatment to hospitals that did not serve indigents according to the financial ability of the institution. The district court overruled a petition to dismiss, including an effort to question the plaintiffs' standing. The court of appeals found standing, but upheld favorable tax treatment for hospitals, even if they did not serve the indigenous to the extent they were financially responsible.

SCOTUS dismissed on standing. Specific individuals failed to show a personal injury redress able by a favorable decision on the tax treatment. An abstract interest cannot substitute for a concrete injury. The organizational complainant had no standing. The individual respondents filed against the U.S. Treasury instead of the offending hospitals, thus leaving little trace between the alleged injuries and the potential sources. The distance between the denial of service and favorable tax codes is far too attenuated than alleged; the plaintiff must show causality between individual injury, traced back to tax policy, and whether a change in tax policy would change or provide remedy for the alleged injury. Individuals cannot attack the tax liability of others when their own liability is not at stake. The court may offer redress only when the injury is traceable to the challenged action, not the independent action by some party not before the court.

Justice Brennan wrote a blistering concurrent opinion that the case simply was not ripe, needing some further contingency, interpretation, or application to bring this before the court. If there is an alleged personal injury, it would provide a constitutionally mandated personal stake sufficient to create the concrete adverseness necessary for Article III justiciability. It is not standing, but the immediacy of future harm. There is nothing in the record that indicates the contested revenue rule, which removes the no- or low-cost requirement but only applies to a subset of nonprofit hospitals, altered the operation of all tax-exempt hospitals. There is nothing in the IRS ruling that encourages nonprofit hospitals seeking tax exempt status to shed their indigent services. The accusation is not ripe because it lacks instantiation. The Court inappropriately forces a chain of causality that is unnecessary for an Article III demonstration. It assumes that the government action complained of encourages hospitals to provide fewer medical services to indigents, and the Court does this to make that demonstration a prerequisite for any legal claims on the revenue ruling. Thus, the hospitals would be dependent upon the revenue ruling; without it, there would be no encouragement, and that without it the services would be available.

The injury is to low income peoples' opportunity and ability to receive medical service. On this issue, there is an allegation of insufficient injury. The Court instead has argued that, were it not for the revenue ruling, free or below cost medical services would have been available. What SCOTUS demands is not determinative of a hospital's future conduct; matters like changes in the economic climate, donor contributions, or potential threats of future illegal policy determinations and so on may change determinations. The question is not understanding the past but immediacy of a future threat or future encouragement. Had the record demonstrated in any way that the tax-exempt status related to the tax ruling, it would entitle the plaintiff to judgment; alternately if not, summary judgment against them would have been in order. The only constitutionally mandated elements of standing are a personal stake that creates concrete adversity. The Court instead adds a further injury-in-fact dimension, that electing to forgo favorable tax treatment would result in free or below cost of medical services. Based on unrestricted discretion given to itself, and its vague holdings on "zone of interests" or "fatally speculative pleadings," the Court may decline to adjudicate claims that it does not wish to hear.

Abood v. Detroit Bd. of Educ., 431 U.S. 209 (1977) serves as an interesting comparison with the *Elrod v. Burns*, 427 U.S. 347 (1976) case. Michigan statutes allow an agency shop for local government employees, that is, those represented by a union in collective bargaining must pay fees even if they are not members of the union. Plaintiffs wanted to avoid these service fees because they oppose the political support offered by the union to various candidates, and because they oppose collective bargaining and other matters related to unions. They did not appear willing to negotiate individual contracts at a level below the collective bargaining agreement. This is a classic example of the collective action problem, where free riders wish to partake of the benefits of collective action without helping to pay for it. SCOTUS ruled the agency shop valid and the union could collect fees for collective-bargaining, contract administration, and grievance adjustment purposes. The plaintiff argued that public employment required surrender of First and Fourteenth Amendment rights. SCOTUS points out that unionization does not bar public employees from expressing their viewpoint. The union may not extract that portion of fees spent on ideological clauses not germane to its activities as a collective bargaining agent. Although required to pay the service fee, those opposed to unions or participation in union affairs do not have to do so. The plaintiffs did not wish to pay the service fee, even though they benefited from the collective bargaining contract.

The district court rejected a request for summary judgment against the agency shop clause because the plaintiff failed to specify an actionable claim for relief. While on appeal, the Michigan Supreme Court in another case ruled against the agency shop, but the Michigan legislature expressly authorized an agency shop. The Michigan Court of Appeals ruled that the legislative amendment permitting the agency shop was not retroactive. The same court ruled that the agency shop is consistent with Michigan law and federal law, except for its expenditure for lobbying and political candidates. SCOTUS observed that the plaintiffs should have made their objections to the union as their first course of action. Congress had, nevertheless, found the agency shop conducive to industrial peace. This is not to suggest, however, that public employment is conditional upon forfeiture of First Amendment rights. Unions may engage in political activities beyond their duties as collective bargaining agents, but that portion of its activities must use voluntary funds. Relief goes only to those who have affirmatively opposed the use of funds for political purposes, namely the fraction of the service fees spent on political purposes returned to the plaintiffs. SCOTUS encouraged unions to adopt a voluntary plan, giving dissenters an internal remedy. Using the internal remedy provides restitution without the attendant problem of making one's political preferences public. A concurring opinion, to which Rehnquist is not a party, argued that each expenditure requires justification for collective bargaining purposes, rather than place the burden on the individual to identify objectionable ideological activities to get a rebate.

Rehnquist joins the dissent in *Elrod*, agreeing that patronage was long part of the American tradition and may indeed have contributed to democratization. He further sided with the observation that those who had taken advantage of patronage could not fairly ask for the end of patronage once it is their turn to lose the privilege. Rehnquist compares the patronage system to the collective bargaining arrangement and argues that he sees no constitutional distinction between the requirement that a public employee be Democrat or Republican, or else lose one's job, and the requirement that an employee contribute to collective bargaining expenses. Rehnquist feels his concurrence in *Abood* is consistent with his dissent in *Elrod*.

Standing and the Bill of Rights

Alleged violations of rights enumerated in the Constitution also provide little basis for standing before the Supreme Court. In an increasingly ill-tempered decision written by Justice Rehnquist, *Valley Forge Coll. v. Americans United*, 454 U.S. 464 (1982), SCOTUS swept away objection to transferring surplus property, free of charge using a public benefit allowance, to a religious institution for its use in post-high school education. The transfer involved seventy-seven acres of land northwest of Philadelphia, which was part of a 181-acre parcel used for the army's Valley Forge General Hospital. The plaintiff, an organization and individuals for separation of church and state, sued to have the land transferred back to the federal government because it violated the Establishment Clause of the First Amendment. The district court dismissed the complaint for lack of standing to sue as taxpayers and failure to identify an actual or concrete injury, citing *Flast v. Cohen*, 392 U.S. 83 (1968). The court of appeals agreed that status as taxpayers gave only a miniscule interest in the disposition of the property and hence offered only a generalized grievance rather than an actual or concrete injury. The court of appeals still overturned the district court decision, holding that the plaintiffs had standing as citizens injured by a violation of the First Amendment. The court of appeals found standing, injury in fact, and a complaint satisfying the cases and controversies requirement. A dissenting judge on the appeals court would grant standing to render the Establishment Clause enforceable. The dissenting judge then concluded that the complaint was a generalized grievance too abstract to satisfy injury in fact.

Rehnquist emphasized the need for cases or controversies. Judging the legal rights of litigants in actual controversies defines the constitutional power of federal courts. Standing requires (1) an actual or threatened personal injury resulting from illegal conduct and (2) the link between the injury and illegal conduct is traceable and (3) likely redress able by a favorable decision. Rehnquist further argues that (4) the separation of powers confines the judicial power to cases traditionally thought to be resolvable by the judicial process. Standing requires an actual injury redress able by the Court. It cannot be an abstract debate but a concrete factual context with a realistic appreciation of the consequences of judicial action. Rather than a vehicle for the vindication of the interests, standing gives due regard for the autonomy of those most likely affected by a judicial order.

Exercised unwisely, declaring a legislative or executive act unconstitutional ultimately threatens the continued effectiveness of the federal courts. The courts should also refrain from passing on the constitutionality of an act unless obliged to do so. Third parties cannot assert the rights of plaintiffs. The Court does not consider abstract questions or generalized grievances.

A plaintiff's complaint must fall within a protected or regulated zone of interest. The status of tax payer allows standing only if power exercises under the Taxing and Spending Clause. Even so, the taxpayer needs to show that the exercise of power is beyond that delegated to Congress. Taxpayers in the instant case lack standing because they attacked an order issued by an executive department, rather than attacking the underlying congressional act. The act allowing the transfer of property was not under the Taxing and Spending Clause, but rather under the Property Clause of Article IV.

The circuit court of appeals found that the plaintiff did have standing, not on the grounds of taxpayers, but rather on the grounds of separation of church and state, that is, the desired to live in a country where there is strict separation between church and state. SCOTUS, however, routinely rejects standing based on the rights possessed by every citizen to expect that the government act according to the laws. Standing focuses on the party wishing to come before the federal court, not the issues that they raise. Nor is standing measured by the intensity of point of view. Someone injured in fact contributes to the concrete adversity of the case, but this does not substitute for the injury itself. The possibility that no one would have standing to sue under the Establishment Clause, if the current plaintiffs did not have standing, is still no reason to grant standing. SCOTUS thus overrules the second criterion (giving standing) of the circuit court of appeals.

Standing is a gateway to the federal courts, but the dissenting opinions of Brennan and Stevens in this case helps focus on major points of disagreement. The courts disregard their constitutional duty when they use standing to bar access seeking constitutional protections. The injury in fact requirement permits a personal stake in the outcome of a controversy that assures concrete adverseness sharpening the presentation of views. Precedents have identified two principles for standing: the plaintiff has suffered or has a threat to suffer a distinct and palpable injury; there is some causal connection between the asserted injury and the defendant's actions. Instead of blind application, what constitutes an injury may include the nature and the source of the claim asserted. The court engages in a disassembling exercise that denies a hearing on a constitutional violation. The Founding Fathers surely intended that the beneficiaries of the Bill of Rights should be able to have legal enforcement in the courts. One perverse conclusion is that a federal court bars someone simply because the alleged violation aggrieves many others. The majority uses a two-pronged test to differentiate *Frothingham* from *Flast*: plaintiff's alleged injury as a tax payer and the alleged violation of the Establishment or Free Exercise Clause of the First Amendment. There is one forbidden exception to the rule that Congress can spend on anything it so desires: a church or religion may not use tax money to support a church or a religion.

The Valley Forge case rejected standing for taxpayers or citizens objecting to a violation of the Establishment Clause. Because establishment is the only spending prohibition in the Bill of Rights, a failure of standing in such a rights case presages the outcome for other policy arenas as well. This is precisely what happens in *Allen v. Wright*, 468 U.S. 737 (1984), albeit with a slight twist. The Internal Revenue Service had authority to deny tax-exempt status to racially discriminatory private schools. Plaintiffs, parents of black students in "desegregated" public schools, argued that the IRS had not developed and applied standards sufficient to accomplish the congressional intent, and that failure to do so allowed private schools with tax exempt status to siphon off white children who otherwise would attend the "desegregated" public schools, resulting in a de facto segregation of the public schools and thus depriving the black children of an integrated schooling. The district court dismissed the complaint; the circuit court of appeals reversed; SCOTUS reversed the appeals court. The plaintiffs had no standing to pursue the complaint. This time around, SCOTUS used the argument that this is a political question and thus Court intervention would violate the separation of powers. The pattern becomes clearer: asserted violations of law are insufficient to grant standing. A violation of equal protection is no exception. SCOTUS does admit that that the failure to get a racially integrated education is a judicially cognizable injury, but it denies a sufficient connection between their school segregation and the IRS tax exemption. The plaintiff would also have to establish that, but for the tax exemption, the private school would alter its policy, or the parent or parents of the white students would remain in the public school. Finally, the faithful execution of the laws lies with the Executive branch.

The black parents pointed out that the IRS requires certification but not implementation of non-discriminatory policies. Perhaps more to point, these private schools expanded with the desegregation order, thus giving white students more opportunity to flee their public school. The consequence is that the white flight to private schools counteracted any efforts at public school desegregation. The tax-exempt status allows the deduction of contributions to these private schools from income taxes. The black parents did not want entry to these private schools; rather, they wanted an effective desegregation plan for their local public schools undefeated, de facto, by white flight to private schools. The black parents asked for prospective relief. Denying the IRS tax exemptions would make alternatives to public school less economically attractive, if not prohibitive. While the case was languishing in the lower courts, the IRS reviewed its rules and proposed tightening them. Congress forbade any changes, for a limited time. It was this intervention of Congress that gave SCOTUS the separation of powers argument.

Justice O'Connor for the majority repeats the oft-cited phrase that the cases-or-controversies doctrine fundamentally limits federal judicial power.

Among the self-imposed limits on justiciability, standing requires the plaintiff to allege personal injury traceable to the defendant's unlawful conduct and that the requested relief likely will provide redress. Even though the various concepts in this requirement are not susceptible of precise definition, evolving case law has given considerable definition. An asserted right to have the government act in one way or another does not establish a judicially cognizable injury. The same applies to an argument about racial denigration; a claimant must demonstrate personal denial of equal treatment. The claim that the plaintiff's children had a diminished capacity to receive an integrated education is a judicially cognizable injury. The current plaintiffs do not meet standing because there is at best a tenuous link between the alleged injury and the illegal conduct. A federal court is not the proper forum for complaints about what the government does or how it goes about its business. Finally, the plaintiff must stand to profit personally by invoking the judicial power.

Justice Brennan's dissent follows much the same as that found in *Valley Forge*. SCOTUS uses standing to slam the courthouse door against hearing the plaintiff's claim on its merits. Standing, of itself, does not raise issues of separation of powers. The plaintiffs seek an injunction requiring the IRS to stop giving tax exempt status to private schools with little or no minority enrollment, located in desegregating school districts, established around the time desegregation began, are racially segregated, or cannot demonstrate that they are not aiding and abetting educational opportunities for white students that help them avoid desegregating schools. The IRS rule change that Congress blocked is quite similar. The plaintiffs' children have a distinct and palpable injury in the inability to receive a desegregated education. The complaint lists three links between the injury and IRS tax exemption: (1) recognition as a charitable organization fosters the development, operation, and expansion of racially segregated private schools; (2) the federal tax exemptions put a federal stamp of approval on racially segregated private schools; (3) these schools undermine the authority to desegregate. Despite the SCOTUS claim to the contrary, the plaintiffs provided quite specific information on school districts where there is a desegregation order and enough racially discriminatory private schools receiving tax exemptions to make an appreciable difference. The causation component of SCOTUS' standing inquiry is a disguise for the Court's view of the underlying merits: indifference.

Justice Stevens, joined by Justice Blackmun, cites the three propositions he feels are clear in the complaint: (1) injury in fact; (2) injury is traceable to the alleged illegal activity; (3) the separation of powers is not an obstacle. SCOTUS has already ruled that tax exemptions and tax deductibility are forms of subsidy that are like cash grants. These subsidies promote some activity. Withdrawing the subsidy changes the incentive structure facing white parents. Constitutionally, the state must steer clear of racially segregated schools and not give significant aid to institutions that practice racial or invidious discrimination. It is the judicial department that must say what the law is. The Court should judge the petition for legal limits on IRS decisions on its merits. The court makes an untenable assumption that tax exemptions and tax deductions do not make private schools more attractive to white students. These exemptions and deductions inhibit the process of desegregation.

The Court developed the justiciability barrier, so they could control the case flow into the courts. Rules evolve for each branch of justiciability. Precedent would suggest that the Court's wiggle-room shrinks with its pronouncements. Sometimes, however, there is an outlier that suggests outside pressure. In *Department of Commerce v. United States House of Representatives*, 525 U.S. 316 (1999), Justice O'Connor announces a decision on standing that deserves close attention. The case arises because the Census Bureau, knowing that some groups had been systematically undercounted, announced that it would supplement the census with statistical sampling. Congress had been hostile to statistical sampling, in part because the under counted groups included some minorities, children, and renters. Two suits arose against the use of statistical sampling. Interestingly, the main affidavit supporting the plaintiffs was a statistical analysis. The first set of plaintiffs were four counties and the residents of thirteen states. The U.S. House of Representatives filed the second suit. The lower courts ruled that the plaintiffs in both cases met the requirements of standing. These courts found that the Census Bureau plan violated the Census Act. These courts granted summary judgment and permanently enjoined the Census Bureau from using statistical sampling to determine population for Congressional Districts.

SCOTUS combined both suits. Each set of plaintiffs had to meet the three requirements that establish standing. Justice O'Connor accepted as injury-in-fact that Indiana faced losing a congressional seat in the 2000 census, and they would surely lose it if the statistical census of the undercounted were to take place. She continues that there is a traceable connection between the use of sampling and Indiana's expected loss of a representative. Finally, upholding the permanent injunction would give Indiana relief. There is no discussion that the shift of population during the last decade of the twentieth century likely deprived Indiana of one of the representatives anyway. O'Connor simply asserts that there is undoubtedly a traceable connection between the use of sampling and Indiana's loss of a representative. She further asserts that the permanent injunction would redress Indiana's loss of a representative, presumably meaning that the results of the 2000 census without sampling would preserve Indiana's representative. The plaintiffs had argued that the sampling would change the state legislative districts in Indiana, thus diluting the votes of those who have it now and do not wish to fix the undercount. SCOTUS thus seems to affirm the claim of diluted voting because some counties have less undercount than others.

The logic here conjures some of the losing reasoning in *Baker v. Carr*. It is possible that SCOTUS had a technology bias, but the decision clearly lacked the intended reforms of *Baker* and *Reynolds*. Although several changes in the census act allowed the use of statistical sampling, SCOTUS concludes that this procedure could not count people in allocating congressional seats because it was not part of the Framers' intentions, presumably because the technology did not exist backed by a narrow construction of "enumeration." The favorable judgment for the first set of plaintiffs removed any federal question for the second set of plaintiffs, and they dismissed that case. Indiana lost the seat anyway.

RIPENESS

Ripeness conjures the adage that we shall drink no wine before its time. How is it, and who is it, that knows when it is time to drink the wine? To be sure, sometimes the criminal, like young wine, are evident, but that does not free us of due process. Indeed, the redundancy in obvious cases is a small price to pay in a free society for the many instances where reasonable doubt is the starting point; we start with reasonable doubt before concluding beyond reasonable doubt.

Ripeness is a rule of justiciability. Like the other rules, it is part of the gateway system by which the Court controls the flow of cases and controversies. The lack of definiteness is clear when SCOTUS invokes ripeness where the lower courts found none, and vice versa. The ambiguity lies in the wide range of issues before the Court and the complexity of the problems entailed. That same ambiguity and complexity allows the Court substantial leeway in assessing ripeness as an element of justiciability. The applicability of ripeness clusters in different policy arenas.

Energy

Thousands of miles of high pressure gas pipelines built to carry pressurized gas from the fields to users, often crossed state lines. Since Congress has plenary control over interstate commerce, the federal government provided the forum for controversies. One touchy issue, occurring time and again, is the state effort to maintain product until meeting domestic demand before allowing the product into interstate commerce. In *Pennsylvania v. West Virginia*, 262 U.S. 553 (1923), the legislature of West Virginia voted to meet all domestic natural gas demand before putting the remainder into pipe trunk lines to Pennsylvania and Ohio. Several public institutions had become dependent upon West Virginia natural gas for heating and lighting. The West Virginia legislative vote threatens to cut off natural gas supplies, leading to these lawsuits. SCOTUS ruled that the complaint was justiciable because it arose from controversy between two states engaged in interstate commerce. The West Virginia statute had just gone into effect when the states asked it declared unconstitutional and that a permanent injunction issue. SCOTUS pointed out that the commerce clause prevented invidious restraint, interference, and other forms of hostile laws. The producing state cannot enforce preference for local consumption at the cost of interstate businesses.

The plaintiffs argue irreparable injury if the statute remains in force. SCOTUS found that the suit met every element of a case or controversy. The suit does not ask an advisory opinion but an injunction against the withdrawal of natural gas. Each plaintiff represents the public facility or school threatened with the interference and the consumer public. The suits came a few days after the statute went into effect, but before the state public service commission made its order according to the law. The injury was pending, and it did not require waiting until enforcement of the threatened injury. A deeply divided court held that the suits were not premature. In the matter of interstate commerce, we are all one people, and natural resources in one are available to all. If one state has it, all states have it. Justice Holmes, in his dissent, articulated the opinion that, until the gas starts to a point outside the state, the state may regulate it. Thus, Holmes does not see any constitutional prohibition on states securing preferences for its own residents. Holmes would accept jurisdiction, then dismiss the bill. Justice McReynolds argues that the case is not even justiciable. Justice Brandeis argued that the suit did not even meet the requirements for a case or controversy; that the mere enactment of a statute does not constitute a threat; that twelve privately owned public service corporations deliver or fail to deliver the gas across state line, yet there is no evidence about the intent of these corporations; and that there is no clear and present danger. Plaintiff fears were at best premature. Absent the necessary inquiries needed for an equitable decision, he would dismiss the bills.

Schools

Exceptions prove the rule, and a particularly valuable exception is *Pierce v. Society of Sisters*, 268 U.S. 510 (1925). The state of Oregon passed a law requiring all children between 8 and 16 to attend public schools. The plaintiff, the Society of Sisters, was a religious corporation offering parochial schooling and directly affected by the Oregon law. Corporations by this time have the status of persons, but not rights, per se. The Society had rights under the Fourteenth Amendment and that, although the interest of corporations in customers was typically not enough to overcome an action of the state, neither were barriers to the plaintiff's request for an injunction. SCOTUS acted before the injury occurred, because the threat was present and real before the "unconstitutional" statute went into effect. Thus, the suit was not premature.

The amendment to the Oregon school law resulted from a state-wide initiative adopted by the people. The initiative permitted limited exceptions, and certainly not for religious-based schools. In addition to the topics normally taught in public schools, there is also systematic religious instruction and moral training according to the tenets of the Roman Catholic Church. The Society made a profit on its schools, and the compulsory education act threatened that income. There is a similar complaint filed by a military academy providing education for boys between five and twenty-one years old. The three-judge panel below issued a temporary restraining order, defining the right to conduct schools as property and the state law a deprivation or property without the due process of law under the Fourteenth Amendment. SCOTUS ruled that the initiative unreasonably interfered with the liberty of parents and guardians to direct the education and up-bringing up children.

Zoning

Two cases after the Society of Sisters follow a more standard pattern. In *Village of Euclid v. Ambler Realty Co.*, 272 U.S. 365 (1926), the plaintiff sought to enjoin a zoning ordinance that would affect the resale value of some property, that is, the deprivation of liberty and property without due process of law. SCOTUS proposed three principles in such cases: the courts could examine the ordinance in its entirety but not bit by bit; the meaning of constitutional guarantees did not change but their application would expand or contract with the nature of the times; under doubt, the legislative judgment prevails. Of course, SCOTUS insisted that the challenge be a concrete case, not an abstract question. SCOTUS found that the ordinance was within the police powers of the city to control residential and industrial development, rather than allowing it to take its natural course. The city violated no property rights.

The following year, in *New York v. Illinois & Sanitary District of Chicago*, 274 U.S. 488 (1927), New York sought to enjoin a proposal to divert waters of the Great Lakes because it would impair navigability and interfere with future water power development. SCOTUS ruled that there was no actual or imminent injury, and thus the paragraph about future water power development was based on an abstract question and strike able, without prejudice, from the bill filed by New York. The remaining part of the bill could continue before the special master assigned to the case.

Loyalty Oath

The issue of ripeness reappears in *Parker v. County of Los Angeles*, 338 U.S. 327 (1949). A county ordinance prescribing a loyalty oath left many open ends. Were there to be penalties for refusing the affidavit? Was this permissible under the Fourteenth Amendment? In a separate order, the county did explicitly adopt sanctions against refusals, but that action is still in the state courts. Because plaintiffs here may benefit from a positive outcome in the state courts, it is premature to raise the constitutional questions and thus they are not ripe for adjudication. Interestingly, the lower courts subsequently dismissed the suits of certain county employees, affirmed by both state district court of appeal and the state supreme court. This time SCOTUS denied discretionary review.

Price Fixing

In a mootness case, *United States v. Munsingwear, Inc.*, 340 U.S. 36 (1950), the United States sued the defendants for violating a price-fixing regulation. The plaintiff asked for an injunction and treble damages. Another suit, based on violations by the company at a later point in time, asked for treble damages in a different court. The second court delayed action until results from the first court's appeal. The first district court originally dismissed its complaint because it found the prices to be within the price regulation. While appeal was pending, the government deregulated the product. The court of appeals dismissed for mootness. A second district court dismissed its bill as *res judicata*. The United States acquiesced when the court of appeals dismissed the case. The United States should have appealed that decision and asked to remand the case to district court for dismissal. The hardship created by failing to do so was its own fault, and the *res judicata* below applies to prevent further litigate sprawl.

Parties

A ripeness question reappears in *Renne v. Geary*, 501 U.S. 312 (1991). Rehnquist joins the majority position. The California constitution prohibited political party or party central committees from endorsing, supporting, or opposing a candidate for nonpartisan office. Nonpartisanship applies to judicial, school, county, and city offices. The complaint focused on the endorsement restriction. Divided lower courts had found on behalf of the plaintiffs, but SCOTUS reversed in a closely divided Court. Justice Kennedy, writing for the majority, linked the non-justiciability of the case to the identity of the parties in the suit. The city and county of San Francisco, its Board of

Supervisors, and other local officials were the plaintiffs. The respondents included ten registered voters in the city and county of San Francisco, the chair and three members of The San Francisco Republican county central committee, and one member of the San Francisco Democratic county central committee. The original respondents, now petitioners, acknowledged that they had been deleting references to a party endorsement from candidate statements in voter pamphlets, based on the constitutional prohibition. The erstwhile plaintiffs complained that the California constitutional prohibition violated the U.S. Constitution's First Amendment. SCOTUS found the issue non-justiciable because the original plaintiffs had not identified a live controversy ripe for resolution. The Republican Party had been endorsing candidates for local non-partisan offices; only the voter guide paid for by San Francisco and San Francisco county eliminated reference to the party endorsement. The Democratic committee declined to endorse any of these candidates to avoid violation of the California constitutional prohibition.

The petitioners assumed that the California provision applied to members and officers of the party central committees. SCOTUS found that the alleged chilling of speech is not redress able by declaring the California constitutional provision invalid or by issuing an injunction against its use; another provision of the same constitution may also prohibit the use of party endorsements. Stevens also questioned whether a member of the central committee could speak for the whole committee, and whether committee members had third-party standing to speak for the candidates as an overbreadth challenge. In this case, justiciability concerns both the standing of the litigants and the timing of the judicial intervention. Plaintiffs do not demonstrate a live controversy. The case had become moot, preventing the application of the repetition yet evading review doctrine. When the Republican committee chose to endorse nonpartisan candidates in 1987, there was no evidence presented that a constitutional doctrine punished the committee or any of its members, or even that the candidates wanted the party endorsement. SCOTUS remanded with instructions to dismiss without prejudice.

Justice Stevens filed a concurring opinion. The central question is whether this case presents a facial challenge or an as-applied challenge. Stevens identifies two additional prudential concerns: ripeness and redressability. Ripeness would obtain if a political party or a party central committee brought the challenge; if a candidate endorsed by a political party brought the challenge, the controversy would also be ripe. Even so, the plaintiffs must present evidence that the political parties would endorse certain candidates and that the candidates would accept the endorsement. Reversibility of the California constitutional provision is unclear because there are two sections in the California law regarding nonpartisan elections.

Justice White, one of two dissenters, argues that only one issue stands before the court: the San Francisco registrar of voters' practice of deleting references to political party endorsements. Three challenges survive: the deletion of portions of valid arguments, the charge of fees for ballot arguments, and the intention of the defendants to continue deleting party references. Only the third charge survives cases and controversies. An injunction would apply only to the defendants in this case. The case does not focus on the constitutionality of the California constitution prohibition. Yet, this is precisely what the lower courts focused upon. The lower courts thus violate prudential rules of the court: never anticipate a question of constitutional law until necessary, and never formulate a rule of constitutional law broader than the facts require. On the narrow grounds, this case is justiciable. The broader source mandating the same action can raise a question of redressability. Whether another provision in the California constitution or statutory law may also require non-partisan labeling does not bar the Court from looking at the constitutionality of the challenged provision. A favorable decision may, by implication, find the other non-partisan provision unconstitutional as well.

Justice Marshall writes the second dissent, joined by Justice Blackmun. The original plaintiffs brought a pre-enforcement challenge to the California constitutional provisions prohibiting identifying party endorsements in a voter brochure. The majority never reaches the merits of this case. The justiciability limitation occurs for the first time in this SCOTUS decision. The record simply does not demonstrate that the plaintiffs have failed to bring a controversy ripe for resolution. The respondents in the initial case explicitly admitted that they would continue the redaction policy. The petitioners want a declaration that the California constitutional provision is unconstitutional, as well as an injunction against current officials for further redaction. The SCOTUS majority asserts that the original plaintiffs lacked standing and that the case was not ripe. Previous cases establish that listeners suffer a First Amendment injury when the state restricts speech for whom they are the expected audience. The injury is traceable to the redaction, and an injunction against the redaction provides relief. Marshall also rejects the use of overlapping laws as a means for defeating redressability. A pre-enforcement challenge is ripe, on a case-by-case basis, by meeting the following: likelihood that the complainant will disobey the law, certainty that the disobedience will take a predicted form, the threat occasions a present injury, and the likelihood of enforcement will ensue. This case meets all four conditions. Reaching the merits, the original plaintiffs claim that the provision as-applied violates the First Amendment and that on its face it violates the First Amendment (over-breadth challenge). Generally, we favor the as-is approach over the overly-broad approach. The first approach would require the plaintiff to prove a right to the suppressed information. The over-breadth challenge is more abstract: Constitutional prohibition goes far beyond the simple redaction of party endorsed information, but rather to party speech itself. These respondents' defense of the over-broad challenge reduces to state paternalism and the odd proposition that the state wants to protect voters from information that may rationally affect their choice.

POLITICAL QUESTION

Treaties and Foreign Policy

The evolution of the political question doctrine was as slow as it was momentous. The early variants derive from majoritarian contractarianism. The government decisions flowing from the social contract of citizens are the law, and judicial scrutiny is inapposite. In *Ware v. Hylton*, 3 U.S. 3 Dall. 199 (1796), Justice Chase summarized that the people were the genuine source and fountain of power exercised within their limits; they had an unquestionable right to grant that power to whom they pleased under whatever restrictions they thought proper; only the Constitution bounds the legislative law of any nation. That law is obligatory upon the courts of the state and nation. The Constitution is singularly sovereign over both. Sovereignty passed from Great Britain to Virginia, modified in limited terms by the Articles of Confederation, until finally transferred to the United States of America. When the British creditor became an enemy to the Commonwealth of Virginia, he forfeited his debt first to the Commonwealth of Virginia, then as modified by the Articles of Confederation, and finally as modified by the Constitution of United States of America.

As the ultimate sovereign in a chain of sovereignty so passed, the laws and treaties of the latter govern the disposition of private debt. A treaty of this inclusive sovereign may be retroactive regarding the debts of private individuals but cannot restore property properly confiscated during the sovereignty of each link in the chain. If restitution will be part of the order of peace, then so be it. The latest holder of sovereignty may order the restitution of private debts even if surrendered or collected in part or whole by its sovereign predecessors. Each successive sovereign had the right to confiscate all or part of a private debt. The remainder passes for disposition to the new sovereign. By the Constitution of the United States, treaties are ultimately sovereign, and they may restore a private debt existing before the various sovereign changes. If the final treaty so specifies, debts are due, even if existing before the sovereign changes; any intervention of intermediary sovereigns into that relation are transparent to the original debt holder. Intermediary intervenors may owe obligations to the debtors for resources it gains upon those debts, but the treaty itself is blind to those operations. National differences should not affect private bargains.

Ware considers treaties derived from the laws of nations and, except for points of disagreement among nations, they are the laws of the peoples and thus more fundamental than changing sovereignties beneath them. In the American framework, the Executive branch negotiates treaties and the Senate ratifies. The Constitution does not put treaties before the most populous branch of government for a vote.

On another foreign policy matter, the President has the power to call out the militia (*Martin v. Mott*, 25 U.S. 12 Wheat. 19 (1827)), and it is his decision alone in determining whether the requisite constitutional exigencies exist. The same would hold if a statute authorizes executive discretion, such as the act of 1795 which allowed the President to call-up troops to suppress an insurrection or repel invasions in the execution of the laws of the Union. Individuals refusing induction are subject to the rules and articles of war. Warrants may issue seizing goods in payment for fines assessed for refusal to serve. When a statute gives discretionary power to an executive, he is the sole and exclusive judge of the facts that might trigger that power. The most populous branch, the House of Representatives, has the power of the purse. Both Houses of Congress must declare war. Checks on the use of presidential power lie at the ballot box and at the hands of elected representatives. Legality nevertheless depends on the facts, not the orders of the President, and a dispute may go to a jury.

Ministers and Executives

If treaties and foreign policy are generally off-limits, *Decatur v. Paulding*, 39 U.S. 14 Pet. 497 (1840) extends this to leaders of the various offices under the President. SCOTUS distinguishes between ministerial and executive responsibilities. The latter require judgment and discretion, and the head of that office, when making executive decisions, is beyond the supervision of courts. (If the office head fails to perform a ministerial duty, *Kendall v. United States ex. Rel. Stokes*, 37 U.S. 12 Pet. 524 (1838) makes it clear that a writ of mandamus may issue.) In *Decatur*, Congress had passed a pension act for widows of officers dying in naval service. That same day Congress adopted a resolution or private bill giving substantially the same benefits to the widow of Captain Stephen Decatur, Susan Decatur. She received benefits under the general act but claimed resources under the resolution as well. The Secretary of Navy denied that second claim, as did the successor Secretary. She then appealed through the D.C. Circuit Court, which had the power to and refused to issue the mandamus. SCOTUS agreed but, per the U.S. Attorney General, she could choose among the two. When exercising executive authority in a government agency, therefore, the courts had no jurisdiction to intervene. Justice Catron, who would dismiss the bill and affirm the Secretary's decision, raised the problem that now the Court would become the final arbiter of what is a ministerial and what an executive act.

Despite the constitutional clause that the federal government would guarantee republican government in the states, SCOTUS decided that this was a political issue best left for the federal legislature in *Luther v. Borden*, 48 U.S. 7 How. 1 (1849). After the American revolution, Rhode Island continued to use its charter governments set up by Charles II, with appropriate adjustments. The charter government had no provision for constitutional amendments; the balance between rural and urban representation only got worse, and the charter government essentially disenfranchised the urban labor vote. In 1841, groups of concerned citizens established a convention for drafting the constitution of a new government. A mass convention of the people ratified the new government, obtained electoral approval from both the newly enfranchised voters and the voters enfranchised under the charter government, and held elections for a new governor, legislators, and other officers.

The charter government rejected the new government, set up its own convention in 1843, and drew up its own constitution. The electorate rejected the proposed charter constitution but approved the alternate constitution. The existing charter government then declared martial law, attributing their electoral failure to Luther and other Dorr colleagues, who the instant government thought to be assembling arms in various parts of the state. During martial law, the infantry broke into and entered his home dwelling to arrest Luther on charges of aiding and abetting of the enemy. There ensued a search and seizure on the premises. If the Charter government were the legal government, then martial law would justify the breaking and entering, although in Justice Woodbury's concurrence, the martial law itself violated English, state charter, and national constitutional limits. If the Dorr constitution were the legal one, then the breaking and entering was illegal. The Charter forces under martial law prevailed; they arrested the shadow governor Thomas Dorr and convicted him of treason. The charter government commissioned yet another constitution, this one providing increased representation to the growing urban populations. This revised government tried and convicted Dorr. Still, SCOTUS engages in a bit of circular reasoning necessarily finding on behalf of the sitting government. Using those premises, the Constitution of 1789 itself would fail.

The Court held that Congress must decide which delegation of representatives to seat. In seating the delegation chosen under the old Charter government, Congress had *de facto* certified that the government of Rhode Island and its constitutional successor met republican standards. The sitting government had declared martial law to meet the challenges of the rump constitution supporters. Before the circuit court was a complaint by the rump government that the charter government had ceased with the rump constitution vote, and that all decisions and acts of that state were null and void since the time the charter government refused transfer of power to the rump government officials. The Rhode Island Supreme Court found on behalf of the charter government and treated the rump government as insurgents and criminals. SCOTUS was unclear how a state court could make such a major decision. Judicial power presumes an established government; acceptance of a controversy recognizes the authority of the government from which it derives. The general SCOTUS rule has been to adopt the decisions of the state courts in matters of state laws and the state constitution. The circuit court accepted the decision of the Rhode Island Supreme Court, but SCOTUS found no ground for that action either.

The political department has the power to act in this situation, not the judicial. Congress did not face the issue of seating senators and representatives from the rump government, but Congress had that power nevertheless. The circuit court should have sought information authentic and available before the formal introduction of testimony. The President may call out the guard to suppress a state insurrection only upon the request of the state's governor. One of the governments must have the right to make such a request. A dissenter to the companion case in *Luther* argued that the Court is an intermediary body between the people and the legislatures, to keep the latter in line. The Courts may also monitor the decisions of the executive, but it is the judiciary that is best suited to check legislative power. The executive, by pursuit and interest, is best suited to make rules which the Courts can then expound and enforce. The only question left to the Court is the martial law arresting and charging Dorr and others with treason. The defendant was not part of the military; arresting him under a limited and different kind of military law is inappropriate; breaking into a home in this instance is also inappropriate. Martial law is not appropriate in times of peace or civil strife.

Blurring Political and Federal

The border line between political questions and the federal questions became increasingly blurred after the Civil War. One of the so-called political questions emerged after the war from Georgia, the same state that destroyed the Cherokee civilization and began the Trail of Tears. Georgia complained that certain acts of Congress would abolish and destroy the corporate existence of the State of Georgia in *Georgia v. Stanton*, 73 U.S. 6 Wall. 50 (1867). Under the reconstruction acts, Congress divided rebel territory into five military districts, each with a military officer charged with protecting all people in their rights; and charged with suppressing insurrection, disorder, and violence; and to punish criminals and disturbers of the peace, until a rebel state forms a new constitution in conformity with that of the United States. Voting would include all males, white and black, who have been residents for a year and not disfranchised by the rebellion.

Georgia objected to the reconstruction act requirements of registration and proof of affirmation and causing a general election to occur in the state under its terms. The court noted that there is a large difference between personal and property rights, on the one hand, and political rights, on the other. Georgia prayed for a bill focused on the rights of sovereignty, political jurisdiction, corporate existence, and constitutional powers and privileges. Like the *Cherokee* case, SCOTUS dismissed the bill for want of jurisdiction.

That is not how the governments of the Northern states assess the situation, but the Southern states had yet to gain representation in Congress. The Northern states wanted new constitutions for the Southern states that would include the newly franchised black population. Congress passed the Reconstruction Act of 1867 to accomplish that purpose. Shortly thereafter, Georgia filed its appeal. SCOTUS found the appeal to be a political question and therefore dismissed the bill for want of jurisdiction. Georgia claimed that the reconstruction acts would destroy its corporate existence, including real and personal property. (Both reconstruction acts passed over the veto of the president.) The military commanders exercised police powers, until Congress accepted the new state governments. Voter registration was to include the newly enfranchised blacks but exclude those who had participated in the rebellion or civil war. Georgia recognized that the reconstruction act essentially overthrew the old state governments in favor of ones developed under the terms of Congress. It was the old form of government in Georgia that appealed to the Supreme Court against the reconstruction acts. The old Georgia government wanted SCOTUS to protect its political rights. Ironically, SCOTUS felt that the question before it was of the same political form underlying the *Cherokee Nation v. Georgia*. The rights of sovereignty, a political jurisdiction of government, are not cases of government infringement on private rights or property. SCOTUS has no jurisdiction over the relief sought by the older government of Georgia.

Giles v. Harris, 189 U.S. 475 (1903) might have been a footnote to lack of federal jurisdiction, were it not for the twists and turns in the decision penned by Justice Holmes. By the turn-of-the-century, most of the Southern states had begun experimenting with ways to deny black residents the vote. Alabama devised a constitutional strategy where white voters in 1902 needed to meet one set of requirements before registered to vote, while those registering in 1903 and beyond requiring a much more stringent set of requirements. Black men lacked the vote in 1902, thereby triggering the stricter rules of 1903. To register to vote in 1902, the potential voter must first register. Registrants in

1902 registered for life. The 1902 requirements included state (two years), county (one year), and precinct (3 months) residency. Registrants had to pay poll taxes, had to have served honorably in one of the United States' wars (including the Civil War) or be lawful descendants of same. If not registered in 1902, an Alabama registration systematically excluded black men in 1902, then the 1903 requirements included the ability to read and write an article of the U.S. Constitution in English, ownership or husbandry of forty acres of the Alabama land upon which they reside, or ownership of real and personal estate assessed for taxation at $300 or more, if owners paid taxes or have them under contest. By preventing blacks from registering in 1902, the Alabama board of registry could block blacks from voting in 1903 and beyond. Would be voters beyond 1902 would also have to give addresses where they have lived in the past five years, names by which they have been known, and the names of their employers.

The plaintiff sued the county board of registry on his own behalf, and on behalf of all others similarly situated, for the right to vote and for a declaration that the offending sections of the Alabama constitution be null and void. By the time the lawsuit got to the Supreme Court, the November 1902 election had come and gone. Relief was not available for the 1902 election but registration before January 1903 would provide lifelong registration. The circuit court judge issued a single certification to the Supreme Court: whether the circuit court had jurisdiction. The circuit courts generally could take cognizance of a case if it involves more than $2,000 in damages. SCOTUS earlier had ruled that a deprivation of political or social rights had damage in at least this amount. Because the plaintiff argued that the constitution of Alabama violated the Constitution of the United States, the appeal could have come before the Supreme Court even without the circuit court certification.

On behalf of a badly split court, Holmes then goes on to argue that SCOTUS cannot provide the relief requested. Holmes argues that relief in equity does not traditionally extend to political rights. He admits that the times are a-changing, so this issue was not fatal to the case. First, relief was not available because compelling black registration would, under the plaintiff's theory, make the Court a party to an illegal scheme (the Alabama constitution). Admitting that the plaintiff may be correct, registration could not cure the fraud. Second, equity cannot enforce political rights. The state appears to be a co-conspirator, but the plaintiff cannot sue the state, given the expansive interpretation of the Eleventh Amendment under *Hans v. Louisiana*, 134 U.S. 1 (1890), which additionally prohibits a citizen suit against its own state. The circuit court is without appropriate relief in this case, save direct supervision of Alabama elections. The people of the state must right such a political wrong through the legislative and executive branches of government.

Clever though it may be, the majority's opinion was not persuasive for the Court's minority. In his dissent, Justice Brewer argued that, whether in law or equity, access to the permanent registry was relief. By contrast, Justice Harlan in his dissent argues that SCOTUS should never have reviewed the case on its merits because the lower court could not take cognizance of the case unless at least $2,000 were in danger. Even if the lower courts failed to make that assessment, it was the obligation of SCOTUS to make that assessment. In either alternative, failure to meet the $2,000 standard meant that the courts should not review the case merits. This case aside, Justice Harlan agrees with Justice Brewer that the courts could grant relief in cases such as this.

The issue of state versus national sovereignty comes up in many cases. The *Texas v. Interstate Commerce Commission*, 258 U.S. 158 (1921) case presented a set of abstract questions more akin to an advisory opinion, lacking the appropriate case or controversy and lacking SCOTUS original jurisdiction. Texas essentially asked that actions by the Railroad Labor Board and the Interstate Commerce Commission be unconstitutional and their enabling act, The Transportation Act of 1920, be an unconstitutional invasion of state rights. The relevant parties had not joined the suit; the United States must be a defendant, as well as the Commissions. The bill also failed to notice decrees previously upheld.

Commonwealth of Massachusetts v. Mellon, 262 U.S. 447 (1923), a case examined earlier under the standing of federal taxpayers, also poses a political question aimed at the dual sovereignty issue. The federal government created a board of maternity and infant hygiene. Relevant administration officials compromised the board members. Using its standard cost-sharing arrangement, the federal government promised money to each state that accepted a bureau for administering the maternity law according to its terms and complete annual filing requirements. The states could either opt in or opt out. If a state opted out it received none of these monies. Once again, SCOTUS dismisses these bills for want of jurisdiction. SCOTUS does note, however, that a maternity act did not invade the powers of the state, since intergovernmental obligations did not reach to the state's till. When a state is involved in the lawsuit, SCOTUS has original jurisdiction, but a case or controversy is still necessary. Questions of a political or governmental character typically are not justiciable. The requested action must be of a legal not simply a moral obligation, and one state cannot enforce the penal code of another. SCOTUS will accept jurisdiction when the case involves proprietary rights.

In the instant case, the plaintiff argues that the federal program violates rights reserved to the states. SCOTUS points out that the bill requires the states to do nothing, and it is difficult to identify a burden. Taxation lies on the individual citizens of the United States, not the State of Massachusetts.

Whether Congress has usurped reserve powers of the state is a political question. The court cannot consider abstract questions of political power, sovereignty, and government. If the state believes it is acting as *parens patriae*, the state needs to understand that citizens of Massachusetts are also citizens of the United States and the latter is more often *parens patriae*. This case would result in the state initiating judicial proceedings for citizens of the United States against acts by its own government.

The crescendo of the political question doctrine is *Pacific States Tel. & Tel. Co. v. Oregon*, 223 U.S. 118 (1912). SCOTUS rules that the Guarantee Clause of the U.S. Constitution is a political question beyond the jurisdiction of the courts. It is for Congress, not the courts, to decide when a state has ceased being a republican form. The state of Oregon amended its Constitution in 1902 to allow the people (1) power to propose laws and amendments (initiative); (2) to enact or reject laws and amendments at the polls (referendum); (3) reserve power to approve or reject at the polls acts of the legislative assembly.

Oregon used the initiative to pass a 2 percent tax on gross revenue on business within the state. The state sued to enforce payment and penalties on the Pacific States Telephone and Telegraph Company. Pacific claimed that the constitutional amendment adding the initiative and referendum violated the Guarantee Clause by depriving the previous lawful government of its republican character. Pacific also claimed violation of the Equal Protection Clause of the Fourteenth Amendment. SCOTUS found the scope of power needed for such determination lay with the Congress as a political act and beyond juridical jurisdiction. It quickly dismissed the Fourteenth Amendment claim because a circular argument finds anything passed by initiative as inherently lacking the nature of republican legislation and detracting from it. If the judiciary were to have the power claimed by the plaintiff, it would be guaranteeing to the states a certain image of republicanism by rendering the federal government un-republican. SCOTUS dismisses the writ of error for want of jurisdiction. These are considerations of policy: courts of justice are entirely incompetent for consideration, examination, and decision on matters of extreme magnitude.

Political Parties

Political parties occupy a unique position in the American government. They are not in the Constitution, but they have become the virtual gateways to federal office. Parties also structure the Congress, and they may have profound effects upon the separation of powers. Both parties had rules that leaned toward elitism, but the fiasco at the Chicago Democratic convention in 1968 put those up for review. For the 1972 elections, the Democratic Party set up the McGovern-Fraser Commission which lead to significant changes in party rules and a dramatic increase in party primaries. The Republican Party resisted these democratization efforts, and it indeed has rules that favor party regulars and republican strongholds. The pressure for change in the parties raised many questions, some philosophical such as whether a semi-oligarchy should control recruitment to office in a semi-democracy. The pressure also led to very touchy legal issues, such as the extent to which parties should enforce guarantees in the Bill of Rights within the party structure, and whether intra-party disputes could go before the federal courts. This was virgin territory for the courts and there was very little precedent upon which to lean. The Democratic party's credentials committee unseated certain delegates from California and Illinois. The unseated delegates pressed their case in federal court, but the district court dismissed the bills. The court of appeals reversed both dismissals, considered the merits, and offered relief to the California delegates but not the Illinois delegates. SCOTUS weighed in through *O'Brien v. Brown*, 409 U.S. 1 (1972), staying the judgment of the appeals court and questioning whether the courts should hear the cases on the merits at all.

The O'Brien decision, with Rehnquist joining the majority, questioned whether such cases were justiciable. That decision lies with the national convention. Long before *Bush v. Gore*, 531 U.S. 98 (2000) decided the presidency in 2000, SCOTUS ruled in 1972 that the court should not interject itself into the deliberative processes of a national political convention. The 1972 Rehnquist argued need for great caution and restraint, while the 2000 Rehnquist entered with gusto, threw caution to the wind, and voted for an outcome that reflected the political party of the justices. In 1972, SCOTUS raised the justiciability issue, the reach of the Due Process Clause, whether the rights of association were involved, and concluded that these issues needed argument before the court, research, and then weighed carefully. The Court then stayed the orders of the court of appeal, effectively removing the federal courts from the fray. Shortly thereafter, Rehnquist considered whether he should issue a stay in *Republican Committee v. Ripon Society*, 409 U.S. 1222 (1972). The district court had issued an injunction stopping the awarding of the bonus delegates to states casting all their electoral votes for Republicans. The court of appeals denied a stay. Serving as a circuit judge, Rehnquist cites the O'Brien case as reason enough to issue the stay so that matters could be subject to study and reason. Rehnquist had been a Republican Party activist in Arizona and saw no problem in allowing the party to continue as it had in the past, until the Court considers all the issues and implications at some future date.

In his scathing dissent in the O'Brien case, Justice Douglas argued that the granting of stays was an abuse of the power to issue one. By the time the justices vote on petitions for certiorari the case will be moot. Douglas then described the issuing of stays as an oblique and covert way of deciding the merits. Justice Marshall, with whose dissent Douglas joined, averred that these are not political questions but are justiciable federal questions. There is no conflict between the court and coordinate branches of the government; being about a political party does not mean it is a political question. It would be a bit odd to argue that political parties are inherently non-justiciable, given their role in our governmental system. Marshall considers party primaries as part of governmental action, and that the primaries now have become infused with state action. Constitutional issues are present, and it is the court's duty to hear the controversies on their merits.

STATES AND RIGHTS

After the *Laird v. Tatum*, 408 U.S. 1 (1972) case, in which SCOTUS found no First Amendment problems with the U.S. Army establishing a data-gathering system on domestic civil disorders, non–justiciability changes, with the expected results in *Gilligan v. Morgan*, 413 U.S. 1 (1973), and a changed basis for non-justiciability. After years of student unrest on college campuses across the nation, the governor of Ohio ordered the National Guard onto the campus of Kent State University. Somehow, in the quest to maintain order, the National Guard killed four students. Several students filed suit for restraint against the governor and the National Guard for future violation of student rights. The District Court dismissed the suit outright, but the court of appeals cut the basis of justiciability to one issue: whether by training, weaponry, and orders the Ohio National Guard used excessive force in responding to civil disorders. By the time the case reached SCOTUS, the university and state officials had left office, and the guard had adopted different use of force rules and revised civil disorder training. SCOTUS would not dismiss the case on the grounds of mootness. SCOTUS argued instead that the relief sought to substitute court supervision for powers vested in the executive and legislative branches of government. The case was not justiciable because the relief sought violated the separation of powers and thus is a political question. Rehnquist was part of the court majority. SCOTUS closely divided on this case. The dissent wanted the case dismissed on the grounds of mootness. A mootness dismissal would provide less precedent power.

The Vietnam Era Court was more than willing to leave tension-based decision-making to the other branches of government, similar in many ways to the Court's hibernation during the McCarthy Era. Just as the post-McCarthy Court found itself, the post-Vietnam Court did much the same, albeit from opposite ends of the political spectrum. The deference on what constituted s political question diminished and the Court found bolder cases justiciable (*Elrod v. Burns*, 427 U.S. 347 (1976)). The support staff in the Cook County sheriff's office changed each time the party-out-of-power became the party-in-power. The election of a Democrat led several Republican non-civil service appointees of the out-going Republican sheriff suing to keep their jobs. The new Democratic sheriff would replace them under the long-standing patronage practice, giving the new party's affiliates the spoils.

The Republican non-civil service employees suing to keep their jobs had gained their positions through the same spoils system. The district court rejected the appeal for declaratory and injunctive relief, but the court of appeals reversed, and SCOTUS upheld that decision. SCOTUS announced a very important principle, namely, neither political questions nor federal questions apply to relations between the federal courts and the states. SCOTUS granted relief under the First and Fourteenth Amendments. The existence and practice of patronage rewards true believers; ending it may require politically associating with those with whom you do not share the same party belief.

The plurality argued that the case was not a political question because no other branch of government could resolve the controversy. The connection to elections was irrelevant. The question focuses on First and the Fourteenth Amendment rights, and only the courts can address these. The plurality answers the separation of powers argument by pointing out that that question focused on the interrelation of different branches of government, where this case focused solely on the relation between the courts and the states. There can be no impairment of executive power if the act violates a constitutional provision. The First Amendment protects both political association and political expression. The concurrent decision, creating a Court majority, only agreed that political belief is no basis for the discharge of non-policymaking, non-confidential government employees who otherwise satisfactorily perform their job.

Interference with First Amendment rights requires strict scrutiny, so the burden of proof is on the state. The state argued that political patronage motivated workers to perform more effectively. The Court plurality found greater inefficiency in the wholesale replacement of public employees, absent those positions involved in policymaking. The plurality found the threat of dismissal an irreparable injury and that, with a high probability of prevailing, deserved the injunction.

Three members of the court file dissenting opinions. In his dissent, Chief Justice Burger pointed out that half the sheriffs staff constituted tenured career personnel with the balance left to the choice of the elected head. Burger argues that wrapping this case around the First Amendment trivializes a constitutional adjudication. Burger would confine this choice to the legislature.

Justice Powell argues that the Court had now held unconstitutional a practice with a significant contribution to the democratization of American politics.

Political patronage encourages participation in the political process, and in so doing increases the volume of political discourse in society. Patronage strengthens political parties. The plaintiffs have failed to identify a cause of action, particularly since they are the beneficiaries of the same practice under the previous sheriff. These employees understood the contingency of their employment. The plurality underestimates local government interest in patronage hiring. The plurality showed disturbing insensitivity to political realities. Powell argues that patronage in state and local government makes a sufficiently substantial contribution to the function of our democratic system as to overcome minor intrusions on the First Amendment.

SCOTUS rejects the concept that constitutional rights turn upon the denial or making conditional a public benefit or privilege. This includes patronage. If it is to survive, the practice or pattern must have a compelling reason. While the plurality found patronage dismissals unconstitutional, Rehnquist joined the dissent. SCOTUS has left this area alone for 185 years. It typically has been a function of the states or of Congress. States often govern through patronage. The Tenth Amendment speaks of matters reserved to the states. Contrary to the plurality decision, the dissent concludes that patronage hiring practices sufficiently serve state interests. The plurality judgment unnecessarily constitutionalizes yet another aspect of American life.

REAPPORTIONMENT

Several states reapportioned their state legislatures and Congressional districts at the outset of the twentieth century but failed to follow-up with sequential reapportionment. As the nation urbanized, massive population shifts occurred, leaving control of the state legislatures in rural hands. This was not a self-correcting problem, because it required legislators to vote against their own interests, or themselves as representatives. SCOTUS considered the problem on several occasions after World War I. A benchmark case occurred in the *Colegrove v. Green*, 328 U.S. 549 (1946). Under the Declaratory Judgment Act, three voters sought to stop the next Congressional election under an act from 1901 and have a 1901 apportionment act declared unconstitutional. The voters also sought enforcement of a federal reapportion act passed in 1911 governing compactness and equal population distribution. The three-judge district court dismissed the complaint, and SCOTUS affirmed the dismissal.

The three-judge district court cited *Wood v. Broom*, 287 U.S. 1 (1932) as the basis for dismissal. The *Wood* complaint sought enforcement of the 1911 Reapportionment Act. SCOTUS held that the act applied only to the congressional districts it created for the 1910 census and no others. An act of Congress in 1929 did not repeat the provisions of contiguity, compactness, and equality. SCOTUS ruled that the 1911 law was no longer in force. Congress deliberately dropped the three requirements from the 1929 reapportionment bill. SCOTUS did not pursue the question of whether this type of complaint was justiciable. The lower court had issued a permanent injunction stopping certain state officials from conducting a Congressional election under an act passed by that state's legislature in 1932. The complaint was that the Mississippi state act violated the compactness, contiguity, and equality rule of the 1911 federal act. SCOTUS reversed the district court's permanent injunction decree and remanded the complaint for dismissal.

After Colgrove, *MacDougall v. Green*, 335 U.S. 281 (1948) denied both jurisdiction and a request for an injunction. Illinois required new political parties seeking a place on its ballot to get 25,000 qualified voters, with a minimum of 200 signatures per county and a minimum of 50 counties out of 102. More than half of the state's registered voters were in Cook County alone, and only 13 percent in the 53 least populous counties. Getting the minimum number of signatures from each of 50 counties was a burden for new parties, so the plaintiff sued to stop enforcement of the 200-signature rule. The District Court ruled that it did not have jurisdiction and could not issue an injunction. SCOTUS affirmed. The plaintiff argued that the Illinois statute was discriminatory and denied due process, equal protection, and privileges and immunities of the Fourteenth Amendment and violation of the Seventeenth Amendment. A closely divided Court found the mal-distribution of power appropriate if the state legislature so chose. Political power is not exclusively a function of numbers.

The sole concurring opinion in *MacDougall* focused on the disruption made possible by ordering the party added to the ballot 12 days before the election. The concurring opinion found against the plaintiff because the court should not exercise equity jurisdiction. SCOTUS offered no opinion regarding the constitutional issues. The three dissenters, on the other hand, thought that the Illinois statute requiring the 200 signatures for each of 50 counties violated Equal Protection Clause of the Fourteenth Amendment. The statute favors less populated counties over more populous counties. The Seventeenth Amendment gives people the right to elect senators, and discrimination against any group or class of citizens impairs the integrity of the electoral process. The Constitution sanctions inequalities in some phases of the political system, but that does not justify the state creating more. The dissent also pointed out that the court had no authority to assume that any injunction would interfere with the orderly process of the election.

What constitutes a political question underwent significant change with *Baker v. Carr*, 369 U.S. 186 (1962). Many legislatures failed to reapportion their legislatures for decades. Some ignored state constitutional requirements to do so. Rural legislators held concentrated power; they must vote themselves out of power by transferring more seats to urban areas. In the hearing before the Supreme Court, respondents admitted that the state would not reapportion but that the U.S. Supreme Court had no power to do so. The court gingerly separated political questions of policy from questions of political structure and ordered reapportionment. SCOTUS found no rational connection between a state purpose and this level of mal-apportionment. The political question doctrine does not stand in the way. SCOTUS determined that the plaintiffs had standing, and that relief was possible. Hence, the case was justiciable under the Equal Protection and the Due Process Clause of the Fourteenth Amendment. (The ruling explicitly excluded the Guarantee Clause case.)

A companion case to *Baker v. Carr*, *Reynolds v. Sims*, 377 U.S. 533 (1964) establishes the one-man one-vote rule for state legislatures. *Wesberry v. Sanders*, 376 U.S. 1 (1964), earlier that year, ruled that the states must draw Congressional districts so that one person's vote was worth as much as that of another. In *Reynolds*, several voters in Alabama brought an equal protection suit against discriminatory reapportionment practices and plans. The plaintiffs also wanted the Alabama senate proportioned by population, rather than patterned on the U.S. Senate, substituting counties for states. A three-judge federal panel declined an at-large primary election, giving the legislature more opportunity to develop a reapportionment plan. None of the plans developed by the legislature, nor the plan in place, remedied the invidious discrimination, so the district court combined elements of the two new reapportionment plans as a temporary measure for the general election. SCOTUS agreed that Alabama debased its suffrage, that it violated the Equal Protection Clause, and that malapportionment presented a justiciable controversy. The court ordered substantially equal representation in both houses of the state legislature. SCOTUS allowed greater flexibility in the relative district sizes for the state legislative seats as opposed to congressional seats. SCOTUS also found that ensuring some voice for political subdivisions in at least one legislative body may justify some deviations from population-based representation. Congress cannot validate an unconstitutional state legislative apportionment. Reapportionment should be serially revisited, with a decennial adjustment more appropriate. The last apportionment in Alabama was based on the 1900 census.

One of the concurring opinions complained that the equal population principle went beyond what was necessary. Justice Clark blamed the overreach on *Gray v. Sanders*, 372 U.S. 368 (1963). The Gray decision addressed the primary system in Georgia, where the winning candidate for one party effectively became the next senator and the same for state-wide officials. Georgia by statute used a county unit system, which systematically watered-down numbers as counties became more populous. As a statutorily prescribed system, it is state action under constitutional scrutiny. SCOTUS found this election system a violation of equal protection of the Fourteenth Amendment. All who participate in the election must have an equal vote: one person, one vote. The three-judge district court held the case justiciable and the county unit system violating the Fourteenth but suggested that state elections might use some modified version of the county unit system. SCOTUS affirmed justiciability, the violation of equal protection, and its injunction in so far as it stopped the current system but did not go along with the inequality standard for state elections. SCOTUS also found that restrictions on primary voters were state action restrictions on elections.

Justice Harlan penned a lengthy dissent. The ruling, affecting most states, makes the federal judiciary a pervasive overlord. He cites *Wesberry* and *Gray* as part of the over-reach, and he argues that the Fourteenth Amendment does not impose the population principle on the states and does not authorize the Court to do so. Adding the Fourteenth Amendment to the Guarantee Clause is an amendment by Court. Harlan would have dismissed all these cases for lack of cause of action. He argues that the second section of the Fourteenth Amendment empowers the states and that, in any event, its original purpose was not the equal population principle. Harlan argued that many states, both loyal and re-admitted, had apportionment plans, constitutional or statutory, that did not meet the equal population principle, particularly for the upper house. Harlan also pointed to a judicial history that did not conform to the *Baker* decision. He argued that reapportionment cases are not amenable to developing judicial standards and will encourage gerrymandering. Although the decision allows some vague consideration of political subdivisions, the decision forbids the use of history, economic or other group interests, area, geographical considerations, effective representation for sparsely settled areas, access of citizens to their representatives, state theories of bicameralism, occupation, balancing urban and rural power, and the majority preference in the state. The judiciary should not be relied upon for political reform.

The exclusionary domain of political questions is severely truncated *in Baker v. Carr*, which made representation a justiciable issue. *Reynolds v. Simms* established one-man, one-vote. Once states and localities had to reapportion their districts, some of them became very creative in drawing district boundaries. It was a practice well-known to the Founding Fathers: gerrymandering. It comes as little surprise that political gerrymandering should become a question of justiciability. Comparing the districts in terms of how close or far away they got from equal balance point in numbers is one exercise, determining what constitutes political gerrymandering is another matter and much more difficult to determine.

In *Davis v. Bandemer*, 478 U.S. 109 (1986) the Supreme Court faced the first of many gerrymandering cases. Using the 1980 census, Indiana set up single member senate districts, seven triple member house districts, nine double member house districts, and sixty-one single member House districts. The mismatch between the proportion of the vote gained and the number of seats awarded became the basis for a Democratic suit on gerrymandering. The district court invalidated the reapportionment plan, enjoined further elections under that plan, and ordered the preparation of a new plan. SCOTUS reversed, but by a plurality and a concurrence using different principles. Most important, SCOTUS found the question justiciable. This is a political case, not a political question. SCOTUS held that the judiciary was a more proper point of decision-making than any other co-equal branch of government. The Court believed that there were judicially discernible and manageable standards for making a decision. The question before the court thus becomes whether each political group, as opposed to racial groups, should have the same chance to elect representatives as any other political group. Under equal protection, there must be a prima facie demonstration of discriminatory vote dilution. Absence of proportional representation does not prove unconstitutional discrimination. SCOTUS did not dismiss the district court finding that there was discrimination by intent; the question is whether there is discrimination in fact. Anytime a state legislature does redistricting one can presume that there is a political motivation. The data provided to the district court, and upon which it reached that decision, does not meet the threshold. Unconstitutional discrimination requires an arrangement that systematically degrades a voter's or voters' influence. One election does not determine a persistent statewide pattern. This complaint focused on state-wide disparities rather than individual districts.

Justice O'Connor, joined by Justice Rehnquist, argued that the question of partisan gerrymandering was non-justiciable. O'Connor could find no judicially manageable standards for resolving the gerrymander claims. Nor does the equal protection clause guarantee a share of power to different political groups. Legislative redistricting is a fundamental partisan and political affair. Proportional representation, an expansion of equal protection, is inconsistent with the American tradition and political institutions. If we allow partisan groups to bring an equal protection claim, we must allow every identifiable group with distinct interests. The door opened by partisan gerrymandering as a justiciable question also invites unwarranted judicial superintendence of reapportionment. *Reynolds v. Sims* focused on the dilution of an individual's vote; this case focuses on group rights. The only place there is a strong nexus between individual and group rights is race. There is also an overextension of equal protection from a district to statewide results. A voter in one district cannot vote in another, so we have left the link between equal protection and individual rights. Why not go one step further and allow the Congressional delegation of one state to challenge the Congressional districting in another state? The search for judicially manageable standards ultimately implies a prior policy decision best left to coordinate branches of government as a political question. How to incorporate independents into the partisan voting scheme is yet another problem.

The *Bandemer* test required intentional discrimination against a political group and a discriminatory effect upon that group. The individual challenge would focus on the dilution of his votes; a statewide challenge involves direct or indirect influence on the elections of the whole state legislature. The original plaintiff suggests that predominant intent replace the *Bandemer* test of disadvantage to the plaintiffs group. That change motivates a shift from using race in a single district to a partisan pattern across the state. Presumably, the predominant intent test means that the partisan goal was first among many other goals used in the redistricting plan. That is vague, and virtually inapplicable when there is a third-party or sizable independent constituency. What if partisanship motivates some but not all the districts? Redistricting is the start of a republican system and it will always have partisanship at its heart.

Considerable time has passed since the appearance of the notorious governor's salamander district in 1812. The practice goes back to the early days of the Republic and continues to the present day. Although the state legislatures draw the original Congressional district boundaries, Congress constitutionally had the power to make or alter those districts. By the turn of the twentieth century, Congress was insisting on contiguity, compactness, and equality of population. The requirements appear for the last time in the apportionment legislation of 1911, although the single member district remains. Writing for the plurality in *Vieth v. Jubelirer*, 541 U.S. 267 (2004), Justice Scalia repeats the six tests for a political questions as identified in *Baker v. Carr*: (1) a textually demonstrable constitutional commitment of the issue to a coordinate political department; or (2) a lack of judicially discoverable and manageable standards for resolving it; or (3) the impossibility of deciding without an initial policy determination of a kind clearly for non-judicial discretion; or (4) the impossibility of a court's undertaking independent resolution without expressing lack of the respect due coordinate branches of the government; or (5) an unusual need for unquestioning adherence to a political decision already made; or (6) the potentiality of embarrassment from multifarious pronouncements by various departments on one question. Scalia focuses on #2: judicial power is not what judges choose to do, but to act in a manner consistent with American and English courts. Courts pronounce principled and rational law and reasoned distinctions. The legislature is free to be inconsistent, illogical, and ad hoc. Scalia concludes that gerrymandering claims are non-justiciable, and Scalia holds *Bandemer* wrongly decided.

The current plaintiff wishes to substitute an effects prong for the *Bandemer* test of "denied its chance to effectively influence the political process." To demonstrate effect, the plaintiff now suggests (1) the plaintiffs shown that districts systematically pack and crack the rival party's voters (2) the court's examination of the totality of circumstances confirms that the proposed map can thwart the ability to transfer majority votes into majority of seats. Unlike race, partisanship is not an immutable characteristic. The Constitution does not give partisan groups the right to proportional representation. Political parties compete for seats; it is not just a partisan alignment that changes with reapportionment, but also candidates, campaigns, money, and issues.

Scalia identifies five standards that Souter wishes to use, as stated in his dissent: (1) the plaintiff is a member of a cohesive political group; (2) the district of his residence paid little or no heed to traditional districting principles; (3) there are specific correlations between the district's deviations from traditional districting principles and the distribution of the population of that group; (4) a hypothetical district exists which includes the plaintiff's residence, remedies the packing or cracking, and deviate less from traditional districting principles; and (5) the defendants acted intentionally to manipulate the shape of the district to pack or crack his group. Scalia suggests that the criteria appear eminently scientific, but that the last four fail for vagueness, and even the ordering of these criteria presents a problem. A solution needs a statement of the problem or goal, and goals like unfairness are even more difficult, then checking to see if a partisan group has some type of effective influence in the political process, or the partisan group can translate majorities of votes into majorities of seats. Regardless of intention, cracking and packing may be consistent with compactness and respect for political subdivision lines. Commenting on Justice Breyer's dissent, Scalia concludes that we do not know precisely what Breyer is testing for or what fails the test. We cannot hold an issue justiciable until such day as the standards for judgment become available. We must overrule *Bandemer*.

Between *Bandemer* and *Vieth* we find *Shaw v. Reno*, 509 U.S. 630 (1993), the majority decision written by O'Connor and joined by Rehnquist, Scalia, Kennedy, and Thomas. Those doing redistricting had discovered that political gerrymandering was a reasonable fix to the one-man, one-vote requirement in *Reynolds v. Sims*. The racial cracking and packing of gerrymandering could overcome, at least in part, the one-man, one-vote requirement of *Reynolds v. Sims*. SCOTUS was certainly aware of the practice, as *Vieth* demonstrates, but the fix was more problematic. The *Shaw* case illustrates the problem. States already under federal scrutiny via Title 5 of the Voting Rights Act of 1975 could not make a change in standards, practice, or procedure without federal authorization. North Carolina submitted a proposed Congressional redistricting with one black minority district to the U.S. Attorney General. She took issue with only one minority district because North Carolina legislators could reasonably create two. North Carolina obliged by creating a 160-mile long, narrow corridor along I-85. Five white North Carolina citizens sued state and federal appellees under Equal Protection. These citizens alleged violation of traditional standards of compactness, contiguity, and political subdivision. The three-judge federal panel dismissed the complaint against both sets of appellees, because the plaintiffs had failed to state an equal protection claim, because favoring racial minorities to set up the second district was not constitutionally discriminatory. SCOTUS reversed the dismissal against the state, holding that the appellants had stated a claim by alleging reapportionment so irrational or bizarre that it implies racial segregation. If the district court, upon remand, could find no compelling state reason except its need to comply with the Voting Right Act, then the District Court must reject the second plan. An earlier case, *United Jewish Organizations v. Carey*, 430 U.S. 144 (1977), did not serve as the basis for dismissing the North Carolina complaint, because the latter focused on racial groups while the former focused on political groups. The post-Civil War amendments clearly elevate the racial consideration into strict scrutiny.

THE REHNQUIST ERA

Impeachment

The district court, court of appeals, and SCOTUS all agreed that the problem posed in *Nixon v. United States*, 506 U.S. 224 (1993) was a political question and hence non-justiciable. Rehnquist wrote a long majority SCOTUS opinion with four concurrences. A criminal court convicted Nixon, chief justice of a federal district court, and it sentenced him to prison. The House of Representatives drew up articles of impeachment and presented them to the Senate. The Senate conducted hearings by special committee that, in turn, reported on the floor of the Senate. The Senate voted to convict Nixon and it removed him from his judgeship. Nixon filed for a declaratory judgment and reinstatement of his judicial salary and privileges. He argued that the Senate rules, used to form the special committee, prohibited the entire Senate from hearing the case, even though that is what the Constitution demanded. Rehnquist cited two premises from *Baker v. Carr*. The case is non-justiciable if (a) there is a textually demonstrable constitutional commitment of the issue to a coordinate political department; (b) there is a lack of judicially manageable standards. The latter standard may reinforce the first standard.

The Constitution assigns impeachment to the Senate. Nixon's quibble over "try" seeks to impose a judicial-style trial on the full Senate, but SCOTUS found the word lacking the precision necessary to provide a judicially manageable standard of review. The specific requirements found in the impeachment clause suggest that the framers did not intend to impose other limitations on the Senate proceedings. Nixon also quibbled over the word "sole." Rehnquist argues against these quibbles using the naturalness of the reading, consistency with expressed limitations, the constitutional convention's history, and contemporary commentary. The impeachment process requires finality and timeliness, and it would require judicial relief beyond setting aside the Senate's conviction. Rehnquist cites with approval *Powell v. McCormack*, 395 U.S. 486 (1969), where SCOTUS held that the exclusion of Powell from his Congressional seat for an elected term was unconstitutional. In Nixon, the Senate has final authority over the meaning of the word "try." The courts do, however, possess the power to review legislation that transgresses identifiable textual limits.

Rehnquist concludes early in the decision that the case before SCOTUS is non-justiciable. Instead of the ending further inquiry, he then goes on to consider elements of the case. Based on various definitions of the word "try," SCOTUS cannot conclude that the Senate cannot transfer the hearings to a subcommittee. The framers did not impose specific guidelines for impeachment, but the very precision of these guidelines suggest that the framers intended to add no further limitations. Nixon's use of the court in this matter violates the separation of powers. The Constitution gives the impeachment power to one house, and the ability to convict given to another house of the legislature. The required two thirds super majority for a conviction also minimizes the chance that the Senate will usurp the judicial review generally. Judicial review in this matter would also cause lack of finality and would raise the problem of what relief is appropriate. In the Powell case, the Constitution sets the qualifications for members of the House of Representatives, and the House may only judge whether a member meets those criteria.

The concurrence by Justice Stevens focuses on judicial restraint, so there is little significance in the inferences drawn from the words "sole" or "try." Another concurrence, this by Justice White, holds that the Constitution does not forbid review of the contentions raised by the plaintiff. There are several instances where the Constitution assigns an issue to a governmental branch. The issue is whether the Constitution has given that branch final responsibility for interpreting the scope and nature of its power. Courts often must infer a political question from the text and structure of the Constitution.

The majority's effort to infer non-justiciability does not follow from the framers' arguments supporting the Senate's power to try impeachment. The majority erroneously concludes that the framers conferred upon Congress impeachment as a tool of legislative dominance but immune from judicial review. The majority also attempt to put the word "try" beyond judicial interpretation. In one variant, the majority argues that it cannot ascertain the sense of "try" which the framers employed, thereby negating judicial review. The argument is disingenuous because the word "try" certainly has a legal sense. In a second variant, the majority argues that "try" does not permit a judicially manageable standard. The word "try" has a definable meaning and is thus judicially manageable. White also concludes that a Senate fact-finding committee is perfectly consistent with the power to try impeachments. Justice Souter' concurrent opinion affirms the complaint as a non-justiciable political question. The political question label requires a case-by-case inquiry. Justice Souter repeats the guidelines for political questions found in *Baker v. Carr*.

Treaties

A sharply divided court introduces a new twist on the political question doctrine (*Japan Whaling Ass'n v. Cetacean Soc'y*, 478 U.S. 221 (1986)). An international convention for the regulation of whaling (ICRW) established an International Whaling Commission (IWC) with the power to set harvest quotas; it not only had no sanction power but also had a procedure through which any member nation could file an objection essentially removing itself from the quota obligations. Congress passed two amendments designed to add unilateral sanctions to violators. The operative phrase in both amendments was "diminish the effectiveness." The First Amendment gave the President the discretion to impose sanctions, while the second made the sanctions mandatory, after certification of the Secretary of Commerce and subject to "diminish the effectiveness." The IWC set a zero quota for sperm whales for 1985 and ordered a five-year moratorium. Japan essentially removed itself from that quota. In 1984, Japan and the United States concluded an executive agreement by which Japan could continue harvesting limited numbers, but cease by 1988, without certification and thus no U.S. economic sanctions. Before the United States signed the agreement, conservation groups filed suit for a writ of mandamus requiring certification by the Secretary of Commerce. The District Court granted the writ, accepting that continued Japanese whaling "diminished the effectiveness" of the ICRW. The Court of Appeals affirmed, but SCOTUS reversed.

SCOTUS ruled that the political question doctrine did not bar judicial resolution. Politics, it would appear, limits the range of the political question doctrine. The Courts could interpret international treaties, executive agreements, and congressional legislation. The Courts may enter even if there are political overtones. SCOTUS held that the executive agreement would meet the amendment requirements as producing the same or better result than the certification/sanction cycle. There is no statutory language defining "diminish the effectiveness." It is this ambiguity that allows the Secretary to certify or not certify each year, at his discretion. The second of the two amendments removed the President's discretion but left the Secretary to judge "diminished the effectiveness." Justice White delivered the majority decision; Rehnquist signed onto the dissent.

The SCOTUS majority held that, whether the Secretary certified a country as diminishing the effectiveness of the IWC quotas was a purely legal question. The Court admits its exercise moves into foreign relations, but that it nevertheless has the role of interpreting statutes and thus the issue is justiciable. The Court holds that certification is not mandatory when a country clearly violates its quota. SCOTUS next argues that, if a statute is silent or ambiguous, the Court generally accepts the executive department's interpretation of the Congressional hearings meant to use "diminish the effectiveness" in the statute, subject to enactment evidence to the contrary. Evidence SCOTUS deduced from the Congressional hearings was that "diminish the effectiveness" gave the Secretary of Commerce a range of certification discretion.

Justice Marshall wrote the dissent, joined by three other members of the Court, including Rehnquist. Marshall argues that Congress was unhappy with the discretion exercised by the President under the "diminish the effectiveness" amendment. The Secretary had limited discretion under the First Amendment. The second of the two amendments intended to rewrite the President's use of sanction discretion on the fishery issue, but it did not substitute Secretary discretion for presidential discretion. The Senate author of the Second Amendment sought, and received, assurances from the Secretary that he would certify as diminishing the effectiveness a nation ignoring the IWC moratorium. Despite his action, the Secretary could not change the penalty, and the statute operated to punish past violations, not to withhold certification to gain compliance at some future time.

CONCLUSION

When SCOTUS claimed the right of the judicial review, it also claimed the right to have the final word on constitutional and statutory disagreements. The domain of this claim is broad indeed, so the Court used rules of justiciability to narrow the range of cases considered. We have looked at three of these rules in this chapter: standing, ripeness, and political question. These rules could constitute a formidable filter for potential cases. Each rule gets crisper understanding and crisper exception over time. Despite some formidable exceptions, the rules get narrower in some areas of interpretation, its filter grows weaker; other rules maintain their filter throughout.

The court used standing to control its gateway and deny entry to many. Marshall thought this was a good mechanism to control the Court's capital, so when the court needed to weigh in on a pressing issue, the other branches of government would take the decision seriously. If Marshall's argument in *Marbury* is brilliant, Marshall seriously miscalculated in the Cherokee cases. In the first of the two cases Marshall found limited standing for domestic dependent nations. Indian nations were neither foreign states nor one of the united states. In the first Cherokee case, Marshall's review of different sovereignties led to the conclusion, like *Marbury*, that the Cherokee had no standing before the Supreme Court under original jurisdiction. The numerous treaties between the Cherokee and the United States apparently conveyed little of the protections conveyed to foreign states or one of these united states.

The second Cherokee case ultimately failed as well. A missionary, originally invited by the Cherokee, failed to get the proper occupancy credentials from the Georgia governor after the governor severed the Cherokee from their land. The state indicted Worcester, convicted him, and sentenced him to hard labor. SCOTUS could now take jurisdiction by writ of error. Marshall announced that the Cherokee had full right to their lands, that they were a distinct community, and that they had direct intercourse with the federal government. The Court ordered Worcester's release. Georgia ignored the order. The President ignored the order. Worchester remained in jail until Georgia changed its own laws.

The Cherokee were not the only large group of people kept from the courts. Ordinary taxpayers to the federal government have no standing to complain about how the federal government spends its money. The Court eventually relented somewhat by allowing a taxpayer standing who complains that Congress is spending tax monies for unconstitutional purposes. Of course, a nexus test must establish a case or controversy. SCOTUS outdoes itself with the Hatch Act's impact on federal and state employees. Only employees who have violated the Hatch Act's prohibition on political campaigning and who face removal from their jobs have standing before the Court. Because the Act attempts to forbid administrative or statutory review of employment release, SCOTUS could issue a declaratory judgment, but chose not to do so, because these terminations, for political management or campaigning, were not unconstitutional. One dissent found the provision facially unconstitutional. Why shouldn't federal and state employees participate in political life beyond the ballot box?

Standing served as an early blockade for environmentalism. The issues were multi-fold, but the results were profoundly simple. Could corporations represent the public interest? Did destruction to ecology or aesthetics constitute a legal wrong under the Administrative Procedures Act? SCOTUS answered that it had to be a personal injury or threatened injury. The workaround was equally simple: make the environmental claim in the name(s) of some people claiming personal harm. Environmental haggling continued over the limits of liability, should a nuclear power plant accident occur. SCOTUS found justiciability, but limited liability ceilings to estimates corresponding to considerations originally set by Congress. A but-for logic established the case or controversy requirement; the plaintiffs argued that the Congressional liability limit allowed building the plant. Rehnquist concurs in reversing the lower court decision favorable to the plaintiffs, but argues that this case, along with a companion case, is not even justiciable.

Standing has barred large groups and significant problems from the federal court docket, but its inconsistency on constitutional violations after the Civil War amendments is more troubling. The urban turmoil of 1968 led the President to order army surveillance of civilians. Plaintiffs argued that this violated the historic understanding of the role of the military in civilian life and chilled free speech. Rehnquist voted with the SCOTUS majority in holding too distant a relation between the army surveillance and constitutional rights and thus the case was non-justiciable. It was, SCOTUS claimed, a political disagreement. A dissenter referred to it as a cancer in our body politic. SCOTUS also denied standing to both veterans and taxpayers who complained that the Incompatibility Clause forbid members of the military reserve from also holding office in either the House or Senate. SCOTUS claimed again that it was just a political disagreement.

The Warren Court does give standing a breather. Simple taxpayers have no claim to complain about programs and policies of the federal government, but there are limits on the Tax and Spend Clause. Spending must be within constitutional bounds, and that explicitly includes the establishment of a religion. Congress exceeds its constitutional power when it furnishes resources to religious schools and it violates its own constitutional limit and right of the taxpayer affected by a violation of the Establishment Clause. This decision was a bit pyrric when, a few years later, five different sets of plaintiffs affected in different ways by a discriminatory zoning ordinance lacked standing. SCOTUS found no case or controversy or too generalized a grievance. Rehnquist, now on the Court, votes in the majority. Rehnquist pens a later decision defending the transfer of surplus federal property to a religious organization that ultimately got 77 acres of prime land for free. Rehnquist summarizes standing requirements: personal injury tied to illegal conduct, redress able, and typically a judicial question under separation of powers. Rehnquist concludes that petitioners in this case lack standing because they attack an executive order rather than the underlying Congressional legislation authorizing such a decision. Even so, violating a right possessed by every citizen does not provide a basis for standing. Under this logic, it is possible that no one would have standing to sue under the Establishment Clause.

Standing continues its strict gateway services when SCOTUS found no standing for those complaining about favorable IRS treatment of hospitals that nevertheless failed to serve indigents according to their financial ability. SCOTUS cited lack of personal injury addressable by a more favorable tax treatment. The plaintiffs lacked personal stake with concrete injury. The Court required further proof of injury-in-fact by showing that hospitals foregoing the favorable tax treatment were providing appropriate indigent services. Plaintiffs again lacked standing in a case where Congress authorized the IRS to deny tax exemption to discriminating private schools. The plaintiffs argued that the tax exempt private schools were draining white students from the public schools, creating de facto public-school segregation. The plaintiffs did not want admission to the private schools; they wanted to change the cost calculus for whites who might, but for the tax exemption, remain in public schools. As SCOTUS was considering the matter a political question and thus subject to separation of powers, the IRS proposed tightening its tax emption rules, but the Congress intervened forbidding that rule change. When Indiana challenged the Census Bureau's intention to supplement counts with statistical sampling, the Court gave Indiana standing on the prospects of losing a seat in the House of Representatives because counting minorities would benefit other states at the cost of Indiana's representation. The counter-factual of the purpose of representation in the first place, SCOTUS forbid the use of statistical sampling to save the Indiana seat, which it lost anyway.

The Court had been a natural enemy of collective bargaining during the Lochner Era. Once legalized, the Court deferred to the legislature for a while and then began tightening the reigns. The agency shop, where the winning union collected fees from everyone, became a contentious point between union-supporting employees and union-opposing employees. In collective action, a free rider is someone who takes advantage of the collective benefits but does not pay for them. Complainants did not want to pay union fees but also did not want to bargain down their own wages through individual contracts. SCOTUS seemed to understand this dilemma but continued its reservations with unions. SCOTUS held that the union could collect dues from all employees but cannot collect or keep the portion of the fees used for political purposes, even though the role of unions in politics was to use the weight of labor to get political and legislative support for union agendas. SCOTUS differentiated the union's role in the workplace from the union's place in the political forum, with the latter threatening the 1st and Fourteenth Amendment rights of those who disagreed with unions generally.

The prior year, SCOTUS struck down political patronage. Administrative and service jobs not under civil service were spoils for the winning party. Each time the opposite party won, there would be a wholesale exodus of those appointed under the previous administration while supporters of the winning party would occupy the vacated positions. The SCOTUS majority found the patronage practice unacceptable, although dissenters argued that patronage helped forge the American democracy and encouraged political participation. Rehnquist supported limiting union fee collections for political activities but in this case joins the dissenters in supporting patronage. Rehnquist compares political patronage, not to the political activity portion of the union fee, but to the collective bargaining component of union fees. He concludes that he sees no constitutional difference between patronage and collective bargaining. His comparison is interesting, because the political party, like the union, is extra-constitutional, but Rehnquist gives the spoils to the party but not the union.

The justiciability rule of standing does Herculean work keeping significant sets of plaintiffs out of federal courts. Ripeness is also part of the justiciability gateway system, but it lacks the power given to standing. Just as the Indiana standing is more striking for its political than legal reasoning, the ripeness rule is sufficiently ambiguous to allow considerable political preference to seep into judgment. Policy arenas rather than sets of plaintiffs distinguish the application of ripeness.

Oil and gas technologies resulted in the transport of these natural resources from the production fields to consumers across the nation. The typical mode of transport were high energy gas and oil lines that crossed state boundaries. Producing states often tried to satisfy domestic markets before putting surplus into inter-state transportation. This puts the state legislatures in charge of interstate commerce, an enumerated power of the federal government. The questions are many, but two are particularly important. Can one state legislature effectively legislate the use of its natural resources in another state? How imminent must the threat be before a case is ripe for judicial review? SCOTUS generally argues that the states are all in this together, so one may not exercise a privilege in interstate commerce not available to all others. In an extremely divided case, SCOTUS holds that the legislative intention is sufficient to make a case ripe, even though the regulatory agency had yet to issue its order. Some dissenters would wait until the product left state lines before justiciable; some felt the case was not ripe; others felt it unjusticiable.

An extraordinary event occurs when the people of Oregon passed a statewide initiative requiring students attend public schools. SCOTUS issued an injunction before the law went into effect, thereby preserving Catholic private school education without interruption. The lower courts used the standard Lochner logic that schools were property and hence the law was a deprivation of private property. SCOTUS introduced a line of reasoning that later would become important, that parents and guardians had the liberty to rear their children as they saw appropriate and thus the injunction necessary. A year later the state wins when zoning, as a use of local police power, was not a deprivation of liberty and property without due process. Another year later, SCOTUS decided a New York complaint that Illinois intended to divert waters of the Great Lakes was not ripe for review.

Auguring what is to come, plaintiffs raised whether a required loyalty oath for county employees was constitutional. When first passed, the ordinance was without sanctions. A later ordinance added sanctions, and another group of plaintiffs brought the sanctions before state court. SCOTUS argued that the outcome of the state court procedure may affect the ordinance procedure in federal court, so the Court found the complaint was not ripe. Once the state court decision upheld the sanctions, the federal plaintiffs sued again on constitutional grounds, but SCOTUS refused to take up the case a second time.

Another punch-counter punch story emerged in a price-fixing scandal brought before two different district courts for two separate charges, with the second lagging the first in timing of the offense. The second court took notice of action pending in the first court and held the proceedings not ripe. The first district court rejected the claim and the case went to appeal. While under appeal, the government deregulated the product's pricing. The court of appeals dismissed for mootness. The second court rejected as *res judicata*, because the United States as plaintiff accepted the outcome of the first appeals court without remanding that case for dismissal. Clearing the second court docket prevented litigation sprawl, but it also prevented any hearing on the second violation.

Rehnquist joins the majority in a case on nonpartisan local elections. SCOTUS invoked several rules of justiciability in refraining from a decision in a badly fractured Court. In California, citizens elect candidates for local offices such as state and county officers on non-partisan ballots and the state parties supposedly refrains from any endorsements. SCOTUS ultimately dismisses complaints against such endorsement on several grounds. The plaintiffs included numerous local officials, several registered voters, and local party officials. SCOTUS drew its first line at ripeness; there was no live controversy when filing the original case. Second, the complaint was not redress able because there were two state constitutional provisions mandating no partisan identifiers. SCOTUS questioned who could speak for whom and even whether the party committee members could serve as third-party spokesperson for the candidates. Fourth, there was questionable evidence for a case or controversy, lacking evidence either of punishment or whether the candidates wanted partisan endorsement. Even if redress able, the court action would apply only to the current candidates, not create a general ruling.

The ripeness rule of justiciability essentially says that conditions are not yet in place for this case to come before the courts. Mootness is the mirror image of ripeness in the sense that it says that conditions are no longer in place for the case to come before the courts. If, in the case of ripeness, the stars are not yet in alignment, in mootness the stars have moved out of alignment.

Ripeness and mootness focus on the conditions that make a case or controversy. Dismissing a case because it is a political question focuses on the separation of powers. The Constitution explicitly assigns some powers to each branch of the federal government. The Court infers other powers as derivative of or necessary for the operation of the enumerated power. Inference boundary lines quickly become fuzzy; the court claims power to make the decision in case of vagueness or indeterminacy. This power allows politics to seep into judicial decision-making. In a simple majoritarian environment, the law is what the majority or their representatives say it is. Constitutionalism trumps majoritarianism with the common law argument that there are fundamental laws and regularities that majorities must observe but cannot change.

In American constitutionalism, the status of treaties magnifies the tension because their terms have the same status as statutory law. The Executive branch makes treaties with the advice and consent of the Senate. The Constitution does not put treaties before the popular branch of government, the House of Representatives. The result is an odd combination of laws made by the Executive and Senate and laws that include participation by the House. The Court considers treaty terms as even transcending changes in sovereignty, say between the Articles of Confederation and the Constitution of the United States.

The range of this tension is clear in issues of property rights. The status of property rights is intricately bound with sovereignty. A treaty under a succeeding sovereignty may restore property confiscated by its predecessor sovereignty. In the transitions following the Revolutionary War, sovereignty passed from Great Britain to one or another of the colonies. The Articles of Confederation modified that sovereignty, but the Constitution of the United States transfers those individual sovereignties to the United States of America. British creditors forfeited debt under some former-colony sovereignties. The reigning sovereignty, in this case the United States, controls disposition of these debts. If governing treaties make retroactive decisions, they cannot restore property taken under preceding sovereignties, but they can offer restitution. These are political questions; the structure and charge of the courts change with sovereignty.

When the Executive gets discretion over some action, such as calling out the militia, it is the Executive that decides whether conditions merit use of the given power. Checks on executive discretion are often indirect. The House controls the power of the purse. Both houses of Congress must declare a war.

The citizen has power at the ballot box. The courts must confine themselves to questions of fact. Executive power generally includes ministerial decisions. The Executive also decides whether the states have the constitutionally-required republican form of government. The Constitution assigns impeachment to the Senate, and SCOTUS agreed that the Senate had final decision in an impeachment case. All these are political questions left to a non-judicial branch of government under the separation of powers.

International agreements generally are the domain of the Executive branch, but in a complex and interconnected world these extend to public and environmental issues such as whaling. The executive agreements are generally non-justiciable, but occasionally the court offers a new twist on a political question not barred from judicial resolution. In the instant case, the controversy centered on the interpretation "diminished the effectiveness." The Executive branch attempted to strengthen a multi-lateral treaty using Congress-approved sanctions. Japan's violations of the treaty would escape U.S. sanctions if it ceased the whaling practice after a few years. SCOTUS claimed the ability to interpret international and executive agreements. SCOTUS approved an Executive work-around for the certification/sanction cycle based on the Executive's interpretation of "diminish the effectiveness." This decision opened the door for SCOTUS to enter matters of foreign affairs, even if the case had political overtones. In the instant case, Congress had attempted to limit executive discretion, but the SCOTUS intervention upheld the executive's interpretation of an important clause on "diminish the effectiveness" in a whaling certification. Rehnquist joined the dissent.

In addition to the separation of powers, or horizontal fragmentation of power, the federal system also contained a division between national powers and those reserved to the states, or vertical fragmentation of power. SCOTUS also considered the vertical division of sovereignty to be a political question. The results are mixed when considering political parties. These extra-constitutional arrangements institutionalized the very factions that Madison sought to prevent. In 1972, with Rehnquist joining the majority, the Court decided that intra-party issues were not justiciable. In 2000, Rehnquist and SCOTUS, along party lines, determined the winner of the 2000 presidential election by requiring far more county recounts in Florida than were possible to meet the state election certification. As early as 1976 SCOTUS, over Rehnquist's objection, ruled against party patronage systems. The Court plurality ruled that a political patronage case was not a political question because the case focused on the relation between courts and the states, not on the separation of powers. Besides, the plurality concluded, no other branch of government could resolve the controversy.

The reapportionment cases of the early 1960s blazed the pathway taken in the political patronage case. What other institution besides the federal courts could fix the malapportionment in the various states? This was not a political question, SCOTUS maintained, because it involved violation of the Fourteenth Amendment. These decisions were largely in stark contrast to the non-justiciable decisions on similar complaints in the 1940s. The reapportionment decisions did not solve the contiguity, compactness, and equality standard that characterized the gerrymandering problem. Clever gerrymandering could undercut some of the gains of one-man, one-vote, but finding a solution proved far more difficult. SCOTUS recognized that gerrymandering was a problem of political structure, not a political question. Rehnquist argued that gerrymandering was non-justiciable. Scalia repeats that conclusion decades later in a plurality decision holding that there were no judicially-discoverable standards that could solve the gerrymandering problem.

Chapter 8

Federal Question

THE MARSHALL COURT

The avowed Federalist John Marshall joined the court as Chief Justice after the Eleventh Amendment had constrained the Court's jurisdiction. Marshall's interpretive genius quickly reversed the temerity of the Court as he found it. We see a much more confident Court in *Martin v. Hunter's Lessee*, 14 U.S. 1 Wheat. 304 (1816). The *Martin* case involved a writ of error to the Supreme Court of the state of Virginia. SCOTUS issued a writ of mandamus to the circuit court that the Virginia Supreme Court conform to the opinion SCOTUS expressed. The Virginia Supreme Court questioned the jurisdiction of the U.S. Supreme Court and thus declined to obey the mandate. SCOTUS was unanimous in its response. Justice Story, writing for the Court, spared few words in defending both SCOTUS' jurisdiction and its ability to review questions of fact as well as questions of law. SCOTUS once again reversed the decision of the Virginia Supreme Court, but SCOTUS did not issue a writ of mandamus. It expected the Virginia state court to obey as a matter of comity.

Excepting one justice, SCOTUS held that the terms of treaties became part of the larger body of laws governing judicial decisions. In a conflict over land, the terms of a treaty, and whether the treaty applied, should be part of the judicial decision process. The other major part of that decision process involved the terms of the Constitution itself. Justice Story demonstrated both the Courts' constitutional jurisdiction and the importance of treaty terms. All justices agreed that the terms of the treaties of 1794 and the peace treaty of 1783 protected a land title given by English kings and approved by colonial legislatures. The Virginia state government had laid claim to the land title and its subsequent assignment to Hunter. Justice Story used a reasonably simple form of semantic analysis, certainly when compared to the convoluted logic of Scalia in *District of Columbia v. Heller*, 554 U.S. 570 (2008), to demonstrate the intentions of the U.S. Constitution. All members of SCOTUS agreed that the U.S. Supreme Court was the court of final appeal from the state supreme courts. The people authorized the U.S. Constitution, not the state legislatures. SCOTUS' jurisdiction, therefore, extended not merely to the circuit courts of the federal justice system, but to the supreme court of each state justice system.

Nowhere in the Eleventh Amendment is there a reference to state sovereignty. If SCOTUS had only anti-Federalists on the bench, they might have use the "spirit" of the Eleventh Amendment, instead of its words, for a different result in this case. Even Justice Johnson, a passionate advocate for the states, found no basis to deny SCOTUS the capacity to review state court decisions involving a constitutional issue. Johnson properly cautioned that a uniformity of the law compelled states to admit national sovereignty in that arena. If state courts could make final decisions on national constitutional issues, it would reduce the national government to little more than the coalition of states found under the Articles of Confederation. A multitude of the final decision makers on U.S. constitutional law would virtually guarantee conflicting interpretations. Marshall had even grander plans, but everyone on the court agreed that the states were incompetent to settle issues of national constitutional law. Neither Rehnquist nor the originalists could legitimately sustain a broad rebuke of the U.S. Constitution in the motivation for, or wording of, the Eleventh Amendment. There is no such original intent of "state sovereignty" in the text of the Eleventh Amendment without arguing that it was a necessary implication of the Eleventh Amendment. Even Justice Johnson found no such implication. Modern originalists are being creative.

Marshall makes a strong statement about Supreme Court jurisdiction in *Cohens v. Virginia*, 19 U.S. 6 Wheat. 264 (1821). Any decision of a state's highest court that questions a treaty, a U.S. statute, other authority exercised by the federal government, or a constitutional matter, will be subject to appeal by the U.S. Supreme Court. Marshall explicitly point out that, whether one party is a state and the other a citizen of that state, does not affect SCOTUS jurisdiction. The Eleventh Amendment forbids jurisdiction when the defendant is a state and the plaintiff is either a citizen of another state or a foreign citizen or subject. The amendment is silent on suits where a citizen of a state meets its own state before the Supreme Court.

Marshall reviews three claims made by Virginia. First, the U.S. Supreme Court has no jurisdiction, because one of the parties is a state and the other party is a citizen of that state. Marshall responds that the Constitution grants the Court jurisdiction over two types of cases: those depending on the character of the cause and those depending on the character of the parties. The first includes all cases, in law or equity, arising under the Constitution, the statutes of the United States, and treaties, now or in the future. The second includes cases involving controversies between two or more states, a state and citizens of another state, or a state and either foreign states, citizens, or subjects. If a case depends on the construction of a constitutional or statutory clause, it is within the jurisdiction of the Court.

Second, Virginia argued that the U.S. Supreme Court could not exercise any power over a state court. Marshall points out that Virginia surrendered part of its sovereignty when it joined the Union, and it cannot use sovereignty as a shield in those arenas. The Supremacy Clause says much the same: the general government has limited powers, but it is supreme in those powers. In cases between a state and its citizen, the Supreme Court has only appellate powers. Marshall continues his analysis by focusing specifically upon the Eleventh Amendment. Preserving the dignity of the state is not its motivation, but to shield states from their creditors. It extended only to suits prosecuted by individuals but not by states. A writ of error acts not on the parties to a suit but on the record. There is no restitution to the defendant, but a superior court judgment on constitutionality or conformity to federal statute. Because a writ of error is not a suit, the Eleventh Amendment can be no bar. Even if this were not the case, the writ of error is among the cases and controversies over which the Supreme Court may judge cause, irrespective of party to the suit.

The last set of claims argues that the Judiciary Act does not give jurisdiction. The Lottery Act of Washington, D.C., is a law of the United States because the Constitution gives Congress exclusive jurisdiction over the District of Columbia. The Supremacy Clause then makes that legislation superior to any competing state legislation. The question becomes whether the Cohens pushed the D.C. legislation, made by a corporation created by Congress, beyond its boundaries, not whether the Virginia statute trumped the laws derived from an act of Congress. Prosecution under Virginia laws by a Virginia court exceeds the powers of Virginia. Congress has the power to make its decisions effectual, and thus enforcement can extend beyond the District limits. Marshall concludes that the entire merit of the case consists of the construction of the Constitution and an act of Congress. The U.S. Supreme Court has jurisdiction here.

Marshall continues his assault on the Eleventh Amendment in *Osborn v. Bank of the United States*, 22 U.S. 9 Wheat. 738 (1824). Marshall again makes use of the distinction between cases with causes and cases with parties. He goes one step further in separating the occupant of an office from the office itself. If the occupant is enforcing an unconstitutional law, he loses restrictions on suability. Marshall's logic here clearly foreshadows *Ex Parte Young*, 209 U.S. 123 (1908). The Bank was another corporation created by Congress, and upon the incorporating law lies all the actions and rights of that creature. The court has jurisdiction when the state has an interest in the outcome of a decision rather than being a party to it. Thus, the Eleventh Amendment only limits those lawsuits in which the state is the party of record.

The occurrence of mixed partnerships in suits before the court created a serious problem, given the Eleventh Amendment. In *Strawbridge v. Curtiss*, 7 U.S. 3 Cranch 267 (1806) Marshall delivers an uncharacteristically short decision to the effect that, in cases of joint interest, all parties must be sue ably competent. This decision applies only to cases where representing a joint interest but left for another day are cases where the interests are several. That same decade, SCOTUS continues to look at the legal status of corporations in *Bank of the United States v. Deveaux*, 9 U.S. 5 Cranch 61 (1809). The act of incorporation confers no right to sue in federal courts. The corporation, in its organic capacity, is not a citizen. If the members, in whose name the corporation sues, are eligible to sue, then that corporation may do so under its name so long as its actual members meet suability criteria. This applies to any federal diversity suit when the originating plaintiff is either an alien or a citizen of another state.

Marshall affirms the judgment in *Osborn* rather than *Deveaux*, and he extends that logic further in *Bank of United States v. Planters' Bank of Georgia*, 22 U.S. 9 Wheat. 904 (1824). To give the Supreme Court original jurisdiction, the plaintiff or defendant must be a state and be the party of record. A suit against a corporation is not a suit against the incorporator. Thus, the state is not a party, *ipso facto*. Because SCOTUS could not have taken original jurisdiction, the case is not within the Eleventh Amendment prohibitions. It is the character of the plaintiff in this case, and not that of the defendant, that determines the right to sue in federal court. Marshall articulates the premise that, when a state partners in a company, its transactions are more like a person than that of a state. It cannot transfer its sovereignty against suits to the corporation. There also can be no diversity requirement or focus on the citizenship of its members; we look to whether the corporation's charter gives it the right to sue, not whether the Judiciary Act confers the right to sue. Justice Johnson dissents, pointing out that if *Planters' Bank* stands, then SCOTUS should overturn *Deveaux*.

Justice Marshall delivers an important federal question decision in *Barron v. Mayor & City Council of Baltimore*, 32 U.S. 7 Pet. 243 (1833). A citizen sued its state for taking private property without just compensation. The Marshall court ruled that the Fifth Amendment applied only against the federal government, and each state uses its own constitution and provides the limitations and restrictions it so desires. As the city paved streets and regulated grades for paving, it ruined a private wharf with deep water. In changing the natural course of certain streams of water, the streams carried sand and earth into wharf waters, destroying its use. The city never made compensation.

The plaintiffs won in district court, but had the case reversed in the court of appeals, and then it pleaded to SCOTUS in a suit against the municipal corporation. The Constitution restricts states only in the areas where the federal government has power explicitly granted to the federal government, such as treaties and foreign agreements. The Bill of Rights is not applicable to the states. (This holding later flips through incorporation of Amendments I-VIII under the Fourteenth Amendment.) SCOTUS then ruled it had no jurisdiction of the case, based on the Fifth Amendment, and dismissed it.

ELEVENTH AMENDMENT

The most convoluted and malleable issue of justiciability concerns the Eleventh Amendment. In article III, section 2 of the U.S. Constitution, the judicial power extends to controversies between the state and citizens of another state, and between a state, or the citizens thereof, and foreign states, citizens or subjects. The Eleventh Amendment strips from the judiciary any suit in law or equity of the citizens of one state against another state, or by citizens or subjects of any foreign state against a state. The Eleventh Amendment effectively cancels some of the powers given to the judiciary in the Constitution. There is a bit of asymmetry between the clauses in the Constitution and those in the Eleventh Amendment. A citizen of one state may not sue another state, but the Eleventh Amendment does not prohibit the reverse. Similarly, citizens or subjects of a foreign state may not sue a state, but again, it does not prohibit the reverse. Although successful in the short-term, the Eleventh Amendment proved impractical in the long term. The Supreme Court cleverly began end-runs on the Eleventh Amendment, only adding to the malleability of the amendment in practice.

The Eleventh Amendment supposedly overturned the results of *Chisholm v. Georgia*, 2 U.S. 2 Dall. 419 (1793). States like Georgia had accumulated considerable debt during the Revolutionary era. Chisholm, a citizen of another state, sued Georgia to recover debt it owed to him. The court notified Georgia about the bill of assumpsit, but the state refused to appear before the Supreme Court, on the grounds of its sovereignty against suit. The states had clearly given up sovereignty over such matters as foreign affairs and interstate commerce, but the question was how far the alienation of sovereignty would go. SCOTUS threatened to enter judgment for the plaintiff if, after a reasonable notice, the state of Georgia refused to appear or show cause to the contrary. The court divided as to whether it could maintain this suit. Judge Iredell argued for no questions of assumpsit against the crown in England, and by analogy, none against one of these states. The Supreme Court had original jurisdiction over cases to which one of the states is a party, except between a state and its citizens, between state and citizens of other states, or aliens. Over the latter, SCOTUS had original but not exclusive jurisdiction. Iredell further limited "controversies" to civil cases. He considers the judicial power legislatively limited, not just in terms of its organization but also in terms of its proceedings. Iredell then reasons that no state authorized a compulsory suit for the recovery of money at adoption of the Constitution or when passing the judicial act. Lacking a law common among all the states, Iredell then points to the common law from England and remedies against the crown. No one may sue the king but by express permission. Given the powers reserved to the states, the same principles must apply to each of the states.

Although Iredell's conclusion was politically correct, the argument ignored the explicit words of the Constitution. Justice Blair pointed to those very words and argued that the asymmetry that would result from allowing a state to pursue a suit but not allowing the reverse was simply untenable. Justice Wilson rhetorically asked, "do the people of the United States form a Nation?" He points out that the word "sovereign" is nowhere in the Constitution. The *people* of Georgia retained sovereignty unto themselves; the Georgia government is thus not a sovereign state. After reviewing examples from other countries, past and present, including the practice in England after the Norman invasion, Wilson celebrates the use of "the people of United States" as the proper testimony of sovereign authority in the United States. The Constitution of the United States operates on the people, not, as did the Articles of Confederation, on the states. The national legislature, the national executive, and the national judiciary bind the several states.

Justice Cushing agrees that the judicial power extends to "controversies between states and citizens of another state." Finally, Chief Justice Jay submits that the recent revolution transferred sovereignty from the British Crown to the American people. "We the people of the United States" established the Constitution of the United States. The state of Georgia sues citizens of another state (*Georgia v. Brailsford*, 2 U.S. 2 Dall. 415 (1793)) at the same time it denies the right of citizens in other states to sue the state of Georgia. A suit against the United States of America stands in different relation to a suit against the state because the executive power of the national government backs up the latter, where as there is nothing to back up a suit against the nation itself. This distinction aside, justice is the same whether it is due from one man or a million.

The Supreme Court ordered Georgia to appear as a defendant. It chose not to do so, and the court declared for the plaintiff and issued a writ of inquiry. Because of the eventual intervention of the Eleventh Amendment, the writ was neither served nor executed. SCOTUS heard another suit in equity against a state, this time Virginia (*Grayson v. Virginia*, 3 U.S. 3 Dall. 320 (1796)). In this case, SCOTUS announced two procedural rules that it would follow for suits against a state. First, the processor should serve upon the governor and attorney general of that state. Second, the processor should serve the defendant sixty days before the expected return date for that process. The attorney for Grayson has not made a motion for a distringas (a request that the sheriff intervene against goods and chattels of the state that will compel it to appear.) Because the distringas could only operate in the future, the attorney requested an alias subpoena (repeat of the first subpoena) instead.

Finally, SCOTUS took official notice of the Eleventh Amendment in *Hollingsworth v. Virginia*, 3 U.S. 3 Dall. 378 (1798). The Attorney General of the United States requested that the Court supersede all pending or future suits against states, in lieu of the Eleventh Amendment's constitutional adoption. The court agreed that the Eleventh Amendment led to the dismissal of any such case past or future. In *Bingham v. Cabot*, 3 U.S. 3 Dall. 382 (1798), we observe the first of many twists and turns. The circuit court found for the plaintiff in the case of assumpsit. The case appeared before the Supreme Court on a writ of error, but the court found the record incomplete because it lacked the citizenship or foreign alienage of both plaintiff and defendant. The Supreme Court ruled that the circuit court had no jurisdiction if there were no diversity of citizenship. It struck all other cases of similar description off the docket.

The pre-Marshall Supreme Court continued to circumscribe its jurisdiction in *Respublica v. Cobbett*, 3 U.S. 3 Dall. 467 (1798). The state of Pennsylvania, in its corporate form, sued Cobbett for libel. The court released him on his own recognizance, subject to good behavior, and subject to a surety. Cobbett continued his "libelous publications," so the Supreme Court of Pennsylvania called him back. At that time, Cobbett asked for transfer of the case to the federal circuit court. In this case, the state was plaintiff and thus the Eleventh Amendment did not prohibit this action. Cobbett claimed that the judicial act gave circuit courts original and concurrent jurisdiction with the state courts over all suits of a civil nature.

Technically, the state court recalled Cobbett because he violated terms of the recognizance, not for hearing on the libel charges themselves. The Pennsylvania court would interpret the violation as criminal under this Pennsylvania statute, and rescue under the First Amendment was not an option. Whether violating the terms of recognizance was civil or criminal was a bit less clear, especially because a surety underwrote the recognizance. Without a chance for removal, independent fair justice might be in question because the plaintiff was also the judge. SCOTUS concluded that compelling Pennsylvania to transfer the case to circuit court would itself be a violation of the Eleventh Amendment. Besides, SCOTUS otherwise would have to have original jurisdiction. Had Cobbett allowed sentencing for violating his recognizance, he might then petition to the Supreme Court for a writ of error.

Pennsylvania argued that the recognizance was part of the criminal process itself. SCOTUS agreed and rejected Cobbett's petition.

BEYOND MARSHALL

By 1840 SCOTUS had returned to the logic of Deveaux in *Commercial & Railroad Bank v. Slocomb, Richards & Co.*, 39 U.S. 14 Pet. 60 (1840). SCOTUS looks beyond the corporation, per se, and back to its members. In a diversity suit, all members of the plaintive corporation must be from a different state than the state of the defendant. Each member of the plaintiff must be able to sue, and the same applies to members of the defendant. Following this logic, SCOTUS concludes that the circuit court in Mississippi should not have taken jurisdiction. The court asserts that it has always followed the doctrine in *Strawbridge* and *Deveaux*. Both the *Deveaux* and *Osborn* lines of reasoning agreed on one detail: the corporation is not a citizen and that it has rights less than those of a citizen.

CIVIL WAR ERA

In the decades before the Civil War, no federal question was more significant than that of fugitive slaves. Article IV, section 2 specifies:

> No Person held to Service or Labour in one State, under the Laws thereof, escaping into another, shall, in Consequence of any Law or Regulation they are in, be discharged from such Service or Labour, but shall be delivered up on Claim of the Party to whom such Service or Labour may be due.

Although this could read as consistent with the "Full Faith and Credit Clause," it is clearly inconsistent with the "Privileges and Immunities Clause." The simple key to the distinction lies in treating slaves as property rather than human beings. We ignore here why slaves were relevant for representational purposes. The fugitive slave provision occupies an unusual place in the text of the new Constitution, further developed under the fugitive slave Law of 1793.

Pre-civil war SCOTUS approaches the fugitive slave issue with the same asymmetry, found in two book-end cases: *Prigg v. Pennsylvania*, 41 U.S. 16 Pet. 539 (1842) and *Strader v. Graham*, 51 U.S. (10 How.) 82 (1851). In the *Prigg* case, a slave and her children escaped from a slave state into a free state. In the *Strader* case, slaves who had routinely visited free states or territories as musical performers eventually fled to Canada. In the *Prigg* case, captors forcibly took the slave from the state of Pennsylvania and returned her to the owners in Maryland. In the *Strader* case, the master in Kentucky lost the slaves but he claimed restitution from the Ohio steamboat that aided and abetted their flight. In the *Prigg* case, Pennsylvania indicted for kidnapping the man who forcibly removed the slave from the state of Pennsylvania and returned same to Maryland.

A Pennsylvania ordinance of 1826 made such a forcible removal a crime. Upon a warrant, Prigg asked a local Pennsylvania constable to take her before a magistrate, but the magistrate refused cognizance, and Prigg then forcibly remove her to Maryland. SCOTUS reaffirmed the right of recapture or seizure. Congress had exercised its necessary and proper powers regarding the fugitive slaves; that power was exclusive; and state legislation could neither add nor subtract. Justice Story makes a sharp distinction between the police powers of the states, which they never alienated, and the federal fugitive slave law of 1793. Thus, the act of Pennsylvania permitting the kidnapping charge was null and void. Further, the constitutional clause requires the national government to carry out the rights of recapture or seizure, and thus this is not dependent upon any state legislation, nor does the federal government require state action. Congressional legislation on this topic is superior to state legislation and, by implication, prohibits it.

Holmes v. Jennison, 39 U.S. 14 Pet. 540 (1840) presents a simple problem about whether Vermont can legally honor a Canadian request for return of an American citizen, but Canadian resident accused of a murder in Canada. The Constitution grants the federal government plenary powers in foreign policy, so it is questionable whether the governor of Vermont can answer a Canadian request to return the alleged murderer for trial. SCOTUS uses *Holmes* for an extensive discussion of the justiciability of federal questions. Justice Taney, writing for four members of the Court, takes notice from the U.S. Secretary of State that no treaty is in place for such action, and therefore the President has no authority to comply with the Canadian request. Taney defines the problem as federal and justiciable on a writ of error by the plaintiff against the Vermont Supreme Court denying liberty on a writ of habeas corpus and continuing his custody, honoring the governor's order to hold the plaintiff. Taney accepts the Supreme Court of Vermont as the final, lawful decision under state law. Taney reaffirms Justice Marshall's argument that a right litigated between parties in a court of justice meets the requirements of a "suit." Taney points out that the power exercised by the Vermont governor was not part of the state police powers but of foreign intercourse. The general government has the constitutional treaty-making power. The Constitution forbids states to exercise this power, and such exercise is inconsistent with the constitutional grants of power to the general government. Vermont does not, and could not, have any agreement to deliver up fugitives charged with offenses in Canada.

The general government has chosen not to act in this area, and it refuses all such requests.

Each dissent raises a different issue. Justice Thompson argues that the Court has no jurisdiction over this case whatsoever. Appellate jurisdiction fails if the issue does not arise in the court below and the courts below made no decision on that point. The court below did not consider the authority under which the governor issued his order and thus there is no decision on the issue. Section twenty-five of the Judiciary Act describes three classes of cases: the validity of a treaty; the validity of a state statute where lower courts have affirmed its constitutional or treaty-based validity; the Fifth Amendment, which does not apply to the states. There is no question regarding the construction of a clause in the Constitution or of a treaty. The decision below is hostile to a claim by either party. Besides, the Court has no power to execute a judgment reversing the state supreme court.

Barbour offers a premise that he would apply to any power not expressly forbidden to the states: when states, before the current Constitution, exercised powers now granted to the federal government, and there is no prohibition on the concurrent use of that power unless expressly forbidden, and the federal government's use of that power has been dormant, the states retain that power. Repugnancy of state action can only occur when the central government has exercised the same power. If it remains federally dormant, the states are free to exercise that power. Taney responds that the federal government's choice not to exercise a power is itself a choice to leave that area free of legislation, and thus there can be no concurrent jurisdiction. Justice Catron argues that the governor of Vermont exercised the warrant, not because Vermont law permits it, but because the governor is the spokesman for the state.

We see another confrontation of free-state and slave-State legislation in the *Strader* case. The laws of Kentucky totally govern the domestic and social situation of slaves. No law in Ohio can govern their right to freedom. Neither the constitution of 1789, nor the Northwest ordinance of 1787, govern the laws of Kentucky on this subject. There is nothing in the Constitution that permits the federal government to control in any way the laws of Kentucky on this matter. If losing slaves, Kentucky law allowed a suit for damages by attaching the steamboat that carried the slaves to freedom, and if they are unsuccessful, directly upon the owners. Having made these and several other observations, Chief Justice Taney then dismissed the case for lack of jurisdiction. Justice Barbour also concludes that SCOTUS has no jurisdiction over this case unless it fits within one of the three classes of cases mentioned in the twenty-fifth section.

A request for habeas corpus in *Ex parte Yarbrough*, 110 U.S. 651 (1884) revealed a detailed examination of SCOTUS jurisdiction in the decades following the Civil War. Article III of the Constitution, plus the Judiciary Act, define the jurisdictions, original and appellate, for SCOTUS and the inferior courts. The circuit courts have criminal jurisdiction, not reviewable or appealable, including alleged errors of law. If SCOTUS determines that the circuit court has ruled on matters outside its jurisdiction, even in criminal cases, then SCOTUS may inquire and issue habeas corpus, if justified. In the instant case, several white men conspired to and did intimidate a black man in the exercise of his vote for a Congressman. The disguised white men, and the severely beaten black man, as perpetrators and victim, respectively, were parties of a crime embraced by the Constitution of the United States. SCOTUS cautioned that any construction of the Constitution included matters implied as well as those expressed, because words cannot express all derivative powers. Federal elections adopt state voter qualifications, but the right to vote derives from the Constitution, and Congress may adopt laws for the free, pure, and safe exercise of that right. The Fifteenth Amendment only indirectly provides the affirmative right to vote. The habeas request asked for release from federal sentencing of the eight white perpetrators, following conviction of conspiracy to intimidate a black voter in a federal election, arguing that the circuit court decision was illegal, null, and void.

Questioning jurisdiction of the circuit court in holding the white perpetrators gave SCOTUS habeas corpus review. SCOTUS cannot issue a writ of error in a criminal case within the jurisdiction of the circuit court. If the indictments in this case were questions of law, the sentence was within the proper jurisdiction of the circuit court. A writ of habeas corpus cannot substitute for a writ of error for law wrongly applied. Congress passed many statutes under the Civil War amendments, but two were germane to the conviction here. A republican government must have the power by appropriate laws to secure elections from violence, corruption, and fraud. Absence of express words to that effect does not mean that Congress may not protect its elections. The protection here arises not from the interest of individuals, per se, but the interest of Congress in providing elections free from uncorrupted choices. The use of intimidation, like the excessive use of money, presents cause for anxiety in a republic. SCOTUS has jurisdiction but denied the writ of habeas corpus.

From Race to Railroads

The passage of the civil rights amendment opened an entirely new chapter on the application of the Eleventh Amendment. In *Cotting v. Kansas City Stock Yards Co.*, 183 U.S. 79 (1901), SCOTUS faced both a Fourteenth Amendment and an Eleventh Amendment controversy. The Kansas legislature had passed a taxing arrangement that effectively would distinguish the stockyards at Kansas City from all other stockyards in the state, subjecting it to a greater tax. The bill itself did not single out the Kansas City stockyards, but rather focused on the definition of what a "public stockyard" is. Although early readings of the Fourteenth Amendment tied very closely to post-slavery problems, interpretations of the Fourteenth Amendment gained breadth and depth over the next several decades. By the turn-of-the-century, SCOTUS invoked the equal protection clause against the legislative bill that distinguished stockyards, based solely on the volume of capital processed on average. The Kansas legislature used this classification system.

When a public interest infuses a private business, qua *Munn v. Illinois*, 94 U.S. 113 (1877), a legislature could intervene into that private business. Of course, the power to regulate should not be the power to destroy. The question in *Cotting* was not whether the legislature could intervene, but whether the legislature could intervene in a way that classified some stock yards imbued with the public interest while others were not so classified. Both the Kansas Supreme Court and the United States Supreme Court brought the Fourteenth Amendment to bear on this problem. The juxtaposition between classification systems and equal protection is a critical one. Equal protection does not require abolition of all classifications. Instead, we look for classifications that lack any reasonable support under the Fourteenth Amendment. Separating stockyards by the average daily value of cows they process is not a classification system that would withstand Fourteenth Amendment scrutiny.

This case consolidates two suits of stockholders against corporate management and the attorney general for the state of Kansas. A true controversy did exist between stockholders and management, but the inclusion of the attorney general for the state of Kansas raised the question of whether the stockholders were suing the state of Kansas. The Eleventh Amendment bars a suit against a state by persons from another state. When served with the process, the attorney general did not raise the Eleventh Amendment issue and, for that matter, did not raise whether the suit was an attempt to interfere with criminal proceedings. This issue arises at the preliminary for the final decree. SCOTUS concluded that the state had not raised the Eleventh Amendment issue in a timely manner and that the decision should go forward on merits. SCOTUS dismissed the suit against the attorney general, without prejudice. SCOTUS settled the suit on Fourteenth Amendment grounds. Anticipating *Ex Parte Young*, 209 U.S. 123 (1908), the court suggested separating an office from the occupant of that office when considering application of the Eleventh Amendment. Whether the Eleventh Amendment barred hearing the suit in the first place was for another day.

Whether the Eleventh Amendment barred jurisdiction grew critical as more and more states barred colored people from voting. The U.S. Constitution created federal legislators for the House of Representatives, but their election rules came from the requirements of the most populous house in each state legislature. This resulted in different qualifications across states for federal elections. The mixing of state and federal sovereignties allowed enduring racial tensions that juxtaposed state and federal constitutions. *Giles* provided no relief for the disfranchised. The same outcome occurs in the earlier case of *Wiley v. Sinkler*, 179 U.S. 58 (1900). Courts considered denying the right to vote to exceed $2,000 in damages, so the circuit court would have jurisdiction. Because U.S. constitutional issues were involved, an appeal from the circuit court to the Supreme Court of the United States was in order. The state of South Carolina demurred on the alleged damage and insufficient facts to establish a case or controversy. This suit was against election officials rather than the state of South Carolina, thus avoiding the Eleventh Amendment prohibition. The plaintiff claimed that he had registered to vote, but the bill contained no evidence to that effect. On those grounds, SCOTUS affirmed the circuit court's judgment and refused relief.

In the *Giles* case, the plaintiff asked the court to declare certain sections of the Alabama constitution unconstitutional. The plaintiff petitioned his addition to the voter rolls, at the same time the plaintiff was impugning that very process. The combination doomed the case. In *Wiley*, the plaintiff wanted the right to vote without showing he had met the state's registration requirements. The plaintiff wanted the registration system itself declared unconstitutional. Like *Giles*, the Court confronts a logical conundrum: the plaintiff wanted on the voter rolls of an election system he wants declared unconstitutional. The *Wiley* decision found insufficient facts to establish a cause, but SCOTUS develops the conundrum in the text of the decision anyway.

These race cases cast a blurry shadow on political questions as nonjusticiable. Some justices have great faith in the legislature as a source of relief on difficult social and economic questions. What happens when we know in advance, not merely the legislature's decision, but also that the legislature intends to disenfranchise a significant portion of its citizens? The legislature, in this instance, clearly is not capable of providing relief. The Civil War amendments are not self-enforcing. The Court guided much of the early civil rights legislation passed at the national level. The inference, it would seem, is that we have a collision in the separation of powers, that the abolition of slavery is not complete if the former slaves can never become political citizens.

While the federal courts were hesitant on the justiciability of race, they were certainly not hesitant to claim jurisdiction on railroad rates. Politicians elected in the populist and progressive eras of United States history were not friends of the railroad. These very large corporations stood against the little man. Legislatures in populist and progressive states sought to provide relief for the little man by regulating and reducing railroad rates. SCOTUS soon found ways to circumvent the Eleventh Amendment and sought new justifications for imposing judicial relief for corporations and for striking down legislative relief for the little man.

Texas established a railroad commission in 1891, empowered to classify and regulate rates (*Reagan v. Farmers' Loan and Trust Co.*, 154 U.S. 362 (1894)). In a diversity suit, the plaintiff, aggrieved and injured by the rates, sued the commissioners. The Texas statute allowed suits against the commission, but the burden of proof lay with the plaintiff. The Texas attorney general joined the suits on behalf of the railroad commission. The lower court found on behalf of the plaintiff; the defendant then filed an appeal to the U.S. Supreme Court. The Court interpreted the Eleventh Amendment sufficiently broadly such that suits against its officers, agents, and representatives were really suits against the state and the Eleventh Amendment forbade that. An exception allowed a suit against an officer of the state acting under color of an unconstitutional statute, doing wrong to a plaintiff who has acquired a contract with the state. The defense in *Reagan* argued it was a suit against the state, but SCOTUS disagreed, arguing that only the shippers and carriers had a pecuniary interest, and that the state had no pecuniary interest at all. "A state cannot tie up a citizen of another state, having property rights within its territory invaded by unauthorized acts of its own officers, to suits for redress in its own courts." SCOTUS did not need to rely upon this reasoning to assert the general powers of the federal court, because the Texas statute gave express authority for a suit against the commission. The court need not even seek a state waiver, because the language of the statute is indefinite with respect to what court could hear the suit, save that it at least had jurisdiction in a county.

SCOTUS further asserts that the charter of a corporation is a contract protected by the contract clause in the U.S. Constitution. A state may not pass any laws impairing the obligation of contracts. The SCOTUS position raises the question, although not settled, whether such a charter or contract guarantees some profitable return to those who have invested money in the enterprise. SCOTUS affirms that a state may regulate railroad rates and that it may do so through a commission. Although the railroads so argued, SCOTUS refused to accept the premise that a state would deliberately cripple or destroy such institutions, but instead would be sincere in doing justice to the owners of the railroad property. For the sake of argument, because the Court did not rule on two of the sections, SCOTUS concedes that penalties for a violation of the rules might be unconstitutional and that the rates might not be *prima facie* evidence of what is just and reasonable. Even if unconstitutional, the rest of the statute survives the excision. The courts cannot set rates, but they can judge them.

SCOTUS pushes the contract logic in *Davis & Farnum Mfg. Co. v. Los Angeles*, 189 U.S. 207 (1903). The bill stands on diversity of citizenship and finds an unconstitutional municipal impairment of the obligation of contract. The municipality is an agent of the state and hence its acts are of the state itself. The obligation of contract opens the entire case to SCOTUS scrutiny. This is important because a court in equity cannot stay a criminal proceeding unless instituted by a party already before it. A supplier to a company contracting with the city does not have a contract with the city, per se, and thus no standing in court and it must seek response from the company with which it has a contract. The owner of the property got permission to commence erection of the gas works, but subsequent ordinances rescinded that permission, resulting in arrests, abandonment of partly finished fixtures, and further arrests. The subcontracting company, not the owner of the land with a city contract, not the company with which she contracted, but a subcontractor of the latter seeking relief from the state. There is a special exception when the stockholders of a corporation try to restrain their own corporation against enforcement of an unconstitutional law. These stockholders must allege under oath that their suit is not collusive to get U.S. court jurisdiction, allege that the directors have refused to institute the proceedings on behalf of their corporation, and that the plaintiff tried and failed to get the directors to act. The rules do not apply to subcontractors, who have only an indirect interest. This case is unlike *Reagan*, because its bondholders were the equitable and beneficial owners, and hence could invoke the judgment of the federal courts on contract rights. In the instant case, the original plaintiff showed no legal interest and no lack of a complete and adequate legal remedy. SCOTUS affirms the lower court in dismissing the suit.

The federal government and the state governments established railroad commissions to regulate the rates for passengers and for freight. The conflict between the federal courts and the railroad commissions took place at many levels. One of the basic conflicts focused on the powers of these railroad commissions. The democratic forces in the states favored majority rule, simultaneously exercising executive, legislative, and judicial powers. Writing for the majority in *Prentis v. Atlantic Coast Line Co.*, 211 U.S. 210 (1908), Justice Holmes took special care to note that state constitutions were free to mix judicial and legislative powers in administrative vehicles like the railroad commissions. Plaintiffs sued the members and clerk of the Virginia State Corporation Commission to prevent enforcement of passenger rates. The plaintiffs charge that the passenger rates were confiscatory and qualify as a taking of private property without just compensation under the Fourteenth Amendment. Hearings before the commission were judicial in nature and the federal courts forbidden to enjoin. The plaintiffs won in the lower courts, so the commission as a defendant appealed to SCOTUS. The core question is whether the federal courts have jurisdiction to intervene.

SCOTUS accepts the commission as a judicial court. When the commission contemplates issuing an order, it must publish that fact four weeks prior to implementation, so that the commission may hear objections to and evidence against the new rule. Once an order has passed, there is another four-week waiting period before going into effect. The supreme court of appeals in the state may reverse that rule and substitute its own, only based on the evidence before the commission. It may enforce commission rules by fines and penalties, after another hearing, and that order is again subject to scrutiny. In the instant case, the commission issued an order fixing passenger rates on a tier system. Under the commission's judicial power, it could then proceed against an offending railroad to enforce the order and punish a breach. No federal court could intervene here, because issuing the new order is a legislative act. The question of judicial intervention is not whether but when: their proper and ordinary course. The railroads still have open to them a writ of error to the Supreme Court of Appeals in Virginia. Litigation arises only after passing the legislation. The plaintiff railroad incorporations include a general set of rules that constitute a contract about profits, and the Constitution protects contracts.

As part of its normal legislative procedure, Congress increasingly authorized judicial review of decisions made by administrative boards such as the *Civil Aeronautics Board C. & S. Air Lines, Inc. v. Waterman S.S. Corp.*, 333 U.S. 103 (1948). The same act authorizing judicial review also indicated that the President must sign off on orders granting or denying applications for air transportation routes. Amidst conflicting decisions from different circuit courts of appeals, one such court considered a decision by the Civil Aeronautics Board to be incomplete until judicial review and before it went to the president for approval. The president's approval was an exercise of political discretion, and hence not reviewable in court. The Congressional acts specifically exempted judicial review of foreign routes. SCOTUS noted that, when legislation conferred the power of judicial review in broad terms, the courts would decline the opportunity to magnify their jurisdiction.

SCOTUS rejected the plaintiffs' argument that air transportation was simply an outgrowth of surface-bound transport. In the case of the Civil Aeronautics Board, Congress inverted the normal relationship between administrative unit and the president, by requiring presidential approval of administrative decisions before they became final. The courts may not review a decision by the president, and it may not review an order of the Board before it acquires finality. If the courts were to act between the decision of the CAB and the president, the president would be free to simply disregard the court's decision. Often, the president modifies parts of the CAB's decision, while the president does not modify others. Foreign policy is necessarily political, so there can be no review of the portions changed by the president. Even so, the vitality of the entire order derives from the president's discretion and is unreviewable. If judicial review comes between the Board's decision and the president's decision, a revision, overturn, or refusal of full faith and credit by another department would not be lawful. In short, judicial intervention between or after a decision becomes final is untenable. The Board's order is immature and thus not judicially reviewable, but when the president makes it final, it is not reviewable because the president has discretion over political matters.

It is in *Ex Parte Young*, 209 U.S. 123 (1908) that railroad rates finally collide with the Eleventh Amendment. It is difficult to underestimate the importance of this case, both for the clever way it sidesteps the Eleventh Amendment and the changing view of the legislature as a source of relief. In the words of Justice Marshall in *Cohen v. Virginia*, 6 Wheat. 264–404: "It is most true that this court will not take jurisdiction if it should not; but it is equally true that it must take jurisdiction if it should. The judiciary cannot, as the legislature may, avoid a measure because it approaches the confines of the Constitution." A stockholder sued a corporation to enjoin its directors and officers from obeying a state statute. The surface conflict aside, this clearly was a suit between a corporation and the state of Minnesota. Such a suit directly against a state violated the Eleventh Amendment, but a suit between a stockholder and the corporation to ignore a state statute was simply to invite retaliation by the state.

The twists and turns in this case make for great legal drama. A court must have jurisdiction before issuing a citation of contempt. Whether a railroad rate, set by state statute, is confiscatory raises a federal question and gives the circuit court jurisdiction under the Constitution of the United States. If state penalties for violation are so enormous as to preclude use of the courts, the statute denies equal protection and due process of the laws, raises a federal question, and gives the circuit court jurisdiction. If a state official enforces an unconstitutional statute, it is an illegal act, and the officer is subject in person to the consequences of that action. He loses his official character. The courts cannot control the discretion of an executive officer, but an injunction against enforcing an unconstitutional statute is not such interference. If standard rules of procedure, such as no federal court intervention in a criminal case pending in state court, the rules do not apply if they enforce an unconstitutional state statute under inquiry in a federal court. In such an event, the federal court has jurisdiction over both civil and criminal cases to the exclusion of all other courts. If the state officer becomes a party to a suit as representative of the state, thereby attempting to preclude federal jurisdiction under the Eleventh Amendment, a federal court may enjoin him. The injunction may not extend to the restraint of the state court or action of the grand jury. A confiscatory rate is beyond the intelligence of a jury and a court of equity should determine the taking of expert opinion and referring the matter to a master.

Defendant Young, attorney general for the state of Minnesota, asked the state court to issue a writ of mandamus enforcing a state statute judged by the federal court to be unconstitutional and against which it issued a temporary stay. Attorney General Young refused to comply with the injunction, the Court cited him for contempt, and took him into custody. Young argued that the circuit court had no jurisdiction, because the suit was really against the state of Minnesota, to which the state had not consented, and that the Eleventh Amendment protected the state. The court issued the contempt against the person of the attorney general rather than the office. Minnesota officials requested that the Supreme Court order a writ of habeas corpus; the marshal responded with the terms of the circuit court contempt, which included a $100 fine and ordered him to dismiss his mandamus proceedings.

In the SCOTUS opinion written by Justice Peckham, the suit by railroad stockholders presented a federal question, thus giving the circuit court jurisdiction. Young denied that there was a federal question, or even a dispute that rises to the level triggering the Fourteenth Amendment's Due Process and Equal Protection Clauses. The question was really a simple matter of fact, whether the rates set by the legislature and the railroad commission were confiscatory. On the contrary, SCOTUS reasoned that a taking of property without due process did raise a federal question. Further, railroad officials could not challenge the constitutionality of the act because of severe penalties, if mistaken. The *de facto* penalties of the challenged rates violate the Equal Protection and Due Process Clause of the Fourteenth Amendment. The rates may also trigger the Interstate Commerce Clause, but not necessary to pursue that issue. SCOTUS concluded that the circuit court did have jurisdiction. Laws making it impossible to test their validity are on their face unconstitutional. The circuit court has the jurisdiction to permanently enjoin the railroads from implementing the rate changes. The circuit court found the rates confiscatory and the act creating them unconstitutional.

Addressing the charge that the circuit court violated the Eleventh Amendment, SCOTUS examined both the Eleventh and the Fourteenth Amendments. The two seem to have contradictory effects. The Eleventh Amendment prohibits a suit against the state by citizens of another state or any foreign state. The Fourteenth provides that no State take a person's life, liberty, or property without due process of law and equal protection of law. *Hans v. Louisiana*, 134 U.S. 1 (1890) extends the Eleventh Amendment to include a state's own citizens. SCOTUS found that the plaintiff's rights rested on the Fourteenth Amendment, but SCOTUS declined to examine whether the Fourteenth implied a limit on the Eleventh Amendment. *Poindexter v. Greenhow*, 114 U.S. 270 (1885) allowed a suit to go forward against a tax collector who, under color of office, refused to accept tender as payment for taxes. Because the law under which the tax collector operated was unconstitutional, the suit would be against the person rather than the state *qua* tax collector's office. Justice Peckham also repeats Justice Marshall's holding in *Osborn v. Bank of the United States*, 22 U.S. 9 Wheat. 738 (1824) that the circuit court may restrain an officeholder who executes an unconstitutional state statute.

A state officer, *qua* office, connects to the enforcement of an act; this allows a personal charge against the officer. The threat to enforce a statute is sufficient to authorize a suit. The court cannot control an officer's use of discretion, but it can compel ministerial acts. An injunction is appropriate to restrain an officer from enforcing an act when he has no legal right to do so. This is not an interference with executive discretion. Securing a writ of mandamus under color of the state's authority is an illegal action. Because the officer has violated the supreme law of the land, the state may offer him no immunity; the violation strips the officer of his official character. In general, a court of equity cannot enjoin criminal proceedings, but the federal court, already hearing a suit involving the enforcement of an unconstitutional statute, may maintain jurisdiction, to the exclusion of all other courts, until it performs its duties. When an unconstitutional statute threatens property rights, a criminal proceeding under the void law is an unlawful interference and a court of equity may intervene. This power does not extend to another court or grand jury.

Getting an employee to violate the statute and then face prosecution to get the act tested, does not save the agent from imprisonment in the meantime. Similarly, the plaintiff may lose the property while awaiting the results of proceedings in the state court. Remedies at law are inadequate, but the court of equity could provide appropriate remedy. The lower federal courts would not issue an injunction unless the issue is free from doubt. To illustrate the supremacy of federal law, a state recognizes a writ of *habeas corpus* for a person in state custody and the state does not consider it a suit against itself.

Justice Harlan, in dissent, points out that the original suit was against Young as the attorney general, not Young as an individual. The suit was, in effect, a suit against the state. The circuit court injunction is void. The contempt order is also null and void. The state can only act through its officers, and the federal seizure of that officer clearly violates the Eleventh Amendment. This judicial assertion would make the states dependencies or provinces. We must assume that the state courts will secure every right guaranteed in the Constitution. If they fail, appeal lies from the highest court in this state to the U.S. Supreme Court. The circuit court has assumed that questions regarding the enforcement of the statute were beyond the competency of the state court. This court has effectively prevented its own law officer from representing the state. The excited claim that the attorney general put officers and property of the railroads in grave danger has little basis in fact, including the attorney general's testimony that he sought no further state court action against the railroads, except the existing writ of mandamus. There is no cause to deny him the writ of habeas corpus. SCOTUS appears very aggressive in asserting jurisdiction regarding railroad rate cases.

SCOTUS sometimes denied jurisdiction on race cases because it could not provide appropriate relief. SCOTUS shows a similar distance regarding its state-level liquor management. The case of *Murray v. Wilson Distilling Co.*, 213 U.S. 151 (1909) is particularly revealing because it appears one year after the *Young* decision. SCOTUS invokes the Eleventh Amendment against liquor vendors suing the state liquor dispensary. South Carolina created a control board for the management of liquor traffic in 1892. A commissioner bought and distributed the liquor used for consumption. SCOTUS found some provisions in an 1895 act unconstitutional because the state's purchase of liquor discriminated against the products of other states. Shortly thereafter, the state adopted a new constitution, giving the general assembly full management of liquor within the state. Income from liquor sales was for specified public purposes. A new statute established a state board of control empowered to purchase all liquor. The legislature empowers a new commissioner to distribute liquor to various state dispensaries. The 1896 statute, amended again in 1897, passed SCOTUS scrutiny as part of the police powers of the state and consistent with national legislation on the topic. A 1907 law established local control, repealing the 1896 statute. The governor appointed county boards that, in the name of the state, authorized the purchase liquor.

The state limited its liability to the sum of the assets of a local dispensary. A special commission would liquidate state dispensary assets, which would also attend to outstanding claims. The commission asked for original books of entry showing the previous transactions as well as the oral examination of certain witnesses. Some of the claimants refused this request and filed suit in the federal circuit court against members of the commission. The liquor distributors relied upon the diversity of citizenship to maintain the suit in federal court, requesting an injunction against the commissioners' disposal of the asset fund until they properly paid claimants. The court issued a temporary injunction, and the commissioners responded that the suit was really against the state of South Carolina, and therefore illegal under the Eleventh Amendment, because the state had not consented. The court continued the restraining order until the final disposition of the suit, and one of the cases added banks holding the dispensary funds as defendant respondents.

The legislature passed a new act giving the commission additional power and giving the claimant the right to appeal to the South Carolina Supreme Court. The legislature also required the commission to pay into the state treasury $15,000 to cover criminal prosecution expenses for violating laws relating to the now defunct state dispensary. The commission did not comply, citing the federal court injunction. The attorney general sought a writ of mandamus to compel compliance. The South Carolina Supreme Court determined that the state was the actual purchaser of the liquor, and that the commissioners were officers of the state. Accordingly, the South Carolina Supreme Court found the federal circuit court without jurisdiction.

Responding to appeals, the circuit court appointed members of the commission as receivers of the liquidation fund, and the court ordered them to hold the funds, pending further orders from the court. The circuit court subsequently entered an order establishing a three-person receivership, two of these members coming from the state-appointed commission. Given the conflicts among the South Carolina Supreme Court, the circuit court, and the liquor distributors, two cases now consolidated into one, asked that trustees holding the liquidation proceeds had a valid, binding, and irrepealable contract protected by the contract clause in the U.S. Constitution. The appeal asked that the legislative act mandating the $15,000 transfer was repugnant to the Constitution of the United States and its Fourteenth Amendment. The circuit court amended its own order to permit $15,000 payable to the attorney general. The state appealed the remainder of the circuit court order to the circuit court of appeals. That court affirmed the lower court, and SCOTUS issued a writ of error. SCOTUS ruled that the state itself was the debtor and the lower court could not compel performance of a contract because of the Eleventh Amendment. The federal circuit court thus had no jurisdiction. SCOTUS also ruled that if a state consented to suit in its own courts, it gives no right to sue in federal court. SCOTUS reversed both the court of appeals and the circuit court, remanding the case to the circuit court for dismissal.

The *Young* logic took quick and firm hold as a vehicle around the Eleventh Amendment, as illustrated in *Truax v. Raich*, 239 U.S. 33 (1915). Immigration is an explicit power of the federal government, but that has not prevented the states from unconstitutional intervention. In the instant case, a state initiative protected U.S. citizens in employment against noncitizens. The state legislature interpreted the initiative results to require employers of more than five people to employ 80 percent or more qualified citizens, regardless of class of work. Employer violations were punishable by fine and imprisonment. The plaintiff's employer sought to meet the requirements of the new law, so intended to fire the plaintiff. The plaintiff filed in district court under the Equal Protection Clause of the Fourteenth Amendment, seeking a declaration of unconstitutionality and restraining action. The plaintiff filed for an injunction *pendent lite* (during litigation) and his employer arrested; the district judge, realizing that the other cooks also faced release, granted a temporary restraining order. The state claimed that it had not consented to a suit, that this was a criminal law, that there was no cause in equity, and that the plaintiff could not sue. A three-judge district panel issued an injunction for the plaintiff against the employer. SCOTUS found that the suit was not against the state but the wrongful behavior of some of its officers, and that suits in equity can, under certain circumstances, extends to criminal prosecutions as unconstitutional acts against the rights of property, absent an adequate remedy at law. SCOTUS made a particularly interesting observation that employment at will, rather than term, does not make it subject to the will of others. Typically, a servant cannot complain against its master, but the distinction here is idle because the law, and only that law, forces a decision by the master. Thus, any distinction making the injury remote or indirect is idle. If the act is unconstitutional, equitable relief is in order. The Fourteenth Amendment applies to any *person* within its jurisdiction, and thus does not require citizenship. The Fourteenth Amendment guarantees the personal freedom and opportunity for such matters as common occupations. Denying employment to some is not equal protection, and the state is acting in hostility to exclusive federal power. The state's restriction falls only upon aliens lawfully admitted under federal law. Justice McReynolds' dissent argued that the Eleventh Amendment prohibited the Court's action.

What difference a century makes is abundantly clear in *New Jersey v. Sargent*, 269 U.S. 328 (1926). New Jersey sought certain sections of the Federal Waterpower Act of 1920s declared unconstitutional because they related to waters within or bordering upon the state itself. The defendant, the Attorney General of the United States, argued that the New Jersey complaint did not constitute a case or controversy. SCOTUS cannot pronounce an opinion on the abstract constitutionality of the law unless it threatens rights or property under judicial cognizance. Political rights do not fall under the cognizance of the court. A bill requesting that Congress has exceeded its authority cannot, without demonstrating the prejudicial effect upon the state, be sufficient to justify an action by the court. SCOTUS dismissed the bill for want of jurisdiction.

Arizona confronts the use of federal power in *Arizona v. California*, 283 U.S. 423 (1931). An Arizona statute required state approval before constructing a dam over a river designed to improve navigation. State assertions to the contrary, SCOTUS had evidence that the lower reaches of the Colorado River had been navigable, but the accumulation of silt prevented current navigation. Engineers estimated that a dam would control both the silt problem and the irregularity of water flow, restoring the river to navigability. Although the river was currently not navigable, and therefore not available for commercial use, this status did not constitute abandonment or prohibit federal control over the river. Construction of a hydroelectric plant would render the project solvent. An interstate compact involving all states for which the river flowed except Arizona, specified that the needs of irrigation should come before navigability. The act of approving the dam included this compact. Arizona sought to enjoin the project because it invaded Arizona's interests, especially in future irrigation projects within the state. SCOTUS ruled that the project did not require state approval; the dam and reservoir were clearly within the powers of Congress; the fact that the federal government had other purposes (irrigation and power) beyond navigation was of no avail. The Boulder Canyon Project Act specified navigation as the first purpose; the Colorado River compact specified irrigation is the first purpose. Although the project act incorporated the compact, the canyon project would resolve the inconsistency relative to the order of purpose. The state wanted access to unallocated water resources for new irrigation projects within the state, in addition to projects already in operation, but the compact, enforced by the act paving the way for a damn and reservoir, would prevent new Arizona irrigation projects. SCOTUS rejected the claim for an injunction against the dam or the compact, because there was no actual or threatened impairment, but only assumed impairment of Arizona's rights. Since Arizona was not a signatory to the compact, its terms did not bind Arizona. SCOTUS could not issue a declaratory decree. SCOTUS dismissed the Arizona bill without prejudice.

As industrialization changed America after the Civil War, SCOTUS became increasingly fixed on the commerce clause in what has come to be known as the *Lochner* era. Although the era would formally end in 1937, cracks in the blind enforcement of the Contracts Clause appeared earlier, especially *Home Building & Loan Assn. v. Blaisdell*, 290 U.S. 398 (1934). As a country sinking deeper into the Civil War, states, particularly those controlled by the populists, made efforts to protect their individual citizens against corporations. SCOTUS recognized the emergency of the situation, cautioned that constitutional power did not change with emergency, but that occasionally emergencies would trigger powers possessed but seldom exercised. What made the Minnesota case a federal question was the commerce clause in the U.S. Constitution. SCOTUS argued that the debates at the Constitutional Convention could not determine the exact scope, or prohibitions, of the commerce clause prior to legislation. SCOTUS argues that an appropriate modification of relief does not impair the Contracts Clause itself. The state has reserve powers to safeguard the vital interests of its people. The Minnesota law extended the time before foreclosure on and sale of existing mortgages. SCOTUS also found the law consistent with the Due Process Clause of the Fourteenth Amendment.

The mortgage moratorium extended only for a brief time. A period of redemption would postpone deficiency judgments. On appeal to SCOTUS, a mortgagee appealed a decision favoring a Minneapolis couple requesting temporary mortgage relief. After remand from the state supreme court, the trial court granted temporary relief, subject to payments on taxes, insurance, interest, and mortgage indebtedness. The state court took notice that most of the firms had ceased investing in mortgages or their renegotiation. SCOTUS found that the Contracts Clause is not an absolute and unqualified restriction on the power of the state. In his dissent, Justice Sutherland argued that a provision of the Constitution cannot admit to distinctly opposite interpretations. A constitution cannot change or declare so because it appears ill-adapted to the present situation. Sutherland also pointed out the long list of case precedents providing the stricter interpretation of the Contracts Clause. Sutherland agrees that the Court can alter the remedy, but not if in so doing it changes the contract itself. Whatever postpones or makes difficult the enforcement of a contract, the action has weakened the obligations of contract.

REHNQUIST

Not since the Jackson administration had SCOTUS faced so much contempt from the executive branch of government than under the imperial presidency of Richard Nixon (*United States v. Nixon*, 418 U.S. 683 (1974)). To preserve Nixon's own interests, the President determined what was justiciable. A special prosecutor investigating federal statute violations requested tape recordings from the Oval Office relating to precisely identified meetings and conversations between the President and certain others. Nixon wanted the subpoena quashed because the conflict was intra-executive and that the courts could not review claims of executive privilege. Nixon argued that in either case the controversy was non-justiciable. SCOTUS ruled that the intra-executive argument was to no avail, and that the claim of executive privilege did not preclude judicial review. SCOTUS pointed out that separation of powers, or the executive's need for confidentiality in high-level communications, did not create an absolute immunity from the judicial process. Rehnquist, who had worked in the Nixon White House, recused himself from this case.

The sought information followed a grand jury indictment of seven named individuals for conspiracy to defraud and obstruction of justice. The indictment named Nixon as an unindicted co-conspirator. The President attempted to shield those indicted under the claim of executive privilege. Nixon also requested that the court expunge the grand jury's action naming Nixon an unindicted co-conspirator and sought protective orders against the disclosure of that information. The district court denied these motions. The President and the special counsel then filed a flurry of writ requests, until docketed before the Supreme Court. The court waived certain rules of finality in this case because application of the rule would require the President to disobey a court order to get a review. The President resisted the special prosecutor request for information in that it was a political question protected by the grant of power under Article II of the Constitution. The President argued that power within the sphere of the executive was absolute and it insulates the President from a judicial subpoena. The legislation authorizing the special prosecutor gave explicit power to contest the invocation of executive privilege. SCOTUS found that the request for information arises in the normal course of a federal criminal prosecution, and thus is within Article III powers. The generalized interest in confidentiality cannot prevail over due process of law and criminal justice. The Supreme Court, not the executive, is the ultimate interpreter of the Constitution.

Whether motivated by a need to reduce pressure on the Supreme Court agenda or to celebrate states' rights, *California v. Grace Brethren Church*, 457 U.S. 393 (1982) celebrated a cooperative federal-state scheme by finding that state courts provided plain, speedy, and efficient remedies, and ruling that the district courts did not have jurisdiction to issue declaratory or injunctive relief under the tax injunction act. The act provided benefits to unemployed workers by requiring employers to pay an excise tax on wages paid to employees. Mandatory coverage was exempt for organizations operated primarily for religious purposes and where principally supported by a church or convention of churches. Fearing excessive entanglement under the Establishment Clause, a district court permanently enjoying the state from collecting unemployment taxes from religious schools. The district court left un-enjoined the federal defendants, lacking knowledge about the possible response of the Secretary of Labor instituting decertification proceedings for failing to collect the taxes. Though the district court did not explicitly find the tax act unconstitutional as applied to religious schools unaffiliated with churches, the thrust of its several findings did just that. SCOTUS claimed jurisdiction because a federal court had declared an act of Congress unconstitutional. SCOTUS found that the tax injunction act prohibited the district court from issuing either declaratory or injunctive relief. Congress wanted to limit drastically federal court interference with the assessment and collection of state taxes. Although the district court exercised jurisdiction, SCOTUS would not consider the merits of taxpayers' First Amendment claims.

The district court distinguished three categories or classes of religious employers: category one is schools that are part of a corporate structure of the church or association of churches; category two are schools that are separate corporations but do not belong to a church or association of churches; category three are schools operated primarily for religious purposes, but not operated, supervised, or control by a church or convention of churches. The secretary of labor eventually exempted both category one and the category two schools. The District Court incorporated category three under claims of excessive entanglement. SCOTUS repeats the importance of minimizing the mandatory docket of the court. SCOTUS then concludes that the tax injunction act deprived the district court of jurisdiction over category one, category two, and the category three schools and that it cannot issue injunctive or declaratory relief. SCOTUS further found that the state did indeed provide plain and efficient administrative and judicial procedures. The dissent argues that this is a federal-state program administered according to federal requirements, and hence only federal questions are involved. Thus, the district court may issue a declaratory judgment. The dissent accuses the majority of nimble law-making.

The Court tries to signal what it will do when a case may or not have a statutory basis for resolution as well as a federal basis in *Michigan v. Long*, 463 U.S. 1032 (1983). The case involves a warrantless search of an automobile whose driver appears to be under the influence and on whose floor-board is a hunting knife. After a pat-down, an officer spotted marijuana under an armrest and a later warrantless search found marijuana in the trunk. Lower courts affirmed the conviction on possession, but the Michigan Supreme Court reversed. SCOTUS first asserts that it will not look beyond a state court decision based on state law, but that if the state court decision depends on federal law and is intermixed with federal law, then the Court will assume that the state court made its decision because federal law required it. SCOTUS then reversed the Michigan Supreme Court on the pat-down and passenger compartment search and remanded for further consideration the trunk search.

Both the state and federal courts can consider a federal question, but the federal courts may review a state court decision involving a federal issue. *ASARCO v. Kadish*, 490 U.S. 605 (1989) raises such an issue. The Federal Enabling Act of 1910 granted Arizona certain federal lands, except mineral lands, for a public-school trust. Arizona could sell the land, but they had constraints by requirements regarding advertisement, bidding, and appraisal. Arizona incorporated these requirements into the Arizona Constitution. A growing effort to distinguish known mineral lands from unknown ones would only exclude the former from sale. In 1927 Congress revised the land grant to exclude all mineral lands from sale. Congress revised rules for leasing the mineral lands in 1936 and 1951, with the latter eliminating the advertising, bidding, and appraisal on the lease of lands for developing hydrocarbons. Plaintiffs included taxpayers in Arizona and a state teachers' association. Respondents included mineral lessees and the State Land Department. The trial court upheld the extinguishing statute, but the state supreme court reversed, pointing out that the advertising, bidding, and appraisal rules were in the Arizona Constitution and thus the extinguishing statute was unconstitutional regarding non-hydrocarbon mineral lessees.

SCOTUS considered the Arizona Supreme Court the final decision in the state courts, and so a case would next come before the U.S. Supreme Court.

There are two exceptions to the finality requirement: (1) the federal issue is conclusive; (2) the federal questions that could come before SCOTUS have been adjudicated by the state court. The original plaintiffs to this suit would have lacked standing in federal court, but the Court is now considering a state decision that causes direct, concrete, and certain injuries to the lessees. The state decision links to the injury, and relief is possible. Article III of the Constitution does not bind the state courts, but their decisions on federal questions are. The controversy here is clearly justiciable. If there were an independent state ground for the state court's decision, the state courts would alone have the case. Their discussions focus on the federal statutes. Additionally, the defendants are the ones entering federal court for the first time; the plaintiffs brought the non-justiciable case to state court, itself not bound by federal justiciability rules. The rule enunciated by the Court is: "when a state court has issued a judgment in a case where plaintiffs in the original action had no standing to sue under the principles governing the federal courts, we may exercise our jurisdiction on certiorari if the judgment of the state court causes direct, specific, and concrete injury to the parties who petition for our review, where the requisites of a case or controversy are also met."

SCOTUS then decided that the sale or lease of mineral lands must conform to the mandatory requirements of advertising, bidding, and appraisal. Justice Rehnquist concurred in part and dissented in part. In the dissent, he argued that the original plaintiffs, the state taxpayers and the teachers' union, lacked Article III standing when they sued in state court and they did not demonstrate injury in fact. He would have dismissed the appeal. The logic seems to be that state courts, even if not bound by Article III standing requirements, should get no SCOTUS review unless they have met Article III standing requirements. There is also the issue that SCOTUS inferred justiciability requirements, including standing, through case law. They are not in Article III, per se.

Nevada v. Hall, 440 U.S. 410 (1979) now allows suing states in the court of another state. A Nevada-owned vehicle on official business crashed into California residents in a car on a California highway. The Californians filed for damages in California court. The trial court denied the petition, but the California Supreme Court reversed and held Nevada amenable to suit. Nevada tried to invoke its statutory protections with waiver of immunity under the Full Faith and Credit Clause. The doctrine of sovereign immunity which protects the sovereign against suit creates no immunity against another sovereign. There is no constitutional mention of the power California exercised, but neither Article III not the Eleventh Amendment forbids it. Sovereignty referenced in Article I section 8 or Article IV section 2 is comity, not obligation. The Full Faith and Credit Clause does not require one state, against its own public policy, to apply the law of another state. It does require one state to honor the official acts of other states. On rare occasions, the courts of one state may apply the law of another. The statutes of one are generally inoperative in another state, particularly if they conflict with the public policy of that state.

It is important to keep in mind that the statutes of one or the other state will prevail, thus meaning a restriction on state sovereignty. The U.S. Constitution also places certain limits on the sovereignty of the states. The decision in the case was by plurality. The dissent focused on the implications. Once establishing jurisdiction, a sovereign state may become a litigant in another state's courts. Justice Blackmun argued that if there is no constitutional source of state sovereignty, one is free to treat any other as a litigant. He would find a constitutional basis, admittedly not in the words of the Constitution, but in its spirit. Rehnquist penned another dissent. People build a constitution upon shared experience and common understanding. The document engrains tacit postulates underlying the plan of the constitution into the fabric of the document and have as much force as the express provisions. Here, Rehnquist rejects literalism in favor of understanding of the Framers and doctrinal evolution of concepts of state sovereignty, including reference back to the Articles of Confederation. Rehnquist argues that the states ratifying the Eleventh Amendment understood it to cover one state hauling another state into its courts. The plurality's use of cooperative federalism will lead to a series of bailing operations. Rehnquist concludes that expressed appropriate limits on state sovereignty constitute the appropriate limits and *Nevada* transgresses that limit.

Justice Rehnquist makes another decision restricting court access in *Goldwater v. Carter*, 444 U.S. 996 (1979). Senator Goldwater sued President Carter for unilaterally cancelling a treaty with Taiwan, which the Senate approved years earlier by two-thirds vote. In a plurality decision written by Justice Rehnquist, the plurality over-ruled the appeals court and it directed the district court to dismiss the suit because it was a political question and therefore was non-justiciable. Rehnquist cites *Coleman v. Miller*, 307 U.S. 433 (1939) as the precedent mandating dismissal.

In Coleman, after an unsuccessful try, Kansas passed the Child Labor Amendment to the U.S. Constitution, with the tie in the Kansas senate broken by the vote of its lieutenant governor. The losing Kansas senators challenged the right of the lieutenant governor to cast the deciding vote, and they challenged the Amendment's vitality because of ratification failure within a reasonable amount of time. They sought an injunction stopping Kansas' formal ratification. The state courts accepted the writ for action, but the state supreme court upheld ratification. The case next goes to the Supreme Court for *certiorari*, which accepted the complaint as a proper federal question.

SCOTUS split between those who felt the lieutenant governor question justiciable, and those who thought it was political question. Whether a state can ratify an amendment, once it has rejected it, is a question for Congress, which sent forth the amendment in the first place. SCOTUS cannot and will not enjoin the secretary of state in Kansas from certifying the ratification.

Congress also has the power to determine whether the amendment has lost its vitality and is now moot. The system needs finality and the Court lacks judicial rules, so SCOTUS will lean toward the political departments. In Coleman, SCOTUS reversed the state supreme court, but the court did consider the merits, not dismiss the *writ of certiorari*. The losing Kansas senators challenged that the plaintiffs had no standing, and they wanted the writ dismissed, but SCOTUS found otherwise. Although SCOTUS had found the ordinary taxpayer has no standing regarding federal policy, the taxpayer does have standing in state and municipal matters. The twenty senators claim that, only with the lieutenant governor's intervention was the amendment ratified. The state proceedings raised a constitutional issue under Article V, on amending the Constitution, not a statutory issue. The questions raised, whether justiciable or political, are federal questions, and appropriately appear before the three-judge panel and then appealed to SCOTUS. Chief Justice Hughes also pointed out that both the ratification withdrawal problem and the sequence of failure to ratify and then ratify occurred with the adoption of the Fourteenth Amendment, but the Secretary of State certified and Congress approved by two-thirds vote of both Houses. These issues are properly considered left to the political departments.

The same holds for the length of time a proposed amendment has vitality. Congress has that power, but it does not follow that the Court should act if Congress does not do so. Political questions are not justiciable; the need for finality and the lack of criteria for a judicial determination conclude the issue. The same applies to our foreign relations. Internally, we have applied the political question to the Guarantee Clause in the Constitution. That it is a political question is the basis for affirming the decision of the Kansas Supreme Court. The concurrence warns that no court, state or federal, may pronounce any control over the amendment process, because the Constitution gives complete control of the Amendment process to Congress. Any judicial admonition is merely advisory, and thus wholly without constitutional authority. The petitioners should have no standing in this Court. To what and to whom the Kansas courts are open is a matter for Kansas to decide; Kansas cannot define the contours of federal court authority. SCOTUS cannot take up political questions of political concern and belong to all. If a state court decision obstructs an official in the performance of his duty to invoke a federal constitutional protection, then that individual may ask this Court to remove the fetters improperly imposed upon him. Where there is no private damage, there is no jurisdiction.

Rehnquist understood the challenge in *Goldwater* to fall under the foreign relations remark in Coleman that these were, for the most part, political questions and thus non-justiciable. The conduct of foreign relations involves the authority of the President and the extent to which the Senate or Congress can negate executive decisions. The Constitution is silent regarding rejection of a once ratified treaty. The standards for settling this dispute must come from the political departments; they are not judicially manageable. The plurality ruling does not include internal affairs, only external relations. He then argues that SCOTUS should set aside the court of appeals decision, with an order to the district court to dismiss the complaint. Drawing from practice in mootness cases, the dismissal process will prevent the finding from generating unexpected legal consequences. This is a political question that the lower court should not have decided and not considered the merits. Ironically, the decision from the Supreme Court did exactly that, spawn unexpected legal consequences.

The concurring opinion to the plurality also would have the complaint dismissed, but as not ripe for judicial review. Each of the branches to the controversy should have asserted constitutional authority which, in turn, the Court could review once reaching a constitutional impasse. One of the dissents agrees with the grant of certiorari but would set the case for oral argument. Another dissent would affirm the court of appeals decision to recognize the President's authority to recognize, or withdraw recognition from, foreign governments. Brennan, in this dissent, argues that Rehnquist profoundly misapprehends what a political question is. A decision of foreign policy is a political question, but the constitutional repository of decision-making power is not. This is a matter of constitutional law. The Constitution gives the power of recognition to the president, and the Court's decision need go no further.

CONCLUSION

Like many other components of justiciability, the problem of federal questions gave SCOTUS considerable wiggle-room. The Eleventh Amendment was a major constraint in the flexibility of this tool. That amendment, consequent to the effort of a citizen of one state to reclaim debts incurred by another state during the Revolutionary War, essentially prohibited suits against a sovereign state by citizens of another or by foreigners. The *Hans* case at the end of the nineteenth century added a suit by the citizens of the state against itself. The Marshall court faces restrictions of the Eleventh Amendment, so

John Marshall spent considerable effort crafting ways around it. There is no reference to state sovereignty in either the Constitution or the Eleventh Amendment.

Marshall distinguishes between state supreme court cases, in law or equity, arising under the Constitution or statutes or treaties of the United States, and those more properly covered by the Eleventh Amendment. Cases of the first type remain under the jurisdiction of the Supreme Court; only the latter type of cases affect Supreme Court jurisdiction. Controversies between two or more states are also under Supreme Court jurisdiction. Cases requiring construction of a constitutional or federal statutory clause are also under SCOTUS scrutiny. A writ of error operates on the record of a case, not the parties to it.

Marshall continues to restrict the Eleventh Amendment in *Osbourne*, where he makes a distinction between cases with causes and cases with parties. In anticipation of events to come, Marshall also separates the occupant of the position from the position itself. And a position does not protect an occupant pursuing an unconstitutional law. If the state has an interest in the outcome of a case, it can no longer be a party to it. If a joint interest occurs, all parties must be sueable. There is an asymmetry here; a state could still sue an individual. In the early part of the nineteenth-century, corporations did not have the standing of a person; the act of incorporation, *per se*, conferred no right to sue. When determining the status of parties to a lawsuit, the question becomes whether we should look behind the corporation back to its members, or should we stop at the corporation boundaries. What appears at first to be a minor discrepancy becomes a major issue when deciding whether a suit against a corporation is a suit against its incorporators. Whether the state is the incorporator, or a member of the incorporators, further complicates the problem. The answer to this question may directly affect the parties to diversity suits.

In the decades before the Civil War, it became increasingly apparent that there was a discrepancy between the fugitive slave clause and the privileges and immunities clause, unless slaves were property rather than humans. Justice Taney threw his weight behind the former. Marshall also reaches a significant decision that the Fifth Amendment applies only against the central government, not against the states. That meant that incorporation of the Bill of Rights could not occur until SCOTUS used the Due Process Clause of the Fourteenth Amendment, adopted after the Civil War, for that purpose. Scotus gives an even more complexing decision in distinguishing a writ of error and habeas corpus. The circuit courts have jurisdiction over criminal cases, and there is no review on matters of law beyond that. If, however, SCOTUS decides that the circuit court operates outside its jurisdiction, SCOTUS can issue a writ of habeas corpus, bringing the decision of the lower court before it. This is a round-about, because SCOTUS can affirm circuit court jurisdiction and uphold the lower court, or it can question jurisdiction and perhaps overturn the lower court.

SCOTUS was generally less hesitant to get involved in matters of the railroad. The Court was in the heyday of the Contracts Clause at approximately the same time the state legislatures tried to cut back the power of railroads. SCOTUS used a combination of the Tenth Amendment to limit national regulation and then the Contracts Clause to limit state regulation. The recipe slowly disintegrated after creation of the Interstate Commerce Commission. During the growth of the administrative state, SCOTUS began interpreting suits against the officers, agents and representatives of administrative units as agents of the state protected by the Eleventh Amendment. Suits by state-level administrative units became suits by states, which the Eleventh Amendment did not prohibit. SCOTUS then argued that the charter of a corporation was a contract, protected by the Contracts Clause. SCOTUS often assumed that the states would not deliberately destroy corporations.

Ex Parte Young reduced the footprint of the Eleventh Amendment by formally separating the office from its occupant, making the latter subject to prosecution for enforcement of an unconstitutional law which, of course, SCOTUS determines. In many ways, this was the climax case between state legislatures bent on populist politics and a SCOTUS bent on contractarianism. SCOTUS won this round, but the proliferation of the administrative state at all levels of government meant that SCOTUS would fall behind its own logic of contracts and corporations.

SCOTUS inherits Rehnquist from the Nixon administration in the days and months leading to the fall of Nixon's empire. Renchberg, as Nixon knew him, brought an anachronous view of state rights back to the Court. Asserting that state courts were more speedy and efficient that federal courts does not make them so, but it does ensure that the patchwork of 50+1 sets of laws is not self-coordinating. The Rehnquist influence facilitated the growth of uniform national moral and establishment laws, on the one hand, and the proliferation of social and economic laws, on the other hand. The mismatch is more obvious precisely because each domain sheltered a different logic. Appeals to a national moral code conjure the natural law beliefs of centuries past. The increasingly interlocking economies of the states, evidenced in *Nevada v. Hall*, the transportation revolution of the last century and the information revolution of this century betray the increasing fragility of Rehnquist's ideology in the face of changing conditions on the ground. Justiciability becomes an increasingly unbecoming variant of dodge-ball.

We end as we begin, with one continuity but two countervailing changes. The initial antagonism between the Federalists and anti-Federalists continues in the tension between national and state sovereignty. Two things have changed: the facts on the ground and legal precedent. The world has changed considerably since the tension between Hamilton and Jefferson. Hamilton would approve. Industrialization, transportation, communication, and administration have made a new America; it does not fit into the old skins of Jefferson's yeoman farmer tradition. Legal precedence has followed apace. The division of physical and mental labor united America into a dynamically integrated whole. Case precedent sometimes reluctantly, sometimes haltingly, followed. We can give lip-service to state sovereignty, but we cannot give life to an idea still-born with the Constitution of 1789.

The substantively empty conflict between levels of sovereignty still has a utility. It is not and will not be, in the foreseeable future, a description of alternate realities. What some believe to be real is not without its consequence. Ideas in conflict put the burden of demonstration and necessity upon the descriptive reality; must the Court go anywhere the nationalists want it to go? It is the existence of a counterclaim, not its realty or claim to an alternate reality, that subjects the dominant view to its reality check. In the best of thought experiments, we can test the truth-value of the dominant claims, what is their superiority to any alternate universe, and we can still learn by comparing the two. It is our ability to keep the two in tension, not through the choice of alternate realities, but through the choice of making our reality better.

Bibliography

Jefferson, Thomas. 1801. "First Inaugural Address." Washington, D.C.

Kuhn, Thomas S. 2012. *The Structure of Scientific Revolutions*. Chicago: The University of Chicago Press.

Llewelyn, Karl N., and E. Adamson Hoebel. 1941. *The Cheyenne Way*. Norman: University of Oklahoma Press.

Madison, James. 1961. "Federalist # 40." In *The Federalist Papers*, edited by Clinton Rossiter, 247–255. New York: The New American Library.

Madison, James. 1920. "Letter from James Madison to George Washington, April 16, 1787." In *The Debates of the Federal Convention 1787*, edited by G. Hunt and J. B. Scott, 592–595. New York.

Popper, Karl. 1945. *The Open Society and Its Enemies*. 2 vols. Princeton, NJ: Princeton University Press.

———. 1999. *The Poverty of Historicism*. London: Routledge.

Tocqueville, Alexis de. 2003. *Democracy in America*. New York: Penguin.

Warren, Charles. 1923. *The Supreme Court in United States History*. 3 vols. Boston: Little, Brown.

Cases Cited

A. L. A. Schechter Poultry Corp. v. United States, 295 U. S. 495 (1935)
Abood v. Detroit Bd. of Educ., 431 U.S. 209 (1977)
Adair v. United States, 208 U.S. 161 (1908)
Addyston Pipe & Steel Co. v. United States, 175 U.S. 211 (1899)
Aetna Life Ins. Co. v. Haworth, 300 U.S. 227 (1937)
Alaska Packers Assn. v. Industrial Accident Commission, 294 U.S. 532 (1935)
Allen v. Wright, 468 U.S. 737 (1984)
Allenberg Cotton Co., Inc. v. Pittman, 419 U.S. 20 (1974)
Allgeyer v. Louisiana, 165 U. S. 578 (1897)
Allstate Insurance Co. v. Hague, 449 U.S. 302 (1981)
Almy v. California, 65 U.S. 169 (1860)
Altvater v. Freeman, 319 U.S. 359 (1943)
American Radio Assn. v. Mobile S.S. Assn., 419 U.S. 215 (1974)
American Steel & Wire Co. v. Speed, 192 U.S. 500 (1904)
Anderson v. United States, 171 U. S. 604 (1898)
Arizona Pub. Svc. Co. v. Snead, 441 U.S. 141 (1979)
Arizona v. California, 283 U.S. 423 (1931)
Armco, Inc. v. Hardesty, 467 U.S. 638 (1984)
ASARCO v. Kadish, 490 U.S. 605 (1989)
Asbell v. Kansas, 209 U.S. 251 (1908)
Ashley v. Ryan, 153 U. S. 436 (1894)
Ashwander v. Tennessee Valley Auth., 297 U.S. 288 (1936)
Atherton Mills v. Johnston, 259 U.S. 13 (1922)
Atlantic & Pacific Tel. Co. v. Philadelphia, 190 U.S. 160 (1903)
Atlantic Coast Line R. Co. v. Riverside Mills, 219 U.S. 186 (1911)
Austin v. New Hampshire, 420 U.S. 656 (1975)
Babbitt v. United Farm Workers Nat'l Union, 442 U.S. 289 (1979)

Bacon v. Illinois, 227 U.S. 504 (1913)
Bailey v. Drexel Furniture Co., 259 U.S. 20 (1922)
Baker v. Carr, 369 U.S. 186 (1962)
Baldwin v. Fish & Game Comm'n of Montana, 436 U.S. 372 (1978)
Baltimore & Ohio R. Co. v. ICC, 221 U.S. 612 (1911)
Bank of the United States v. Deveaux, 9 U.S. 5 Cranch 61 (1809)
Bank of United States v. Planters' Bank of Georgia, 22 U.S. 9 Wheat. 904 (1824)
Barker Painting Co. v. Painters Union, 281 U.S. 462 (1930)
Barnum v. Okolona, 148 U.S. 393 (1893)
Barron v. Mayor & City Council of Baltimore, 32 U.S. 7 Pet. 243 (1833)
Baugh case: *Baltimore & Ohio R. C. v. Baugh*, 149 368 (1893)
Bingham v. Cabot, 3 U.S. 3 Dall. 382 (1798)
Blake v. McClung, 172 U.S. 239 (1898)
Bowman v. Chicago & Northwestern Railway Co., 125 U.S. 465 (1888)
Boy Scouts of America v. Dale, 530 U.S. 640 (2000)
Bradford Electric Light Co., Inc. v. Clapper, 286 U.S. 145 (1932)
Brennan v. Titusville, 153 U.S. 289 (1894)
Brown v. Board of Education of Topeka, 347 U.S. 483 (1954)
Brown v. Maryland, 25 U.S. 419 (1827)
Building Trades v. Mayor of Camden, 465 U.S. 208 (1984)
Bush v. Gore, 531 U.S. 98 (2000)
C. & S. Air Lines, Inc. v. Waterman S.S. Corp., 333 U.S. 103 (1948)
Cairo v. Zane, 149 U.S. 122 (1893)
California Retail Liquor Dealers Assn. v. Midcal Aluminum, Inc., 445 U.S. 97 (1980)
California v. Grace Brethren Church, 457 U.S. 393 (1982)
Carolina v. Baker, 485 U.S. 505 (1988)
Carroll v. Greenwich Ins. Co. of New York, 199 U.S. 401 (1905)
Carroll v. Lanza, 349 U.S. 408 (1955)
Carter v. Carter Coal Co., 298 U.S. 238 (1936)
Chambers v. Baltimore & Ohio R. Co., 207 U.S. 142 (1907)
Chassaniol v. City of Greenwood, 291 U.S. 584 (1934)
Chemical Waste Management, Inc. v. Hunt, 504 U.S. 334 (1992)
Cherokee Nation v. Georgia, 30 U.S. 5 Pet. 1 (1831)
Cherokee Nation v. Southern Kansas Ry. Co., 135 U.S. 641 (1890)
Chicago & Grand Trunk Ry. Co. v. Wellman, 143 U.S. 339 (1892)
Chicago, M. & St. P. Ry. Co. v. Solan, 169 U.S. 133 (1898)
Chicago, Milwaukee & St. Paul Railway v. Ross, 112 U.S. 377 (1884)
Chisholm v. Georgia, 2 U.S. 419 (1793)
City of Milwaukee v. Illinois, 451 U.S. 304 (1981)
City of Philadelphia v. New Jersey, 437 U.S. 617 (1978)

Cleveland, C., C. And St. Louis Railway Company v. Backus, 154 U.S. 439 (1894)
Cohens v. Virginia, 19 U.S. 6 Wheat. 264 (1821)
Cole v. Cunningham, 133 U.S. 107 (1890)
Colegrove v. Green, 328 U.S. 549 (1946)
Coleman v. Miller, 307 U.S. 433 (1939)
Colgrove, MacDougall v. Green, 335 U.S. 281 (1948)
Commercial & Railroad Bank v. Slocomb, Richards & Co., 39 U.S. 14 Pet. 60 (1840)
Commission of Wisconsin v. McCartin, 330 U.S. 622 (1947)
Conner v. Elliott, 59 U.S. 591 (1855)
Cooley v. Board of Wardens, 53 U.S. 299 (1851)
Corfield v. Coryell, 6 Fed Cas. 546, no. 3,230 C.C.E.D. Pa. 1823
Corp. Commission of Oklahoma v. Federal Power Commission, 415 U.S. 961 (1974)
Cotting v. Kansas City Stock Yards Co., 183 U.S. 79 (1901)
Crandall v. State of Nevada, 73 U.S. 35 (1867)
Crossman v. Lurman, 192 U.S. 189 (1904)
CSC v. Letter Carriers, 413 U.S. 548 (1973)
Daniels v. Williams, 474 U.S. 327 (1986)
Davis & Farnum Mfg. Co. v. Los Angeles, 189 U.S. 207 (1903)
Davis v. Bandemer, 478 U.S. 109 (1986)
Dayton-Goose Creek Ry. Co. v. ICC, 263 U.S. 456 (1924)
Decatur v. Paulding, 39 U.S. 14 Pet. 497 (1840)
Department of Commerce v. United States House of Representatives, 525 U.S. 316 (1999)
Diamond Match Co. v. Ontonagon, 188 U.S. 82 (1903)
District of Columbia v. Heller, 554 U.S. 570 (2008)
Doe v. Bolton, 410 U.S. 179 (1973)
Dombrowski v. Pfister, 380 U.S. 479 (1965)
Doremus v. Board of Education, 342 U.S. 429 (1952)
Duke Power Co. v. Carolina Env. Study Group, 438 U.S. 59 (1978)
East Tennessee, V. & G. Ry. Co. v. ICC, 181 U.S. 1 (1901)
Ellis v. Dyson, 421 U.S., 426 (1975)
Elrod v. Burns, 427 U.S. 347 (1976)
Employers' Liability Cases, 207 U.S. 463 (1908)
Erie R. Co. v. Tompkins, 304 U.S. 64 (1938)
Eureka Pipe Line Co. v. Hallanan, 257 U.S. 265 (1921)
Evers v. Dwyer, 358 U.S. 202 (1958)
Ex Parte Bakelite Corp., 279 U.S. 438 (1929)
Ex Parte Yarbrough, 110 U.S. 651 (1884)
Ex Parte Young, 209 U.S. 123 (1908)

Fair Assessment in Real Estate Assn. v. McNary, 454 U.S. 100 (1981)
Fauntleroy v. Lum, 210 U.S. 230 (1908)
Flast v. Cohen, 392 U.S. 83 (1968)
Flint v. Stone Tracy Co., 220 U.S. 107 (1911)
Fogg v. Blair, 139 U.S. 118 (1891)
Fort Gratiot Sanitary Landfill, Inc. v. Michigan Department of Natural Resources et al., No. 91–636 (1992)
Foster-Fountain Packing v. Haydel, 278 U.S. 1 (1928)
Frothingham v. Mellon and Commonwealth of Massachusetts v. Mellon, 262 U.S. 447 (1923)
Fry v. United States, 421 U.S. 542 (1975)
FTC v. Ticor Title Ins. Co., 504 U.S. 621 (1992)
Garcia v. San Antonio Transit Auth., 469 U.S. 528 (1985)
Geer v. Connecticut, 161 U.S. 519 (1896)
General Oil Co. v. Crain, 209 U.S. 211 (1908)
Georgia v. Brailsford, 2 U.S. 2 Dall., 415 (1793)
Georgia v. Stanton, 73 U.S. 6 Wall. 50 (1867)
Gibbons v. Ogden, 22 U.S. 1 (1824)
Giles v. Harris, 189 U.S. 475 (1903)
Gilligan v. Morgan, 413 U.S. 1 (1973)
Gladson v. Minnesota, 166 U.S. 427 (1897)
Golden v. Zwickler, 394 U.S. 103 (1969)
Goldwater v. Carter, 444 U.S. 996 (1979)
Gordon v. United States, 69 U.S. 2 Wall. 561 (1864) at 117 U.S. Appx. 698.
Gray v. Sanders, 372 U.S. 368 (1963)
Grayson v. Virginia, 3 U.S. 3 Dall. 320 (1796)
Great Northern Life Ins. v. Read, 322 U.S. 47 (1944)
Green v. Van Buskirk, 72 U.S. 307 (1866)
Griswold v. Connecticut, 381 U.S. 479 (1965)
Guaranty Trust v. York, 326 U.S. 99 (1945)
Gulf, Colorado & Santa Fe Ry. Co. v. Hefley, 158 U.S. 98 (1895)
Hammer v. Dagenhart, 247 U.S. 251 (1918)
Hampton v. McConnel, 16 U.S. 234 (1818)
Hans v. Louisiana, 134 U.S. 1 (1890)
Hayburn's Case, 2 U.S. 2 Dall., 409 (1792)
Healy v. Beer Institute, Inc., 491 U.S. 324 (1989)
Hennington v. Georgia, 163 U.S. 299 (1896)
Hollingsworth v. Virginia, 3 U.S. 3 Dall. 378 (1798)
Holmes v. Jennison, 39 U.S. 14 Pet. 540 (1840)
Home Building & Loan Assn. v. Blaisdell, 290 U.S. 398 (1934)
Hopkins v. United States, 171 U.S. 578 (1898)
Houston E. & W. Tex. Ry. Co. v. United States, 234 U.S. 342 (1914)

Hudson County Water Co. v. McCarter, 209 U.S. 349 (1908)
Hughes v. Alexandria Scrap Corp., 426 U.S. 794 (1976)
Hughes v. Oklahoma, 441 U.S. 322 (1979)
Hylton v. United States, 3 U.S. 3 Dall. 171 (1796)
Idaho ex rel. Evans v. Oregon, 444 U.S. 380 (1980).
Illinois Central R. Co. v. Behrens, 233 U.S. 473 (1914)
Illinois Central R. Co. v. Illinois, 163 U.S. 142 (1896)
International Textbook Co. v. Pigg, 217 U.S. 91 (1910)
Interstate Commerce Commission v. Alabama Midland Railway Co., 168 U.S. 144 (1897)
Japan Whaling Ass'n v. Cetacean Soc'y, 478 U.S. 221 (1986)
Joseph E. Seagram & Sons, Inc. v. Hostetter, 384 U.S. 35 (1966)
Joy v. St. Louis, 138 U.S. 1 (1891)
Kaiser Aetna v. United States, 444 U.S. 164 (1979)
Kansas City Sou. Ry. Co. v. Kaw Valley Drainage Dist., 233 U.S. 75 (1914)
Kawananakoa v. Polybank, 205 U.S. 349 (1907)
Keller v. Potomac Elec. Power Co., 261 U.S. 428 (1923)
Keller v. United States, 213 U.S. 138 (1909)
Kendall v. United States ex. Rel. Stokes, 37 U.S. 12 Pet. 524 (1838)
Kraft Gen. Foods, Inc. v. Iowa Dept. of Revenue and Finance, 505 U.S. 71 (1992)
Laird v. Tatum, 408 U.S. 1 (1972)
Lake Shore & Michigan Southern Ry. Co. v. Ohio, 173 U.S. 285 (1899)
Lake Shore and M. S. Railway Company v. Ohio, 165 U. S. 365 (1897)
Lambert Run Coal Co. v. Baltimore & Ohio R. Co., 258 U.S. 377 (1922)
Leisy v. Hardin, 135 U.S. 100 (1890)
Lemke v. Farmers Grain Co., 258 U.S. 50 (1922)
Leo Sheep Co. v. United States, 440 U.S. 668 (1979)
Liberty Warehouse Co. v. Grannis, 273 U.S. 70 (1927)
License Cases, 46 U.S. 504 (1847)
Lochner v. New York, 198 U.S. 45 (1905)
Loewe v. Lawlor, 208 U.S. 274 (1908)
Longshoremen's Union v. Boyd, 347 U.S. 222 (1954)
Lord v. Veazie, 49 U.S. 8 How. 251 (1850)
Luther v. Borden, 48 U.S. 7 How. 1 (1849)
Magnolia Petroleum Company v. Hunt, 320 U.S. 430 (1943)
Marbury v. Madison, 5 U.S. 137 (1803)
Martin v. Hunter's Lessee, 14 U.S. 1 Wheat. 304 (1816)
Martin v. Mott, 25 U.S. 12 Wheat. 19 (1827)
Maryland v. Louisiana, 451 U.S. 725 (1981)
Maryland v. Wirtz, 392 U.S. 183 (1968)
McCready v. Virginia, 94 U.S. 391 (1896)

McCulloch v. Maryland, 17 U.S. 316 (1819)
McElmoyle v. Cohen, 38 U.S. 312 (1839)
Michigan v. Long, 463 U.S. 1032 (1983)
Milk Control Bd. v. Eisenberg Farm Products, 306 U. S. 346 (1939)
Mills v. Duryee, 11 U.S. Cranch 481 (1813)
Mills v. Green, 159 U.S. 651 (1895)
Minneapolis & St. Louis Ry. Co. v. Emmons, 149 U.S. 364 (1893)
Minnesota v. Blasius, 290 U.S. 1 (1933)
Missouri, Kansas & Texas Ry. Co. v. McCann, 174 U.S. 580 (1899)
Montague & Co. v. Lowry, 193 U.S. 38 (1904)
Morehead v. New York ex. rel. Tipaldo, 298 U.S. 587 (1936)
Munn v. Illinois, 94 U.S. 113 (1876)
Murray v. Wilson Distilling Co., 213 U.S. 151 (1909)
Muskrat v. United States, 219 U.S. 346 (1911)
Nashville, C. & St. Louis Ry. Co. v. Wallace, 288 U.S. 249 (1933)
National League of Cities v. Usery, 426 U.S. 833 (1976)
Nevada v. Hall, 440 U.S. 410 (1979)
New Jersey v. Sargent, 269 U.S. 328 (1926)
New State Ice Co. v. Liebmann, 285 U.S. 262, 311 (1932)
New York & New England R. Co. v. Bristol, 151 U.S. 556 (1894)
New York ex. Rel. Silz v. Hesterberg, 211 U.S. 31 (1908)
New York v. Illinois & Sanitary District of Chicago, 274 U.S. 488 (1927)
New York v. Miln, 36 U.S. 102 (1837)
New York v. United States, 505 U.S. 144 (1992)
New York, L. E. & W. Railroad Company v. Pennsylvania, 153 U. S. 628 (1894)
New York, N. H. & H. R. Co. v. New York, 165 U.S. 628 (1897)
Nixon v. United States, 506 U.S. 224 (1993)
NLRB v. Jones & Laughlin Steel Corp., 301 U.S. 1 (1937)
Northeast Bancorp, Inc. v. Governors, FRS, 472 U.S. 159 (1985)
Northern Pacific R. Co. v. Egeland, 163 U.S. 93 (1896)
O'Brien v. Brown, 409 U.S. 1 (1972)
O'Reilly v. Morse, 56 U.S. 15 How. 62 (1853)
O'Shea v. Littleton, 414 U.S. 488 (1974)
Oregon Waste Systems, Inc. v. Department of Environmental Quality of Ore., 511 U.S. 93 (1994)
Osborn v. Bank of the United States, 22 U.S. 9 Wheat. 738 (1824)
Pacific Employers Ins. Co. v. Industrial Accident Commission, 306 U.S. 493 (1939)
Pacific States Tel. & Tel. Co. v. Oregon, 223 U.S. 118 (1912)
Parker v. Brown, 317 U.S. 3451 (1943)
Parker v. County of Los Angeles, 338 U.S. 327 (1949)

Parratt v. Taylor, 451 U.S. 527 (1981)
Passenger Cases, 48 U.S. 283 (1849)
Paul v. Virginia, 75 U.S. 168 (1869)
Pennsylvania v. West Virginia, 262 U.S. 553 (1923)
Pennsylvania v. Wheeling & Belmont Bridge Company, 59 U.S. 421 (1855)
Philadelphia v. New Jersey, 437 U.S. 617, 618 (1978)
Phillips Petroleum Co. v. Shutts, 472 U.S. 797 (1985)
Pierce v. Society of Sisters, 268 U.S. 510 (1925)
Pipe Line Cases, 234 U.S. 548 (1914)
Plessy v. Ferguson, 163 U.S. 537 (1896)
Poe v. Ullman, 367 U.S. 497 (1961)
Poindexter v. Greenhow, 114 U.S. 270 (1885)
Pollock v. Farmers' Loan & Trust Co., 157 U.S. 429 (1895)
Postal Telegraph-Cable Co. v. Taylor, 192 U.S. 64 (1904)
Powell v. McCormack, 395 U.S. 486 (1969)
Prentis v. Atlantic Coast Line Co., 211 U.S. 210 (1908)
Prigg v. Pennsylvania, 41 U.S. 16 Pet. 539 539 (1842)
Printz v. United States, 521 U.S. 898 (1997)
Public Service Comm'n v. Wycoff Co., Inc., 344 U.S. 237 (1952)
Quincy, Missouri & Pacific R. Co. v. Humphreys, 145 U.S. 82 (1892)
Railroad Commission of Ohio v. Worthington, 225 U.S. 101 (1912)
Railroad Company v. Fuller, 84 U.S. 560 (1873)
Railroad Company v. Husen, 95 U.S. 465 (1877)
Railroad Retirement Board v. Alton Railroad Co., 295 U.S. 330 (1935)
Reagan v Farmers' Loan and Trust Co., 154 U.S. 362 (1894)
Reeves, Inc. v. Stake, 447 U.S. 429 (1980)
Renne v. Geary, 501 U.S. 312 (1991)
Reno v. Condon, 528 U.S. 141 (2000)
Republican Committee v. Ripon Society, 409 U.S. 1222 (1972)
Respublica v. Cobbett, 3 U.S. 3 Dall. 467 (1798)
Reynolds v. Sims, 377 U.S. 533 (1964)
Rhodes v. Iowa, 170 U.S. 412 (1898)
Richards v. United States, 369 U.S. 1 (1962)
Richmond & A. R. Co. v. Patterson Tobacco Co., 169 U.S. 311 (1898)
Roe v. Wade, 410 U.S. 113 (1973)
Santa Clara County v. Southern Pacific Railroad, 118 U.S. 394 (1886)
Savage v. Jones, 225 U. S. 501(1912)
Schlesinger v. Reservists Committee, 418 U.S. 208 (1974)
Schollenberger v. Pennsylvania, 171 U.S. 1 (1898)
Seven Cases v. United States, 239 U.S. 510 (1916)
Shaffer v. Carter, 252 U.S. 37 (1920)
Shaw v. Reno, 509 U.S. 630 (1993)

Sierra Club v. Morton, 405 U.S. 727 (1972)
Simon v. Eastern Kentucky Welf. Rights. Org., 426 U.S. 26 (1976)
Smith v. Adams, 130 U.S. 167 (1889)
SouthCentral Timber Development, Inc. v. Wunnicke, 467 U.S. 82, 83 (1984)
Southern Railway Co. v. United States, 222 U.S. 20 (1911)
Sporhase v. Nebraska ex. rel. Douglas, 458 U.S. 941 (1982)
St. Louis, I. M. & S. Ry. Co. v. Taylor, 210 U.S. 281 (1908)
Stafford v. Wallace, 258 U.S. 495 (1922)
Standard Oil Co. of New Jersey v. United States, 221 U.S. 1 (1910)
Steffel v. Thompson, 415 U.S. 452 (1974)
Strader v. Graham, 51 U.S. (10 How.) 82 (1851)
Strawbridge v. Curtiss, 7 U.S. 3 Cranch 267 (1806)
Sun Oil v. Wortman, 486 U.S. 717 (1988)
Supreme Court of New Hampshire v. Piper, 470 U.S. 274 (1985)
Swift & Co. v. United States, 196 U.S. 375 (1905)
Terry v. Adams, 345 U.S. 461 (1953)
Texas and Pacific Ry. Co. v. ICC, 162 U.S. 197 (1896)
Texas v. Interstate Commerce Commission, 258 U.S. 158 (1921)
The Civil Rights Cases, 109 U.S. 3 (1883)
The Slaughter House Cases, 83 U.S. 16 Wall. 36 (1872)
The Sonneborn Brothers v. Cureton, 262 U.S. 506 (1923)
Thomas v. Washington Gas Light Company, 448 U.S. 261 (1980)
Titus v. Wallick, 306 U.S. 282 (1939)
Toomer v. Witsell, 334 U.S. 385 (1948)
Travis v. Yale & Towne Mfg. Co., 252 U.S. 60 (1920)
Truax v. Raich, 239 U.S. 33 (1915)
U.S. Steel Corp. v. U.S. E.P.A, 444 U.S. 1035 (1980)
Union National Bank v. Lamb, 337 U.S. 38 (1949)
United Credit Bureau of America INC. v. N. L. R. B., 454 U.S. 994 (1981)
United Fuel Gas Co. v. Hallanan, 257 U.S. 277 (1921)
United Jewish Organizations v. Carey, 430 U.S. 144 (1977)
United Public Workers v. Mitchell, 330 U.S. 75 (1947)
United States v. American Tobacco Co., 221 U.S. 106 (1911)
United States v. California, 297 U.S. 175 (1936)
United States v. Darby, 312 U.S. 100 (1941)
United States v. E. C. Knight Co., 156 U.S. 1 (1895)
United States v. Evans, 333 U.S. 483 (1948)
United States v. Ferger, 250 U.S. 199 (1919)
United States v. Ferreira, 54 U.S. 13 How. 40 (1851)
United States v. Florida East Coast Ry. Co., 410 U.S. 224 (1973)
United States v. Hamburg-Amerikanische Co., 239 U.S. 466 (1916)
United States v. Joint Traffic Association, 171 U.S. 505 (1898)

United States v. Lopez, 514 U.S. 549 (1995)
United States v. Morrison, 529 U.S. 598 (2000)
United States v. Munsingwear, Inc., 340 U.S. 36 (1950)
United States v. Nixon, 418 U.S. 683 (1974)
United States v. Rands, 389 U.S. 121 (1967)
United States v. Reading Co., 253 U.S. 26 (1920)
United States v. Texas, 143 U.S. 621 (1892)
United States v. Trans-Missouri Freight Ass'n., 166 U.S. 290 (1897)
Valley Forge Coll. v. Americans United, 454 U.S. 464 (1982)
Veazie v. Moor, 55 U.S. 568 (1852)
Vermont Yankee Nuclear Power Corp. v. NRDC, 435 U.S. 519 (1978)
Vieth v. Jubelirer, 541 U.S. 267 (2004)
Village of Euclid v. Ambler Realty Co., 272 U.S. 365 (1926)
Virginian Railway Co. v. Railway Employees, 300 U.S. 515 (1937)
Wabash, St. Louis & Pacific Railway Company v. Illinois, 118 U.S. 557 (1886)
Ward v. Maryland, 79 U.S. 418 (1870)
Ware v. Hylton, 3 U.S. 3 Dall. 199 (1796)
Warth v. Seldin, 422 U.S. 490 (1975)
Watson v. Employers Liability Assurance Corp, Ltd., 348 U.S. 66 (1954)
Welton v. State of Missouri, 91 U.S. 275 (1875)
Wesberry v. Sanders, 376 U.S. 1 (1964)
West Coast Hotel Co. v. Parrish, 300 U.S. 379 (1937)
West Lynn Creamery, Inc. v. Healy, 512 U.S. 186 (1994)
West v. Kansas Natural Gas Co., 221 U.S. 229 (1911)
Western Union Tel. Co. v. New Hope, 187 U.S. 419 (1903)
White v. Mass. Council of Constr. Employers, 460 U.S. 204 (1983)
Wickard v. Filburn, 317 U.S. 111 (1942)
Wiley v. Sinkler, 179 U.S. 58 (1900)
Williams v. Hagood, 98 U.S. 72 (1878)
Willing v. Chicago Auditorium Association, 277 U.S. 274 (1928)
Windward Shipping v. American Radio Assn., 415 U.S. 104 (1974)
Wisconsin R. Co. Commission v. C., B. & Q. R. Co., 257 U.S. 563 (1922)
Wood v. Broom, 287 U.S. 1 (1932)
Woodruff v. Parham, 75 U.S. 123 (1868)
Worcester v. Georgia, 31 U.S. 6 Pet. 515 (1832)
Wyoming v. United States, 255 U.S. 489 (1921)
Zwickler v. Koota, 389 U.S. 241 (1967)

Index

About the Author

Steven T. Seitz began his career teaching and researching on criminal policy and law at the University of Oregon and Florida State University. He served as principal investigator for a multi-city project evaluating court services as alternatives to incarceration. After four years as book review editor for the American Political Science Review while at the University of Illinois, he became the principal investigator for the team that built the U.S. computational model for HIV/AIDS. The two million-line computer program included demographic, epidemiological, and behavioral modules designed to simulate the epidemic, its primary causes, and the extrapolated impact of alternative policies. He served as research scientist for the Department of State in assisting countries around the world use the program simulating their epidemics. This book on constitutional clauses and a later book on clauses in the Bill of Rights are part of a larger project at the university's Computational Modeling Laboratory designed to automate and simulate the American judicial process. The clause research stands on its own as a temporal picture of how the Court parses its power and limitations on that power. Professor Seitz teaches constitutional law, American political thought, and democratic theory in the Department of Political Science at the University of Illinois at Urbana–Champaign.